FINANCIAL SECTOR TRANSFORMATION

Lessons from Economies in Transition

While policy makers need to focus on achieving and sustaining basic macroeconomic stability in the transition of economies from a socialist to a market orientation, financial institutions and reforms play a particularly crucial role in this transformation. The essays in this collection offer overviews of issues in banking sector reform and capital markets as well as specific perspectives on the financial sectors in changing economies of Central and Eastern Europe, China, and Israel. The editors and contributors explore the questions of how much focus needs to be given to macroeconomic stabilization vis-à-vis the dynamics of the financial sector, what may be appropriate time frames for dealing with immediate and longer-term financial problems, and how trends toward economic globalization interact with financial development in transition countries. Original versions of the essays were presented at the Second Dubrovnik Conference on Transition Economies organized by the National Bank of Croatia in June 1996.

Mario I. Blejer is Senior Advisor in the Monetary and Exchange Affairs Department of the International Monetary Fund. He recently served as Walter Rathenau Professor of Economics at the Hebrew University, Jerusalem, for 1996–98. Dr. Blejer has also taught at Boston, New York, and George Washington Universities, the University of Geneva, and Johns Hopkins University, and served as senior advisor to the Europe and Central Asia Regional Department of the World Bank. A specialist on issues of international finance and stabilization, he is the coauthor or coeditor of a dozen works, including *Financial Factors in Economic Stabilization and Growth* (coedited with Zvi Eckstein, Zvi Hercowitz, and Leonard Leiderman, Cambridge University Press, 1996).

Marko Škreb is Governor of the National Bank of Croatia, the host institution sponsoring the Second Dubrovnik Conference on Transition Economies on which this volume is based. Before assuming the governorship, Dr. Škreb earlier served as director of the bank's Research and Analysis Department, executive director of its Research and Statistics area, and subsequently served as Advisor for Economic Affairs to the president of Croatia from December 1995 to March 1996. He has also taught at the University of Zagreb.

FINANCIAL SECTOR TRANSFORMATION

Lessons from Economies in Transition

Edited by

MARIO I. BLEJER
International Monetary Fund

MARKO ŠKREB
National Bank of Croatia

CAMBRIDGE
UNIVERSITY PRESS

CAMBRIDGE UNIVERSITY PRESS
Cambridge, New York, Melbourne, Madrid, Cape Town, Singapore, São Paulo, Delhi

Cambridge University Press
The Edinburgh Building, Cambridge CB2 8RU, UK

Published in the United States of America by Cambridge University Press, New York

www.cambridge.org
Information on this title: www.cambridge.org/9780521640374

First published 1999
This digitally printed version 2008

A catalogue record for this publication is available from the British Library

Library of Congress Cataloguing in Publication data

Financial sector transformation: lessons from economies in transition/
edited by Mario I. Blejer, Marko Škreb.
p. cm.
Papers presented at the second Dubrovnik conference on transition economies.
ISBN 0-521-64037-7 (hardbound)
1. Finance – Europe, Eastern – Congresses. 2. Finance – Israel – Congresses. 3. Finance – China – Congresses. 4. Banks and banking – Europe, Eastern – Congresses. 5. Banks and banking – Israel – Congresses. 6. Banks and banking – China – Congresses. I. Blejer, Mario I. II. Škreb, Marko, 1957– ••. III. Dubrovnik Conference on Transition Economies (2nd: 1996)
HG186.E82F573 1999
332.1–dc21 98-20735
CIP

ISBN 978-0-521-64037-4 hardback
ISBN 978-0-521-08822-0 paperback

Contents

Contributors

Mario I. Blejer, *International Monetary Fund*
Velimir Bole, *University of Ljubljana, Slovenia*
John P. Bonin, *Wesleyan University*
Willem H. Buiter, *University of Cambridge and Bank of England*
Cevdet Denizer, *World Bank*
Thomas Dorsey, *International Monetary Fund*
Jacob A. Frenkel, *Bank of Israel*
Ardo H. Hansson, *Stockholm School of Economics*
Arye L. Hillman, *Bar Ilan University*
Evan Kraft, *National Bank of Croatia*
Ricardo Lago, *European Bank for Reconstruction and Development*
Martha de Melo, *World Bank*
Robert A. Mundell, *Columbia University*
Hélène Rey, *Centre for Economic Performance, London School of Economics and CREST*
Marko Škreb, *National Bank of Croatia*
Velimir Šonje, *National Bank of Croatia*
Franjo Štiblar, *University of Ljubljana, Slovenia*
Triinu Tombak, *Estonian Investment Bank*
Heinrich W. Ursprung, *University of Konstanz*
Paul Wachtel, *Stern School of Business, New York University*

INTRODUCTION

Financial Reforms and Economic Transition: An Overview of the Major Issues

Mario I. Blejer and Marko Škreb

The essays in this volume deal with banking sector reform and capital markets in transition economies.[1] To place these issues in broader context, however, we first discuss here a number of related questions that provide an appropriate framework for the understanding of the specific and crucial role played by financial reforms in the context of post-Communist transformation.

These questions have arisen because various transition economies appear to have achieved a relatively high degree of macroeconomic stability, especially compared with the situation observed at the beginning of the process, in the early 1990s.[2] First, once macroeconomic stability seems to have been achieved, should policy makers continue to pursue macroeconomic stabilization – should it remain a permanent concern in transition economies? Second, since transition should be, logically, a time-bounded process, what is the appropriate time horizon for policy makers? Should policy makers concentrate more on long-term issues or should they focus on immediate transition problems? Third, how do the trends toward economic globalization interact with financial development in transition countries? Finally, what is the role of commercial banks in transition and why are banking reforms so difficult to complete? We attempt to deal with these questions in order to provide a broad analytical framework for the contributions collected here.

[1] All the essays in the collection were presented at the Second Dubrovnik Conference on Transition Economies organized by National Bank of Croatia. The First Dubrovnik Conference on Transition Economies focused on macroeconomic issues. Papers presented in that conference are published in Blejer and Škreb 1996.

[2] See, for example, European Bank for Reconstruction and Development 1996.

SHOULD WE STOP WORRYING ABOUT MACROECONOMIC STABILITY?

Once achieved, the quest for price stability may lose its appeal (especially for politicians), as if, in fact, stable prices were a natural state of the economy. After inflation has been conquered, it is not unusual for macroeconomic populism to reappear, concentrating its efforts on seeking "development" with little concern for maintaining price stability. Situations of this sort seem to have arisen in a number of transition economies. As soon as stabilization is secured, people's impatience about standards of living starts to rise. Questions are asked and politicians, eager to be reelected, seem to like the notion of "instant" growth. The implicit belief about the existence of a long-term Phillips curve is very much alive in the thoughts of many decision makers and the maintenance of low inflation becomes an often neglected policy goal.

Such an approach could be highly dangerous in the long run. Many of those responsible for policy making seem to have reached the conclusion that inflation is, after all, not invincible and, therefore, if it reappears, it would not be such an arduous endeavor to deal with it. This, indeed, is a mistaken belief. It has been said that "inflation fighting is not like elephant hunting, where you first find the elephant, and then you fire." Inflation must be dealt with before it appears, and not be "shot at" only after it has been spotted. Once inflation is revived, it is usually too late to avoid significant social and economic costs.

There is, by now, a broad consensus on the issue of inflation and financial development: without stability it is not possible to have efficient financial intermediation, neither through banks nor through capital markets. Moreover, because of the initial financial underdevelopment prevailing in most of the transition economies, the need for macroeconomic stability in these countries could be even more crucial. On the other hand, it is equally true that stability per se is not enough to deliver increasing welfare (e.g., growth and equity). Therefore, if transition is to be successful, there is an obvious need to link macroeconomic policies with structural measures that promote sustainable economic growth, but it would be imprudent to neglect stability once it has been achieved, usually at a high cost.

Central banks are typically regarded as guardians of stability. Within the framework of promoting economic growth, it seems legitimate to ask whether central banks, in addition to fighting inflation, do more to foster growth. Most economists would probably answer no, particularly because for many economists the meaning of "fostering growth by the central bank" would simply imply a significant relaxation of its monetary policy stance ("printing more money"), which ultimately leads only to higher inflation. Clearly, although temptations are always present, a central bank cannot generate real (as opposed to nominal) growth just by printing money.

But there is indeed a role for the central bank in promoting growth. Central banks should be independent from short-term political influence, have a clear mandate to achieve and maintain price stability, (or an explicit inflation target), publicly announce their goals, and be accountable (Capie, Goodhart, Fischer, and Schnadt 1995). If those conditions are met, central banks can indeed deliver higher economic growth and prosperity by ensuring the necessary long-term stability of the currency and of the financial system, which are essential for higher savings and investment and for the efficient allocation of investments. Both of these elements – high and well-allocated savings – are necessary ingredients for achieving a higher and sustained growth path.

It seems, therefore, that while the focus of attention in transition economies has somewhat shifted from macroeconomic stability issues toward structural microeconomic-oriented questions (such as those discussed in this volume, related to banking and enterprise reforms and to the development of capital markets), it should be pointed out that both, macroeconomic stability and microeconomic reforms, are necessary conditions for attaining and sustaining a high rate of economic growth. Without economic growth, the economy is just playing a constant-sum game, and it would not be able to deliver prosperity, inducing disappointment and undermining institutional credibility.

SHORT-RUN VERSUS LONG-RUN POLICIES

Although it is indeed too early to summarize the lessons from the transition process, it is already evident from the existing experience that the transition is not a one-time effort nor a short-term undertaking, but rather a long-standing, continuous battle, a sociopolitical and economic endeavor that evolves over a long time horizon. Moreover, while it is evident that a successful transition will result in a substantial increase in the well-being of the population, the rewards would only appear gradually and after considerable sacrifices. This, of course, could lead to the design of shortsighted, and therefore wrong, policies or result in significant time inconsistencies in the decision-making process.

While it could be entirely rational for politicians to be tempted to adopt some sort of myopic behavior, given the immediacy of the costs and the heavy discount usually applying to the future benefits (particularly in conditions of political instability), it is crucial to insist that long-term goals should not be neglected. The list of transitional matters that cannot be resolved overnight is a long one, including privatization, enterprise restructuring, and institution building. High in that list, however, we find a number of issues closely related to banking sector reform and capital-market development. We concentrate here on three of these issues: the notion of risk, credibility of economic policy, and the promotion of long-term savings.

Risk is inherent to a market-based economy. Socialism could be seen, in fact, as a big insurance company: enterprises could not fail, and workers did not run the risk of loosing their jobs. In particular, credit and foreign-exchange risks were meaningless concepts since losses of commercial banks were socialized by the state and, frequently, exchange losses were also explicitly covered. The state (broadly speaking) was the main insurer, and insurance premiums were paid independently of the underlying risks. It goes without saying that moral hazard was a dominant force in such a system. Changing this situation, however, is not an overnight task. It not only requires a change in the ways that economic agents reason and react but it also necessitates active training in order to learn risk measurement and risk management techniques. Financial markets would only fulfill their roles efficiently when such changes in mentality and in operational practices become widespread, but this is, indeed, a long-term goal.

A similar long-term outlook should be adopted regarding the issue of policy-making credibility. If the government is unable to send a clear message to the public that it seriously intends to conduct stable policies and to establish and maintain firm financial discipline, the cost of actually pursuing these policies would increase significantly. In the central-planning context the question of credibility of policy making was not present because there was no scope for indirect market instruments and therefore no room for individual discretion in decision making. But building credibility during the process of transition becomes a crucial issue.

This can be particularly appreciated in the context of financial sector development. Unless policy credibility is strengthened, it would be very difficult to generate credibility in the emerging banking system, and without credibility in the banking system there will be no available sources of long-term funds and no available long-term bank financing. The lack of trust in domestic banks would tend to induce long-term capital flight that may, in certain circumstances, coexist with short-term, usually speculative, capital inflows. Since short-term capital inflows do not resolve the problem of scarce long-term funding, it is necessary to focus attention in strengthening credibility, certainly a prolonged process, as the only way of stabilizing the economy's balance of financial resources.

When speaking about credible long-term policies, financial discipline deserves special attention. The role of the government is essential in this process. If the government does not set an example (by meetings its obligations and forcing other agents to do so), it may undermine all the efforts made in other areas of transition. Moreover, without financial discipline on the part of the government, a generalized credibility gap may arise, resulting in financial disintermediation or in "short-termism," a clear consequence of the lack of trust in the banking system.

The third relevant long-term issue relates to the promotion of savings during the transition. If transition economies are to achieve long-term high and sustained rates of growth they must adopt policies that encourage domestic savings. Domestic savings are crucial in financing capital formation and in fostering economic growth. Foreign savings may be able to substitute for the lack of domestic savings, but only temporarily. While capital inflows and foreign direct investments play an important role, the evidence is that, in the long run, sustained high growth rates cannot be achieved without sufficient domestic savings. Aggregate domestic savings were very high during central planning, but have fallen significantly during the transition. There is, therefore, a genuine need to promote policies that increase aggregate savings in all its components – that is, government, enterprise, and household savings. But, promoting saving cannot be achieved immediately, and therefore, again, a long-term, comprehensive approach is called for.

GLOBALIZATION AND THE FUTURE OF TRANSITION ECONOMIES

The future is always uncertain. But there are some clear global economic trends emerging, which are becoming considerably visible and which should not be neglected as economic policies in transition economies are designed. It is evident that the world economy is globalizing rapidly while also strengthening regional currencies and trade blocks. The globalization of the world financial markets and the increasing sophistication of financial instruments (such as derivatives) make it increasingly obvious that crises are contagious. Regardless where they start, they can very quickly spill over to other countries. Therefore, it is not enough for a country to pursue "sound policies at home." It has to watch world developments closely and respond to them promptly. At the same time, globalization also demands permanent "good behavior." Increasing financial integration and greater transparency augment the responsibility of domestic policy makers since their decisions are constantly watched by international economic agents.

As mentioned before, "right" economic policies may not always be popular with voters, and therefore may be shunned by politicians, but the cost of the alternatives could be extremely high. While decision makers cannot, and probably must not, neglect local public opinion, a more global perspective should be adopted. How, then, should transition economies behave in a rapidly changing world? Like Alice in Wonderland, if transition economies want to catch up with the developed world, they have to run twice as fast, which can be achieved only by adopting adequate policies. And there is no more evident area than the financial sector where a promising future depends crucially on the nature of today's decisions.

COMMERCIAL BANKS IN TRANSITION

Schumpeter once said that the only important institution in capitalism is the bank. Banks should collect savings and be responsible for the efficient allocation of resources. In most transition economies, however, financial markets are both shallow and narrow. Given the underdevelopment of their capital markets and their relatively high country risks, raising equity capital either on the stock exchange or through direct foreign investments is indeed more difficult than in developed market economies. Thus, enterprises must rely much more heavily either on self-financing, or on bank lending. Banks fulfill, therefore, a very important function in the overall financial system of almost all transition countries.

Banks in transition, however, cannot fully fulfill one of their most significant roles: the efficient allocation of savings throughout the economy. Starting in most cases from monobanking, old (usually state controlled) banks are not prepared to measure risks adequately, are overstaffed, and frequently are burdened with bad loans. Their decision making is often more influenced by political considerations than by sound banking principles. New, emerging, private banks are usually too small and their influence is not enough to create a competitive banking environment. Thus the thorough rehabilitation and restructuring of commercial banks is an essential ingredient in the creation of a sound banking system. After stabilization has been achieved, bank rehabilitation and bank restructuring (linked with enterprise restructuring) appear as the highest priorities for transition economies.

In practice, however, bank rehabilitation has proved to be a very slow process in transition economies, which has led to the emergence of serious banking crises. Of course, banking sector problems are not restricted to transition economies. Since 1980 about 130 countries have experienced significant banking sector problems, while 36 had serious banking crises (Lindgren, Garcia, and Saal 1996). But banking crises seem to have been particularly endemic in transition economies. Why has it been so difficult to rehabilitate banks in transition countries before a full-blown banking crisis erupts? The usual answer is that bank rehabilitation (including carving out bad loans, bank recapitalization, and restructuring) is very costly and budgetary resources are scarce. This is, however, only partially true as bank rehabilitation appears to be just a redistribution problem. With budgetary expenditures of about 50 percent of the GDP, as is the case in most transition economies, devoting, say, two percentage points to bank rehabilitation does not look like an unattainable objective. The lack of determination to pursue bank rehabilitation is therefore a problem of intertemporal redistribution (because it essentially involves the decision about what budgetary expenditures should be lowered in order to finance the process) and therefore it is largely a problem of social and public choice. Consensus in this area seems to have largely eluded transition economies.

Why is that so? If financing is really not the problem (or at least not the main one), why is bank rehabilitation postponed? Why are optimal decisions in bank rehabilitation not taken? Probably the key to these questions is a correct assessment of the reasons behind the lack of political support for this type of endeavor. Bank rehabilitation is usually faced with significant resistance from various groups of economic agents. Resolving systemic banking problems is a practical exercise in multiple enterprise restructuring. This again means substantial redistribution. In transition economies, banks need restructuring because, in most cases, their loans were granted on the basis of political criteria (without adequate measuring of the risks involved) and not on the basis of sound banking practices. Banks were usually state-controlled, and their decisions were easily influenced by politicians. Banks were managed by individuals who were closely linked with the political elite and their aim was to fulfill certain "duties" (such as "support the economy") rather than to protect bank liabilities (deposits and capital).

It is not surprising that resistance to bank rehabilitation arises from many quarters. The most clearly defined groups that are expected to oppose restructuring include politicians, bank managers, bank personal, and state controlled enterprises. Bank managers were usually appointed by the political elite before the transition. If this political elite has not withdrawn from the scene (or has reemerged as is the case in some transition countries), it may be difficult to change the management of a bank during the process of rehabilitation. Politicians are aware that they will have much less power if stripped of their influence over banks through the appointment of new management. Friendly management can grant loans for wages to enterprises on strike, finance local sports teams, newspapers, and the like.

Bank managers clearly have vested interests within the existing power structure. High wages and political influence are strong enough motives for their active opposition to any change that implies the loss of their position. They may go along with rehabilitation plans as long as they themselves bear no consequences on account of their previous behavior. But if supposedly rehabilitated banks operate under the same management, we are clearly faced with a moral hazard problem and probably minimal efficiency gains could be expected.

Bank personnel resist rehabilitation and restructuring because the process creates uncertainty. Clearly, as most of the old banks need serious downsizing, the fear of layoffs is widespread.

State-controlled enterprises based their existence on soft loans from state-controlled banks. It was common that the largest debtors of a bank were sitting on supervisory boards of the banks, thus creating interlocking incestuous relationships. Those firms would engage their resources in rent-seeking activities aimed at retaining the status quo rather than investing time and effort in restructuring their operations in order to become profitable in a competitive environment. Thus, from the management of those enterprises as well as from their employees one can expect strong resistance to bank rehabilitation.

Clearly, while the implementation of sound banking principles is bound to increase the welfare of the population at large, it would significantly hurt some groups of people. One should, therefore, expect various interest groups to offer strong resistance to banking reforms.

If banks are not rehabilitated, if they continue to extend loans based on political criteria, and if insolvent banks remain in the system, severe banking problems and crises could emerge sooner or later. The costs of banking problems are, in general, huge and can severely affect a country's fiscal and financial soundness. That is why it is extremely important to seek and reach firm political consensus on the necessity of bank restructuring. Without such consensus, bank rehabilitation cannot proceed.

One has to note, however, that even when this consensus is reached, the problems are not eliminated. Governments seldom act quickly and decisively. Delays are usually common and the process could be affected by dilution – that is, by undertaking measures to rehabilitate banks that are not radical enough. In such a case bank rehabilitation may have to be repeated again and again. If this happens, future bank rehabilitation would be more difficult and more costly. Indeed, the only thing that could probably be even worse for the economy than doing nothing about needed bank rehabilitation is to proceed with improper rehabilitation. This is so because improper rehabilitation substantially decreases the government credibility and increases the cost of future bank restructuring.

To summarize, commercial banks play a significant role in the transition process. But to fulfill their demanding task the banking sector must be restructured and depoliticized. In the long run privatization of banks, increasing competition in the banking industry, and integration into world financial markets are the best remedies for ailing banking sectors in transition, but immediate action from the state in this sector appears to be fully warranted. Financial stability (comprising a sound banking sector) is a public good and the state has an important role to play in this particular area.

CONTENTS OF THE BOOK

The themes discussed here are thoroughly treated in the various essays of this volume. The book is comprised of four chapters dealing with issues related to the financial sector in transition from a general perspective and five studies focused on specific country experiences. An afterword summarizes some of the emerging conclusions.

The opening essay, by Martha De Melo and Cevdet Denizer, concentrates on the most significant reforms involving the objectives and instruments of monetary policy during transition. As such, this study provides important elements in order to assess the background within which financial transformation is taking place. The authors examine the implementation of monetary policy in twenty-six transition economies (in Europe and Central Asia), analyzing the period 1989–95. De Melo and Denizer proceed to evaluate the specific impact of six monetary policy instruments, both direct and indirect, on the rate of inflation and on the level of financial depth. After analyzing a rich cross-country, time-series data panal three distinct patterns emerge. First, by the end of the observed period, after roughly six years of transition, about half of the countries rely primarily on market-oriented forms of monetary policy. Second, Central and East European countries moved more rapidly to market instruments compared with the states of the former Soviet Union. Finally, De Melo and Denizer conclude that both inflation control and the level of financial depth (measured by quantitative indicators of the McKinnon-Shaw type) are related more to the *stance* of monetary policy (measured by rates of growth of base money and by the real discount rate) and less to the market orientation of the instruments used.

The next essay, by John Bonin and Paul Wachtel, sets a general framework designed to examine the central aspects of the development of market-oriented banking in transition economies. Based on the comparative experience of the three Visegrad countries, Hungary, Poland, and the Czech Republic, the authors concentrated on four main topics: the restructuring of the banking sector, bank privatization, competition and contestability, and the regulatory structures of banking in transition. One of the definite conclusions reached in their analysis is that simply privatizing the banking sector, though an important element in the development of market-oriented banking, is only part of the story. What is essential, in their view, is the *disengagement of the state from bank governance.* This implies that while state-owned banks must certainly be privatized, privatization alone would not guarantee the nonpolitical allocation of credit as long as the state does not withdraw from direct decision making at the bank management level. At the same time, however, total state disengagement from the banking industry is also highly counterproductive and it is crucial to ascertain what is the appropriate role of the state. After withdrawing from ownership, the state should support the banking sector (typically in the form of deposit guarantees, bank consolidation, recapitalization, etc.) and should put in place and enforce an effective regulatory framework. Bonin and Wachtel conclude that while significant progress has been achieved in the countries considered, the process of transition in the financial sector is still far from completed.

While the Bonin-Wachtel essay provides a useful normative framework to analyze the desired path of transition toward a well-functioning banking system in post-Communist economies, there are open questions regarding the political feasibility and the constraints of following such path. In order to light face shed light on these questions, Arye Hillman and Heinrich Ursprung examine in detail the political economy aspects of banking sector reform in transition countries. They consider questions such as why the best policies are not always chosen or, if chosen, why they are not implemented. Hillman and Ursprung develop a simple model that captures the basic elements of the relations between a large state enterprise and a state bank. The model reflects their view that the banking system has very special characteristics that make the process of reforms much more complex, and that some of these characteristics are sharpened in transition economies. Prudence, honesty, and adequate regulation should be the guiding principles to protect the public interest but not all these principles could be expected to emerge rapidly and therefore it seems realistic to anticipate problems and to foresee financial crises during the transition. Thus, banking failure could be easily predicted. But, due to asymmetric information, it is not possible to say whether "an honest banker has honestly failed, or a dishonest banker has dishonestly failed."

The interactions between the enterprise sector and the stance of financial policies is also the subject of the fourth essay, by Willem Buiter, Ricardo Lago, and Hélène Rey. They concentrate on the financial and macroeconomic influences on enterprise decision making and performance. The starting point of their study is that macroeconomic stability is a critical precondition for effective enterprise management, and it has a direct bearing on their efficiency and performance. After developing an analytical framework to assess the effects and the consequences of macroeconomic stability on enterprise performance, Buiter, Lago, and Rey present rich empirical evidence on the positive influences of a stable financial and macroeconomic environment on enterprise performance. On the basis of such evidence, the authors offer a number of conclusions and policy prescriptions. It seems that, as far as enterprise performance is concerned, fast reformers did better than slow ones and that the eradication of inflation is far more consequential than the adoption of mechanisms, such as indexation, that only alleviate its consequences. On an apparent confirmation of the observation made by Bonin and Wachtel regarding the functioning of banking in transition, the authors conclude that, also for the performance of enterprises, it is of utmost importance to build up and to support actively institutions that assure the maintenance of macroeconomic and financial stability, such as an equitable social safety net, and strong banking supervision and tax administration. Their final conclusion is, therefore, that macroeconomic control is, par excellence, central to the role of the state in promoting transition to a market economy.

The second part of the book is devoted to the study of specific country experiences regarding financial sector reform. While, indeed, the various countries covered here have faced very distinct circumstances, the examination of their experiences, and of the various policy patterns followed, allows the extraction of significant conclusions that strengthen the inferences reached from the general analysis of the previous section.

The first essay in this section, by Ardo Hansson and Triinu Tombak, deals with the banking crises that affected all the three Baltic states. Estonia, Latvia, and Lithuania had undergone minimal reforms before their independence and, therefore, the extent of reforms that had to be implemented at the outset was, indeed, very large, and eventually all three countries faced open banking crises. The essay summarizes the main aspects of these major banking crises and describes the ways in which they were resolved. After analyzing the factors behind the crises, the authors derive general lessons and conclusions. Even though it is acknowledged that each banking crisis is unique and responds to particular reasons, Hanson and Tombak propose, nevertheless, seven general lessons. First, once a banking sector problem arises, it is very important to act quickly. Second, if banks problems are rooted in financial insolvency, neither significant central bank lending nor voluminous transfers of government deposits can resolve the problem. Third, the option of bank liquidation (as opposed to rehabilitation) should be seriously considered. Fourth, when the process of bank privatization advances at a slow pace, there is an argument for favoring liquidation of failed institutions in order to avoid their renationalization. Fifth, rehabilitation should be considered only when clear systemic risks are present. Sixth, restructuring plans developed and promoted by owners of insolvent banks imply, usually, the bailouts of their institutions and therefore lack credibility; and, seventh, resolving banking crises by forcing mergers of good with bad banks is a very risky undertaking because such mergers usually end up contaminating the previously good bank. Without claiming universality, the authors conclude that these lessons, arising from the comparative experience of the Baltic countries, have important policy implications for many other financial sectors in transition.

In contrast with the Baltic countries, the transition experience of Croatia has become a well-known case of antiinflationary success. Less is known, however, about the country's financial reforms and developments. In their Velimir, Šonje, Evan Kraft, and Thomas Dorsey analyze the Croatian experience regarding the relationships between monetary and exchange rate policies, putting special emphasis on the efficiency of the Croatian banking sector. Such an emphasis stresses specifically the links between the postponement of bank restructuring and the emergence of very high levels of real interest rates. A special effort is made to study the main determinants of aggregate interest rate spreads, which have remained substantially high. A central conclusion is that, while the Croatian nonrestructured banking system has not impaired the preservation of macroeconomic stability, further space and more degrees of freedom are now needed in order to improve monetary management, and this can only be achieved through substantial structural supply-side reforms in the banking system.

The next two essay in the volume deal with the case of Slovenia. In the first essay Velimir Bole explores the issue of very high real interest rates and analyzes their relation to the structure of the financial sector. Bole argues that after inflation in Slovenia was conquered, high real interest rates remained as one of the main problems, together with the rapid rate of wage increases. He postulates that the high level of interest rates is due to two sets of factors. The first relates to the way stabilization is managed, both in terms of fundamentals and credibility. The second set of factors involves the quality of financial intermediation, that is, the efficiency of the financial sector. Bole's findings are that distress borrowing, and high interbank mobility of deposits, which forced banks to compete very aggressively for such deposits, were the main factors affecting interest rates.

The second essay on Slovenia, by Franjo Štiblar, deals with bank rehabilitation and emphasizes the experience of Nova

Ljubljanska Banka (NLB), the largest bank in the country. The essay describes in detail the composition and performance of the banking sector in Slovenia and delineates the characteristics of the Slovenian approach to bank rehabilitation. It concludes with an analysis of the achievements in rehabilitating the NLB. Štiblar points out that bank rehabilitation is one of the most complicated and important problems of the transition process. The success of NLB rehabilitation does, indeed, look convincing. This is only one (though the largest) of many banks in Slovenia.

Although most of the effort to understand banking reforms and financial transition has been focused on Eastern Europe and the former Soviet Union, the case of China, a huge country that adopted a particular reform strategy, deserves particular attention. Robert Mundell examines this special case by looking at eight specific financial and monetary issues: inflation and growth, monetary deepening, government credit and inflationary finance, money-financed growth, inflation semielasticities, monetary policy, price stability and currency areas, and financial markets. Mundell claims that China's combination of high growth and (relatively) low inflation has generated envy in other countries but that, given its size and the dual character of its economy (which is only partially monetized), it is very difficult to compare China with other countries in a meaningful manner. However, Mundell predicts that financial deepening in China, which has increased remarkably in the past forty years, will intensify and that the country is bound to become an important financial center in Asia relatively soon. This would happen not only because of China's geographical position, but also because of the incorporation of Hong Kong, one of the most important financial centers of the world. In the long run, Mundell concludes, China will become the dominant power of Asia.

Since financial market reforms and liberalization have been implemented in a large number of market economies (both emerging and developed countries), it is worthwhile to place the experience of transition economies in the broader perspective of reforming practices. This is the objective of the last chapter, by Jacob Frenkel, who reviews in detail the financial market reforms implemented in Israel since 1985, following the macroeconomic stabilization package introduced in that country at the time. Frenkel examines both the objectives and the implementation of the Israeli reforms, which were largely directed toward the deregulation of the financial system, and evaluates the achievements of the process. Overall, he considers the reforms to have attained most of their goals and to have made the various segments of the Israeli economy much more efficient by increasing their degree of integration. His main regret is that the reforms were not started earlier and moved faster, and this is also his main message for the transition countries. He realizes that there is no constituency for structural reforms, but since policy makers know that reforms should be carried out, they might as well do them fast, quickly, and early.

The analytical and applied analysis in this volume covers, indeed, a substantial amount of ground and constitutes a comprehensive attempt to understand both the impact of transition on financial developments and the importance of financial sector reform in determining the nature of the process. Some of these interrelations are summarized in Mario Blejer's afterword. It is evident that progress in reforming the financial sector has been uneven across countries, and not very smooth even in the most advanced ones. A remark that could be made, in conclusion, is that transition economies have no alternative to credible, transparent, and prudent long-term financial policies, and the promotion of efficient banking sectors and well-developed capital markets play a crucial role in the ability to implement those policies.

REFERENCES

Blejer, Mario I., and Marko Škreb (eds.). 1997. *Macroeconomic Stabilization in Transition Economies*. Cambridge: Cambridge University Press.

Capie, F., C. Goodhart, S. Fischer, and N. Schnadt. 1995. *The Future of Central Banking*. Cambridge: Cambridge University Press.

European Bank for Reconstruction and Development. 1996. *Transition Report*. London.

Lindgren, C. J., G. Garcia, and M. I. Saal. 1996. *Bank Soundness and Macroeconomic Policy*. Washington, D.C.: International Monetary Fund.

PART I

General Studies

CHAPTER 1

Monetary Policy during Transition: An Overview

Martha de Melo and Cevdet Denizer

This chapter looks at monetary policy in twenty-six transition countries in Europe and Central Asia from 1989 to 1995. The purpose is to provide a broad characterization of the experience of these countries as they make the transition from a socialist economy, where money and credit were largely determined as a residual, to a market economy, where monetary policy plays an active role in economic management and where economic efficiency is believed to be enhanced by the variety and sophistication of financial instruments. In the process, we classify countries by the extent of market orientation in the use of monetary policy instruments, by indicators of policy stance, and by broad measures of effectiveness. The relationships between these three dimensions are evaluated by cross-country comparison over the transition period and at the time of stabilization.

To place the discussion in context, the first section reviews briefly the nature of money and finance under socialism and provides a snapshot of various financial development ratios at the beginning of transition. The second section discusses countries' policy response to transition and distinguishes two groups – one where a monetary policy framework was quickly developed as part of the economic transformation strategy and another where continued participation in the ruble zone and greater ambivalence toward reform resulted in delayed stabilization programs.

In the third section, we look at how monetary policy has been

We appreciate comments from Jerry Caprio, Stijn Claessens, Nikolay Gueorguiev, Françoise Le Galle, Piroska Nagy, Fabio Schiantarelli, and Ulrich Zachau on an earlier draft. We thank Nikolay Gueorguiev and Kenneth Xu for their valuable research assistance. The findings, interpretations, and conclusions expressed in this paper are entirely those of the authors. They do not necessarily represent the views of the World Bank, its executive directors, or the countries they represent.

conducted. The focus is on the use of specific policy instruments, for which we identify "late socialism," "transitional," and "market-oriented" forms. We then classify countries by the extent of market orientation in their use of both direct and indirect instruments. In order to facilitate comparability, we look at market orientation of monetary instrument use around a common event, namely stabilization, and make some observations about similarities and differences across countries.

The fourth section classifies countries against some crude indicators of policy stance and two broad indicators of effectiveness, namely price stability and financial depth. In the fifth section, we look at the interaction between instrument use, policy stance, and effectiveness. The purpose is to see to what extent the use of instruments and policy stance – rather than nonmonetary factors such as changes in international terms of trade, trade and exchange rate policies, and the behavior of banks – have affected economic outcomes.

The standard caveats on data deficiencies apply to this overview, which covers countries affected by regional conflicts and blockades as well as those free of such disruptions. An attempt has been made to provide comparable data across countries, but the quality and the availability of data vary substantially. High inflation in most countries raises questions about both the estimates of changing prices and the deflation methods. Also, distinguishing between movements in M1 (narrow money) and M2 (broad money) has not been possible since estimates of average stocks of M1 are not available for some countries. For all these reasons, the emphasis here is placed on broad trends that appear to be robust.

MONEY AND FINANCE UNDER SOCIALISM

Money under socialism passively accommodated the financing needs of the central plan, which emphasized production in the real sectors. As is well known, central plans set production targets specified in physical units in each sector to ensure a target growth rate for the economy. The emphasis on growth, given labor force and technology, required new investment; and planners determined the level of sectoral investment using investment coefficients derived from detailed input-output studies. An investment plan was then produced by aggregating the sectoral investment needs.[1]

The role of the financial sector was to fulfill the investment plan as well as other financing requirements of the state enterprises and the government budget included in the credit plan, the financial counterpart to the physical targets. Planners set targets in real sectors, and financial flows were adjusted to achieve them. The central credit plan operated like a global directed credit scheme; interest rates were not a factor in the mobilization and allocation of resources, much less in managing aggregate demand. Money was not a policy instrument, and therefore most instruments of monetary policy found in market economies were not used.

However, this did not mean money and credit were unimportant. For price stability, planners had to ensure a balance between money supply and output. To attain this balance, the system was split into cash and noncash sectors. Noncash transactions between enterprises were accounting entries within the financial system and had no effect on the money supply. Cash transactions were undertaken by households, which received their wages in cash. The equality between the wage bill and consumption goods valued at administratively fixed prices was a key condition for the equilibrium of the system. To the extent that wages paid by the authorities exceeded expenditures on goods sold by state-owned enterprises – often in short supply – money would be printed to finance the gap, generating inflationary pressures (see Sahay and Vegh 1995 for a model of money and prices under socialism).

Similarly, the financial assets of enterprises and households were maintained separately, even though they were all nominally part of the monobank system characteristic of socialism. Household deposits were virtually all directed to the savings bank; the financial assets and liabilities of enterprises were almost entirely held by commercial and sectoral banks.

In sum, the financial institutions that implemented the central bank's credit plan were passive. They had no role in credit allocation, and the basic legal, accounting, and regulatory systems found in market economies were not in place. Knowledge

[1] See Nove 1991 for a fuller description.

of enterprise accounts and investment projects was typically located in the central-planning agency, not in the banks. With this set of initial conditions, it is not surprising that improvements in resource allocation from financial intermediation have been slow in transition economies (Caprio 1995). We inquire later whether instruments of monetary policy used in market economies can be introduced into such an environment quickly and effectively.

By the beginning of political transition – roughly 1989 for most of Central and Eastern Europe (CEE) and 1991 for the former republics of Yugoslavia (FRY) and the former Soviet Union (FSU) – basic financial ratios in socialist countries were relatively high, as shown in Table 1.1. Only in Poland and the FRY, where inflation was high in the late 1980s, were overall ratios of M2 to GDP low.

But financial depth did not necessarily indicate financial development, as it does in market economies. Rather, part of the accumulation of financial assets in the banking system reflected a growing disequilibrium, particularly after the mid-1980s, as wages were raised more rapidly than the availability of consumer goods. This was especially the case in the FSU. With limited consumption possibilities, people had no choice but to convert part of their incomes into bank deposits. These forced savings resulted in a sizable monetary overhang in most socialist countries at the time of the collapse of central planning (see Balcerowicz and Gelb 1994 for estimates of the monetary overhang).

THE POLICY RESPONSE TO TRANSITION

Countries can be classified roughly into two groups based on the speed of their policy response to the break from socialist central planning. The first group, referred to here as the "fast response" group, consists of most CEE countries (except FYR Macedonia and Romania), the Baltics, the Kyrgyz Republic, and Moldova. These countries developed a monetary policy framework as part of their economic transformation strategy relatively quickly. As indicated by the date of adoption of a stabilization program shown in Table 1.2, monetary or exchange rate targets were put in place within the first two years of transition, with the declared objective of regaining price stability.

Table 1.1. *Pretransition financial ratios as percent of GDP*

Countries	Year	Currency	DD	TSD	FXD[a]	Total M2
Central and Eastern Europe						
Albania[b]	1990	9	n.a.	n.a.	0	31
Bulgaria[b]	1989	14	37	52	4	107
Croatia[c]	1991	3	7	5	8	23
Czech Republic[b,d]	1989	9	30	29	0	68
Hungary[b]	1989	10	9	19	1	38
Macedonia[c]	1991	4	11	3	6	24
Poland[b]	1989	4	4	4	11	22
Romania	1989	8	17	23	1	51
Slovak Republic[b,d]	1989	9	30	29	0	68
Slovenia[c]	1991	2	5	6	8	21
Group average		7	15	18	4	42
Former Soviet Union and Mongolia						
Armenia	1991	n.a.	18	56	0	74
Azerbajian	1991	37	19	23	n.a.	79
Belarus[a]	1991	5	28	17	0	50
Estonia[b]	1991	11	25	18	24	66
Georgia	1991	n.a.	n.a.	n.a.	n.a.	n.a.
Kazakstan	1991	13	n.a.	n.a.	n.a.	71
Kyrgyz Republic	1991	13	15	15	n.a.	43
Latvia	1991	10	n.a.	n.a.	7	40
Lithuania[b]	1991	14	24	6	2	47
Moldova[c]	1991	6	n.a.	n.a.	n.a.	70
Russia	1991	9	n.a.	n.a.	8	61
Tajikistan[c]	1991	16	n.a.	n.a.	n.a.	n.a.
Turkmenstan	1991	21	40	3	n.a.	64
Ukraine	1991	9	37	21	0	67
Uzbekistan	1991	22	21	21	n.a.	64
Mongolia	1989	5	25	14	1	46
Group average		14	25	20	5	60

Notes: Monetary stocks are averages of end-year stocks from the specified year and the previous year, except as noted.
[a] FXD include an amount frozen at VEB in Moscow.
[b] Quarterly averages of monetary stocks, except for FXD of Czech and Slovak Republics.
[c] Monetary stocks are end–current year; to account for that, they are deflated by CPI (eop) and GDP is deflated by CPI (pa).
[d] Data for the federation.
Sources: For the FSU, *IMF Economic Review*, various issues, and *IMF Recent Economic Developments*, various issues; for CEE, Central Bank bulletins and *IMF International Financial Statistics*.

Table 1.2. *Monetary policy framework*

Countries	Adoption of stabilization program	Principal nominal anchor in stabilization program	Newly introduced currency
Group 1: Fast response[a]			
Albania	III/92	Money	No
Blgaria	I/91	Money	No
Croatia	IV/93	First money, later exchange rate	Yes, II/94
Czech Republic	I/91	Exchange Rate	No
Hungary	I/90	Money	No
Poland	I/90	Exchange Rate	No
Slovenia	I/92	Money	Yes, I/92
Slovak Republic	I/91	Exchange Rate	Yes, I/93
Estonia	II/92	Exchange Rate (currency board)	Yes, II/92
Latvia	II/92	First money, later exchange rate	Yes, III/93
Lithuania	II/92	First money, later exchange rate (currency board)	Yes, II/93
Kyrgyz Republic	II/93	Money	Yes, II/93
Moldova	III/93	Money	Yes, III/93
Group 2: Slower response			
Macedonia	I/94	Money	Yes, II/94
Romania	IV/93	Money	No
Armenia	IV/94	Money	Yes, IV/93
Azerbaijan	I/95	Money	Yes, III/93
Belarus	IV/94	Money	Yes, IV/94
Georgia	III/94	Money	Yes, III/95
Kazakstan	I/94	Money	Yes, IV/93
Russia	II/95	Money	Yes, III/93
Tajikistan	I/95	Money	Yes, II/95
Turkmenistan	No targets as of IV/95	n/a	Yes, IV/93
Ukraine	IV/94	Money	Yes, IV/92
Uzbekistan	IV/94	Money	Yes, II/94
Mongolia	II/93	Money	No

[a] Countries adopting a stabilization program within the first two years of transition (see Table 1.1 for base year).
Sources: Column 1: Fisher, Sahay, and Vegh 1996; except Mongolia. Columns 2 and 3: IMF and World Bank reports.

Among this group, relatively tight monetary policy was not seen as contradictory to adjustment in the real sector. In fact, the early adoption of a stabilization program appears to be intimately linked to broader reform strategies, as these countries are virtually the same as those that have been elsewhere classified as advanced and high intermediate reformers on economic liberalization (see de Melo, Denizer, and Gelb 1996). Money and credit targets were designed in conjunction with the imposition of hard budget constraints and enterprise reforms, an important element of success (Bruno 1993).

While the objectives of this group were similar, the design of monetary policies differed, most visibly in the choice of a nominal anchor. For example, Czechoslovakia, Poland, and Estonia adopted stabilization programs, backed by International Monetary Fund (IMF) standby arrangements, based on fixed exchange rate regimes after relatively large devaluations. This choice imposes clear constraints on monetary policy to maintain the exchange rate, as further devaluation would severely undermine the program's credibility. It also presumes sufficient foreign reserves, or a sufficiently devalued currency, to maintain the credibility of the nominal peg. For Poland, a major rescheduling of international debt made it possible to adopt this approach.[2] Other CEE countries, Moldova, and the Kyrgyz Republic chose money as the main nominal anchor for their stabilization programs. This was largely due to the expectation that without rapid economic liberalization and fiscal adjustment, maintaining a fixed exchange rate would have been hard if not impossible.

After their independence from the FSU, all three Baltic countries moved to a monetary policy framework within the context of a fixed exchange rate regime. Their experience is of particular interest as they succeeded in stabilizing more quickly than other former soviet republics, shifting decisively away from the socialist money and credit framework (Saavalainen 1995). Estonia led the way as the first of the former soviet republics to issue its own currency, the kroon, and in mid-1992 adopted a currency

[2] See Bruno 1993, Flood and Mussa 1994, Calvo and Vegh 1994 for the issues involved in the selection of the nominal anchor. For a review of performance of exchange rate vs. money as the nominal anchor, see Sahay and Vegh 1995, Citrin et al. 1995, and Bennett 1994.

board–type arrangement, where the central bank is strictly prohibited from lending to government or state enterprises and base money is fully backed by foreign reserves.[3] A currency board is sometimes viewed as renouncing monetary policy altogether, but it has the important advantage of insulating policy from vested interests.

Latvia, not having as ample reserves as Estonia, initially adopted a money-based stabilization strategy. After floating an interim currency, which circulated along with the Russian ruble, the government issued a national currency, the lats, in mid-1993. Without publicly committing itself to a fixed exchange rate regime, Latvia has de facto pegged its currency to the SDR since early 1994. Lithuania's initial commitment to controlling inflation was less firm than in the other two Baltic countries, but the government gradually adopted a tough stabilization program. Like Latvia, it introduced an interim currency in mid-1992 and a national currency, the litas, in mid-1993. In April 1994, Lithuania adopted a currency board arrangement, pegging its exchange rate to the dollar.

The second group of countries includes FYR Macedonia, Romania, and most of the non-Baltic FSU countries plus Mongolia. Their slow response was partly the consequence of institutional arrangements following the break up of the FSU.[4] In particular, the non-Baltic FSU countries, including Moldova and Kyrgyz Republic, remained within the ruble zone for a year or more after gaining independence. Under the ruble zone arrangement, all rubles were printed in Moscow and put into circulation by the Russian Federation. But perverse incentives came into play. The new central banks of the non-Baltic FSU countries, formerly branches of the USSR Gosbank, were able to issue noncash credits to purchase goods from other ruble

[3] It might be noted that restrictions on central bank lending led Estonia to create a variety of budgetary funds that were on-lent through the domestic banking sector to support agriculture, housing, exports, regional development, and small and medium enterprises. By mid-1996, these funds accounted for 10% of the net credit to the private sector.

[4] Following the period covered in this paper, FYR Macedonia embarked on a serious program of stabilization and structural reforms, resulting in single-digit inflation in 1995.

zone members. In the absence of a central credit allocation body or set of rules governing credit issue, the eleven new central banks were able to issue large amounts of credits and pressure the Russian government to supply them with cash as well as noncash rubles.

There were many attempts to create an orderly mechanism for credit allocation within the ruble zone, but the objective proved to be elusive and ultimately nonworkable. The lack of agreement on rules of operation and the attempt to maintain existing employment and output provided strong incentives for countries to extract as many resources as possible from the center, the Russian Federation. Indeed, in the early years following the dissolution of the FSU, Russia's financing of other ruble zone members through credit and cash allocations together was quite large – an estimated 11 percent of GDP in 1992 and 7 percent of GDP in 1993 (Dabrowski 1995). Capturing these resources was in fact the main element of monetary policy of most member countries until the ruble zone collapsed in late 1993.[5] Traditional monetary policy objectives were only adopted after issuing national currencies in 1993 and 1994.

Why did these countries not follow the lead of the Baltics and take control of money and credit after becoming independent states? Their reluctance in this regard can be seen from several angles. First, their haste to disassociate themselves politically from Russia was not as strong as it was for the Baltics. Second, the geographic location of most of these countries made the alternatives to trade with Russia less promising than they were for the Baltics, and participation in the ruble zone was seen as a means of maintaining existing, extensive trade relations. Third, many of these countries were slow reformers, attempting to maintain employment and the existing production arrangements with directed credits to unreformed industrial and agricultural enterprises. Introducing a new currency to aid in stabilization would have also required a hard budget constraint on these enterprises, suggesting that the overall strategy of transition largely determined the evolution of monetary policy.

[5] See also Conway 1995, Granville 1995, and Aslund 1995 for a discussion of the evolution of the ruble zone and reasons for its collapse.

THE USE OF MONETARY POLICY INSTRUMENTS DURING THE TRANSITION

Availability of Instruments

The beginning of transition marked an end to the passive role played by the financial sector under socialism. Authorities were forced to focus on monetary developments, whether their key policy objective was to regain price stability or maintain employment and output. And the interest in monetary developments was accompanied by a focus on available instruments to affect these developments. Table 1.3 distinguishes six separate instruments – three direct and three indirect. Other factors also affect monetary developments, including a country's foreign exchange regime and the size of the fiscal deficit, but the instruments shown here are the major conventional instruments relied on. Directed credit, credit ceilings, and interest rate controls are classified as direct instruments; reserve requirements, refinance or discount facilities, and government and central bank paper are classified as indirect instruments. The discussion here will be confined to them.

In general, direct instruments take the form of regulations while indirect instruments work through markets. As pointed out in Hilbers (1993) and Alexander, Balino, and Enoch (1995), direct instruments generally set limits on prices and/or quantities and are set in motion by central bank initiative. Indirect instruments are established by the central bank but rely on market-determined prices and quantities. As such, they are set in motion by commercial bank initiatives. This difference is not always as clear-cut as suggested, however; for example, it is not always easy to distinguish directed credit, defined to be at central bank initiative, from a refinance window with preferential rates or access, defined as a facility responding to commercial or specialized bank initiative.

The use of direct instruments does not preclude the use of indirect instruments, or vice versa, and they are often used in combination. But the form of instrument use varies. A distinctive feature of Table 1.3 is the definition of three stages of market orientation for each instrument: "late socialism," "transitional," and "market-oriented."

Table 1.3. *Main instruments of monetary policy in CEE/FSU*

Instruments	Use of instruments during transition[a]		
	Late socialism	Transitional	Market-oriented
A. Direct instruments			
1 Directed credits	Enterprises	Banks	Credit auction
2 Credit ceilings		Bank-by-bank ceilings, tradable ceilings	Ceiling on CB net domestic assets, or none
3 Interest rate controls on commercial bank deposit/lending rates	Fixed administered rates	Maximum and minimum rates or margin fixed	None
B. Indirect instruments			
4 Reserve requirements	None	High and/or changing levels	Low and stable
5 Refinance windows	Preferential rates/access	Refinance at single rate	Credit auction
Rediscount/Lombard facilities		Introduction	Fully developed
6 Government and CB bills and bonds	Introduced sometimes with statutory liquidity ratios	Secondary market trade introduced	Open-market type operation or fully developed secondary market trade

[a] The form of instrument use is not necessarily exclusive. Country sheets reflect the dominant use of each instrument.

Notes: See Alexander, Balino, and Enoch 1995 for a further description of monetary policy instruments. CB = central bank.

Appropriate Use of Instruments

On an a priori basis, it was not clear what degree of market orientation would be most effective. On the one hand, there is a general consensus among economists that indirect instruments are more effective than direct instruments in monetary control and that they promote more efficient financial intermediation (Alexander et al. 1995). Also, there is a view that direct instruments can be abused since by definition they depend on discretionary power. Moreover, direct instruments can be circumvented and hence rendered less effective, especially where countries, such as the Baltics and those in CEE, have an open capital account.

On the other hand, while it is desirable in principle to switch to indirect monetary control methods, several observers (Bredenkamp 1993, Mathieson and Haas 1994, and Hilbers 1993) point out that prevailing conditions in transition economies may not warrant their rapid adoption and use. Noting that the effectiveness of indirect instruments depends on the quality and nature of transmission channels – and noting the close links between financial sector reforms, banking reorganization (e.g., privatization, new entry mergers), establishment of an effective legal framework, monetary policy framework, capital markets, and other structural reform policies – these researchers raise two fundamental problems that can be expected to reduce the effectiveness, and hence discourage the use, of more market-oriented instruments during the transition.

The first problem is the large share of nonperforming loans in the portfolios of many banks at the beginning of the reform process. With the administrative allocation of resources and soft budget constraints characteristic of the socialist economy, enterprises were allowed to service their loans through fresh borrowing or debt rollover without any tests of their economic viability. The collapse of trade arrangements and sharp changes in relative prices accompanying transition adversely affected the profitability of many enterprises, undermining their ability to service their loans.

Thorne (1993) estimated that at the end of 1991 nonperforming loans were 37 percent of total bank lending in Romania and 50 percent in Hungary (see also Dittus 1994). More recently, the

World Bank has estimated that almost 80 percent of the financial sector portfolio in the Kyrgyz Republic was nonperforming. The main reason was the structural demand shift and relative price changes that made enterprises unprofitable and hence unable to service previously contracted debts. The policy response of the authorities, particularly in the FSU, did not help to improve things. Most FSU governments continued with directed credit policies and in effect ordered banks to lend to unprofitable enterprises. As a result, the banks – already technically insolvent given their nonperforming assets – became dysfunctional.

As many transition countries lacked an adequate prudential regulation framework, this led to the second, related, moral hazard problem, with insolvent banks continuing to operate and obtaining more funds – from the central bank by persuasion and from the public by raising interest rates. Under such circumstances, interest rates do not serve their allocation role; and, since indirect monetary control methods assume that interest rates allocate funds efficiently, a rapid substitution of indirect instruments could aggravate an already difficult situation. In fact, as a result of this situation in some countries – Kyrgyz Republic, for example – the central bank screened commercial banks for solvency before they were permitted to participate in central bank auctions.

These circumstances suggest that abolishing direct instruments quickly could be premature and also that there is a sequencing issue for monetary reform, requiring prior and parallel reforms in the banking and enterprise sectors. Thus, the introduction of indirect instruments needs to be seen in the context of broader financial and enterprise sector reforms.[6]

Experience with direct and indirect policy instruments elsewhere offers some guidance on the pace of adoption and use in transition economies. As recently reviewed by Farahbaksh and Sensenbrenner (1996), direct instruments, especially credit ceilings, were used in a number of Organization for Economic Cooperation and Development (OECD) countries during the 1960s, 1970s, and 1980s. France, for example, maintained credit ceilings for almost twenty years, until 1987. However, the general trend in OECD countries has been toward reliance on indirect

[6] See Alexander et al. 1995 for further discussion of the benefits and costs of using direct and indirect instruments.

instruments. Many developing countries have also moved toward more indirect instruments; however, credit ceilings are still regarded as useful in other countries for several reasons. One is the ease of implementation and the perception that ceilings facilitate the achievement of monetary and credit targets. Another is that ceilings can be coordinated with directed credit to priority sectors – a common practice in developing countries. Finally, the relatively limited technical capabilities of the monetary authorities in many developing countries have inhibited the adoption of more indirect instruments.

Use of Instruments during Transition

The analysis here was carried out in two steps. First, we prepared twenty-six country data sheets, which indicate the use of instruments according to the schema in Table 1.3; these are included in an appendix as Tables 1A.1–26. Then we classified each instrument in each country in each year as market-oriented or not. For *direct instruments*, market orientation is defined by low reliance on the three direct instruments in Table 1.3 as indicated by: (a) central bank–directed credit less than 25 percent of total credit; (b) an absence of bank-by-bank credit ceilings (some of which may have been replaced by an overall ceiling on central bank net domestic assets); and (c) an absence of restrictions on deposit and loan rates.[7] For *indirect instruments*, market orientation is defined by the introduction and use of market-oriented forms of indirect instruments, namely: (a) maximum reserve requirements equal to 12 percent or less; (b) a refinance window with auction or nonpreferential rates and/or rediscount or lombard facilities; and (c) government or central bank paper used for monetary operations or actively traded in a secondary market. Table 1.5 summarizes the findings, which are used to create an index of market orientation for each instrument, an overall index of MOMPI (Market Orientation of Monetary Policy Instruments), and dummy variables for use in the regression analysis in the section on effectiveness, stance, and instrument use.

[7] These criteria are suggested by Alexander et al. 1995.

During the early phase of transition, all countries seem to have used at least one and often all three direct instruments in the implementation of their monetary policies. Moreover, by late 1994, most countries still had maximum ratios above 12 percent – the somewhat arbitrary level designated above as the cutoff between the direct versus indirect use of this instrument. And some countries had retained interest rate controls and had not yet developed a market for government paper. Other countries, however, had a high or substantial market orientation. On average, CEE countries and "fast response" countries switched more quickly from direct to indirect instruments, but variation within these groups can also be observed. A brief description of the use of instruments during transition follows.

Directed Credit

As late as 1990, all countries except Hungary and Poland had large directed credit programs inherited from the central-planning period. These programs, financed by central bank credit channeled through commercial banks at preferential interest rates, were used to support enterprises in designated sectors, usually including agriculture. About half the countries sharply reduced the share of directed credit with the beginning of reform, and by 1995 the share of directed credit in total credit had fallen to under 25 percent in many countries, although it remained high in "slow response" countries. In these latter countries, directed credits were retained and channeled to state enterprises at subsidized rates, leading to large quasi-fiscal deficits and high inflation (see de Melo et al. 1996).

Credit Ceilings

Credit ceilings were used in several CEE countries in the early 1990s, but the effectiveness of implementation varied. In the Czech Republic, for example, ceilings on commercial bank credits were enforced strictly by the authorities. In Bulgaria, ceilings were exceeded in 1992, and it was only in 1994 that monetary aggregates were brought under control and credit ceilings removed. Most "slow response" countries did not use credit ceilings; limitations on credit expansion would have been inconsistent with the authorities' strategy of using directed credit to maintain employment and output in state enterprises.

Interest Controls

Interest rates on bank deposits and loans have been market-determined since late 1992/early 1993 in most "fast response" countries. The removal of interest rate controls, however, has involved some difficulties and has not always led to positive, moderate real rates, as expected. On the one hand, there are cases, such as Romania, where interest rates were liberalized during the early days of transition but, as a result of collusion among banks, did not become positive before late 1994. On the other hand, there are countries – for example, Slovenia and Macedonia – where real interest rates were quite high. Moreover, many countries in the FSU, as well as Albania, have removed interest rate controls more gradually than those in CEE, even allowing for a two-year difference in the start of reforms. About half these countries have relied on minimum and maximum interest rates, as well as controls on margins. The others have maintained direct controls on nominal deposit and loan rates and, except in Albania, the resulting real rates have been highly negative over the past couple of years, contributing strongly to disintermediation and undermining attempts at stabilization.

Reserve Requirements

Reserve requirements were put in effect by all countries soon after the beginning of reforms. Enforcement lagged especially in the non-Baltic FSU, but by 1995 most central banks were able to enforce them relatively effectively. Ratios were high initially, presumably due to high inflation and the desire of authorities to absorb liquidity. In the non-Baltic FSU, reserve ratios were frequently changed, with a tendency to raise the level to absorb liquidity, contributing to the disintermediation trend discussed earlier. Many CEE countries lowered reserve ratios over time, although in Croatia they rose to 34 percent in mid-1995.

Refinance Window

Most countries also introduced a refinance window, but its use differed. Countries in CEE were more likely to use this instrument in a market-oriented and noninterventionist fashion without preferential access. The refinancing rate was set at the central bank discount rate or established on the basis of auctions. In some countries, there remained small amounts of refinancing for agriculture or housing. Rediscount and Lombard facilities were put in place, and their importance seems to have increased over time. By 1995 commercial bank borrowing from the central bank was mostly carried out through the use of this instrument. In many FSU countries, refinancing facilities were often used to direct credit for specific purposes at preferential rates. The rediscount and Lombard facilities are not as extensively used.

Market for Government Paper

Government, and in some countries central bank, paper was introduced relatively early in CEE countries.[8] In Hungary, this instrument existed since 1988 and by 1993 monetary policy was being implemented mostly through open-market-type operations, using government paper. Although some other countries have introduced secondary market trade, it is limited, and government paper typically is not used for open-market-type operations. In the non-Baltic FSU, this instrument may have been introduced but is typically not yet developed.

By late 1994, there was substantial diversity in the extent to which transition countries were relying on market-oriented instruments of monetary policy. We can distinguish four groups on the basis of the data in Table 1.4, which classify the market-oriented use of six different instruments: At the end of 1994, countries with "high" market orientation met all, or almost all, the criteria of market orientation specified here. To the extent that these countries still relied on direct instruments, they used market-oriented forms; also, they have all introduced the main indirect instruments used in market economies. The speed of introduction differed, reflecting the pace of broader structural reforms, including solving the nonperforming loan problem. For example, the Czech Republic eliminated almost all direct controls in 1992, whereas Bulgaria phased them out in 1994.

Countries with "substantial" market orientation use both direct and indirect instruments for policy-making purposes; in some countries, there have been policy reversals. Implementation diffi-

[8] For issues involved in the use of government versus central bank paper, see Quintyn 1994.

Table 1.4. *Market orientation of monetary instruments at end 1994*

High	Substantial	Moderate	Low
Bulgaria	Croatia	Albania	Armenia[a]
Czech Republic	Lithuania	Azerbaijan[a]	Belarus[a]
Estonia	Macedonia[a]	Georgia[a]	Kyrgyz Republic
Hungary		Kazakstan[a]	Moldova
Latvia		Mongolia[a]	Turkmenistan[a]
Poland		Russia[a]	Tajikistan[a]
Romania[a]			Ukraine[a]
Slovak Republic			
Slovenia			

Notes: High: 5 or 6 instruments; substantial: 4 instruments; moderate: 3 instruments; low: 1 or 2 instruments.
[a] Countries stabilizing relatively slowly (see Table 1.2).

culties are common, often as a result of lack of parallel financial sector reforms. Countries with "moderate" or "low" market orientation continue to rely on either directed credit or interest rate controls, or both, to influence money and credit. They typically have high reserve requirements and have not developed secondary markets for government or central bank paper. However, most have introduced a refinancing facility based on auction or nonpreferential interest rates.

Figure 1.1 shows the average differences in CEE and FSU countries from 1990 through 1994, at which time the CEE countries had switched almost entirely to market-oriented instruments while FSU countries were clearly relying on a combination of both market and nonmarket instruments. The decline in market orientation of FSU countries after 1991 was primarily due to the increase in reserve ratios, designed to absorb liquidity in a highly inflationary environment.

Instrument Use around Stabilization

One difficulty in cross-country comparisons of transition economies is that reforms were initiated at different points in time. In an attempt to control for the timing of reform, we look here at how instruments were used at the time of stabilization. Figure 1.2 shows the sequencing of market-oriented use of monetary instru-

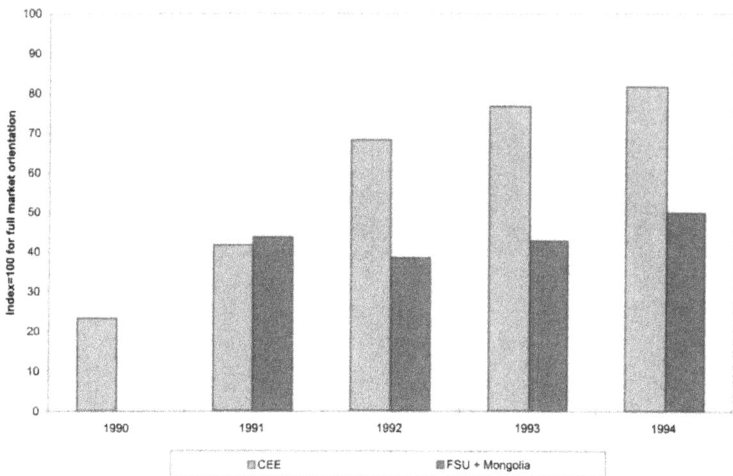

Figure 1.1. Market orientation of monetary policy instruments, group averages, 1990–94.

ments during the year of stabilization (year T, as shown in Tables 1.5b and 1.5c) and also during the years before (year T − 1) and after (year T + 1). With the exception of credit ceilings, which were reimposed by several CEE countries during the year of stabilization, countries on average shifted progressively toward market-oriented instruments. As indicated earlier, FSU tended to raise reserve requirements as inflation persisted, but CEE countries typically reduced reserve ratios and switched from directed credit programs to a more market-oriented refinance window.

Tables 1.5b and 1.5c organize the data in Table 1.5a to show the market orientation of instrument use in CEE and FSU countries around the time of stabilization (year T). The "grand total" for each country is used to define an annual country index for the Market Orientation of Monetary Policy Instruments (MOMPI), used in some simple correlations reported here. The average "scores" on market orientation permit a comparison between CEE and FSU countries at any point in time. It indicates, for example that FSU countries were actually slightly more market oriented than CEE countries in the year before stabilization, perhaps because stabilization occurred somewhat later relative to the

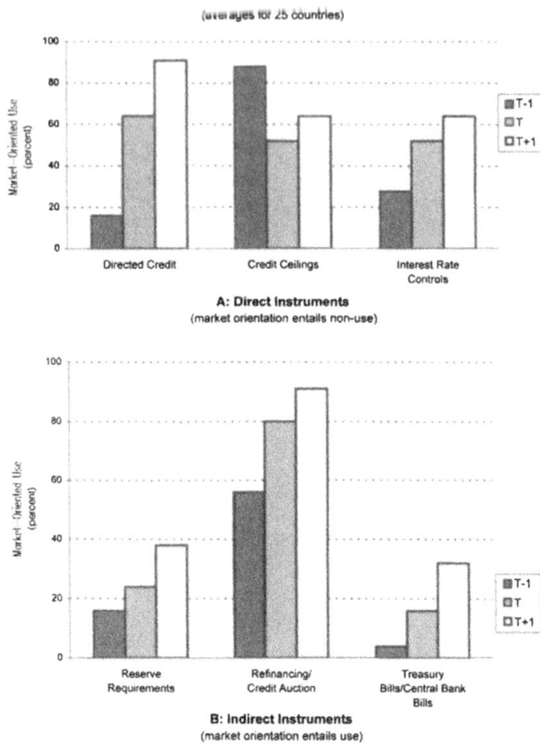

Figure 1.2. Sequencing of market-oriented use of monetary instruments in transition economies during stabilization.

beginning of transition; however, they moved more slowly toward market orientation during and following stabilization.

Table 1.5d shows the average market orientation for specific instruments in index form around the time of stabilization. The indices for "all countries" show that almost all countries had contained directed credit and replaced it with a market-oriented refinance window, and most countries had removed interest rate controls, by the year following stabilization. The use of credit ceilings shows different pattern, in that countries increased their reliance on credit ceilings during stabilization. This was particularly true in CEE and "fast response" countries. Indices for country groups also point up the much slower movement in FSU and Mongolia on the removal of interest rate controls,

Table 1.5a. *Market orientation (1) of monetary instrument use in transition economies*

	Direct instruments[a]															Indirect instruments[b]														
	Directed credit					Credit ceilings					Interest rate controls					Reserve requirements					Refinancing/ credit auction					T-bills/CB bills[c]				
Countries	90	91	92	93	94	90	91	92	93	94	90	91	92	93	94	90	91	92	93	94	90	91	92	93	94	90	91	92	93	94
Albania	0	0	1	1	1	1	1	0	0	0	0	0	0	0	0	0	0	1	1	1	0	0	0	1	1	0	0	0	0	0
Bulgaria	0	1	1	1	1	1	0	0	0	1	0	1	1	1	1	0	1	1	1	1	0	1	1	1	1	0	0	0	1	1
Croatia[d]	0	0	0	1	1	0	1	1	1	1	0	1	1	1	1	0	0	0	0	0	1	1	1	0	0	0	0	0	1	1
Czech Republic[d]	0	1	1	1	1	1	0	1	1	1	0	0	1	1	1	0	0	1	1	1	0	1	1	1	1	0	0	1	1	1
Hungary	1	1	1	1	1	0	0	1	1	1	0	0	1	1	1	0	0	0	0	0	1	1	1	1	1	1	1	1	1	1
Macedonia[d]	0	0	0	0	1	0	1	1	1	0	0	0	1	1	1	0	0	0	1	1	1	1	0	0	1	0	0	0	0	0
Poland	1	1	1	1	1	0	0	0	1	1	1	1	1	1	1	0	0	0	0	0	1	1	1	1	1	0	0	1	1	1
Romania	0	0	0	1	1	1	0	1	1	1	0	1	1	1	1	0	0	1	1	1	0	0	1	1	1	0	0	0	0	0
Slovak Republic[d]	0	1	1	1	1	1	0	1	0	1	0	0	1	1	1	0	0	1	1	1	0	1	1	1	1	0	0	1	1	1
Slovenia[d]	0	1	1	1	1	0	1	1	1	1	0	1	1	1	1	0	0	0	0	0	1	1	1	1	1	0	0	1	1	1
Armenia	—	0	0	0	0	—	1	1	1	1	—	0	0	0	0	—	0	0	0	0	—	0	0	0	1	—	0	0	0	0
Azerbaijan	—	0	0	0	1	—	1	1	1	1	—	0	0	0	0	—	0	0	0	1	—	0	0	0	0	—	0	0	0	0
Belarus	—	0	0	0	0	—	1	1	1	1	—	0	0	0	0	—	1	0	0	0	—	0	0	1	1	—	0	0	0	0
Estonia	—	1	1	1	1	—	1	1	1	1	—	1	1	1	1	—	1	1	1	1	—	0	0	1	1	—	0	0	1	1
Georgia	—	0	0	0	1	—	1	0	1	1	—	0	0	0	1	—	1	0	0	0	—	0	0	1	0	—	0	0	0	0
Kazakstan	—	0	0	0	0	—	1	1	1	1	—	0	1	1	1	—	0	0	0	0	—	0	1	1	1	—	0	0	0	0
Kyrgyz Republic	—	0	0	0	1	—	1	1	1	0	—	0	0	0	0	—	0	0	0	0	—	0	0	1	1	—	0	0	0	0
Latvia	—	0	1	1	1	—	1	1	1	1	—	1	1	1	1	—	0	0	0	1	—	1	1	1	0	—	0	0	0	1
Lithuania	—	0	1	1	1	—	1	0	1	1	—	0	0	1	1	—	1	1	1	1	—	0	0	1	0	—	0	0	0	0
Moldova	—	0	0	0	0	—	1	1	1	1	—	0	0	0	0	—	0	0	0	0	—	0	1	1	1	—	0	0	0	0
Russia	—	0	0	0	0	—	1	1	1	1	—	0	0	0	0	—	1	0	0	0	—	0	1	1	1	—	0	0	0	1
Tajikistan	—	0	0	0	0	—	1	1	1	1	—	0	0	0	0	—	0	0	0	0	—	0	1	1	1	—	0	0	0	0
Turkmenistan	—	0	0	0	0	—	1	1	1	1	—	0	0	0	0	—	0	0	0	0	—	0	0	1	1	—	0	0	0	0
Ukraine	—	0	0	0	0	—	1	1	1	0	—	0	0	0	0	—	1	0	0	0	—	0	1	1	1	—	0	0	0	0
Uzbekistan	—	0	0	0	0	—	1	1	1	1	—	0	0	0	0	—	0	0	0	0	—	0	0	1	1	—	0	0	0	0
Mongolia	0	0	0	0	1	1	1	0	0	0	0	1	0	0	0	0	0	0	0	0	0	1	1	1	1	0	0	0	0	0

[a] Use of direct instruments as of year-end; 0= in use, 1= not used, and thus market oriented; see text for criteria.
[b] Use of indirect instruments as of year-end; 1= in use, and thus market oriented; 0= not used; see text for criteria.
[c] T-bills – issued by the Ministry of Finance; CB bills – issued by the Central Bank.
[d] Instrument use shown for Czechoslovakia and Yugoslavia, as appropriate, prior to breakup.

Table 1.5b. *Market orientation of monetary instrument use in CEE at the time of stabilization*

	Year T-1									Year T[a]									Year T + 1[b]								
Countries	DC	CC	IRC	Total	RR	RCA	TCB	Total	Grand total	DC	CC	IRC	Total	RR	RCA	TCB	Total	Grand total	DC	CC	IRC	Total	RR	RCA	TCB	Total	Grand total
Albania (92)	0	1	0	1	0	0	0	0	1	1	0	0	1	1	0	0	1	2	1	0	0	1	1	1	0	2	3
Bulgaria (91)	0	1	0	1	0	0	0	0	1	1	0	1	2	1	1	0	2	4	1	0	1	2	1	1	0	2	4
Croatia (93)	0	1	1	2	0	1	0	1	3	1	1	1	3	0	0	1	1	4	1	1	1	3	0	0	1	1	4
Czech Republic (91)	0	1	0	1	0	0	0	0	1	1	0	0	1	0	1	0	1	2	1	1	1	3	1	1	1	3	6
Hungary (90)	0	0	0	0	0	1	0	1	1	1	0	0	1	0	1	1	2	3	1	0	0	1	0	1	1	2	3
Macedonia (94)	0	1	1	2	1	0	0	1	3	1	0	1	2	1	1	0	2	4	1	0	1	2	1	1	0	2	4
Poland (90)	1	0	0	1	0	0	0	0	1	1	0	1	2	0	1	0	1	3	1	0	1	2	0	1	0	1	3
Romania (93)	0	1	1	2	1	1	0	2	4	1	1	1	3	1	1	0	2	5	1	1	1	3	1	1	0	2	5
Slovak Republic (91)	0	1	0	1	0	0	0	0	1	1	0	1	2	0	1	0	1	3	1	1	1	3	1	1	1	3	6
Slovenia (92)	1	1	1	3	0	1	0	1	4	1	1	1	3	0	1	1	2	5	1	1	1	3	0	1	1	2	5
Total	2	8	4	14	2	4	0	6	20	10	3	7	20	4	8	3	15	35	10	5	8	23	6	9	5	20	43
Average	0.2	0.8	0.4	1.4	0.2	0.4	0.0	0.6	2.0	1.0	0.3	0.7	2.0	0.4	0.8	0.3	1.5	3.5	1.0	0.5	0.8	2.3	0.6	0.9	0.5	2.0	4.3

Notes: This table is derived from Table 1.4a. A "1" = market-oriented use. Year T refers to the year of the last stabilization attempt, shown in parentheses in the first column (see also Table 1.2).

[a] If year T or T + 1 is 1995, the latest available information is used.

Table 1.5c. *Market orientation of monetary instrument use in FSU and Mongolia at the time of stabilization*

Countries	Year T-1								Grand total	Year T[a]								Grand total	Year T + 1[a]								Grand total
	DC	CC	IRC	Total	RR	RCA	TCB	Total		DC	CC	IRC	Total	RR	RCA	TCB	Total		DC	CC	IRC	Total	RR	RCA	TCB	Total	
Armenia (94)	0	1	0	1	0	0	0	0	1	0	1	0	1	0	1	0	1	2	1	1	1	3	0	1	0	1	4
Azerbaijan (95)	1	1	0	2	1	0	0	1	3	1	1	0	2	0	1	0	1	3									
Belarus (94)	0	1	0	1	0	1	0	1	2	0	1	0	1	0	1	0	1	2	1	1	0	2	1	1	0	2	4
Estonia (92)	1	1	1	3	1	0	0	1	4	1	1	1	3	1	0	0	1	4	1	1	1	3	1	1	1	3	6
Georgia (94)	0	1	0	1	0	1	0	1	2	1	1	1	3	0	0	0	0	3	1	1	1	3	0	0	0	0	3
Kazakhstan (94)	0	1	1	2	0	1	0	1	3	0	1	1	2	0	1	0	1	3	1	0	1	2	0	1	1	2	4
Kyrgyz Republic (93)	0	1	0	1	0	0	0	0	1	0	0	0	0	0	1	0	1	1	1	1	0	2	0	1	0	1	3
Latvia (92)	0	1	1	2	0	1	0	1	3	1	1	1	3	0	1	0	1	4	1	1	1	3	0	1	0	1	4
Lithuania (92)	0	1	0	1	0	0	0	0	1	1	0	0	1	1	0	0	1	2	1	1	1	3	1	1	0	2	5
Moldova (93)	0	1	0	1	0	1	0	1	2	0	1	0	1	0	1	0	1	2	0	1	0	1	0	1	0	1	2
Russia (95)	0	1	0	1	0	1	1	2	3	1	1	1	3	0	1	1	2	5									
Tajikistan (95)	0	1	0	1	0	1	0	1	2	0	0	1	1	0	1	0	1	2									
Turkmenistan																											
Ukraine (94)	0	1	0	1	0	1	0	1	2	0	0	0	0	0	1	0	1	1	1	0	0	1	0	1	0	1	2
Uzbekistan (94)	0	1	0	1	0	1	0	1	2	0	1	0	1	0	1	0	1	2	0	1	0	1	0	1	0	1	2
Mongolia (93)	0	0	0	0	0	1	0	1	1	0	0	0	0	0	1	0	1	1	1	0	0	1	0	1	0	1	2
Total	2	14	3	19	2	10	1	13	32	6	10	6	22	2	12	1	15	37	10	9	6	25	3	11	2	16	41
Average	0.1	0.9	0.2	1.3	0.1	0.7	0.1	0.9	2.1	0.4	0.7	0.4	1.5	0.1	0.8	0.1	1.0	2.5	0.8	0.8	0.5	2.1	0.3	0.9	0.2	1.3	3.4

Notes: This table is derived from Table 1.4a. A "1" = market-oriented use. Year T refers to the year of the last stabilization attempt, shown in parentheses in the first column (see also Table 1.2).
[a] If year T or T + 1 is 1995, the latest available information is used.

Table 1.5d. *Market orientation of monetary policy instruments around stabilization in year T (average indices)*

Instruments	All countries			CEE countries			FSU countries and Mongolia			"Fast response" countries			"Slow response" countries		
	Year T−1	Year T	Year T+1	Year T−1	Year T	Year T+1	Year T−1	Year T	Year T+1	Year T−1	Year T	Year T+1	Year T−1	Year T	Year T+1
Direct															
Directed credit	16	64	91	20	100	100	13	40	83	23	85	92	8	42	89
Credit ceilings	88	52	64	80	30	50	93	67	75	85	38	69	92	67	56
Interest rate controls	28	52	64	40	70	80	20	40	50	31	54	69	25	50	56
Indirect															
Reserve requirements	16	24	38	20	40	60	13	13	25	8	31	46	25	17	25
Refinancing/ credit auction	56	80	91	40	80	90	67	80	92	38	69	92	75	92	89
Government paper	4	16	32	0	30	50	7	7	17	0	23	46	8	8	11
Overall index	35	48	63	33	58	72	36	42	57	31	50	69	39	46	54

Sources: Authors' calculations; see text for definition.

the adoption of more moderate reserve ratios, and the development of markets for government paper. These differences exist, but to a lesser degree between "fast-response" and "slow-response" countries.

The relationship between the adoption of market-oriented instruments and the choice of a nominal anchor in a country's stabilization program is shown in Table 1.5e. In general, countries relying on an exchange rate anchor, either initially or following an initial reliance on a monetary target moved quickly toward more market-oriented monetary policy instruments, while countries relying exclusively on a money anchor did not. In particular, all countries using an exchange rate anchor contained the amount of directed credit and removed interest rate controls.

MONETARY POLICY STANCE AND EFFECTIVENESS

Here we define some indicators of monetary policy stance and effectiveness, in order to relate them to the introduction of market-oriented instruments. No attempt is made to define policy stance in relative terms – for example, relative to the current rate of inflation or to changes in the demand for money – although this would be an important consideration in the formulation of monetary targets. Rather, several simple nominal indicators of average policy stance are considered, and base money growth is chosen as the most appropriate indicator for purposes of classification. Inflation and financial depth are used as indicators of policy effectiveness.

Policy Stance

Four simple indicators of monetary policy stance are provided in Table 1.6: the average growth rate of base money, which reflects the use of directed credit and refinance facilities as well as central bank financing of the fiscal deficit; the average growth of broad money, which is influenced by reserve requirements as well as inflation and other factors; the effectiveness of credit ceilings; and the average real discount rate in 1992–94. The average growth of base money is used as the classification criterion to organize countries into three groups: Group 1: moderate; Group 2: loose; and Group 3: very loose. It is clear from the group

Table 1.5e. *Market orientation of monetary instrument use in CEE at the time of stabilization*

	Year T−1									Year T[a]									Year T + 1[a]								
Countries	DC	CC	IRC	Total	RR	RCA	TCB	Total	Grand total	DC	CC	IRC	Total	RR	RCA	TCB	Total	Grand total	DC	CC	IRC	Total	RR	RCA	TCB	Total	Grand total
Exchange rate anchor																											
Czech Republic (91)	0	1	0	1	0	0	0	0	1	1	0	0	1	0	1	0	1	2	1	1	1	3	1	1	1	3	6
Poland (90)	1	0	0	1	0	0	0	0	1	1	0	1	2	0	1	0	1	3	1	0	1	2	0	1	0	1	3
Slovak Republic (91)	0	1	0	1	0	0	0	0	1	1	0	1	2	0	1	0	1	3	1	1	1	3	1	1	1	3	6
Estonia (92)	1	1	1	3	1	0	0	1	4	1	1	1	3	1	0	0	1	4	1	1	1	3	1	1	1	3	6
Total	2	3	1	6	1	0	0	1	7	4	1	3	8	1	3	0	4	12	4	3	4	11	3	4	3	10	21
Average	0.5	0.8	0.3	1.5	0.3	0.0	0.0	0.3	1.8	1.0	0.3	0.8	2.0	0.3	0.8	0.0	1.0	3.0	0.8	0.8	1.0	2.8	0.8	1.0	0.8	2.5	5.3
Money followed by ER anchor																											
Croatia (93)	0	1	1	2	0	1	0	1	3	1	1	1	3	0	0	1	1	4	1	1	1	3	0	0	1	1	4
Latvia (92)	0	1	1	2	0	1	0	1	3	1	1	1	3	0	1	0	1	4	1	1	1	3	0	1	0	1	4
Lithuania (92)	0	1	0	1	0	0	0	0	1	1	0	0	1	1	0	0	1	2	1	1	1	3	1	1	0	2	5
Total	0	3	2	5	0	2	0	2	7	3	2	2	7	1	1	1	3	10	3	3	3	9	1	2	1	4	13
Average	0.0	1.0	0.7	1.7	0.0	0.7	0.0	0.7	2.3	1.0	0.7	0.7	2.3	0.3	0.3	0.3	1.0	3.3	1.0	1.0	1.0	3.0	0.3	0.7	0.3	1.3	4.3
Money anchor																											
Albania (92)	0	1	0	1	0	0	0	0	1	1	0	0	1	1	0	0	1	2	1	0	0	1	1	1	0	2	3
Armenia (94)	0	1	0	1	0	0	0	0	1	0	1	0	1	0	1	0	1	2	1	1	1	3	0	1	0	1	4
Azerbaijan (95)	1	1	0	2	1	0	0	1	3	1	1	0	2	0	1	0	1	3									

Belarus (94)	0	1	0	1	0	1	0	1	2	0	1	0	1	0	1	0	1	2	1	1	0	2	1	1	0	2	4
Bulgaria (91)	0	1	0	1	0	0	0	0	1	1	0	1	2	1	1	0	2	4	1	0	1	2	1	1	0	2	4
Georgia (94)	0	1	0	1	0	1	0	1	2	1	1	1	3	0	0	0	0	3	1	1	1	3	0	0	0	0	3
Hungary (90)	0	0	0	0	0	1	0	1	1	1	0	0	1	0	1	1	2	3	1	0	0	1	0	1	1	2	3
Kazakstan (94)	0	1	1	2	0	1	0	1	3	0	1	1	2	0	1	0	1	3	1	0	1	2	0	1	1	2	4
Kyrgyz Republic (93)	0	1	0	1	0	0	0	0	1	0	0	0	0	0	1	0	1	1	1	1	0	2	0	1	0	1	3
Macedonia (94)	0	1	1	2	1	0	0	1	3	1	0	1	2	1	1	0	2	4	1	0	1	2	1	1	0	2	4
Moldova (93)	0	1	0	1	0	1	0	1	2	0	1	0	1	0	1	0	1	2	0	1	0	1	0	1	0	1	2
Mongolia (93)	0	0	0	0	0	1	0	1	1	0	0	0	0	0	1	0	1	1	1	0	0	1	0	1	0	1	2
Romania (93)	0	1	1	2	1	1	0	2	4	1	1	1	3	1	1	0	2	5	1	1	1	3	1	1	0	2	5
Russia (95)	0	1	0	1	0	1	1	2	3	1	1	1	3	0	1	1	2	5									
Slovenia (92)	1	1	1	3	0	1	0	1	4	1	1	1	3	0	1	1	2	5	1	1	1	3	0	1	1	2	5
Tajikistan (95)	0	1	0	1	0	1	0	1	2	0	0	1	1	0	1	0	1	2									
Ukraine (94)	0	1	0	1	0	1	0	1	2	0	0	0	0	0	1	0	1	1	1	0	0	1	0	1	0	1	2
Uzbekistan (94)	0	1	0	1	0	1	0	1	2	0	1	0	1	0	1	0	1	2	0	1	0	1	0	1	0	1	2
Total	2	16	4	22	3	12	1	16	38	9	10	8	27	4	16	3	23	50	13	8	7	28	5	14	3	22	50
Average	0.1	0.9	0.2	1.2	0.2	0.7	0.1	0.9	2.1	0.5	0.6	0.4	1.5	0.2	0.9	0.2	1.3	2.8	0.7	0.4	0.4	1.6	0.3	0.8	0.2	1.2	2.8

Notes: This table is derived from Table 1.5a: A "1" = market-oriented use. Year T refers to the year of the last stabilization attempt shown in parentheses in the first column (see also Table 1.2).
[a] If year T or T + 1 is 1995, the latest available information is used.

Table 1.6. *Indicators of monetary policy stance, 1990–94 (CEE and Mongolia) and 1992–94 (FSU and FYRs) (%)*

	Average growth rate of base money[a]	Average growth rate of broad money[a]	Effectiveness of credit ceilings[b]	Average real discount rate, 1992–94[c]
Group 1: Moderate				
Albania	66	79	E	−11
Bulgaria	31	60	E*	−11
Czech Republic[d]	29	18	E*	−4
Hungary	28	23	E*	2
Poland	51	66	E*	3
Romania	78	98	NE	−23
Slovak Republic[d]	24	13	E*	−5
Slovenia	76	77	NU	−12
Estonia	91	52	NU	n.a.
Latvia	64	95	E*	−21
Group average	54	58		−9
Group 2: Loose				
Kyrgyz Republic	284	242	E*	−41
Lithuania	127	175	E*	n.a.
Macedonia	248	970	E	20
Moldova	352	265	NU	−43
Mongolia	144	84	E	−53
Group average	231	347		−29
Group 3: Very loose				
Croatia	534	587	NU	−28
Armenia	1,711	970	NU	−82
Azerbaijan	652	733	NU	−88
Belarus	993	1,115	NU	−80
Georgia	1,978	2,447	NE	−94[e]
Kazakstan	843	600	NE	−72
Russia	650	437	NE	−41
Tajikistan	1,113	722	NE	−56
Turkmenistan	742	875	NU	−91
Ukraine	2,009	1,070	E	−59
Uzbekistan	552	644	NU	−85
Group average	1,071	927		−70

Notes: The group classification is based on average annual base money growth: Group 1: <100%; Group 2: >100% and <400%; Group 3: >400%.

[a] Average of December/December growth rates; broad money includes foreign exchange deposits.

[b] E = effectively used, still used as of end-1994; E* = effectively used, terminated; NE = not always enforced; NU = not used, or used only for a short period of time.

[c] The real discount rate is calculated as [(I + i)/(I + □)]− 1, where i refers to the quoted central bank discount/refinancing rate and □ refers to the quarterly eop CPI-based inflation. The period rate is based on quarterly average rates.

[d] 1990–92: data on the former federation; 1992 – base money estimated from the CB balance sheet.

[e] Average for 1992–93.

Sources: IMF and IBRD reports, country Central Bank bulletins, Banerjee et al. 1995, Citrin et al. 1995, Ebril et al. 1994.

averages that other indicators of policy stance are consistent with this one.

On the one hand, given the void in enterprise governance, especially in the early stages of transition, tight monetary policy forces reallocation of resources toward more productive uses, thus generating growth. On the other hand, as argued by Portes (1993) and Calvo and Coricelli (1993), monetary policy can be too tight, restricting growth. On balance, however, the most recent literature suggests output recovery has occurred in countries that had relatively tight monetary policies (Citrin, Anderson, and Zettelmeyer 1995, Sahay and Vegh 1995), possibly because nowhere was average annual base money growth less than 20 percent.

Effectiveness

We can identify three plausible objectives of monetary policy: price stability; financial depth, as a determinant of economic growth, and growth itself. Table 1.7 provides data for 1990–94 on all three objectives – lower inflation, greater financial depth, and higher real growth in GDP. Countries are grouped, as previously, by policy stance, and it can be seen that achievement of these objectives is associated with a moderate policy stance (Group 1), suggesting that it may have been relatively tight but was not too tight.

In the econometric analysis that follows, we take only price stability and financial depth as measures of effectiveness. Price stability is the traditional objective of monetary policy, and the relationship between financial depth and growth is explained in the remainder of this section. Growth itself is not used as a measure of effectiveness here, as too many other factors affect it to try to separate out the effect of market-oriented monetary instruments.

The importance of financial depth in development was stressed by Mckinnon and Shaw in the early 1970s. Subsequent cross-country comparisons have largely confirmed this relationship (see King and Levine 1993, Fry 1995). The basic idea is that the level of financial intermediation is a proxy for the level and quality of financial services, including entrepreneurial selection, and that effective financial services promote growth through both capital accumulation and improvements in economic efficiency.

Table 1.7. *Indicators of effectiveness of monetary policy (%)*

	Average CPI/RPI inflation					Domestic M2/GDP					Real GDP growth				
	1990	1991	1992	1993	1994	1990	1991	1992	1993	1994	1990	1991	1992	1993	1994
Group 1															
Albania	2	36	226	85	23	31	45	31	26	27	−10	−28	−10	11	7
Bulgaria	26	334	82	73	96	89	37	44	49	41	−9	−12	−7	−2	1
Czech Republic	10	57	11	21	10	64	57	62	63	69	0	−14	−6	−1	3
Hungary	29	35	23	22	19	35	33	36	37	33	−4	−12	−3	−1	3
Poland	586	70	43	35	33	14	22	21	22	22	−12	−7	3	4	6
Romania	5	175	211	256	131	53	26	19	11	10	−6	−13	−9	1	4
Slovak Republic	11	61	10	23	14	64	57	63	57	55	0	−15	−6	−4	5
Slovenia	550	118	201	32	20	15	12	10	13	16	−5	−8	−5	1	6
Estonia	23	211	1,076	90	48	67	49	14	19	18	−8	−11	−14	−7	−3
Latvia	4	124	951	109	36	67	42	12	16	21	3	−8	−35	−15	2
Group average	125	122	283	75	43	50	38	31	31	31	−5	−13	−9	−1	3
Group 2															
Kyrgyz Republic	3	85	855	1,209	280	67	43	13	8	9	3	−5	−25	−16	−27
Lithuania	8	225	1,021	409	72	67	44	11	9	12	−5	−13	−38	−24	2
Macedonia	603	115	1,691	350	122	15	18	8	8	12	−10	−12	−21	−8	−4

Moldova	4	98	1,208	1,283	587	67	n.a.	21	8	6	−2	−18	−29	−1	−31
Mongolia	2	33	203	269	87	54	41	26	11	15	−2	−9	−10	−3	2
Group average	125	111	995	704	230	54	37	16	9	11	−3	−11	−25	−10	−12
Group 3															
Croatia	610	123	666	1,518	98	15	15	9	6	10	−9	−14	−9	−3	1
Armenia	10	100	825	3,732	5,273	67	74	30	11	4	−7	−11	−52	−15	5
Azerbaijan	8	106	616	1,130	1,664	67	79	19	21	12	−12	−1	−23	−23	−21
Belarus	5	84	969	1,188	2,220	67	50	14	8	5	−3	−1	−10	−12	−20
Georgia	3	79	887	3,125	18,922	67	n.a.	22	3	1	−12	−14	−40	−39	−35
Kazakstan	4	91	1,381	1,662	1,880	67	70	15	11	4	0	−13	−13	−12	−25
Russia	6	93	1,353	896	302	67	58	14	10	10	−4	−13	−15	−9	−13
Tajikistan	4	112	1,157	2,195	341	67	n.a.	27	32	n.a.	−2	−7	−29	−11	−21
Turkmenistan	5	103	493	3,102	2,400	67	64	12	13	6	2	−5	−5	−10	−20
Ukraine	4	91	1,210	4,735	891	67	67	22	10	10	−3	−12	−17	−17	−23
Uzbekistan	3	82	645	534	1,568	67	64	33	20	13	2	−1	−11	−2	−4
Group average	60	97	927	2,165	3,233	62	60	20	13	8	−4	−8	−20	−14	−16

Sources: EBRD, IFS, IMF reports.

Transition from a command economy to a market economy has, however, been accompanied by a collapse in financial ratios in many countries. Table 1.8 compares the average annual ratios of domestic broad money to GDP in transition economies to those in other countries classified by income level. As shown, this ratio is higher for high income countries, and in recent years financial depth has increased in high-income countries. In 1989, at the beginning of transition, CEE and FSU countries also had relatively high financial ratios on average. But by 1993–94 financial ratios had declined and, in CEE countries, were comparable with those in lower- to middle-income countries. Ratios in all FSU countries and Mongolia fell dramatically and by 1993–94 had dropped well below those in low-income countries. These trends can be compared with the experience of transition countries in East Asia, namely China and Vietnam, where financial depth has increased.

There are a number of factors that might cause disintermediation and account for the large differences observed in CEE and FSU countries. One factor is the elimination of the monetary overhang, which appears to have been larger in the FSU (see de Melo et al. 1996). Declines in financial ratios in some countries, however, exceed rough estimates of the monetary overhang as a percent of GDP. Other factors are inflation and highly negative ex ante and ex post real interest rates, especially in FSU countries; these have resulted in an erosion of financial savings and little incentive to hold domestic currency in any form. Yet another factor appears to be informal credit in the form of interenterprise arrears (see Citrin et al. 1995). Such credit may substitute for M1 and thus help to explain the observed high velocity in certain transition economies. Also, credibility of reforms and hysteresis effects may account for continuing high levels of currency substitution; foreign currency deposits remain high relative to M2 in Poland and the Czech Republic, for example, despite stabilization and growth.

In the following section, we investigate the extent to which financial depth may be affected by the market-oriented use of monetary instruments. The focus is on domestic liquid liabilities, as they allow the government to generate investible resources in the form of seignorage. The evolution of this ratio in relationship to policy stance is shown in Table 1.6, and Figure 1.3 shows that a

Table 1.8. *Comparison of average financial ratios across country groups*

M2/GDP (including FX deposits)[a]	1989	1991	1993	1994[b]
High income	68	79	80	75
Upper middle income	51	42	47	50
Lower middle income[c]	42	39	40	39
Low income	24	31	29	34
Transition economies[d]				
CEE	55	39	43	42
FSU and Mongolia	54	62	20	17
East Asia	42	50	53	54

Notes: Income groups as defined in the World Bank World Development Reports.
[a] M2 calculated as the average of the year-end figures for the specified and the previous year.
[b] Country breakdown as for 1993, except Portugal is in the high-income group (upper-middle income in 1993).
[c] Bolivia excluded in 1991, because it is an extremely high outlier.
[d] Not included in the previous categories.
Sources: World Bank, *World Development Report* (1991, 1993, 1995); IMF reports.

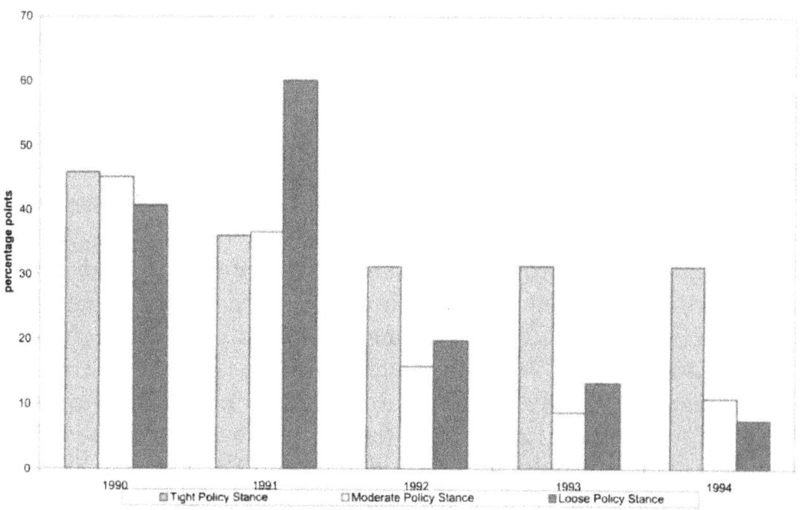

Figure 1.3. Evolution of domestic broad money/GDP ratio, group averages, 1990–94.

similar pattern exists for the ratio of the evolution of total broad money (including foreign exchange deposits) to GDP

EFFECTIVENESS, STANCE, AND INSTRUMENT USE

Association of Effectiveness, Stance, and Instrument Use during Stabilization

Table 1.8 integrates the three dimensions of monetary policy developed here: market orientation of instrument use, policy stance, and effectiveness. Classifications are based on criteria used earlier and applied to the year of stabilization and the year after (see notes to Table 1.9 for further explanation). Three broad observations can be made.

First, neither policy stance nor effectiveness depends on the market orientation of instruments. Albania has implemented a relatively tight monetary policy with low market orientation, and Mongolia has implemented a program that proved effective with low market orientation. (Estonia is somewhat of a special case, in which the adherence to a currency board, which may be the ultimate market-oriented instrument, preempts the use of more traditional market-oriented instruments.)

Second, Table 1.9 suggests an association between market orientation of instruments, moderate policy stance, and effectiveness in the CEE countries and lack of market orientation, loose policy stance, and ineffectiveness in the FSU countries. This association is due to a variety of factors including differences in initial conditions and in the pace of liberalization. CEE countries liberalized earlier and to a greater extent, although the Baltics were not far behind. Initial macroeconomic distortions and dependence on socialist trade were lower in CEE countries, and more favorable experience with inflation and output loss there may have made it easier to conduct a more moderate monetary policy. For the non-Baltic FSU, adherence to the ruble zone – a policy that appeared initially to have some merit but subsequently to delay reform – bound these countries together in a roller-coaster ride into hyperinflation and large declines in real output, both of which lowered dramatically the transactions demand for money.

Third, it seems clear that the FSU countries showing the lowest market orientation and the loosest monetary policy continue to

Table 1.9. *Use of market-oriented instruments, policy stance, and effectiveness during and after stabilization*

Market orientation of instruments	Policy stance		
	Moderate	Loose	Very loose
High (5–6 instruments)	*Slovenia (92)*	*Estonia (92)* Latvia (92) Romania (93)[a] Russia (95)[a,b,c]	*Croatia (93)*
Substantial (4–4.5 instruments)	*Bulgaria (91)* *Czech Republic (91)* Hungary (90) FYR Macedonia (94)[a] (?) *Poland (90)* *Slovak Republic (91)*	Azerbaijan (95)[a,b,c]	Armenia (94)[a,c] (?) Georgia (94)[a,c] (?) Kazakstan (94)[a,c]
Moderate (3–3.5 instruments)		Kyrgyz Republic (93) Lithuania (92) Moldova (93) Tajikistan (95)[a,b,c] Uzbekistan (94)[a,c]	Belarus (94)[a,c]
Low (2–2.5 instruments)	Albania (92)	*Mongolia (93)*[a] Ukraine (94)[a,c]	

Notes: The use of market-oriented instruments is shown as an average of years T and T + 1. Policy stance is also an average for years T and T + 1 with categories for base money growth defined as in Table 1.5. Effectiveness, shown by italics, is defined by inflation in year T + 1 less than 100 and less than inflation in year T and a stable or increasing ratio of M2/GDP by year T + 1. Turkmenistan is excluded, as it had not adopted a stabilization program by end 1995.
[a] Indicates countries stabilizing relatively slowly.
[b] Based on data for year T only.
[c] Base money growth and inflation for 1995 are midyear estimates annualized.

rely on rationing through directed credit and interest controls because direct controls serve their purpose, to provide support to state enterprises despite their failure to restructure. The need for further institutional development is no doubt a limitation, but other FSU countries with similar underdeveloped institutions have made faster strides. Russia and the Kyrgyz Republic, for example, have introduced screening criteria to distinguish better managed, more solvent banks so that market-oriented policy instruments can be introduced on a limited basis in a more stable environment. In reality, it seems that it is not so much underdeveloped institutions that limit policy effectiveness but the policy goal that limits the shift to the full range of market-oriented monetary instruments.

Simple correlations between base money growth, inflation, and the MOMPI index around the time of stabilization are given in Table 1.10. As expected, the correlation between base money growth and inflation is positive and high, although less high during stabilization in the FSU and "fast response" countries. This suggests that the problems of stabilizing quickly in the Baltics, Moldova, the Kyrgyz Republic, and Mongolia were more complex than in CEE countries. There is a strong negative correlation between base money growth and the use of market-oriented instruments in "slow-response" countries the year before stabilization, suggesting that the most rapid money growth took the form of highly subsidized directed credit. This interpretation is consistent with other evidence that stabilization was undertaken at varying stages of reform. Using the cumulative liberalization index (CLI) developed by de Melo et al. (1996), most countries were at an intermediary stage of reform, between 0.5 and 0.8 on a scale of 0 to 1.[9] However, Mongolia and several FSU countries – namely, Armenia, Azerbaijan, Belarus, Georgia, Kazakstan, Tajikistan, and Uzbekistan – stabilized with a CLI between 0.35 and 0.45, indicating less reform; and Ukraine attempted stabilization in late 1994 with a CLI of only 0.26.

Inflation and the MOMPI index were positively and relatively strongly correlated in CEE countries the year before stabilization. But this is not necessarily evidence that the move toward market orientation was premature; rather, it probably reflects the fact that a switch to market-oriented monetary instruments coincided with

[9] In de Melo et al. (1996), an annual liberalization index is constructed for twenty-six CEE and FSU countries for each year from 1989 through 1994. The index is a weighted average of the rankings on liberalization in three areas: internal markets, external markets, and private sector entry. The cumulative liberalization index (CLI) is the sum of a country's annual liberalization indices in any given year and, hence, represents the duration as well as the depth of reform.

Table 1.10. *Simple correlations between base money growth, inflation, and the MOMPI Index*

Correlation coefficients	Year T − 1	Year T[a]	Year T + 1[b]	Average
1. Overall[c]				
Base money growth – inflation[d,e]	0.96	0.86	0.79	0.95
Base money growth – MOMPI Index[d,e]	−0.11	−0.14	−0.12	−0.34
Inflation – MOMPI Index	−0.04	−0.15	−0.20	−0.25
2a. CEE countries				
Base money growth – inflation[d,e]	0.79	0.96	0.86	0.98
Base money growth – MOMPI Index[d,e]	0.22	0.27	−0.26	0.12
Inflation – MOMPI Index	0.52	0.21	−0.34	0.17
2b. FSU countries and Mongolia				
Base money growth – inflation[d]	0.96	0.84	0.71	0.93
Base money growth – MOMPI Index[d]	−0.29	−0.06	0.09	−0.33
Inflation – MOMPI Index	−0.19	0.00	0.03	−0.16
3a. "Fast response" countries				
Base money growth – inflation[e]	0.83	0.73	0.83	0.84
Base money growth – MOMPI Index[e]	0.08	0.12	−0.24	−0.15
Inflation – MOMPI Index	0.11	−0.03	−0.34	−0.18
3b. "Slow response" countries				
Base money growth – inflation[c]	0.96	0.86	0.97	0.94
Base money growth – MOMPI Index[d]	−0.51	−0.22	0.05	−0.49
Inflation – MOMPI Index	−0.37	−0.16	0.01	−0.28

Notes: MOMPI – Market Orientation of Monetary Policy Instruments; see text for definition. The 1995 data are annualized midyear numbers.

[a] The year of the latest stabilization effort as reported in Fisher, Sahay, and Vegh (1995).

[b] The following countries, in which stabilization started in 1995, are excluded: Azerbaijan, Russia, Tajikistan; Uzbekistan is excluded due to lack of data.

[c] Turkmenistan is excluded from all calculations since no stabilization started before 1995. For the following countries and years, domestic broad money growth is substituted for base money growth: Estonia, Latvia, Lithuania in year T − 1 (1991), Latvia in year T (1992), Uzbekistan in year T (1994).

[d] Tajikistan is excluded due to lack of monetary data.

[e] Slovenia is excluded in year T − 1 (1991) due to lack of monetary data.

Sources: Authors' calculations.

price liberalization in these countries. These same two indicators were negatively correlated in "slow-response" countries the year prior to stabilization, suggesting that price liberalization had already taken place and that a switch to market-oriented instruments may have coincided with real structural reforms implemented prior to stabilization. In the year after stabilization, market orientation was negatively associated with both base money growth and inflation for all country groups, suggesting that they were more effective than not.

Effectiveness and Market-Oriented Use of Instruments

Next, using regression analysis, we explore to what extent the market-oriented use of instruments may have promoted or deterred effectiveness. Policy stance is taken into account by using the real discount rate in the equations for financial depth (measured by M2/GDP) and the growth of base money in the equations for price stability (measured by the annual CPI). The time span of data for the regressions, shown in Table 1.11, is typically 1990–94 for CEE (except the former Yugoslav republics) and Mongolia and 1991–94 for other countries.

Three equations are estimated for each dependent variable. In the first equation, we include all the instruments; in the second equation, we include only those instruments that are statistically significant. And in the third equation we substitute the composite MOMPI index for individual instrument dummy variables. In each equation, we specify a lagged independent variable, a policy variable, and two conditioning variables – one representing a time trend and one representing price liberalization. The lagged variable accounts for the influence of omitted variables that have a continuing, or persistent, effect over the period covered. The time trend variable is added to account for time variant factors. The price liberalization variable is defined as the change in the index of domestic price liberalization – one of the three components of the liberalization index developed by de Melo et al. (1996). Where indicated, we used the fixed-effects estimation method to allow for country-specific effects on the dependent variable.

Table 1.12 presents the equations for financial depth, which use the fixed-effects method. Persistence explains about a third

Table 1.11. *Time span of data for the regressions*

	M2/GDP	LNINF[a]
Albania	1990–94	1990–94
Bulgaria	1990–94	1990–94
Croatia[b]	1990–94	1990–94
Czech Republic[c]	1990–94	1990–94
Hungary	1989–94	1989–94
Macedonia[b]	1990–94	1990–94
Poland	1989–94	1989–94
Romania	1990–94	1990–94
Slovak Republic[c]	1990–94	1990–94
Slovenia[b]	1990–94	1990–94
Armenia	1991–94	1991–94
Azerbaijan	1991–94	1991–94
Belarus	1991–94	1991–94
Estonia[d]	—	1991–94
Georgia	1991–94	1991–94
Kazakhstan	1991–94	1991–94
Kyrgyz Republic	1991–94	1991–94
Latvia	1991–94	1991–94
Lithuania	1991–94	1991–94
Moldova	1991–94	1991–94
Russia	1991–94	1991–94
Tajikistan	1991–94	1991–94
Turkmenistan	1991–94	1991–94
Ukraine	1991–94	1991–94
Uzbekistan	1991–94	1991–94
Mongolia	1990–94	1990–94

[a] Natural logarithm of inflation measured by the CPI.
[b] Data for former Yugoslavia used in 1989–90.
[c] Data for former CSFR used in 1989–91.
[d] Estonia is not included as no discount rate is used under the currency board arrangement.

of financial depth, much of the remainder appears to be explained by the policy stance variable and a negative time trend. The relationship between financial depth and the MOMPI index is positive, but not statistically significant; however, there is a significant positive association between financial depth and the market orientation of two specific instruments – the elimination of credit ceilings (CC) and development of the market

Table 1.12. *Effectiveness and market-oriented instruments: Financial depth (dependent variable: M2GDP)*

	Equation 1		Equation 2		Equation 3	
Variable	Coefficient	t-statistic	Coefficient	t-statistics	Coefficient	t-statistics
M2GDPLAG	0.31	2.91	0.294	2.99	0.37	3.83
PLIB	−0.11	−1.35	−0.10	−1.35	−0.16	−2.21
RDR	0.13	3.50	0.12	3.40	0.12	3.31
T	−0.58	−2.88	−0.05	−3.70	−0.05	−3.01
DC	−0.002	−0.05	—	—	—	—
CC	0.07	2.34	0.06	2.13	—	—
IRC	−0.02	−0.37	—	—	—	—
RR.	−0.03	−0.55	—	—	—	—
RCA	0.04	1.10	—	—	—	—
TCB	0.09	1.96	0.06	1.73	—	—
MOMPI	—	—	—	—	0.09	1.02
FE1 (Albania)	0.45	4.07	0.43	5.03	0.37	4.24
FE2 (Bulgaria)	0.49	5.31	0.49	5.85	0.44	4.92
FE3 (Croatia)	0.21	3.15	0.21	3.44	0.24	3.66
FE4 (Czech Republic)	0.53	5.55	0.55	6.33	0.53	5.93
FE5 (Hungary)	0.33	3.73	0.37	5.45	0.38	5.17
FE6 (Macedonia)	0.25	2.69	0.21	2.42	0.19	2.51
FE7 (Poland)	0.29	4.06	0.31	4.68	0.29	4.24

FE8 (Romania)	0.31	3.68	0.29	3.69	0.27	3.09
FE9 (Slovak Republic)	0.51	5.51	0.53	6.19	0.50	5.76
FE10 (Slovenia)	0.16	1.93	0.20	3.04	0.23	3.26
FE11 (Armenia)	0.20	2.47	0.23	3.24	0.24	3.47
FE12 (Azerbaijan)	0.39	2.66	0.39	2.87	0.39	3.04
FE13 (Belarus)	0.26	2.84	0.27	3.41	0.27	3.76
FE14 (Estonia)	—	—	—	—	—	—
FE15 (Georgia)	0.16	2.05	0.19	2.76	0.20	2.98
FE16 (Kazakhstan)	0.19	2.39	0.21	2.70	0.20	2.68
FE17 (Kyrgyz Republic)	0.22	3.19	0.23	3.60	0.24	3.63
FE18 (Latvia)	0.24	3.32	0.24	3.79	0.24	3.49
FE19 (Lithuania)	0.32	3.03	0.29	3.27	0.26	2.62
FE20 (Moldova)	0.15	1.95	0.18	2.71	0.20	3.07
FE21 (Russia)	0.14	1.55	0.18	2.50	0.21	3.18
FE22 (Tajkistan)	0.38	3.92	0.41	4.83	0.42	4.76
FE23 (Turkmenistan)	0.22	2.11	0.24	2.39	0.25	2.48
FE24 (Ukraine)	0.21	2.55	0.24	3.44	0.23	3.36
FE25 (Uzbekistan)	0.31	3.47	0.33	4.33	0.33	4.33
FE26 (Mongolia)	0.37	5.18	0.39	5.78	0.37	5.23
Adjusted R^2		0.82		0.83		0.81
DW		2.10		2.13		2.09

for government paper (TCB). As indicated in Tables 1.5b and 1.5c, many countries imposed credit controls at the time of stabilization, since other regulatory systems were weak or ineffective. However, successful stabilizers removed credit controls rather quickly, providing a strong signal that economic conditions had returned to normal. This signal coincided with, and may have contributed to, an increase in demand for broad money. A significant and positive link between financial depth and TCB could be viewed as the normal and expected outcome, since development of this market is facilitated by normalization of economic conditions.

Table 1.13 presents the equations for inflation. Here, the lagged variable explains close to half of the current inflation, with much of the remainder explained by money growth, a smaller negative time trend than in the previous equations, and price liberalization. The relationship between base money growth and inflation confirms that policy stance operates in the expected way to attain price stability during the transition process and countries that were able to restrict base money growth were able to control inflation. This, of course, does not mean that there were not other factors influencing inflation. As shown by Citrin et al. (1995), for example, increases in energy prices and other shocks affected inflation in the short term. And the PLIB variable here indicates that, given the large money overhang and negative real interest rates in many transition economies, the elimination of price controls led to higher price levels and the erosion of real money balances.

Turning to the use of market-oriented instruments, the elimination of directed credit and the introduction of a market-oriented refinancing window are both negatively and significantly associated with inflation. Most other instruments are negatively related to inflation but are not significant. However, equation 3 shows that the inclusion of the overall MOMPI index results in a fall in the significance of the price liberalization variable. The significant, negative association between the MOMPI index and inflation suggests that – even if the association is explained largely by the fact that countries with lower inflation found it easier to introduce market-oriented instruments – on the whole the introduction of market-oriented instruments did not aggravate the problem of inflation control.

Table 1.13. *Effectiveness and market-oriented instruments: Inflation (dependent variable: Log of inflation (CPI))*

	Equation 1		Equation 2		Equation 3	
Variable	Coefficient	t-statistic	Coefficient	t-statistics	Coefficient	t-statistics
NINFLAG	0.47	7.26	0.43	7.80	0.48	7.92
RESM	0.09	5.67	0.10	6.95	0.10	6.03
PLIB	1.54	2.65	1.55	3.47	0.82	1.36
T	−0.19	−1.44	−0.18	−1.75	−3.1	−2.38
DC	−1.04	−3.02	−0.91	−3.82	—	—
CC	−0.22	−0.81	—	—	—	—
IRC	0.25	0.92	—	—	—	—
RR	−0.12	−0.46	—	—	—	—
CA	−0.55	−2.17	−0.49	−2.19	—	—
TCB.	−0.18	−0.52	—	—	—	—
MOMPI	—	—	—	—	−1.60	−3.07
Constant	1.43	3.11	1.34	4.04	1.78	4.36
Adjusted R^2	0.79		0.74		0.76	

CONCLUSIONS

In this chapter we looked at monetary policy in twenty-six transition economies in CEE and FSU between 1989 and 1994. We provided a schema for classifying the use of six important monetary policy instruments, both direct and indirect, and suggested criteria for defining market-oriented use of these instruments. We then made an assessment of the extent of market-oriented instrument use during the period under review and around stabilization. The impact of instrument use on inflation and financial depth, which declined dramatically during the early years of transition, was also explored.

Our conclusions indicate several clear patterns. First, by end 1994, slightly less than half the countries were relying primarily on market-oriented forms of monetary instruments, and slightly more than half had moderate or low reliance on such instruments. As might be expected, countries that quickly formulated a monetary policy response following the break from socialist central planning were more likely to switch to market-oriented instruments. Second, CEE countries moved more rapidly than FSU countries toward these forms, even when we control for stage of stabilization. Third, the use of credit ceilings was seen to be helpful in the year of stabilization, especially in CEE countries. And the elimination of credit controls was associated with effective stabilization.

Our findings support the view that policy stance, as measured by base money growth and the real discount rate, was effective in helping to reverse undesirable inflation and disintermediation trends. But the relationship between effectiveness and market orientation of monetary policy instruments is less clear. Financial depth is associated with the elimination of credit ceilings and the development of markets for government paper, and inflation is associated with the elimination of directed credit and the establishment of a market-oriented refinancing window. The overall index of the market orientation of monetary policy instruments (MOMPI) is negatively related to inflation, but the direction of causality is unclear.

On balance, the relatively weak link between market orientation of instruments and indicators of effectiveness suggests that inflation control and financial depth are more directly related to policy stance, which is in turn related to broader structural reforms. As concluded by de Melo et al. (1996) and Fischer, Sahay, and Vegh (1996), monetary stability goes hand in hand with adjustment in the real sectors. Subsidies and central bank support of public enterprises to help maintain employment and output are ultimately financed by money creation, reducing the options for monetary policy regardless of the market orientation of the monetary system.

REFERENCES

Alexander, William E., Tomas J. T. Balino, and Charles Enoch. 1995. "The Adoption of Indirect Instruments of Monetary Policy." IMF Occasional Paper no. 126, June, International Monetary Fund, Washington, D.C.

Aslund, Anders. 1995. *How Russia Became a Market Economy*. Washington, D.C.: Brookings Institution.

Balino, Tomas, and Carlo Cottarelli. 1994. *Frameworks for Monetary Stability: Policy Issues and Country Experiences*. Washington, D.C.: International Monetary Fund.

Balcerowitz, Leszch, and Alan Gelb. 1994. "Macropolicies in Transition to a Market Economy: A Three Year Perspective." Paper prepared for the World Bank Annual Conference on Development Economics, Washington, D.C.

Bennett, Adam, G. G. 1994. "Currency Boards: Issues and Experiences." IMF Paper on Policy Analysis and Assessment 94/18, International Monetary Fund, Washington, D.C.

Bredenkamp, Hugh. 1993. "Conducting Monetary and Credit Policy in Countries of the Former Soviet Union: Some Issues and Options." IMF Working Paper WP/93/23, International Monetary Fund, Washington, D.C.

Bruno, Michael. 1993. *Crisis, Stabilization and Economic Reform: Therapy by Consensus*. Oxford: Oxford University Press.

Bruno, Michael. 1995. "Inflation and Growth in an Integrated Approach." In P. Kenen (ed.), *Understanding Interdependence: The Macroeconomics of the Open Economy*, 313–67. Princeton, N.S.: Princeton University Press.

Calvo, Guillermo, and Fabrizio Coricelli. 1993. "Output Collapse in Eastern Europe: The Role of Credit." In Mario Blejer et al. (eds.), *Eastern Europe in Transition: From Recession to Growth?* World Bank Discussion Paper no. 196, World Bank, Washington, D.C. pp. 92–105.

Calvo, Guillermo, and Carlos Vegh. 1994. "Inflation Stabilization and Nominal Anchors." Contemporary Economic Policy 12: 35–45.

Caprio, Gerard, Jr. 1995. "The Role of Financial Intermediaries in Transitional Economies." *Carnegie-Rochester Conference Series on Public Policy* 42: 257–302.

Citrin, Daniel, J. Anderson, and J. Zettelmeyer. 1995. "The IMF's Approach to Stabilization in the Baltics, Russia and the Other FSU Countries." *Economic Policy in Transition Economies* (MOCT) 5, no. 2: 85–100.

Cochrane, John, and B. Ickes. 1995. "Macroeconomics in Russia." In E. P. Lazear (ed.), *Economic Transition in Eastern Europe and Russia*. Hoover Press.

Conway, Patrick. 1995. "Currency Proliferation: The Economic Legacy of the Soviet Union." Princeton Studies in International Finance.

Dabrowski, Marek. 1995. "The Reasons for the Collapse of the Ruble Zone." Studies and Analyses no. 58, Center for Social and Economic Research, Warsaw, Poland.

de Melo, Martha, Cevdet Denizer, and Alan Gelb. 1996. "From Plan to Market: Patterns of Transition." *World Bank Economic Review* (September): 397–424.

Dittus, Peter. 1994. "Bank Reform and Behavior in Central Europe." *Journal of Comparative Economics* 19, no. 3 (December): 335–61.

Easterly, W., and Stanley Fisher. 1995. "The Soviet Economic Decline." *World Bank Economic Review*, no. 3: 341–71.

Easterly, W., P. Mauro, and K. Schmidt-Hebbel. 1995. "Money Demand and Seignorage Maximizing Inflation." *Journal of Money Credit and Banking* 22, no. 2 (May): 583–603.

Easterly, W., and P. Vieira da Cunha. 1994. "Financing the Storm: Macroeconomic Crisis in Russia." Policy Working Paper no. 1240, Policy Research Department, World Bank, Washington, D.C.

Easterly, W., and Holger Wolf. 1995. "The Wild Ride of the Ruble." Mimeographed World Bank, Washington, D.C.

Farahbaksh, Mitra, and Gabriel Sensenbrenner. 1996. "Bank-by-Bank Credit Ceilings: Issues and Experiences." IMF Working Paper no. 63, International Monetary Fund, Washington, D.C.

Fischer, Stanley. 1982. "Seignorage and the Case for a National Currency." *Journal of Political Economy* 90, no. 21: 295–313.

Fischer, Stanley, R. Sahay, and Carlos Vegh. 1996 "Stabilization and Growth in Transition Economies." *Journal of Economic Perspectives* 10: 45–66.

Flood, Robert P., and Michael Mussa. 1994. "Issues Concerning Nominal Anchors for Monetary Policy." IMF Working Paper no. 61, International Monetary Fund, Washington, D.C.

Fry, Maxwell, 1995. *Money, Interest, and Banking in Economic Development*. Baltimore: Johns Hopkins University Press.

Granville, Brigitte. 1995. "Farewell, Ruble Zone." In Anders Aslund, (ed.), *Russian Economic Reform at Risk*, 65–88. New York: Pinter Publishers.

Gros, Daniel, and Alfred Steinherr. 1995. *Winds of Change*. London: Longman Publishers.

Hilbers, Paul. 1993. "Monetary Instruments and Their Use during the Transition from a Centrally Planned to a Market Economy." IMF Working Paper WP\93\87, International Monetary Fund, Washington, D.C.

International Monetary Fund. 1994, 1995. *Economic Outlook*. Washington, D.C.

Kierzkowski, Henryk, E. Phelps, and G. Zoega, 1994. "Mechanisms of Economic Collapse and Growth in Eastern Europe." Working Paper no. 30, Polish Policy Research Group, Warsaw University, Warsaw.

King, Robert G., and Ross Levine. 1993. "Finance and Growth: Schumpeter Might Be Right." *Quarterly Journal of Economics* 108 (August): 717–37.

Mathieson, Donald J., and Richard D. Haas. 1994. "Establishing Monetary Control in Financial Systems with Insolvent Institutions." IMF Paper on Policy Analysis and Assessment PPAA/94/10, International Monetary Fund, Washington, D.C.

Mckinnon, Ronald. 1973. "Money and Capital in Economic Development." Brookings Institution, Washington, D.C.

Mellis, C. L., and M. Cornelius, 1994. "New Currencies in the Former Soviet Union: A Recipe for Hyperinflation or the Path to Price Stability?" Working Paper series, no. 26, Bank of England, London.

Nove, Alec. 1991. *The Economics of Feasible Socialism Revisited*. New York: Harper Collins Academic Publishers.

Portes, Richard (ed.). 1993. *Economic Transformation in Central Europe: A Progress Report*. London: Centre for Economic Policy Research.

Quintyn, Marc. 1994. "Government versus Central Bank Securities in Developing Open Market Operations." In T. Balino and Carlo Cotterelli (eds.), *Frameworks for Monetary Stability*, 691–737. Washington, D.C.: International Monetary Fund.

Ratna, S., and C. Vegh. 1995. "Inflation and Stabilization in Transition Economies: A Comparison with Market Economies." IMF Working Paper WP/95/8, International Monetary Fund, Washington, D.C.

Saal, Matthew I., and Lorena M. Zamalloa. 1994. "Use of Central Bank Credit Auctions in Economies in Transition." IMF Paper on Policy Analysis and Assessment PPAA/94/11, International Monetary Fund, Washington, D.C.

Saavalainen, T.O. 1995. "Stabilization in the Baltic Countries: A Comparative Analysis." IMF Working Paper WP/95/44, International Monetary Fund, Washington, D.C.

Sahay, Ratna, and Carlos Vegh, 1995. "Inflation and Stabilization in Transition Economies: A Comparison with Market Economies." IMF Working Paper no. 8, International Monetary Fund, Washington, D.C.

Shaw, Edward S. 1973. *Financial Deepening in Economic Development.* New York: Oxford University Press.

Sundararajan, V., P. Dattels, I. McCarthy, M. Castello Branco, and H. Blommestein. 1994. "The Coordination of Domestic Public Debt and Monetary Management in Economies in Transition: Issues and Lessons from Experience." IMF Working Paper WP/94/148, International Monetary Fund, Washington, D.C.

Thorne, Alfredo. 1993. "Eastern Europe's Experience with Banking Reform: Is There a Role for Banks in the Transition?" *Journal of Banking and Finance* 17, no. 5: 959–1000.

World Bank. 1992. "Mongolia: Towards a Market Economy." World Bank, Washington, D.C.

Table 1A.1. *Albania: Use of monetary policy instruments*

Instruments	Use of instruments during transition		
	Late socialism	Transitional	Market-oriented
A Direct instruments			
1 Directed credits	Credit plan was in place until 92	Directed credit abandoned in 92; credit guarantees for some enterprises introduced in 93	Guarantees discounted in 94
2 Credit ceilings	Not used	Bank-by-bank ceilings introduced in mid-92; tradable since late 94	Ceilings maintained and lowered in 94
3 Interest rate controls on commercial bank deposit/lending rates	Fixed rates until mid-92	Max. and min. rates since mid-92 aimed at keeping positive real rates	
B Indirect instruments			
4 Reserve requirements	Not used	Introduced mid-92 at 10% for all deposits; poor compliance initially	Rates unchanged since mid-92; by end 93 all banks are meeting RR
5 Refinance window	Not used	Introduced in 93 but limited use	
Rediscount/Lombard facilities	Not used		
6 Government and CB bills and bonds	Primary market introduced in 7/94; limited		

Notes: Abbreviations used in the various country tables include CB = central bank; CD = certificate of deposits; DD = demand deposits; DMB = deposit money bank; FX = foreign exchange; LC = local currency; LT = long term; MOF = Ministry of Finance; NDA = net domestic assets; OMO = open-market operations; RR = reserve requirements; ST = short term; TD = time deposits; TSD = time and savings deposits.

Table 1A.2. *Armenia: Use of monetary policy instruments*

Instruments	Use of instruments during transition		
	Late socialism	Transitional	Market-oriented
A. Direct instruments			
1 Directed credits	Operated under credit plan until 92	In 93 directed credit program transferred to MOF	Directed credit abolished in 1/95
2 Credit ceilings	Not used		
3 Interest rate controls on commercial bank deposit/lending rates		Fixed administered rates for directed credit 92–1/95; minimum deposit and loan rates were introduced in 3/94	Loan rate controls were removed in 6/94 and deposit rate controls in late 94
B. Indirect instruments			
4 Reserve requirements		Introduced in late 93; unified at 15% for all dram and FX deposits in late 94; savings bank is excluded	
5 Refinance window		Preferential rates for directed credit until 94; auction introduced in 5/94 with interest rate minimum	Auction redesigned and expanded in 2/95 without minimum interest rate
Rediscount/Lombard facilities	Not used		
6 Government and CB bills and bonds	Not used		

Table 1A.3. *Azerbaijan: Use of monetary policy instruments*

Instruments	Use of instruments during transition		
	Late socialism	Transitional	Market-oriented
A. Direct instruments			
1 Directed credits	Used according to credit plan until 92	Used extensively 92–95; share decreasing since late 94	
2 Credit ceilings	Not used		
3 Interest rate controls on commercial bank deposit/lending rates		3% margin for lending rates in 91, increased to 10% in 93	
B. Indirect instruments			
4 Reserve requirements		Introduced in 91 with 15/12/10% by maturity; 4 largest banks exempt 7/93 extended to FX deposits; low compliance; RR extended to all banks in 1/94, high variability in 95	
5 Refinance window	Preferential refinancing since 92	Since 1/95 refinance at single rate	Refinance rate based on auctions since 3/95
Rediscount/Lombard facilities	Not used		
6 Government and CB bills and bonds	Not used		

Table 1A.4. *Belarus: Use of monetary policy instruments*

	Use of instruments during transition		
Instruments	Late socialism	Transitional	Market-oriented
A. Direct instruments			
1 Directed credits	Used according to credit plan until 93	15% of DMB loans must be for investment in 94; CB-directed credit continues at subsidized rates in 95	
2 Credit ceilings	Not used	No bank-by-bank ceiling but a 5% of GDP ceiling on CB credit to government in 93	
3 Interest rate controls on commercial bank deposit/lending rates	A 3% margin between deposit and loan rates, later canceled, lending rate set at 25% in 91; 9/94 margins controlled but changing; savings bank deposit rates controlled in 93–94	Min. rates on time deposits in 10/94, average rates' margin reset at 3% in 1/95, raised to 5% in 6/95	
B. Indirect instruments			
4 Reserve requirements		Introduced in 88; 7/91 indicative ratios 15–12% by maturity; 2/92 raised to 20%, 2/93 RR differentiated by banks 8–15%; savings bank exempt in 10/93; 4/94 uniform for all banks 15% on DD and 10% on TSD; 10/94 RR set at 5.5% and FX included; 7/95 RR set at 12% on LC and 10% on FX deposits	
5 Refinance window	Introduced in 91; preferential rates for directed credit	Auctions started in 2/93; suspended in 10/93; resumed in 4/94; limited because of other cheap credit	
Rediscount/Lombard facilities	Not used		
6 Government and CB bills and bonds	Government paper introduced 2/94; CB bills launched 6/95, primary markets only		

Table 1A.5. *Bulgaria: Use of monetary policy instruments*

Instruments	Use of instruments during transition		
	Late socialism	Transitional	Market-oriented
A. Direct instruments			
1 Directed credits		Agricultural loans directed through banks 91–95	
2 Credit ceilings		Bank-by-bank ceilings introduced in 2/91; two large banks exempt but included in 1/92; ceilings made tradable in 7/92	Abandoned in 8/94
3 Interest rate controls on commercial bank deposit/lending rates	Fixed rates abolished in 2/91		Formally market determined but influenced by CB refinancing rates
B. Indirect instruments			
4 Reserve requirements		Introduced at 7% in 2/91 on all types of deposits; no change 2/91–8/94; upward drift and 3 changes 8/94–8/95 increasing to 12%	
5 Refinance window	For agricultural loans at preferential rates since 1/91 to 1/95 date	Some refinancing at the discount rate 91–93; auctions of CB deposits at DMBs introduced in 9/91 but terminated in 94	
Rediscount/Lombard facilities	Introduced in late 91; funds limited to 90% of collateral's face value	Funds limited to 70% of collateral's face value in 92	Fully developed
6 Government and CB bills and bonds	Introduced in 7/91	Secondary market trading since 93	OMO after 8/94

Table 1A.6. *Croatia: Use of monetary policy instruments*

Instruments	Use of instruments during transition		
	Late socialism	Transitional	Market-oriented
A. Direct instruments			
1 Directed credits	Preferential credit to agriculture on demand 6/91–4/92	Quotas on preferential credit introduced in 4/92; and subsumed under general refinancing 1/93	
2 Credit ceilings			Bank-by-bank ceilings used only 5/95–7/95 to cope with a transitory surge in credit demand
3 Interest rate controls on commercial bank deposit/lending rates	Note used		
B. Indirect instruments			
4 Reserve requirements		Introduced in 12/91; DD and TD with maturity less than 3 months 13%, other TSD 5.5%; obligatory NBC bills at 8.6% of all deposits subsumed under enforced RR; obligatory CB bills reintroduced early 95; as of 7/95 average RR was 34%	
5 Refinance window	A quarterly quota on ST refinancing 6/91–9/93	General purpose refinancing discontinued in 9/93	
Rediscount/Lombard facilities		Lombard facility introduced in late 93	
6 Government and CB bills and bonds	CB bills introduced in late 91; government bonds are LT and low interest, illiquid	No secondary trade in government securities; primary sales and secondary trade of CB bills	

Table 1A.7. *Czech Republic: Use of monetary policy instruments*

Instruments	Use of instruments during transition		
	Late socialism	Transitional	Market-oriented
A. *Direct instruments*			
1 Directed credits	Not used		
2 Credit ceilings		Bank-by-bank ceilings starting 1/91; ceilings terminated in 4/92 for small banks and 10/92 for big banks	
3 Interest rate controls on commercial bank deposit/lending rates		Ceiling on lending rates introduced 1/91–4/92	Market-determined since 92
B. *Indirect instruments*			
4 Reserve requirements		Introduced in 1990, high initial levels (16–18%); lowered and differentiated by deposit maturity in 2/92	Unchanged since 8/94, DD: 3%; TSD: 12%
5 Refinance window		Introduced in early 91	Auctions introduced in early 1992 and terminated in 6/94
Rediscount/Lombard facilities		Introduced in 93	Fully developed since 94
6 Government and CB bills and bonds	Introduced in early 1992	Secondary market trade	OMO started since 93

Table 1A.8. *Estonia: Use of monetary policy instruments*

Instruments	Use of Instruments during transition		
	Late socialism	Transitional	Market-oriented
A. Direct instruments			
1 Directed credits	Not used		
2 Credit ceilings	Not used		
3 Interest rate controls on commercial bank deposit/lending rates			Fully market based since mid-92
B. Indirect instruments			
4 Reserve requirements		Introduced in late 91 at 10% on all deposits	FX and government deposits subjected to RR in early 1994; strictly enforced
5 Refinance window	Not used		
Rediscount/Lombard facilities	Not used		
6 Government and CB bills and bonds	No government securities issued; budget surplus since 91	CB CDs auctioned off to provide instruments for collateral since 5/93	

Table 1A.9. *Georgia: Use of monetary policy instruments*

Instruments	Use of instruments during transition		
	Late socialism	Transitional	Market-oriented
A. Direct instruments			
1 Directed credits	Used according to credit plan	Used directly for firms and through banks at preferential rates in 92 and 93	Practically eliminated by late 94
2 Credit ceilings		Bank-by-bank ceilings introduced in early 92 abandoned in late 92	
3 Interest rate controls on commercial bank deposit/lending rates		Formally liberalized in 91, except the savings bank	Market-determined by mid-94
B. Indirect instruments			
4 Reserve requirements		Introduced in 91 at 5–10%; state banks de facto exempt; lax enforcement; increased to 20% on local currency deposits in 93; FX deposits became subject to RR in early 94 at 15%; increased to 20% in late 94; RR compliance improved in 95	
5 Refinance window	Not used	Refinancing auction introduced in 12/93 and suspended in 5/94	Auctions resumed in 4/95; interbank auction introduced in 5/95
Rediscount/Lombard facilities	Not used		
6 Government and CB bills and bonds	Not used		

Table 1A.10. *Hungary: Use of monetary policy instruments*

Instruments	Use of instruments during transition		
	Late socialism	Transitional	Market-oriented
A. Direct instruments			
1 Directed credits	Preferential program since 89	Sectoral coverage of preferential programs reduced sharply by 93; preexport finance and privatization credits put in place at low rates	By 95 directed credit less than 25% of total and diminishing in importance
2 Credit ceilings		Bank-by-bank credit ceilings in place in 89; eliminated in late 91	
3 Interest rate controls on commercial bank deposit/lending rates	Fixed rates for enterprises until 87 and for households until 91–92		Market-determined since 93
B. Indirect instruments			
4 Reserve requirements		Introduced with differentiated rates in 87; simplified and unified in 90 at 18%; changed 5 times 90–95 and reduced to 12% in late 94; increased to 14% in 2/95	
5 Refinance window	Automatic access and preferential rates used for selected activities since 89	Quotas on automatic refinancing of selected activities introduced in 91; switch to refinance auctions also in late 91; multiple refinancing rates exist but their importance is declining	
Rediscount/Lombard facilities			Discount rate applicable to nondirected credit; Lombard facility introduced in 93
6 Government and CB bills and bonds	Introduced in 88	Secondary market dominated by CB; significant direct sales to general public in 94	OMO used since 90; OMO became main policy instrument, was in 93 when repos and reverse repos were introduced

Table 1A.11. *Kazakstan: Use of monetary policy instruments*

Instruments	Use of instruments during transition: Late socialism	Transitional	Market-oriented
A Direct instruments			
1 Directed credits	Used according to credit plan until 92	Bank-by-bank quotas since 92; one-time direct lending to enterprises to clear their arrears; tightening of quotas late 94	Virtually eliminated in early 1995
2 Credit ceilings		Bank-by-bank ceilings 12/90, often exceeded until late 94	Ceiling put on CB net domestic assets in 95
3 Interest rate controls on commercial bank deposit/lending rates	Fixed interest rates before 92	Formally market-determined since 93, but heavily influenced by subsidized CB refinance rates for most directed credit	Mainly market-determined since 95
B Indirect instruments			
4 Reserve requirements		Introduced in 91, differentiated up to 15%; unified at 18% in 92, increased to 30% in 94 for domestic deposits and 15% RR imposed on FX deposits	RR unified at 20% on all types of deposits in 2/95
5 Refinance window		Introduced in 91 on a quota basis; switch to monthly auctions since 1/93; intentions to auction all CB credit since 4/95 not yet achieved	
Rediscount/Lombard facilities			Introduced in 9/95
6 Government and CB bills and bonds		Secondary market trade started in the second half of 95	Short-term CB bills introduced in 6/95; used for sterilization of FX inflows

Table 1A.12. *Kyrgyz Republic: Use of monetary policy instruments*

	Use of instruments during transition		
Instruments	Late socialism	Transitional	Market-oriented
A. Direct instruments			
1 Directed credits	Used according to credit plan until 92 at preferential rates	Bank-by-bank credit quotas since 91	Directed credit virtually eliminated since late 94
2 Credit ceilings	Not used	Bank-by-bank credit ceiling set to zero in 94	Ceilings in CB NDA in 95
3 Interest rate controls on commercial bank deposit/lending rates	Rates of savings bank fixed until end 91	Since 92/93, rates liberalized except directed credit	Virtually all interest rates are market determined since late 94
B. Indirect instruments			
4 Reserve requirements		Introduced in 91, differentiated up to 15%, limited application; rates progressively raised to 30% RR enforced since early 95 at continuing high rates	
5 Refinance window		Introduced at single rate in late 93 but tightly controlled	
Rediscount/Lombard facilities		Introduced 8/93 for limited short-term borrowing; emergency liquidity facility introduced late 94	Fully developed since early 95
6 Government and CB bills and bonds	Introduced 5/93 at fixed interest rates; maturities lengthened and fixed interest rates abolished since mid-94		

Table 1A.13. *Latvia: Use of monetary policy instruments*

Instruments	Use of instruments during transition		
	Late socialism	Transitional	Market-oriented
A. Direct instruments			
1 Directed credits	Used according to credit plan until mid-92	Phased out gradually after curency reform in mid-92	Eliminated by 93
2 Credit ceilings		Quarterly ceiling on CB NDA with indicative ceilings on banking systems' NDA between 7–12/92	CB NDA ceiling replaced by quarterly base money ceiling in 93; the former reinstated in mid-94 plus indicative ceilings on base money and NDA of the banking system
3 Interest rate controls on commercial bank deposit/lending rates			DMBs liberalized interest rates an Bank of Latvia discontinued all subsidized lending in mid-92
B. Indirect instruments			
4 Reserve requirements		Introduced in 91 at 15% on all deposits; RR increased to 20% and differentiated in 7/92	Unified and lowered to 8%, including FX deposits in 7/93; enforced
5 Refinance window		Refinance facility available at the discount rate in 91; switch to auctions in late 93; emergency refinance facility introduced in 2/95	
Rediscount/ Lombard facilities	Not used	Lombard introduced in mid-93 with rate 5% above the discount rate	Since 10/95 all refinancing required collateral introduced at CB
6 Government and CB bills and bonds	Primary market started in 12/93	Secondary trade window in 4/94, limited OMO; interest ceiling eliminated 6/95	

Table 1A.14. *Lithuania: Use of monetary policy instruments*

Instruments	Use of instruments during transition		
	Late socialism	Transitional	Market-oriented
A. Direct instruments			
1 Directed credits	Used in very small amounts under certain occasions under directions from government or parliament		
2 Credit ceilings		Tradable bank-by-bank ceilings and ceiling on net domestic assets of the CB introduced in 92	Bank-by-bank ceilings removed in 7/93; CB net domestic asset ceiling discontinued after 3/94 with the introduction of currency board
3 Interest rate controls on commercial bank deposit/lending rates		Lending rate ceilings until 2/92, then replaced by a minimum deposit rate; ceiling on lending rates put back in 9/93	Market determined by 95
B. Indirect instruments			
4 Reserve requirements		Introduced in 92 at 10% on all deposits; increased to 12% and extended to FX deposits in 93; strictly enforced	Reduced to 10% in 4/95
5 Refinance window Rediscount/Lombard facilities	Not used Not used		Auction based since 5/93
6 Government and CB bills and bonds	Introduced in 7/94, mostly 1–3 month bills		

Table 1A.15. *Macedonia: Use of monetary policy instruments*

Instruments	Use of instruments during transition		
	Late socialism	Transitional	Market-oriented
A. Direct instruments			
1 Directed credits	Not used	Credit directed to agriculture and export finance subject to quotas 4/92–3/94	
2 Credit ceilings	Not used	Bank-by-bank ceilings, not tradable, introduced in 94	
3 Interest rate controls on commercial bank deposit/lending rates			Market-determined rates since monetary independence in 4/92
B. Indirect instruments			
4 Reserve requirements	Min. liquidity ratio (quasi RR) introduced in 91 at 2.5%	RR introduced at 15–30% for DD, 5.5% for TSD in 92	Declined to 8% for DD, 3.5–5.5% for TSD by 1994; enforced
5 Refinance window		Prior to 94 all selective credits automatically refinanced at single rate	
Rediscount/Lombard facilities	Not used	Discount facility introduced 93–94	
6 Government and CB bills and bonds	Compulsory CB bills introduced in 92; primary T-bills auctions since 1/94		

Table 1A.16. *Moldova: Use of monetary policy instruments*

Instruments	Use of instruments during transition		
	Late socialism	Transitional	Market-oriented
A. Direct instruments			
1 Directed credits	Used according to the credit plan through 91	During 92–93 credit was directed to agro-industry, agriculture, and energy sectors at preferential rates; by end 94 directed credit declined to 30% of total	
2 Credit ceilings	Not used		
3 Interest rate controls on commercial bank deposit/lending rates		Ceiling on DMB loan rates introduced in 1/92; margins imposed for lending rates 11/93–4/94	Rates liberalized after 4/94 for other than directed credit; rates heavily influenced by CB auction rate
B. Indirect instruments			
4 Reserve requirements	Not used	Introduced in 93; 5 changes 93–94; DD 10–28, TSD 7.5–17%	RR unified at 12% on all deposits in 12/94
5 Refinance window		Introduced in late 92	Switch to auction-determined refinance rates in 11/93
Rediscount/Lombard facilities	Not used		
6 Government and CB bills and bonds	Primary market introduced in 94; small amounts		

Table 1A.17. *Mongolia: Use of monetary policy instruments*

	Use of instruments during transition		
Instruments	Late socialism	Transitional	Market-oriented
A. *Direct instruments*			
1 Directed credits	Used according to the credit plan until 91	Issued to priority sectors and oil imports at low rates; volume 1/3 of the total in 93	Terminated in mid-94; a CB facility used for the purpose terminated in 1/95
2 Credit ceilings		Bank-by-bank ceilings introduced in 1/91; removed in 5/91; reinstated in late 92; on monthly basis since 9/93; still used as of end 95	
3 Interest rate controls on commercial bank deposit/lending rates		DMB rates liberalized in 8/91; min. deposit rate introduced in late 92	Nonbinding guidelines to reduce DMBs spread to 5% in 94
B. *Indirect instruments*			
4 Reserve requirements		Introduced in 8/91 at 20% on business deposits, 15% household DD, 5% on TSD; 8/93 RR unified at 14%; 6/94 raised to 17%	
5 Refinance window	General refinancing available at preferential rates		Regular auction refinancing at market-determined rates since 3/95
Rediscount/Lombard facilities		ST liquidity credit issued via a clearing window 93–95; limits on its use since 1/95	
6 Government and CB bills and bonds	11/93 CB introduced its bills; used frequently		

Table 1A.18. *Poland: Use of monetary policy instruments*

Instruments	Use of instruments during transition		
	Late socialism	Transitional	Market-oriented
A. Direct instruments			
1 Directed credits		Used for priority sectors since 80s	Discontinued by 93
2 Credit ceilings		Informal bank-by-bank ceilings 89–early 93	
3 Interest rate controls on commercial bank deposit/ lending rates	Fixed administered rates until 8/89 for priority sectors	Basically liberalized in 1/90 but strongly influenced by CB	Market-determined since early 93
B. Indirect instruments			
4 Reserve requirements		Introduced 1/90 with high and changing levels; range; DD 9–30%; TD 5–15%; SD 5–10%; in late 94 lowered DD 20%	
5 Refinance window	Available at preferential rates since 1/90	Refinance operations more market-oriented	Fully developed
Rediscount/Lombard facilities		Available since 8/90	
6 Government and CB bills and bonds	CB bills introduced 7/90 and replaced by government bills in 5/91	1–3 year bonds introduced in 92; limited secondary market	OMO since early 93; fully developed

Table 1A.19. *Romania: Use of monetary policy instruments*

Instruments	Use of instruments during transition		
	Late socialism	Transitional	Market-oriented
A. Direct instruments			
1 Directed credits	Special credit to deal with interenterprise arrears end 91; repaid mid-92	92–93 special credit lines for LT credit to various sectors at preferential rates	Special credit lines marginalized in 8/93; some directed credit at official discount rate still available in 95
2 Credit ceilings		Used for some time in 91 but lifted in the second half of 92	
3 Interest rate controls on commercial bank deposit/lending rates		Savings bank rates controlled for some time	Market-determined by 95
B. Indirect instruments			
4 Reserve requirements		Introduced for enterprise deposits in 92; 12/92 RR extended to HH deposits; generally enforced; FX deposits included in early-94; government deposits exempt	
5 Refinance window		For ST at the discount rate introduced in 92; auctions started in 92, rates can not fall below discount rate; limits on each bank's share in auction credit	As of 95 weekly refinancing auctions are held
Rediscount/Lombard facilities		Not used; a very short-term and collateralized emergency facility introduced in 92	
6 Government and CB bills and bonds	Primary market started in 3/94		

Table 1A.20. *Russia: Use of monetary policy instruments*

	Use of instruments during transition		
Instruments	Late socialism	Transitional	Market-oriented
A. Direct instruments			
1 Directed credits	Used intensively for various sectors	Declining importance since 94	Directed credit under 10% of total in the first half of 95
2 Credit ceilings		Quarterly ceilings on CB credit to DMBs since 93; reasonably enforced in 94	Ceiling on the CB's NDA in 94
3 Interest rate controls on commercial bank deposit/lending rates	Savings bank rates fixed and 25% limit on lending rates in 91	All controls on DMB rates lifted except for savings bank in 1/92 and a margin for directed credits	Market-determined by 95
B. Indirect instruments			
4 Reserve requirements	With savings bank exempt introduced in 91 at 2%	Raised to 10–15% according to maturity in 2/92; to 15–20% in 4/92 including savings bank	2/95 adjusted to 10–22%
5 Refinance window	Introduced in 91	Liquidity refinancing at rate started in 92	Auctions introduced in 2/94
Rediscount/Lombard facilities			Lombard expected end 95
6 Government and CB bills and bonds	Introduced in 91; negligible amounts until 94	6/94 emergence of a secondary market; foreign participation restricted	

Table 1A.21. *Slovak Republic: Use of monetary policy instruments*

Instruments	Use of instruments during transition		
	Late socialism	Transitional	Market-oriented
A. Direct instruments			
1 Directed credits	Not used		
2 Credit ceilings		Bank-by-bank ceilings introduced 1/91 and terminated in 92; reintroduced 1/93 and largely eliminated in 12/94	
3 Interest rate controls on commercial bank deposit/lending rates		Ceilings on lending rates introduced 1/91; abandoned in 4/92	Market-determined since 4/92
B. Indirect instruments			
4 Reserve requirements		Introduced in 90, 16–18% on all deposits but not effective; 2/92 lowered and differentiated 2–9%; continuing difficulties with compliance	
5 Refinance window	Introduced 91; preferential refinance for exports and agriculture important in 93	Auctions introduced in early 92	After 12/93 mainly auction based with occasional suspensions
Rediscount/Lombard facilities		Introduced 93	Since 12/93 fully developed at 1% above auction rate
6 Government and CB bills and bonds	Introduced early 92	Secondary market trade dominated by CB	Since early 95 active OMO with CB bills

Table 1A.22. *Slovenia: Use of monetary policy instruments*

Instruments	Use of instruments during transition		
	Late socialism	Transitional	Market-oriented
A. Direct instruments			
1 Directed credits	Not used		
2 Credit ceilings		Used only in 10/91	
3 Interest rate control on commercial bank deposit/lending rates	Not used		
B. Indirect instruments			
4 Reserve requirements			Relatively low and stable since 2/92; arranged according to maturity detailed FX cover regulations after 2/92
5 Refinance window		In 92–93 special liquidity credits for 3 troubled banks	
Rediscount/Lombard facilities	Introduced 10/91 but limited to 5% DMB CB bill holdings	Lombard introduced 7/92 with some restrictions	
6 Government and CB bills and bonds	Government bonds introduced? LC and FX CB bills introduced in 91		

Table 1A.23. *Tajikistan: Use of monetary policy instruments*

Instruments	Use of instruments during transition		
	Late socialism	Transitional	Market-oriented
A. Direct instruments			
1 Directed credits	Used according to the credit plan until 91	Used extensively in 91–95 with interest-free credits extended to priority sectors and government	
2 Credit ceilings	Not used	Ceiling on CB NDA but not observed; 2/95: a 60-day freeze on all lending to the economy and the budget, followed by bank-specific credit ceilings	
3 Interest rate controls on commercial bank deposit/ending rates		92: DMB lending rates limited to 6% over CB refinancing rate; deposit rates free except savings bank; loan rates to private sector freed in 93 except priority sectors; 95: all rates liberalized except those for relending directed credit to the economy	
B. Indirect instruments			
4 Reserve requirements		Introduced in 11/91: 15/12/10/0% depending upon maturity; savings bank exempt	
5 Refinance window	Introduced in 91; preferential rates for almost all public sector firms; highly negative in real terms	A temporary liquidity facility established in 95 to assist in case of large cash withdrawals; new currency introduced in 5/95	
Rediscount/Lombard facilities	Not used		
6 Government and CB bills and bonds	Not used		

Table 1A.24. *Turkmenistan: Use of monetary policy instruments*

Instruments	Use of instruments during transition		
	Late socialism	Transitional	Market-oriented
A. Direct instruments			
1 Directed credits	Used according to the credit plan until 92	New directed credit policy channels CB funds through banks at low rates despite high inflation; decreasing importance in 95	
2 Credit ceilings	Not used		
3 Interest rate controls on commercial bank deposit/lending rates	Fixed in 90–91 with a 3% margin between deposit and loan rates	Since 1/92 nominally liberalized rates, but continued controls for directed credit and savings deposits; lending rates capped at 15% in 2/95	
B. Indirect instruments			
4 Reserve requirements		Introduced in 92 with major exemptions: DD 15%, TD 10%; uniformly set 20% in 11/93; 2/94 RR differentiated and lowered; increased in 1/95	1/96: unified at 11% on all types of deposits
5 Refinance window	Automatic access for directed credits at concessional rates	Auctions introduced in 8/93; not successful due to availability of cheap financing	As of 1/96, all CB refinancing is to be channeled through auctions
Rediscount/Lombard facilities	Not used	Rediscounting possible, but rarely done as a matter of policy	
6 Government and CB bills and bonds	Not used: the CB finances the budget on demand		

Table 1A.25. *Ukraine: Use of monetary policy instruments*

	Use of instruments during transition		
Instruments	Late socialism	Transitional	Market-oriented
A. Direct instruments			
1 Directed credits	Used according to credit plan until 92	Used regularly in 92–94; DMBs required to lend 10% of their credits to agriculture	Stopped in principle in 95, except occasional loans to the budget
2 Credit ceilings		10/94 CB NDA ceiling introduced; also ceiling on the net banking system credit to government	
3 Interest rate controls on commercial bank deposit/lending rates		Margins on lending rates, 3% in 91; no formal controls on deposit rates but dominated by savings bank rates; ceiling on lending rates in 94	
B. Indirect instruments			
4 Reserve requirements		Introduced in 91 at 10% only on DD; 1/92 raised to 15%, weak enforcement; reset at 25% in 3/93 with better enforcement; 9/93 temporary additional 7% RR introduced; 3/94 lowered to 15%	
5 Refinance window	Introduced in 91 at preferential rates	Auctions introduced in 5/93; refinancing rates closely aligned with auction rate	In 10/94 all refinancing became auction-based
Rediscount/Lombard facilities	Not used		
6 Government and CB bills and bonds	Introduced in 3/95; small volumes; CB also issued CDs		

Table 1A.26. *Uzbekistan: Use of monetary policy instruments*

Instruments	Use of instruments during transition		
	Late socialism	Transitional	Market-oriented
A. Direct instruments			
1 Directed credits	Based on the credit plan until 92	Highly subsidized rates for priority sectors via DMBs; directed credit share began to decline in 95	
2 Credit ceilings	Not used		
3 Interest rate controls on commercial bank deposit/ lending rates		Formally deposit rates freed in 92, except savings bank; caps on loan rates; subsidized CB loans discontinued but interest subsidy proided by MOF	
B. Indirect instruments			
4 Reserve requirements		Introduced in 8/91; 15% on DD, 12% on TD, and 0% on deposits more than 3 years; poor compliance; in 5/94 RR increased to 30% on deposits less than 3 years and 10% on rest	
5 Refinance window	Used in conjunction with directed credit policy at subsidized rates	Refinancing auction introduced in 8/93 on a very limited basis; expanded by 95 but preferential rates remain	
Rediscount/Lombard facilities	Not used		
6 Goverment and CB bills and bonds	Not used		

CHAPTER 2

Toward Market-Oriented Banking in the Economies in Transition

John Bonin and Paul Wachtel

Privatization of the banking sector is usually viewed as the way to create market-oriented banking sectors in formerly planned or transition economies. However, bank privatization is only part of the requisite story. Market-oriented banking requires the disengagement of the state from direct governance of banks (whether they are state-owned or privatized) and the simultaneous development by the state of an effective regulatory framework for the banking sector. At one and the same time, the governments should be getting out of the banking business and getting into the regulatory or supervisory business. It is no wonder that managing these two seemingly contradictory tasks is often so difficult.

In practice in the economies in transition (EITs), bank privatization involves only partial divestiture of the state's ownership claims. Hence, a necessary condition for privatization to be deemed a success is that the state remain as a passive investor only. Successful regulatory policy requires the state to assume an arms' length role as regulator and supervisor of the banking sector without any direct involvement in the conduct of the banking business. The simultaneous tasks of disengagement from banking and involvement in regulation are the topic of this chapter. We undertake a comparative analysis of the experiences in three Visegrad countries (Czech Republic, Hungary, and Poland) to determine the approaches that are most likely to result in the

This chapter draws on the research for an Institute for EastWest Studies study, the Comparative Privatization Project on *State Withdrawal: Creating Market-Oriented Banking Sectors for the Economies in Transition*. Research from that project can be found in Bonin, Mizsei, Székely, and Wachtel 1998. A set of policy recommendations for the banking sector was prepared from the project and published by the institute (Bonin, Mizsei, and Wachtel 1996).

independent governance of the banking sector and an effective regulatory structure.

Transition policy should be based on several fundamental principles. To begin, governance of the banks must become independent of the state. This is likely to imply that the state-owned banks should be privatized, but privatization does not always guarantee that the allocation of credit in the economy is not politicized. The more fundamental dilemma for the EITs is to determine the proper mix between state support (e.g., explicit or implicit deposit guarantees, recapitalization of insolvent banks, consolidation of small weak banks to take advantage of economies of scale) and state withdrawal from direct governance of the banks.

Successful bank privatization should lead to the establishment of entities that are not only independent of the state but also independent of control by insiders. In the EITs, independence from insider control is often as important as independence from state control. The inherited legacies of planning mechanisms encourage a continuation of negotiated credit allocation that is not based entirely on strict commercial conditions. The existing relationship between the government and bank management leads more often to antagonistic bilateral bargaining than to consensus building. Interlocking arrangements between a bank and its large clients result in excessive accumulation of bad debt in hostage-like situations. Due to a lack of expertise, bank personnel are often incapable and unwilling to monitor company behavior. Hence, insider control should be avoided unless management is changed from the top down.

For independence from state control to be a credible policy, the banks must be financially able to operate independently. Hence, privatization policy must acknowledge the need to augment the capital base of what would be an insolvent bank if its loan portfolio were to be "marked to market." In EITs, public funds have been used to recapitalize banks, usually by substituting government securities for nonperforming loans, prior to privatization.[1]

[1] In Hungary, the securities are serviced from general revenues and the Ministry of Finance (MOF) acquired a substantial ownership stake from the recapitalization. In Poland, funds made available by donor countries and international financial institutions are available to service the securities once the SOCBs have been privatized. In the Czech Republic, ownership transfer of the large banks occurred through the mass voucher privatization program that generated no new capital for the banks but recapitalization was financed from the National Property Fund.

On the other hand, revenues from privatization transactions have gone to the government privatization agency rather than to the banks. The link between privatization and bank independence, both financially and from the governance perspective, has not been clearly established.

Next, resources must be allocated to the rapid development of the institutional infrastructure necessary for effective banking supervision and regulation. This is not a simple matter of putting legislation and bureaucracies in place. It entails the development of institutions that are able to provide credible regulatory threats to the banks.

Finally, the state must insure the contestability of the banking sector in order to foster efficiency. The last condition requires both the strengthening of the financial capabilities of domestic banks and the encouragement of foreign competition by entry to the market of foreign banks and cross-border banking. Unfortunately, initial regulatory policy in the EITs achieved the opposite by encouraging, in the name of competition and private sector development, the proliferation of small undercapitalized domestic banks and (with the notable exception of Hungary) preventing foreign banks from entering the market in greenfield operations through licensing policy.

Each of the Visegrad countries followed different approaches to the reform of the banking sector. Hungary has attempted to attract a strategic foreign financial investor (SFFI) by first recapitalizing the state-owned banks with public funds and allowing majority foreign ownership. Poland has taken eclectic approaches combining the search for a SFFI, subsidized distribution to insiders, and a public offering with a large and small investor tranche. The Czech Republic included the banks in the first wave of voucher privatization and has effectively blocked sizable foreign investment.

RESTRUCTURING THE BANKING SECTOR

Even before the political transition began, state-owned commercial banks (SOCBs) were created as joint-stock companies from separating the commercial portfolios of the national banks and dividing the clients along regional (e.g., Poland) or sectoral (e.g., Hungary) lines. Savings banks, one in Hungary and the Czech

Republic and two in Poland, and the commercial foreign trade bank in each country also became joint-stock companies with almost full state ownership.

When created as part of the two-tier banking system, the SOCBs were sources of revenue for the state budget. At just the time when the SOCBs needed to become financially stronger, governments tended to drain liquidity from the banks through tax and dividend policies. According to domestic accounting practice, accrued interest was part of the tax base so that nonperforming loans provided taxable income but no cash flow. This philosophy carried over to the privatization process, as selling state-owned bank shares was expected to bring in significant government revenues. The future financial strength of the bank was not of primary interest. Dividend policy often reflected the desire of the state owner to draw liquidity from the banks. As the poor quality of the portfolios of the banks began to be recognized, rapid provisioning and state recapitalization were needed if banks' own capital was to meet the newly adopted regulatory requirements.

The financial needs of the newly born banks and the fiscal needs of the state were often at odds in the early period of the transition. The banking sector must have additional capital to develop adequate lending capabilities in a business environment that has both great growth potential and high risk. Therefore, the preparation stage for privatization should recognize the following two points. First, when created as joint-stock companies, the SOCBs must be viewed as independent financial entities in need of internal accumulation of capital in order to strengthen their lending capacity and not as sources of revenue for the fiscal budget. Second, the inherited loan portfolio with its accompanying inherited client base was the accumulation of decisions made on noncommercial terms. Therefore, these legacies must be prevented from affecting adversely new credit decisions that should be based on strictly commercial principles only.

The symptoms of financial distress are well known; the litany includes large spreads, undercapitalized banks, and loan portfolios with substantial "holes" if they are marked to market. In market economies, financial distress usually results from overly aggressive lending activity followed by a macroeconomic shock. In the EITs, the root cause of financial distress is different. The newly created banks inherited loan portfolios that were established on a noneconomic basis with clients who were often wedded to one of the SOCBs. Whether a client could be expected to service a loan had not been a criterion for credit allocation. Hence, the SOCBs inherited both a loan portfolio and a customer base (of state-owned enterprises) from a discredited political regime without financial compensation (e.g., loan-loss reserves). The transition resulted in three significant shocks to the financial sector, namely, a transition-induced recession, a trade reorientation shock with the demise of the Soviet bloc, and a relative price shock (including a terms-of-trade shock). The legacies and the shocks notwithstanding, the new banking legislation in EITs requires SOCBs to classify loans according to Western market standards and abide by prudential regulations.[2] Since financial distress in EITs has both familiar and idiosyncratic roots, policy for transition economies must be designed with these differences in mind.

Much of the literature on banking reform in EITs focuses on the problem of nonperforming loans in the portfolios of the SOCBs. Dittus (1994) provides a comparative analysis of financial reform and bank behavior through 1993 in Poland, Hungary, and the Czech/Slovak Republics with extensive references to bad loans. Marrese (1994) analyzes bank restructuring strategies in these same countries. Recommendations include early cleansing of bad loans from the banks' balance sheets (Beggs and Portes 1993) and linking bank recapitalization to bank privatization (Levine and Scott, 1992). Abel and Bonin (1994) discuss privatization of SOCBs as a crucial element of financial sector reform in Hungary. The literature offers no consensus to policy makers in EITs nor does the experience of the faster-reforming countries provide consistent lessons.

In all EITs, the state placed the burden of supporting ailing state-owned enterprises (SOEs) on the SOCBs when it eliminated direct fiscal subsidies. The banks had little choice but to protect their clients. Hence, nonperforming loans were rolled over, interest arrears accumulated, and fresh credit was even extended to

[2] A phase-in period is often specified as in the Hungarian Banking Act whereby banks were given a three-year period to satisfy gradually the provisioning requirements against the nonperforming part of the portfolio.

some of the better-connected but ailing clients. Good companies, those that serviced their debt, paid for these subsidies in the form of the high cost of services and high borrowing rates. What had been transparent fiscal support of nonprofitable SOEs was transformed into nontransparent support intermediated by the SOCBs. Furthermore, the SOCBs left with poor credit risks as clients turned to government securities for both a better risk-return package and the liquidity needed to accumulate the loan-loss reserves required by the new regulations. Hence, the banks in the EITs charged high spreads, undertook little new commercial lending, and had a high proportion of bad loans.

To alleviate financial distress, partial recapitalization of the insolvent banks was undertaken. Any government bailout program faces a moral hazard problem. How can the government commit credibly to a once-and-for-all recapitalization? Since the quality of the portfolios are influenced significantly by the shocks mentioned, basing recapitalization on inherited loans rated as bad by some past date has proved ineffective.[3] Choosing an instrument to fill the hole in the bank's balance is also problematic. If the securities used are highly liquid and yield a market rate of return, as recommended by Beggs and Portes (1993), inflation management will be difficult as banks would essentially be receiving cash. Hence, the securities chosen have been long-term government bonds with some restrictions on transferability.[4] In essence, these securities are actually worth less than their face value due to restrictions and nonmarket return.

Any publicly financed bailout of bank management and shareholders has moral hazards attached to it unless there are appropriate terms conditionally attached to it. To the extent that the bad debt is truly inherited, management can not be held accountable for it; to the extent that it results from poor governance, it must not be forgiven unconditionally. Management and the current shareholders (usually state-owned agencies and organizations) should share in the cost of recapitalization. To the extent that all existing shareholders are public institutions, the issue may look like an accounting exercise. However, the

[3] For examples, consider Hungary's first recapitalization program in 1992 (Abel and Bonin 1994) and Bulgaria's program (Dobrinsky 1994).

[4] For examples, see the Polish program (Bonin, Leven, and Schaffer 1996) and the Hungarian 1992 program (Abel and Bonin 1994).

incidence of recapitalization may not be purely distributional; rather the cost borne by certain groups (e.g., municipalities or pension funds) may affect their activities. To date, any conditionally accompanying recapitalization in EITs has focused on changing bank governance and not on distributing some cost to shareholders.

Loan workout in EITs may involve removing loans from bank balance sheets or requiring the banks to arrange for their collection. Loan consolidation involves identifying and packaging effectively the bad debt so that the resulting portfolio can be managed to maximize the present discounted value of the eventual return. Efficient workout requires a match between expertise in managing the portfolio and the necessary financial information. In Poland, the SOCBs have been identified as the agents to work out bad debt and assist their clients in restructuring. In Hungary and the Czech Republic, policy involves a combination of centralized and bank-based workout of bad debt with restructuring of SOEs left to the government or the courts.

In Poland, an integrated bank-led restructuring program was designed in which bank recapitalization and bad-debt workout are linked together. In addition to the existing court-based option (basically, chapter 7 bankruptcy) and the liquidation option under the Polish privatization law, the 1993 Polish legislation offered a new financial instrument for resolving bad debts, namely, the bank conciliatory procedure (BCP). As the agent for all creditors, the lead bank is involved in designing both a financial restructuring plan and a "revitalization" or business plan (operational restructuring). From the bank's perspective, financial restructuring consists of rescheduling (principal plus accrued interest), refinancing with a decrease in the interest rate, writing down the face value (partial write-off), engaging in a debt-equity swap, or pursuing some combination of these. Approximately four hundred BCPs, mainly with the largest borrowers due to lower transaction costs, have been initiated in Poland covering 59% of the eligible loans. The average agreement covers three years, and only 30 percent of all BCPs involve debt-equity swaps (Bonin, Leven, and Schaffer 1996). Encouraging banks to take equity holdings in their clients leads to the well-known conflict of interest between the lending facility and the ownership objective, especially in periods of financial distress. Furthermore, it strengthens the ties between banks and their inherited troubled clients when the reverse is the appropriate policy.

An alternative to making the SOCBs responsible for loan workout is to set up a centralized "sink" or "hospital" bank. In 1991, the (then) Czechoslovakian government created such a bank, Konsolidacni Banka (KOB). KOB took over a portfolio of revolving credit loans with low fixed interest and noncollateral attached (TOZ loans). The transfer of TOZ loans reduced both sides of the SOCB's balance sheet as liabilities of equal value were also removed and the bank was effectively downsized. KOB was given a mandate to restructure these to seven-year maturity loans bearing a market rate of interest. Since TOZ loans (working capital) were held by virtually all enterprises of any significant size in the country, the portfolio of KOB was not all bad debt. In fact, the performance of KOB's restructured portfolio has been better than average for Czech banks.[5] KOB has also been used as a repository for bad loans by the major Czech commercial bank, Komercni Banka (KB). In 1992, KB was allowed to pass bad loans amounting to about 5.5 percent of its loan portfolio to KOB in return for a capital injection. KB had also been partially recapitalized in 1991 with government securities in exchange for bad loans totaling more than 8 percent of its portfolio. Hence, the Czech Republic has used a combination of a centralized and bank-based workout.

After using a combination of programs, Hungary settled on a bank-based one similar to the Polish scheme. Of the loans included in the 1992 recapitalization, the Hungarian Investment and Development bank (HID) took over about one-third in value to work out. HID then packaged the loans and auctioned them off in secondary markets. The remainder were left with the banks to work out, using incentive contracts to encourage recovery. The second major bank recapitalization in Hungary in 1993–94 involved a workout procedure similar to the bank-based one in Poland in that it used a fast track, chapter-11-type procedure to facilitate financial restructuring. However, a three-year time limit was placed on any bank's holding of equity in a restructured company resulting from a debt-equity swap.

[5] The portfolio was split into a Czech part and a Slovak part when the two republics separated.

To date, market-based strategies involving the sale of loans at auctions, thus transferring the rights to work out the bad debt to the purchasing agent who values it most highly, have not met with much success. In the 1993 Polish restructuring program, public sales have been the preferred option in terms of the number of loans, but these account for less than 20 percent of the total value of bank debt in the program. Furthermore, the recovery rate has been low at about 21 percent of face value (Bonin, Leven, and Schaffer 1996). Since the banks have the best financial information on debtors, auctions are not likely to be effective in matching expertise with information, especially for large debtors.

Two propositions are extractable from the recapitalization experience in EITS. First, banks should be capable of divesting themselves of old clients and encouraged to do so when this is appropriate on commercial grounds. As a corollary, industrial policy should be financed transparently by the fiscal authorities, not hidden on the balance sheets of SOCBs. Second, as created, the SOCBs were basically insolvent and, hence, in need of recapitalization. However, the financial support they receive must be a credible one-shot occurrence and must not tie the SOCB's governance more closely to the government. Programs like Poland's integrated program violate the first proposition. Hungary has made the largest expenditure of public funds to recapitalization. In doing so with repeated bailouts of banks and enterprises, it has fallen into the moral hazard trap – that is, the difficulty of making a credible commitment to avoid subsequent bailouts. A closer linking of recapitalization to privatization will facilitate the likelihood of independent governance of SOCBs resulting from transitional policy toward banks.

BANK PRIVATIZATION

Bank privatization policy must acknowledge the conflict among multiple objectives and, thus, the need to choose a primary goal. Our candidate for the latter is to maximize the speed with which the governance of the bank becomes independent from both the state and existing management. As a corollary, the privatization strategy should maximize the likelihood of attracting an SFFI that would bring to the bank financial capital, independent governance, technical expertise, and reputational capital. The latter is most important as it provides the incentives for good governance. Unfortunately, the goal commonly pursued in EITs is to maximize revenues to the state from the sale of ownership shares in an SOCB. We argue that such a goal is at odds with the goal of rapid achievement of independent governance.

Privatization methods can be divided into three approaches, namely, sales by initial public offering (IPO), seeking an SFFI by tender, and give-away. An example of the third is the inclusion of banks in the first wave of voucher privatization in (then) Czechoslovakia at the end of 1992. The benefits of this approach are the speed of transfer of ownership, the egalitarian nature of the process, and the avoidance of having to set a price administratively for the transaction. The obvious cost is the lack of capital raised for the bank or revenues for the treasury. As we argue later, this method is likely to result in disperse ownership and is not conducive to achieving the primary goal of independent governance.

If banks are sold, either by tender or IPO, a selling price must be determined. Allowing the price to be determined by tender runs the risk of establishing too low a selling price due to the imbalance between the supply of seekers and the demand from prospective takers for whom nondiversifiable systemic risk creates an option value to waiting. The alternative of setting the price administratively in negotiation with an SFFI that may have been selected by tender is also problematic. The political cost of selling banks to foreigners in what appears to be a fire sale is severe.[6] However, undue preoccupation with "getting the price right" is likely to retard significantly progress toward achieving the primary goal of independent governance. In EITs, the IPO method encounters two additional impediments, namely, the underdeveloped infrastructure for handling the processing of claims from a large number of small owners and the lack of absorption capacity of nascent domestic capital markets in which bank stocks dominate market capitalization.

Experiences with bank privatization in the three Visegrad countries correspond roughly to prototypes for each of the three methods, voucher give-away, selling to SFFI, and selling by IPO (see Bonin 1995). In the Czech Republic, voucher privatization

[6] As we develop further in the case of Bank Slaski in Poland.

has led to mixed results. Although the state and the voucher funds have large stakes in the banks, existing management is often firmly entrenched. The Hungarian program has progressed erratically, but now boasts the first successful bank privatization according to our criterion. Four of Poland's nine state-owned regional banks have been privatized with plans for two more privatizations proceeding smoothly. Poland is currently entertaining the consolidation of the remaining three regional state-owned banks to strengthen their balance sheets prior to privatization. The Polish program has taken an eclectic approach to selling the banks with the emphasis shifting from SFFI to IPO to SFFI over time. We will discuss all three approaches starting with the Polish experience.

Privatizations in Poland

In Poland, bank privatization policy focused on the nine regionally concentrated SOCBs. Poland with some inducement from the G7 donor countries and the international financial institutions set a clear timetable for privatizing these banks. In order to obtain financial support from the Polish Bank Privatization Fund for recapitalizing seven of the nine, Poland agreed to privatize all nine by the end of 1996.[7] The original blueprint had the treasury retaining a 30 percent ownership stake, employees purchasing on preferential terms up to 20 percent, and the remaining half divided between a large and small investor tranche. The small investor tranche involved a domestic IPO while the large investor tranche was intended to attract an SFFI core investor by tender. The first two banks to be privatized, Wielkopolski Bank Kredytowy (WBK) in Poznan and Bank Slaski (BSK) in Katowice, were chosen for their financial strength and quality of management (Bonin 1993). Preparation of these two began in the summer of 1991, and WBK was privatized first on 15 March 1993.

WBK issued new shares to obtain a capital injection – 28.5 percent of the augmented share base. The government intended

[7] The donors agreed to make about $700 million available from monies originally provided but never used to support the fixed exchange rate anchor of the stabilization program in 1990. Two of the banks were ineligible for support because they were already privatized when the financial restructuring program was designed in 1993.

to sell these shares to an SFFI but after an unsuccessful search contracted with the European Bank for Reconstruction and Development (EBRD) at a price of $6.89 per share for $12.6 million of new capital. The same price was applied to a 27.2 percent stake in an IPO divided into a large investor tranche (7.2%) and a small investor tranche (20%). The former was subscribed mainly by Polish investors (80%) and the latter entirely by domestic investors. The employee stake is about 15 percent. WBK opened for trading on the Warsaw Stock Exchange (WSE) on 22 June 1993 at a price of $19.66. The approximately threefold increase from issue price tracked the increase in the market index, WIG. Slawomir Sikora, the person responsible for bank privatization at the Ministry of Finance (MOF), claimed that the stock market run-up was due to the privatization of WBK because that act convinced investors that the government was seriously supporting privatization and the market.

In March 1995, Allied Irish Banks (AIB) participated in a second new share issue by WBK and acquired a 16.26 percent stake for $20 million. AIB had been WBK's twin but declined to participate in the initial privatization. The new issue reduced EBRD's stake to 23.9 percent, and AIB signed an agreement with EBRD to purchase its stake at a future date. Recently the MOF announced its intention to sell a 20 percent stake in WBK, and AIB has expressed interest. The pending offering plus the option on the EBRD's stake would give AIB a controlling interest in WBK.

Did AIB benefit from the option value of waiting? On the one hand, AIB paid $20 million for a smaller stake than EBRD currently holds and had obtained for $12.6 million two years before. On the other hand, the share price of WBK was $2.50 as of 26 January 1996, significantly lower than the price ($6.89) that EBRD paid in 1993. Only the results of the subsequent negotiations between AIB and both EBRD and the MOF, respectively, will afford a definite answer.

The privatization of BSK was consummated in December 1995 following a canceled tender. In a prospectus dated 31 August 1993, both a public tender and an IPO were announced. The tender for large investors initially involved 45 percent of BSK's shares and was designed to attract a SFFI. The IPO for small investors was allocated a 15 percent stake with the total 60 percent stake being sold from the state's holdings as BSK issued no new shares. From mid-September to mid-October, bids specifying quantity requested and price offered above the minimum share price of PLZ 230,000 ($11.50) were accepted.[8] The minimum price was set so that the value of the total shares outstanding equaled the book value of the bank. The strike price was to be determined in the tender and then applied to the IPO.[9] The clear intention was to let the competitive tender process determine the price for the IPO as well.

After a change in the composition of the coalition government, the tender was canceled reportedly due to a lack of sufficient demand. At the time, the strike price would have been slightly above the minimum at $12.50 per share even though the run-up in the WIG had continued into the fall.[10] The MOF allocated more shares to the IPO, bringing the total to a 30 percent stake and accepted offers for a minimum of 10 shares and a maximum of 5,000. The price set for the IPO was determined administratively at $25 per share yielding a value of approximately twice the book value of the bank for the total shares outstanding. Even with the additional allotment, the IPO was seriously oversubscribed. Reserved for the employees of BSK was a 10 percent stake on preferential terms (half price). In early December, the Dutch bank, Internationale Nederlanden Group (ING), showed renewed interest in BSK after having participated in the tender bidding earlier.

The process resulted in ING taking a 25.9 percent stake in BSK for $60 million (2 million shares at $25 per share) on 13 January 1994, employees taking a 10 percent stake and receiving their shares early enough to register them for trading in January, and 817,644 small investors receiving three shares each in the IPO. The terms of the contract with the SFFI require ING to hold the shares for at least three years. The large number of small shareholders led to widely dispersed ownership of 30 percent of BSK shares. The state retained a 33 percent stake. When BSK opened

[8] At the minimum bid price, the smallest allowable stake in the tender would have cost $2,127,500. Clearly the tender was intended to attract large investors (mainly foreign).

[9] The MOF reserved the right to reallocate a 15.1% stake (amounting to 33.6% of the shares in the large-investor tranche) from the tender to the IPO (small investor tranche).

[10] WBK traded at around $35 or six times its issue price during this period.

for trading on the WSE on 25 January, the market-established price was $337.50 or thirteen and a half times the issue price! Trade volume amounted to 32,410 or about 0.35 percent of the total shares. To be tradable on the exchange, shares must be registered at an approved brokerage house. BSK employees were advantaged both in receiving their shares earlier than the public and in having ready access to BSK's brokerage facilities. The other 800,000 plus shareholders had difficulty registering their shares in a timely fashion. Hence, much of the first-day selling was presumed to be employee shares. Since these were purchased at $12.50 per share, the profit per share for those selling on the first day would have been $325.

Public outcry surrounding the BSK affair focused on the special treatment accorded BSK employees and the information about excess demand in the IPO available to ING before it committed to its investment at what was perceived to be a "bargain-basement" price. From an ex post perspective, the obvious problems were the lack of adequate capacity to handle the number of shareholders attempting to register in a short period of time and the below-equilibrium price in the IPO. Neither could have been anticipated in advance, and both are clearly interdependent. A higher price would have reduced significantly the number of shareholders. The pricing problem had substantial political costs as Stefan Kawalec, the deputy finance minister responsible for setting the price, was dismissed and left to face charges of wrongdoing.[11] The price as of 26 January 1996 for BSK shares was $73.12 still significantly above its dollar issue price. The lesson in Poland is clear: beware of pricing bank stocks administratively, especially when the secondary market is thin and the trading infrastructure is underdeveloped.

The third SOCB privatized was Bank Przemyslowo-Handlowy (BPH) in Krakow. In 1993, Credit Suisse First Boston (CSFB) was engaged to supervise the privatization and locate an SFFI. Both CSFB and ABN-Amro (BPH's twin) found the offer price at about twice book value too high. The chief executive officer of BPH, Janusz Quandt, was arguably not interested in ceding responsibility to an SFFI. Hence, the BSK affair was sufficient fod-

[11] When Marek Borowski, the minister of finance, learned of Kawalec's dismissal, he resigned in protest.

der to allow Mr. Quandt to dictate privatization by IPO only. A prospectus dated 9 November 1994 announced that purchase orders for a 50.2 percent stake would be accepted over a four-week period with the maximum allowable stake set at 10 percent.[12] The strike price was determined on a special market day with a minimum price set at $29.66 to avoid the pricing problem associated with the BSK privatization. Unfortunately, the WIG lost about two-thirds of its value from a March 1994 high by the end of the year, and the Mexican crisis dampened foreign interest in emerging markets. As a result of lack of demand, the strike price was at the minimum and EBRD as underwriter was left with a 15 percent stake. ING and BSK each took a 5 percent stake and increased their combined stake to 15 percent by purchasing the shares remaining with a second underwriter at a later date. The state is currently left with a 43 percent stake while 27 percent of the shares in BPH are widely held.

Although no core investor emerged from the privatization of BPH, in our opinion by design of the chief executive officer, the partnership of ING and BSK expressed interest in its sister Silesian bank.[13] With the EBRD holding a significant share, the possibility of the ING/BSK duo eventually taking a core investor stake in BPH exists. However, recent announcements by the MOF indicate alternative plans. When the legislation is passed to facilitate consolidation of banks currently owned by the state, the MOF is considering placing the state's remaining shares in BPH with a consolidated group. This would effectively block any attempt by ING/BSK to take an active investor role in BPH. Discussion continues in Poland as to whether this is a viable option. It is clear that, by retaining a core-investor stake in a bank, the government can pursue banking policy directly through governance in addition to indirectly through regulation.

The fourth privatization of an SOCB was that of Bank Gdanski (BG) for whom ING had been the twin. The plan called for a two-pronged IPO with one-third of the shares sold to foreign portfolio investors using global depository receipts and one-third sold to

[12] An additional 6.8% of the shares were reserved for sale at a discount to holders of Exchange Treasury Bonds.

[13] Interestingly, Mr. Quandt was dismissed by the supervisory board of the bank two months after the privatization for having led an ineffective advertising campaign to increase interest in BPH's shares.

domestic investors at a price of $9.70 per share. Employees were expected to take a 4 percent stake and the state retained the remainder (30%) of the shares. An interested core investor emerged from the domestic sale. Bank Inicjatyw Gospodarczych S.A. (BIG), a widely held private Polish bank, took a 24.1 percent stake and immediately increased this to 26.75 percent with a block purchase on the WSE after BG opened for trading. Evidently, Polish financial core investors are now preferred to SFFIs by the MOF.

The Polish experience with privatizing four SOCBs identifies three impediments to an effective transfer of governance to an independent core investor. First, pricing is problematic because of the political costs associated with the perception that banks are being sold at bargain prices in fire sales. Second, speed may prevent tailoring privatization plans to the conditions of the market and foreign demand. Both the absorption capacity of the domestic market and the option value of waiting must be taken into account. Third, a strong CEO can prevent the transfer of governance to nonstate outsiders. With the state retaining a core-investor stake, the result of dispersed ownership is then continued insider-state bargaining over bank policy. A fourth lesson from Polish experience is the need to develop the transactional infrastructure before the privatization transaction. The political costs incurred in the BSK privatization due to an overloading of the trading infrastructure could have been avoided if properly anticipated.

Privatizations in Hungary

By the end of 1995, Hungary had privatized three formerly state-owned banks, of which two are controlled independently by outside nonstate investors. The first successful bank privatization was Magyar Kulkereskedelmi Bank (MKB), the Hungarian Foreign Trade Bank and the third largest bank in Hungary, in July 1994. Discussions with Bayerische Landesbank Girozentrale Bank (BLB), a German state-owned bank having long-standing business relations with MKB, began in 1991. Privatization involved a new share offering worth $19 million; BLB and EBRD paid a total of $54 million for stakes of 25 percent and 16.7 percent, respectively. The state retained a 27 percent stake with the other 31.3

percent of the shares held widely by Hungarian and foreign investors.

The purchase price per share for BLB and EBRD was $122.55 but the sale involved an equity-based, price-adjustment clause for EBRD only (see Kormendi and Schatterly 1996 for a description of the deal). If the pretax profits for MKB in the last half of 1994 and the first half of 1995 exceeded respective hurdle figures, the price would be adjusted upward by 30 percent and 25 percent respectively. The hurdles were set rather low by historical standards, and both were met.[14] The final price paid by EBRD (but not BLB) turned out to be close to $190 per share. Given the conservative nature of the hurdles, the contract suggests that EBRD was concerned about prompting MKB to avoid bad-case outcome in the period immediately following the privatization. Clearly BLB was able to free-ride on this incentive. Nonetheless, by negotiating a performance-based price adjustment with EBRD, the participants on both sides reduced the risks associated with not getting the transaction price "right."

In February 1995, the German Investment and Development Corporation (GIDC) bought 8.33 percent of the shares in MKB from its treasury portfolio. Both BLB and GIDC agreed to vote together their combined stake of 33.34 percent, which is sufficient to block major policy changes requiring a two-thirds majority vote. Recently the AVP Rt (the Hungarian State Holding Company) sold its remaining stake to BLB to bring the latter to majority shareholder status with a stake of 51 percent. Hence, BLB by any measures can now control the governance of MKB, and the Hungarian state has divested itself fully of its ownership stake in the bank.

The privatization of Orszagos Takarekpenztar es Kereskedelmi Bank (OTP), the national savings bank founded in 1949 and the largest bank in Hungary with 430 branches, was the second completed major bank privatization in Hungary. The expatriate financier, George Soros, had expressed interest in acquiring a large stake in OTP but his offer was successfully rebuked by a strong chief executive officer. Toward the end of 1994, 2 percent of

[14] The first required MKB's earnings in 1994 to be more than about two-thirds of its 1993 earnings. The second proscribed first-half earnings in 1995 on an *annualized basis* to be about one-half of 1993 earnings.

OTP's shares was transferred to municipalities and, in May 1995, 20 percent of the OTP share capital was transferred to the two state social security funds. The state retained an ownership stake of 25 percent with AVP Rt and sold 34 percent of OTP's shares to portfolio investors (20% foreign using GDRs and 14% domestic). Another 20 percent is widely held by Hungarian investors. The chief executive officer of OTP has retained his position and his insider control with the state as the only significant outside investor.

The first privatization of an SOCB in Hungary was delayed when CSFB pulled out of the final stages of negotiation with Budapest Bank (BB) in March 1995. In December 1995, GE Capital and EBRD paid $87 million to BB which the bank used to pay a short-term capitalization loan coming due on 15 December (see Kormendi and Schatterly 1996). GE Capital received a 27.5 percent ownership stake and a contract giving it full management control. EBRD took a 32.5 percent stake with the state retaining 22 percent of the shares. Another 18 percent is widely held mainly by domestic investors. In addition to the state agreeing contractually to be only a passive investor, GE Capital and EBRD were protected against downside loss with a put option for their entire 60 percent stake at a predetermined price. GE Capital, as the bank's management, was also given the option to turn over to the government certain bad loans during a three- to five-year period. Finally, GE Capital was given a call option to purchase both the EBRD's and the state's stake at a predetermined price within some time frame.[15] GE Capital is in a position to reap all the upside gain of its management decisions in BB without incurring the risk of any downside loss. BB has independent governance, and GE Capital has its reputation on the line. If BB's performance over the near term is sufficiently strong, the naysayers who complain about the government having "given the bank away" may be quieted.

The major lesson from Hungary's experience with bank privatization is that the search for an SFFI takes time but is likely to be worth the effort and patience. The transaction price is not as important as securing the governance of an independent foreign investor. Performance-based incentive contracts can attract SFFIs

[15] The specifics of the put and call options are confidential.

willing to put up their own reputational capital, which is likely to be of more lasting value to the bank than any up-front financial capital. This is especially true when the financial capital from the privatization transaction goes to the state and not to the bank. As a corollary, a strong chief executive officer can prevent the transfer of governance to an outsider, as was evidenced in the case of OTP.

Privatization in the Czech Republic

In Czechoslovakia in 1992, three of the big four Czech banks participated in the first wave of voucher privatization. Komercni Banka (KB), created from the Czech part of the commercial portfolio of the national bank, Ceska Sporitelna (CS), the Czech savings bank created in 1969, and Investicni a Postovni Banka (IPB), formed by a merger of the investment bank and the network of deposit-taking post office branches, were the participants. Investment funds (IPFs) dominated the first wave of voucher privatization, collecting about 72 percent of the points allocated. These three Czech bank funds (KB, IPB, CS) were among the five largest, with the Harvard group the only nonbank fund in the top five. Hence, banks were on both sides of bank privatization transactions while the state retained a large ownership stake in the "privatized" banks.

With KB, the state's total ownership stake is 50.5 percent consisting of the 48 percent held by the National Property Fund (NPF) and a 2.5 percent stake held by the Restitution Investment Fund (RIF). As of 10 June 1995, the other major shareholders in KB were the Harvard group with 8.4 percent, the IPB funds with 5.3 percent, the Vseobecna Uverova Banka (Bratislava) fund (VUB) with 3.5 percent, KB's own fund with 3.3 percent, and the CS fund with 3.3 percent. No other shareholder, including any IPF, held a stake in excess of 2 percent at that time. The aggregate stake held by IPFs at the end of 1995 is 33 percent. Individual shareholders hold only 7.5 percent of the shares while foreign institutions have a 9 percent stake. Hence, the state has a majority ownership position in KB, IPFs in the aggregate have a core-investor stake, and the remaining shares are held widely by domestic individuals and by foreign portfolio investors. Insider governance is firmly entrenched at KB under a strong chief executive officer, Richard Salzmann.

In the case of CS, municipalities hold 14.75 percent of the shares in addition to the 45 percent stake held by the NPF and a 3 percent stake held by RIF, bringing total government ownership to 62.75 percent. Immediately after the voucher privatization of CS, the Harvard Group held 12.9 percent of the shares and the major bank funds held the following stakes: IPB, 8.8 percent; KB, 3.9 percent; and VUB, 1.6 percent. Viktor Kozeny, the founder of the Harvard Group, attempted to influence governance at CS but failed. By the end of 1995, the total holding of privatization funds was 32.5 percent of the shares in CS with the remaining 4.75 percent of the shares widely held by individual investors. As in KB, the government holds a clear majority ownership position, and IPFs as a group hold a core-investor stake in CS. The probability of a nonbank core investor emerging is low given the current ownership configuration and the constraints on concentration of ownership by any single IPF.[16] Hence, the governance of the two largest banks in the Czech Republic remains in the hands of the state and insiders at this time.

The case of IPB is slightly different. The state holds a core-investor stake of 39.6 percent consisting of the NPF's 32.8 percent and the RIF's 6.8 percent. The next largest individual stake at 14.7 percent is held by the IPB's own fund management company (Prvni Investicni AS or PIAS). The Czech insurance company (Ceska Pojistovna) holds 7.5 percent of the shares and the remaining 38.2 percent are held by IPFs and institutional investors. Again the state's ownership stake is dominant although not a majority holding. More interestingly, IPB's own investment fund group has a large stake and 45.7 percent of the shares are held by portfolio investors. The insider-state nexus retains a hold on governance in IPB as the major "outside" investor is IPB's own investment fund.

Voucher privatization in the Czech Republic has resulted in significant cross-ownership patterns and strengthened the nonmarket relationships between banks and their company clients to the detriment of the governance of both. Furthermore, voucher

[16] Czech regulations prohibit any IPF from owning more than a 20% stake in any company.

privatization has led to bifurcated ownership structure in which the state retains a core-investor-size stake, while the preponderance of the rest of the shares are held widely. Such a configuration provides ample opportunity for insider-state or solely state control. Although voucher privatization is quick and politically expedient, it requires a second round of ownership transfer to bring about independent nonstate governance. In the interim, it may entrench informal nonmarket relations that will be difficult to break in the future. Voucher privatization of banks with a large state residual share is not likely to be market friendly.

Progress in achieving bank governance that is independent from both the state and entrenched insiders has been slow in EITs. Three lessons can be drawn from the experiences of these three countries. First, the state's retention of a "core-investor" stake in the banks leads to the perpetuation of state dominance of bank governance. Second, a forceful chief executive officer in a yet-to-be privatized bank can exercise significant influence over the process and often insure insider control. Third, the process of finding a suitable SFFI takes time and, once found, the ceding of governance authority to the SFFI is at odds with other goals. Whether the cost in terms of time and political capital is worth the transfer of governance to an independent outsider depends crucially on the reputational capital that the SFFI puts on the line.

COMPETITION AND CONTESTABILITY

A competitive banking sector is of broad macroeconomic importance because it leads to an efficient allocation of investment resources. The importance of competition was recognized early in the reform of banking systems in the EITs. As discussed already, the large state-owned monobanks of the Soviet era were broken up in most EITs in the very earliest stages of transition. However, these efforts often created banks with monopolies in either geographical or industrial segments of the financial services market. As a consequence, the initial restructuring of the banking system did little to create a competitive environment, and further efforts to create a competitive industry followed quickly (see Miklaszewska 1995).

In the next stage of transition, policies that encouraged new entrants into banking were introduced in order to create a more competitive banking environment. In order to increase quickly the number of competitors in banking, minimum capital requirements for a bank license were set at fairly low levels, and the review process for new entrants was rather lax (procedures and personnel for licensing review simply did not exist). The number of banks increased very rapidly. The number of banks (excluding saving cooperatives) reached about 75 in Poland, about 55 in the Czech Republic and almost 40 in Hungary. (In Russia the number of banks has swelled to 2,600.) Throughout the region there were far more banks than made sense for an efficient level of operations. In most instances, the formerly SOCBs retained large market shares, and the new entrants had little influence on the industry, except where their poor banking practices created large systemic risks.

The increase in the number of banks was problematic for at least two reasons. First, a large number of inefficient and poorly capitalized banking institutions may not improve the efficiency of financial intermediation. Second, the proliferation of small banks can be destabilizing. Poorly capitalized banks that undertake risky activities have systemic implications that extend well beyond the individual institution. Larger systemic risks can have negative effects on the efficiency of the financial system as a whole. Since banks play an essential role in maintaining the stability of the payments system and the means of payment, a large number of poorly capitalized banks can have negative systemic effects that outweigh any of the advantages of increased competition. In fact, the weak structure of many new banks meant that they did little to foster competition.

Competition in banking does not require a large number of banks. Most countries (both small and large) have relatively few banking institutions; the situation in the United States is the exception and not the rule. Competitive pressures in the industry come from the structure of the financial system generally and the extent to which other nonbank financial institutions compete with the banks. The Visegrad countries have opted for universal banking that allows the banks to conduct both traditional banking and investment banking activities (see Buch 1995). In Hungary, the investment banking activities are restricted to bank affiliates that can be fully owned and controlled by the parent bank. The only other limits on bank activity are limits on the ownership of firms and limits on the ratio of equity holding to the bank's capital. In the Czech Republic, notification and approval is required when bank ownership exceeds 10 percent of a firm's capital or if equity holdings exceed 25 percent of the bank's capital. Similarly, in Poland banks cannot hold more than 25 percent of their capital in shares without special permission. In Hungary, the limit on equity holdings is 60 percent of the bank's capital and banks cannot hold more than 15 percent of their capital in any one enterprise. These restrictions allow other financial intermediaries to compete with the banks for much of the capital markets' business.

Other structural issues that affect competition in banking are, importantly, the entry of foreign banks and the threat of new entrants or the provision of banking services by other institutions – the contestability of the financial services market. Contestability of the market can lead banks in a highly concentrated, seemingly protected market to operate as they would under pure competition. Also, contestability and the entry of foreign banks and nonbank competition can create a competitive framework for banking without increasing systemic risks.

In the EITs, foreign banks play an important role in fostering a competitive environment (see Wachtel 1995) and recent privatizations in the Visegrad countries suggest that banking authorities have recognized this. By allowing foreign bank entry (as new entrants, strategic partners, or merger partners), competition will emerge with lesser risks. Foreign banks bring in modern banking technology and business practices that will affect the whole industry. Even when foreign banks enter with little actual capital at risk (which is true in many instances, such as the GE Capital investment in Budapest Bank), they are likely to be making a significant commitment because they are placing their international reputational capital at risk. A drawback of foreign bank entry is that it creates a two-tier system in which the strong banks with foreign partners attract the best customers and the other banks are left the dregs. An approach to this problem is for the government to orchestrate foreign-bank entry by promoting joint ventures and equity investments in existing banks. Thus, the foreign entry is a catalyst for the transformation of the banking system.

Nevertheless, there is often considerable resistance to the entry of foreign banks (see Wachtel 1995) for nationalistic reasons. In providing a payments' system and defining the money asset, banks have a pervasive importance in the economy. Countries are loath to have the national currency subject to foreign influence, and foreign ownership of the banks seems to convey the appearance of foreign control. However, the appropriate way to judge foreign ownership of the banks is to consider it as one would consider any foreign direct investment in industry (in this case the financial services industry). A foreign commitment to the banking industry is a direct investment in a major services industry and not a means of some unspecified form of exploitation.

After the initial stage of rapid expansion of the number of banks, there was considerable resistance to further foreign entry into banking. Issuance of new banking licenses was suspended in Poland and Hungary. However, the potential benefits of foreign direct investment in banking were soon realized and the authorities began to encourage alliances between existing banks and foreign banks. By 1995, foreign banks were playing a major role in bank privatizations in all of the Visegrad countries.

The most effective route to a competitive banking structure in Poland is competition among the original nine large SOCBs. It is unclear how to achieve this because of tension among the MOF to identify local strategic investors, the preference of existing management for IPOs that are likely to secure their continued control, and the interest of SFFI in privatizations (see our earlier discussion). Nevertheless, SFFIs have played an important role in the privatization of two of the large SOCBs and it is likely that SFFI will continue to play a role in further privatizations or consolidations.

Seven foreign banks were licensed in Poland by 1992 when the government decided to limit foreign entry. After a two-year hiatus, five more foreign bank licenses were issued. In 1994, BNP/Dresdner was given a license for commercial banking operations. Reports are that this was a reward to Dresdner Bank for its efforts in negotiating with the London Club the reduction of Poland's debt. In 1995, several other German and Dutch banks – West LB, Hypo Bank, ABN-Ambro, Rabobank – acquired or were planning to acquire stakes in Polish banks.

The distinguishing characteristic of the Hungarian banking sector is the inroads into the banking business by foreign banks. In

1994, foreign banks and joint ventures accounted for 16 percent of total bank assets and about one-quarter of entrepreneurial deposits and credits. Although a number of small foreign banks had closed, local ventures by some major foreign banks were becoming increasingly active on the domestic market. The growth in market share of the foreign banks in Hungary demonstrated that markets are contestable, and this had a significant influence on attitudes toward privatization of the large SOCBs. Policy makers and bankers were willing to accept an SFFI when faced with competition that had the potential of reducing the market shares of the SOCBs significantly.

Thus, at the end of 1995, after several false starts with other suitors, the largest commercial bank, Budapest Bank, was privatized. (The complex transaction involving GE Capital and the EBRD was described earlier.)

Banking in the Czech Republic remains highly concentrated as a consequence of the cross-ownership that resulted from voucher privatization. Nevertheless, the small foreign banks have already made significant inroads into banking. By late 1994, majority foreign-owned banks had a 32 percent market share of lending to private and cooperative enterprises and a 55 percent share of lending to foreign controlled firms. Thus, banking markets can be contestable even in a highly concentrated industry.

The competitive pressures from contestable markets can cause even a monopolist to behave as if the market is competitive. In fact, it is likely that the large Czech commercial banks have already begun to react. In May 1996, the state (via the National Property Fund) is reducing its ownership of Komercni Bank with a public offering on international equities markets via Global Depository Receipts. Such an offering can only be successful if the state has significantly reduced its involvement with the bank.

The entry of foreign banks in the initial stages of transition in all of the Visegrad countries has resulted in markets that are to a large extent contestable. The large SOCBs are more open to change when they discover that their market shares would wither away over time. This occurs because open capital markets make many aspects of banking easily contestable markets. Foreign branches and small foreign banks can provide many banking services. For example, commercial lending is an area where entry or the threat of entry will force changes in banking practices. However, retail deposit collection may not be an easily contestable market because of the costs of building a branch network. Thus, the contestability of markets might not be sufficient to force the large formerly SOCBs to transform themselves into market-oriented banking institutions.

In conclusion, the proliferation of new banks creates more problems for the banking system than it solves. The moral hazard problems and the increase in systemic risks far outweigh the benefits of marginally increased competition. However, limited foreign entry, as occurred in all of the Visegrad countries by the early 1990s, creates a contestable environment. The threat of competition can cause existing institutions to transform themselves into competitive financial services enterprises that require capital and expertise. As a result, attitudes toward SFFI have been changing.

REGULATORY STRUCTURE

As noted earlier, the EITs must develop an effective bank regulatory structure at the same time that they reduce the government involvement with the banking sector. This apparent contradiction makes the task extremely difficult because there is a great temptation to use the regulatory structure as a means of maintaining government influence or control over the activities of banks.[17]

Many, if not most, of the EITs have adopted a basic formal and legal framework for prudential regulation of the banking industry (see EBRD 1995). The key issues at the present time are to make sure (a) that the regulatory structure is independent of any residual state involvement in the banking business, (b) that the credibility of bank supervisors and regulators is unquestioned, and (c) that the formal regulatory structure is applied.

The appropriate design of bank regulatory structure is not a problem that is restricted to the economies in transition. Both developed and less developed countries have been debating how to define the appropriate institutional framework for banking. In the wake of recent banking crises, both large and small countries

[17] For an overview of the elements of prudential regulation, see Polizatto 1992.

around the world are grappling with the issues (see Udell and Wachtel 1995, Honohan and Vittas 1995). Authorities have come to realize the importance of a well-designed structure for bank regulation. Moreover, it is clear that no matter how well intentioned, the regulatory framework must also be managed in ways that make regulatory discipline credible. The challenge for the economies in transition is designing a structure for bank regulation that can also be quickly and effectively implemented.

Recent large-country experiences illustrated the importance of these issues. For example, in the United States, although an inadequate regulatory structure was not, in all likelihood, responsible for the crisis in the thrift industry in the 1980s, the inadequacies of the regulatory response probably made the crisis more severe than it needed to be. A similar argument can be made regarding the ongoing crisis in Japanese banking. Although a regulatory structure is in place, it has not responded in as timely a fashion as it should. A design of a regulatory structure that insures a timely and well-informed response to problems as they develop is a topic of international interest. These experiences in major countries suggest that conventional forms of bank supervision may not be able to stem bank failures in all situations. Perhaps the implicit understanding that authorities will rescue any bank in collapse and, at the very least, make the depositors whole creates an insurmountable moral-hazard problem.

The regulatory framework should not serve as a substitute for the salutary effects of market discipline but as a complement to it. The regulatory authorities in New Zealand have come to this realization and are introducing a system in which conventional bank regulation will be augmented by market discipline; no deposit insurance will be provided and there will be extensive requirements for banks to publish regularly information on their condition.

The bank regulatory powers can be located in various agencies – in the government (e.g., Ministry of Finance), in the central bank, or in an independent bank regulatory authority (see Tuya and Zamalloa 1994). The disadvantages of placing bank regulatory authority (including the power to close banks) under the authority of a cabinet member are obvious; bank regulatory agencies should be protected from political pressures.

The central bank, especially when its independence has been

firmly established, is a logical agency for bank regulation. The principle function of a central bank is to act as the source of liquidity for the financial sector, which is both a macroeconomic monetary policy and a bank regulatory function. The macroeconomic function relates to the aggregate amount of liquidity that is provided. The regulatory function relates to how and how much liquidity is provided to particular financial institutions. The central bank can determine whether to provide liquidity to a particular bank and what the terms of such loans should be. The central bank will often have a broader supervisory role as well because it is more able to attract and pay capable staff than other government agencies.

The existence of a liquidity facility implies that the central bank, as a lender, will want to have the information any lender would require. Thus, the central bank's role as bank examiner follows from the existence of central bank lending facility. However, central bank lending should not be distorted into a means of providing government support to the banking system. The lender of last resort facility is needed to provide liquidity by discounting bank assets and should only be made available after an appropriate assessment of the bank's creditworthiness. It should not be used to provide government assistance to failed or failing banks or to augment bank capital. Separate and distinct facilities should be utilized for the recapitalization of banks.

Regulatory oversight should not be the responsibility of the central bank alone for at least two reasons. First, macroeconomic credit goals of the central bank and the liquidity needs of individual banking institutions may be in conflict. For example, the central bank may well be reluctant to take regulatory actions that might lead to increased demand for central bank loans if, at the same time, macroeconomic policy dictates that credit expansion be constrained.[18] Second, in the event that the central bank does not provide liquidity to a troubled banking institution, another regulatory structure to monitor and deal with the troubled institution needs to be in place. That is, there needs to be an independent

[18] Perhaps a more likely and less desirable scenario occurs when the central bank is adding liquidity to the economy in order to finance or monetize the government's debt. In such situations, the central bank is unlikely to refuse bank demand for liquidity and may well be less than diligent in fulfilling its regulatory functions.

regulatory agency that can either close down or sustain failed banks.

Thus, in our view, there should be two tiers to the regulatory structure. The first tier is the central bank, which provides a liquidity facility and a supervisory and monitoring function in order to judge when liquidity should be provided. The second tier should be provided by an independent agency that licenses banking activity (granting and removing licenses), determines the scope of acceptable bank activities, and provides guarantees of banking operations (deposit insurance). The precise division of regulatory responsibilities between the central bank and the independent bank regulatory agency will vary from situation to situation. As long as some state ownership of the banks continues (as is likely), the state's ownership role must not be confused with its regulatory functions. The state's residual ownership powers should not be vested in the central bank or any other agency responsible for bank supervision. We now turn to the regulatory structures in the Visegrad countries in order to see how they match with or differ from this idealized structure.

Bank Regulation in Hungary

In most of the transition economies, bank regulatory functions are housed in the central bank. An exception where there really are two distinct tiers to bank regulation is Hungary. The prudential regulation of banks is shared between the State Banking Supervisor (SBS) and the National Bank of Hungary (NBH). The SBS was established in 1987 as part of the Ministry of Finance when the two-tiered banking system was created from the Soviet monobank. It is now a quasi-independent government agency (the president of the SBS is appointed for a six-year term). The SBS is responsible for bank licensing and is given the mandate to protect depositors and promote the stability of the financial system. In order to do so, it examines banks and collects accounting data needed to monitor operations. The SBS needs the approval of the Banking Supervisory Committee (consisting of representatives of the SBS, the MOF, and the NBH) in order to issue regulations or set standards or to take regulatory action (e.g., withdraw a banking license or limit a bank's activities).

Since 1993, the NBH also has a bank supervisory department

that monitors the day-to-day liquidity positions of the banks. In order to identify liquidity problems early, the NBH uses a standard framework for risk assessment. Thus, there are two agencies that monitor the soundness and safety of individual banks. There is some overlap of function, but that simply serves to increase the reliability of bank supervision efforts.

Bank Regulation in Poland

The regulatory structure for banking in Poland dates back to 1982 when the National Bank of Poland (NBP) was separated from the MOF. The role of the NBP was more clearly identified in 1989. The president of the NBP is appointed for a six-year term which insulates the bank from direct political influence. The central bank is responsible for both the strength of the currency (monetary policy) and the proper operation of the banking system (prudential regulation). The NBP is responsible for all regulatory functions – bank licensing, collecting information, bank examination, prudential regulations. State ownership of the banks was left in the hands of the MOF. Additional legislation in 1992, reinforced the supervisory functions of the NBP and also strengthened the independence of the bank from the government.

The NBP has a broad range of regulatory powers: it determines the activities that are allowable to banks and the allowable banking activities of nonbanks, gives consent to all significant changes in ownership, licenses banks, can order liquidation or a takeover when capital decreases by half, and can order remedial action in order to restore liquidity. At the same time, the NBP is responsible for the tools of monetary policy. It conducts refinancing for the banks, extends lombard loans, and sets mandatory reserve requirement ratios.

The concentration of regulatory powers – both bank supervision and monetary policy – in the NBP is an issue for some concern. There is great potential for conflict between the two and a need to develop appropriate safeguards.

Bank Regulation in the Czech Republic

The restructuring of the banking sector dates only to 1990 when a two-tier banking system was created in Czechoslovakia (see

Hrncir 1994 for a discussion of bank regulation). This important step was taken in 1987 in Hungary and 1988 in Poland. From 1990 until 1992 the central bank maintained strict control of the banks through credit and interest rate ceilings. At the same time, the central bank introduced standards for bank examination, oversight of foreign exchange activities, credit limit exposure, and capital requirements.

The minimum risk-adjusted capital requirements were set at 8 percent for new entrants, and existing banks were given a five-year period to make the transition to that target by the end of 1996.

Central Bank Independence

In the EITs, as well as elsewhere, there are efforts to make the central banks independent of the government (see Siklos 1994 for a discussion of central bank independence in the Visegrad countries). The central bank laws in the EITs are often modeled after the Bundesbank, presumably with the hope that the German inflation record will follow suit. However, a much more stringent definition of independence would be desirable because of the inherent involvement of central banks in transition economies with the problems of the banks and the fiscal problems of the government.

Central bank independence and its ability to follow an antiinflationary monetary policy are limited because the central bank is also playing a role in the restructuring and recapitalization of the banks. Similarly, the independence of monetary policy is limited when the central bank is the fiscal agent of the government in an economy without any developed government securities markets. There are statutory limits on the extent to which the central banks can monetize the deficit. Such limits are not effective, however, when government debt is an important asset of the banks and the central bank discounting is a major liability.

In a formal sense, the Czech central bank may be more independent than others because price stability is its sole stated macroeconomic responsibility, whereas the Polish and Hungarian central banks have to support government macroeconomic policy. All three central banks have presidents with six-year terms that exceed the election cycle. However, in all three countries the institutional culture that determines the extent of government influence on central bank decision making is still evolving.

Deposit Insurance

Since it is almost impossible (in the EITs or elsewhere) to envision a deposit insurance fund that is sufficiently well capitalized to provide insurance against all risks, the deposit insurance agency should have sufficient power to minimize the calls on the insurance funds. Thus, the deposit insurance agency should also have extensive regulatory powers over banks. Otherwise, the deposit insurance scheme is simply the cashier that pays the bill when other regulatory functions fail. In such cases, it is unlikely that the insurer will have sufficient funds. The insurer should be able to act before there is a need to call on its limited insurance funds (see Kaufman 1997, 1998).

In order to make the deposit insurance scheme credible, its rules should be as transparent as possible and should be uniformly and consistently applied. Any deviation from specified rules will create the expectation that the government is willing to guarantee the continued existence of banks, which simply encourages moral-hazard problems. The formal deposit insurance schemes that have been introduced in the Visegrad countries are yet untested. It is not clear what additional government responses would be made to protect all depositors and/or avoid liquidation of any bank. That is, the existence of a well-specified and limited deposit insurance scheme does not clearly provide an answer to the question of whether all banks are too big to fail.

The Hungarian National Deposit Insurance Fund was introduced in 1993 in accordance with European Union (EU) recommendations. It is designed to provide limited protection for depositors who would have difficulty assessing the quality of financial institutions. The fund is an independent entity although the presidents of both the NBH and the SBS are on its board. Membership is mandatory for all depository institutions. The insurance coverage maximum is 1 million forints (about $7,500) which would cover more than 90 percent of all household deposits. The fund's income comes from a one-time admission fee (0.5% of bank capital) and a premium on eligible deposits of up to 0.2 percent per year, which can be raised to 0.3 percent for banks that are risky. The fund's assets are invested in government securities and the fund is allowed to borrow from the NBH or in the money markets. Lending by the fund is government guaranteed and is to be repaid from special contributions from the member banks.[19]

The Polish Bank Guarantee Fund started operating in June 1995. The fund is an independent body governed by a council that includes representatives of the NBP, MOF, and the bankers association. It was capitalized by the MOF, and the NBP and the banks will pay a compulsory premium of 0.4 percent of risk-adjusted assets. Other details of the fund are similar to those in Hungary – it can borrow from the NBP and ask the government to increase the premiums.

The Polish deposit insurance scheme has three parts. First, 100 percent of deposits in the state-owned savings banks are guaranteed by the state treasury. Second, the Bank Guarantee Fund provides compulsory insurance for other deposits: fully for deposits up to 1,000 ECU and 905 for deposits between 1,000 and 3,000 ECU. Third, the legislation allows for agreements among the banks and the guarantee fund for the extension of the deposit insurance system. Although the preferential treatment for state savings banks are supposed to expire at the end of 1999 and the modest limits on the other insurance are supposed to increase, the differential treatment distorts depositor behavior. The system serves to sustain the state savings banks.[20]

The ability of the Bank Guarantee Fund to intervene is limited. It has to first submit a bank audit to its own board and then get central bank approval for any assistance to a failing bank. Finally, the extent of such assistance cannot exceed the fund's insurance liability to the bank. It is difficult to imagine that the fund will be a major force in bank supervision or in regulatory responses to banking crises.

By the end of 1995, the Bank Guarantee Fund paid out about one-third of its assets to depositors in twenty-nine failed coopera-

[19] Information is from a presentation by Elemer Tertak at the International Conference on Deposit Insurance, Institute of EastWest Studies and Federal Reserve Bank of Atlanta, December 1995.

[20] The information on the Polish bank Guarantee Fund was from a presentation by Jan Szambelanczyk at the International Conference on Deposit Insurance, Institute for EastWest Studies and the Federal Reserve Bank of Atlanta, December 1995.

tive banks and two failed commercial banks. There have been additional bankruptcies or suspensions of cooperative banks and commercial banks. There are considerable disputes with depositors on the fund's obligations and a large number of additional cooperative banks are in very poor condition. The existence of the guarantee fund has been viewed as an alternative to considering how to recapitalize and restructure the cooperative banks. As a result, the Polish fund is headed for crisis in a very short period of time.

The adequacy of the fund arrangement is impossible to judge. The experiences of the United States, however, indicate that deposit insurance funds are only adequate when the insurance agency has sufficient banking powers to intervene in failing banks before the fund has to make restitution. The Hungarian deposit insurance fund has only limited powers to intervene. The fund can undertake rescue of failing banks if the Banking Supervisory Agency approves. The fund can also expel members that would prevent the bank from collecting deposits. These arrangements are fairly weak because the former is subordinated to the decisions of the bank supervisors and the latter is too strong to ever be used as a preventive measure. Thus, the deposit insurance fund is entirely reliant on the quality of bank supervision to prevent all bankruptcies. Its capitalization is too small to cover any but the smallest banks.

With respect to all aspects of bank regulation, it is important that there be a credible commitment to the structure and the rules. In both large countries and small, the efficacy of bank regulation is undercut when all the players – bankers, governments, and others – believe that, in the event of any bank failure, there will be some provision of liquidity or government-financed recapitalization that guarantees the continued operation of the bank in trouble. Instead, the bank regulators should specify a set of corrective actions and responses to bank weakness and failure that are transparent and to which strict adherence is maintained. Experience with a transparent set of regulatory responses will quickly establish the credibility of the entire regulatory structure. In this way, corrective action will limit the need to actually call on the deposit insurance funds.

The desire to gain international recognition is an important force that influences bank regulatory policy. In particular, the association agreements with the European community and the desire to enter the EU have been a catalyst for change on several fronts. For example, international accounting standards and standards for the classification of loans have been introduced. In addition, all of the Visegrad countries have restrictions on bank equity holdings that are consistent with EU directives on large single exposures. These rules are of two types. First, there are limits on equity investments (total and/or single large exposure) as a proportion of bank capital. This reflects the need for portfolio diversification and limits on risk exposure. Second, there are restrictions on the size of bank positions in equity investments that limit bank control over enterprises. These rules influence the development of the banking sector and the banks' role in the restructuring of firms through debt-equity swaps. As a result, exceptions to the limits are common, and limits can be evaded in Hungary through investments made by bank subsidiaries and in the Czech Republic through bank control of privatization funds.

Bank regulators in the EITs have imposed the minimum risk-based capital requirements in the Basle agreements. In the Czech Republic a 6.25 percent minimum capital adequacy ratio (using Bank for International Settlements definitions) was introduced at the end of 1993, and banks are supposed to reach 8 percent by the end of 1996. In Hungary the 1991 banking act set an 8 percent target risk-weighted reserve ratio for the end of 1994. Similarly, in Poland BIS standards and an 8 percent target were set.

Regulators seem quite satisfied to be able to use the BIS standard for banks in a region. However, regulators should understand that the minimum capital standards are based on risk levels inherent in developed countries. Higher overall riskiness argues for higher capital-asset ratios in the EITs than in the major industrial economies. The 8 percent standard was designed for well-run banks in a rather stable macroeconomic environment and is far too low for banks in the economies in transition. Higher capital ratios are appropriate in many instances, and regulators should develop rules for a gradual adjustment to these standards.

Regulators are often lax in applying their own rules for loan evaluation and capital adequacy. If loans are appropriately classified, then write-offs will lead to banks that are undercapitalized and perhaps insolvent. Thus, there is great incentive to ignore the rules. Appropriate bank regulation goes beyond simply structuring the regulatory organizations. Important issues of implementation also can be very difficult to solve. In fact, the banking crises that have occurred in major Western countries are usually due to errors in implementation and not to the inadequacies of the regulatory structure.

Coordination of regulatory authority is particularly important when banks may be viewed as being too big to fail. In such instances, which are very common, regulatory action must be timely because closing the bank with or without deposit insurance guarantees may be impossible for any of several reasons. Bank closure may be politically unfeasible or systemic consequences on the economy may be feared and closure may often impose costs that are beyond the capabilities of the deposit insurance scheme. If closure is precluded, then effective regulation takes the form of examining and disciplining the bank's activities. The regulators should have a clear understanding of the types of sanctions that can be imposed on a bank prior to closure. There should be a plan of action for dealing with failing banks that enables the regulators to forestall bank activity prior to failure.

The failure of the regulators to respond promptly to poor banking practice when the banks are too big to fail will lead inevitably to renationalization of the banking sector. In all likelihood, situations will arise in which governments decide that extraordinary interventions are warranted. Any such interventions should be limited to very rare circumstances and should not be accepted as part of the normal sequence of regulatory responses. Regulators should have the tools to deal with failed or failing banks. They should be able to arrange the sale, merger, or recapitalization of banks without forcing bankruptcy or resorting to the renationalization of banks.

CONCLUSION

A market-oriented banking system will emerge in the economies in transition when governments have made significant progress on both fronts discussed here – disengagement from the banks and establishment of a regulatory framework. In both instances, there are enormous problems that inhibit progress and they have basically been the topic of our extended discussion. However, it is probably more appropriate to focus on the enormous progress that has been made in the countries examined in a very short period of time. The institutional structures for a market-oriented banking system have been established. With further improvements in the macroeconomic environment and strengthening of the democratic structures, many of the problems noted here can be solved and pitfalls avoided.

REFERENCES

Abel, István, and John P. Bonin. 1994. "Financial Sector Reform: Towards the Privatization of State-Owned Commercial Banks." In Bonin and Székely 1994, 109–26.

Beggs, David, and Richard Portes. 1993. "Enterprise Debt and Economic Transformation: Financial Restructuring in Central and Eastern Europe." *European Economic Review* 37: 396–407.

Bonin, John P. 1993. "On the Way to Privatizing Commercial Banks: Poland and Hungary Take Different Roads." *Comparative Economic Studies*, 35, no. 4: 103–19.

Bonin, John P. 1995. "Banking in the Transition: Privatizing Banks in Hungary, Poland and the Czech Republic." Institute for East West Studies Policy Paper, New York, October.

Bonin, John P., Bozena Leven, and Mark E. Schaffer. 1996. "Unlocking Frozen Assets and Creating Market Culture: Hungary and Poland Take Different Approaches." In H. Brezinski, E. Franck, and M. Fritsch (eds.), *Microeconomics of Transition and Growth*. Cornwall: Edward Elgar.

Bonin, John P., Kálmán Mizsei, István Székely, and Paul Wachtel. 1998. *Banking in Transition Economies: Developing Market Oriented Banking Sectors in Eastern Europe*. Cornwall: Edward Elgar.

Bonin, John P., Kálmán Mizsei, and Paul Wachtel. 1996. "Toward Market-Oriented Banking for the Economies in Transition: A Summary of Policy Recommendations." Institute for EastWest Studies, Prague.

Bonin, John P., and István Székely (eds.). 1994. *The Development and Reform of Financial Systems in Central and Eastern Europe*. Cornwall: Edward Elgar.

Buch, Claudia. 1995. "The Emerging Financial Systems of the Eastern European Countries." Working Paper no. 716, December, Kiel Institute of World Economics, Kiel.

Dittus, Peter. 1994. "Bank Reform and Behavior in Central Europe." *Journal of Comparative Economics* 19, no. 3: 335–61.

Dobrinsky, Rumen. 1994. "Reform of the Financial System in Bulgaria." In Bonin and Székely 1994, 317–46.

European Bank for Reconstruction and Development. 1995. *Transition Report*. London.
Honohan, Patrick, and Dimitri Vittas. 1995. "Bank Regulation and the Network Paradigm: Policy Implications for Developing and Transition Economies." Paper presented to the World Congress of the International Economic Association, Tunis, December.
Hrncir, Miroslav. 1994. "Reform of the Banking Sector in the Czech Republic." In Bonin and Szekely 1994, 217–52.
Kaufman, George. 1997. "Lessons for Transitional and Developing Economies from U.S. Deposit Insurance Reform." Paper prepared for the International Conference on Deposit Insurance, Institute for EastWest Studies and Federal Reserve Bank of Atlanta, December. Reprinted in George M. von Furstenberg (ed.), *Regulation and Supervision of Financial Institutions in the NAFTA Countries and Beyond*, 16–35. Boston: Kluwer.
Kaufman, George. 1998. "Designing an Efficient and Incentive Compatible Government-Provided Deposit Insurance Program for Developing and Transition Economies." *Review of Pacific Basin Financial Markets and Policies* 1: 1–13.
Kormendi, Roger C., and Karen Schatterly. 1996. "Bank Privatization in Hungary and the Magyar Kulkereskedelmi Bank Transaction," William Davidson Institute, Ann Arbor, Mich., March.
Levine, Ross, and David Scott. 1992. "Old Debts and New Beginnings: A Policy Choice in Transitional Socialist Economies." World Bank Policy Research Working Paper Series no. 867 World Bank, Washington, D.C.
Marrese, Michael. 1994. "Banking Sector Reform in Central and Eastern Europe." In Joint Economic Committee, U.S. Congress, (ed.), *East-Central European Economies in Transition*, 111–32. Washington, D.C.: Government Printing Office.
Miklaszewska, Eva (ed.). 1995. *Competitive Banking in Central and Eastern Europe*. Krakow: Jagiellonian University Press.
Polizatto, Vincent P. 1992. "Prudential Regulation and Bank Supervision." In Dimitri Vittas (ed.), *Financial Regulation: Changing the Rules of the Game*, 283–319. EDI Development Studies. Washington, D.C.: World Bank.
Siklos, Pierre L. 1994. "Central Bank Independence in the Transitional Economies: A Preliminary Investigation of Hungary, Poland, the Czech and Slovak Republics." In Bonin and Szekely 1994, 69–97.
Tuya, Jose, and Lorena Zamalloa. 1994. "Issues on Placing Banking Supervision in the Central Bank." In Tomas J. T. Balino and Carlo Cottarelli (eds.), *Framework for Monetary Stability*, 663–90. Washington, D.C.: International Monetary Fund.
Udell, Gregory, and Paul Wachtel. 1995. "Financial Systems Design for

Formerly Planned Economies: Defining the Issues." *Financial Markets, Institutions and Instruments* 4, no. 2: 1–60.

Wachtel, Paul. 1995. "Foreign Banking in the Central European Economies in Transition." Institute for EastWest Studies Policy Paper, New York, October.

CHAPTER 3

The Trials and Tribulations of Banking in Transition Economies: A Political Economy Perspective

Arye L. Hillman and Heinrich W. Ursprung

The banking sector has been a consistent source of concern in transition economies. A substantial literature provides detailed advice for providing the foundations for sound banking in the transition and for avoiding difficulties – including Fabrizio Coricelli and Alfredo Thorne (1992), John Bonin and Istvan Szekely (1994), Gregory Udell and Paul Wachtel (1994), John Bonin, Kŕlmŕn Mizsei, and Paul Wachtel (1996), and Jorge Roldos and Kenneth Kletzer (1996).

Consider, for example, the following recommendations of Bonin et al. They propose that capital requirements should be increased both for new bank licenses and for existing banks that were created under the laxer regime to encourage mergers and takeovers of undercapitalized small private banks. That is, there is a fear for the viability of undercapitalized banks. They further propose that the supervisory structure must be strengthened to the point where it is competent to exercise effectively discretion over who should be allowed to set up a bank. The supervisory agency must offer adequate compensation to attract capable and competent personnel. This recommendation reflects the fear of bank failure due to opportunistic behavior or incompetence of bankers. Bankers should be qualified to evaluate the prospects of borrowers and should be honest. Those monitoring the bankers should also be competent and honest, which requires a remuneration structure that makes employment by the regulatory authority attractive and succumbing to bribes unattractive. Further, the "hole" or negative net worth arising from marketing to market the

This is a revised version of the paper presented at the second Dubrovnik Conference on Transition Economies, Dubrovnik, 26–28 June 1996. The conference discussant Vito Tanzi and an anonymous referee have provided very useful comments. The collaboration for this research was undertaken with the assistance of the Max-Planck Prize for Economics.

asset portfolio should not be filled solely by public funds without strong assurances that management practices and personnel will behave prudently in the future (e.g., removal of current management and provision of proper incentive contracts). This recommendation reflects the concern that governments will persist in bailing out insolvent banks and, in so doing, will throw good money after bad. Also, bank management should not have any explicit or implicit obligation to continue lending to enterprises that are not appropriate credit risks. If necessary, subsidies to firms should be provided directly by the government and not channeled through the banking system. This recommendation reflects the propensity of banks in transition economies to act as life supports for ailing and chronically indisposed state "enterprises." If governments wish to subsidize factories, it is recommended that this be done by transparent budgetary procedures, and not via directed credits of the banking system.

The foregoing recommendations provide advice regarding how to ensure a prudent and viable banking system. The recommendations are well founded and reflect a considerable consensus on the policies governments should follow. Yet the recommendations have not preempted difficulties in the performance of banks in the transition economies.

Why then do banks fail or find themselves in severe difficulties? The individual behavior underlying the problems of the banks is in general private information, and so is not directly observable by outsiders. Often observations on bankers' behavior come from no more than journalistic reporting (or speculation) and rumors. The ambiguities permit different viewpoints regarding the origins of the problems, and thereby the nature of solutions. Perhaps governments have been lax in regulation. Or perhaps banks are in distress despite the correct policies. That is, unfortunate outcomes can be the consequence of indecisive government or inappropriate policies, or can have arisen despite worthy attempts at following the correct policy advice. There is also a further possibility, that neither incompetence nor laxity of regulators nor simple bad luck in the face of exogenous uncontrollable events, is the source of the problems of the banking sector, but rather that the problems that arise reflect inappropriate pursuit of private interest.

The possibility that there may be a contradiction between private interest and socially desirable policies brings us into the realm of economic analysis known as political economy (see Hillman 1994 for a political economy perspective on different aspects of the transition). Whereas economists may formulate and set out the correct policies to be followed (as just explicated), a political-economy perspective seeks to explain why such policies, once made known to government decision makers, are not necessarily chosen or, if chosen, why the correct polices are not implemented. The reason for self-serving behavior by a political agent may be pursuit of private wealth, or political support from a particular constituency. The government officials or bureaucrats who have the responsibility to implement policies may further not be independent of their political masters, or may have sufficient discretion to conduct policy based on their own personal agendas.

Such political and bureaucratic discretion has been exercised in a context of initial ambiguity of property rights. The transition from socialism began with social ownership and proceeded to permit claims to private ownership, with much former social property privately contestable (see Gelb, Hillman, and Ursprung 1996). The contesting of private rights of ownership has been expressed in the inefficiencies described in the economic literature on rent-seeking activity (see Nitzan 1994 for a comprehensive review of this literature); that is, individuals have confronted incentives to use resources unproductively in attempts to secure for themselves a greater share of what is available, rather than productively contributing to output. The mechanisms through which the claims to ownership have been contested have often involved the banking system.

Even if someone has succeeded in staking a claim to former state property, the claim has not necessarily been respected by others. There has rather been a perception that property or resources that had previously belonged to the state or to society, and thereby to no one in particular, could not be claimed indefinitely as personal property by any private individual. The political or bureaucratic discretion that people suppose must have been exercised in securing the property, or asset, or position with access to special income did not necessarily grant a privilege that was respected. Contestability could therefore be an ongoing affair.

The ongoing contestability and attitudes are part of a more

general cynicism and lack of trust by large parts of the population in the objectivity and fairness of postsocialist allocation mechanisms. Even where property rights were assigned to the public at large by voucher schemes, supplementary assignment processes gave incumbent managers and workers, and foreign investors in other cases, discretionary capabilities that limited the returns to the broader population of owners. The cynicism has often been reflected in the unwillingness of large segments of the population to participate in schemes that were ostensibly providing them with free or discounted access to state property.

It is within the standards and norms of this framework of persisting ambiguous property rights, private self-interest expressed via political and bureaucratic processes, cynicism, and lack of trust, that we must consider the functioning of the banking system in the transition.

THE BANKING SYSTEM: AN OVERVIEW

The idea of "reform" implies that existing arrangements or policies can be improved upon, to secure better policies and better outcomes. "Reform" thus implies a precondition that something exists that can be changed for the better. Yet a banking system as understood in the context of a Western market economy (see Fama 1985) was nonexistent under socialism, and by continuity did not exist at the time of exit from socialism. A "bank" under socialism could not be a financial intermediary that took private savings and spread risk of private lending among borrowers in a capital market. There could be no capital market if all capital was owned by the state, while risk sharing was already present in the social ownership of capital. "Banks" under socialism were accounting houses that matched financial flows with the real variables of the plan. Each "bank" had a specialized purpose, such as taking deposits for personal savings, facilitating foreign trade transactions of state factories, or acting as an accounting division of a particular state enterprise sector. There was, most importantly, no concept of repayment of loans. After a decision had been made that a factory would receive a certain piece of capital equipment, an offsetting transfer was made to match the real investment. In principle, the offsetting nominal value of such a transfer was of no great importance.

There did exist entities that could be associated with the idea of a bank in a market economy, such as the state savings bank and the foreign trade bank. The beginning of the transition introduced these entities and the sectorally specialized accounting and disbursement institutions into a new market environment, with functions in principle of banks in market economies. We say "in principle" because the end of planning did not immediately change behavior of factory managers or conceptions of the relation between "banks" and factories. The response of factory managers to the system change was to continue as far as possible to do what they had previously done. Traditional relationships and inertia guided behavior. Goods continued to be shipped to the same destinations to which they had previously been shipped. Factories received their intermediate inputs from other factories and proceeded to make the transformations assigned to them. In the new market environment, a request for delivery of goods should, however, precede shipment and should be accompanied by payment, or a credible obligation that payment will be made to the supplier in the future. If in particular there is no demand for final consumption, the accumulation of inventories and absence of payment feed back in the chain of intermediate suppliers to create a chain of arrears of payment. At the same time, although the banks did not receive the prior offsetting financial transfers (since planning had ceased), bank officials cooperated by continuing to behave as they had previously and "financed" (or simply recorded) the transactions among factories.

The factories thus accumulated liabilities to the banks. Since there was no tradition of need for repayment, there was also no conception of the meaning or implication of the accumulating liabilities. The socialist production system had after all no need for "money" as understood in a Western market economy. "Money" had not mattered in securing claims for resources for the factory; more important was the ability to convince the responsible ministry or planning authority of the "need" for the equipment or inputs.

At some point came the realization that the rules had changed and that financial obligations had been incurred. State enterprises, however, now owed the banks money, which they had no way of repaying, and the banks had "assets" on their books, which were for the most part irredeemable liabilities. If the state factories now went bankrupt, so would the state banks. Concern for viability of the banks provided an incentive to keep lending to the factories (see Buch 1995). The fate of the state banks was therefore intertwined with the fate of the state enterprises. Recognizing the truth about the financial position of the enterprises entailed recognizing the truth about the balance sheets of the banks.

Where privatization was sought by direct sale, the nexus placed a brake on progress with sought policies. Who would wish to purchase enterprises so burdened with debt? Bank privatization was also impeded. For who would wish to buy shares in banks with such dubiously repayable loans on their books?

Credit and corresponding real resources were thus diverted from potentially productive activities in the new emerging private sectors or from more successful state enterprises, to ailing state factories. A common ending is for liabilities of the state enterprises, expressed in the nonrepayable loans from the banking system, to be transformed to government obligations in a restructuring program that simultaneously saves enterprises and banks. By this process, the liabilities are nationalized, and assets with positive value privatized.

VIEWS OF THE SAME PHENOMENON

We shall presently (in the following section) formulate a model that takes a political-economy view of the relation between banks and state factories. Our model supposes that private agents adopt the viewpoint that state firms can be used as sources of private profit. The model proposes rational individual behavior and is set in the institutional environment of the ambiguous property rights of the transition and the associated prevailing personal norms of behavior. Underlying the model is asymmetric information or, in another terminology, "rational ignorance." The population of ordinary people chooses rationally to be "ignorant" when there is inadequate prospect of personal gain from acquiring information. They remain outside the domain of contestability of state assets and incomes that derive from these assets. This provides greater latitude for active participants in distributional contests. Although large parts of the population are "rationally ignorant," they are nonetheless exposed to more blatantly evident or indirect manifestations of the contests that are taking place, as, for example, an inordinate number of untimely and unresolved deaths of bankers.

Our model is, of course, one of different ways of looking at the problems of the banking sector. A macroeconomic model would, for example, look at the consequences of potential failure of the banking system in terms of the aggregate variables of the economy. The same macroeconomic framework is, however, often applied to widely differing underlying institutional structures and incentives, since governments in all countries confront decisions regarding budget deficits, interest rates, monetary policy, exchange rates, and, in particular with regard to the banking system, reserve requirements, capitalization, and the scope and type of regulation. The macroeconomic uniformity conceals differences in the norms of individual behavior and institutions among countries, and the focus on aggregate variables does not permit a consideration of the distributional issues that can well be expected to underlie economic and political behavior. Our model stresses these distributional issues.

Alternatively, a paternalistic model would emphasize prospective benevolence in the motives for the bank lending that keeps insolvent state enterprises alive, and would propose that the bank credits reflect genuine care for the well-being of the workers. Paternalistic motives for policy can of course be indistinguishable from political motives. The large state factories that the banks keep alive are more than economic entities. The failure of a factory, in particular where the factory is the basis for the livelihood of a town or region, may be difficult to countenance, for paternalistic reasons or because of the political consequences for the government.

Paternalistic motives might thus well be present. Our model nonetheless points to the inevitable presence of opportunities (see Bogetić and Hillman 1995) for private profit from state factories. A state factory cannot be restructured, and private ownership and profit motives cannot be introduced, as long as there remain overbearing financial obligations to the banks. The nexus between factories and banks thereby "protects" the factory from privatization, and thereby protects private profits. The state enterprises are kept alive for reasons of private profit, even though a glance at the formal books of these enterprises reveals a picture of complete or near insolvency.

A MODEL OF THE NEXUS

Consider one state firm and one state bank. At any point in time, the firm's losses are given by:

$$V = wL + R + rD - E, \tag{1}$$

where E denotes the firm's revenues from sales of output, wL is wages paid to workers and management salaries, R is private rents taken from the enterprise, r is the interest paid to the bank on the firm's debt, and D is the firm's stock of outstanding debt.

The rents R taken from the enterprise are discretionary. We do not here specify who takes the rents. The rents are, however, a private gain. The method of taking the rents can be direct appropriation of either money or physical output, or transfers made by the prices at which the state enterprise transacts with private agents.

The losses V need to be financed, and the source of finance is bank credit, provided by the bank to which the debt D has already been incurred. Denote by B the bank's change in loans to the firm to finance the loss. Then

$$V = B. \tag{2}$$

This is a condition for the survival of the firm. The firm has only the bank to finance its losses, and survives if the bank covers its losses with new credits. Equation (2) thus describes the change in the liabilities of the firm and in the assets of the bank.

The bank also lends to the private sector, to which it has outstanding loans H. The balance sheet of the bank is

$$Z + J = D + H + S, \tag{3}$$

where Z denoted deposits, J the bank's own capital, and S the bank's reserves. D and H are the loans outstanding to the state firm and to the private sector.

The bank's profits consist of the interest paid by the state firm and the private sector, minus its own interest payments to depositors. Denote the interest paid by the bank to depositors by i. The bank's profits are

$$\prod = r(H + D) - iZ. \tag{4}$$

We can now consider the changes that take place over time. The change in the firm's debt is

$$\dot{D} = B. \tag{5}$$

The bank's profits are added to its capital, and hence

$$\dot{J} = \Pi. \tag{6}$$

Since the state firm requires additional credits to survive and repays neither principal nor interest, the profitability of the bank hinges on the interest received from the loans made to the private sector. Denote the stock of loans demanded by the private sector by $\overline{H}$. The supply of loans by the bank is H. Since loans to the private sector are profitable and loans to the state firm only add to questionable debt, the bank prefers if possible to lend to the private sector, but needs to lend to the state firm to keep the state firm alive. The question now is whether, after the "loans" to the state firm have been made, the bank can satisfy the demand of the private sector. The two possibilities are reflected in

$$H = \begin{cases} Z + J - D, & Z + J - D < 0 \\ \overline{H}, & Z + J - D \geq 0. \end{cases} \tag{7}$$

In the first case in equation (7), there is unsatisfied private sector demand for loans; in the second case, the demand is satisfied. The inequalities in equation (7) reflect the incentive for the bank to satisfy the private sector demand whenever possible, and the bank's need at the same time to satisfy the state firm's demand for additional credits to finance losses.

This system remains viable if both the firm and the bank can survive. This requires that the following condition be satisfied:

$$D \leq Z + J. \tag{8}$$

That is, the state-enterprise debt cannot exceed the sum of the bank's deposits and capital (supplemented by profits from private sector lending), which is all that the bank has to lend. Or equivalently from equation (3) the condition for joint survival is that

$$A = S + H \geq 0. \tag{8a}$$

That is, reserves plus private sector lending must be positive. If this condition is not satisfied, the bank has already used up its reserves in financing the losses of the state firm, and once the reserves are gone, the bank fails, and with the bank gone, the firm fails.

From equations (3), (5), and (6) we see that

$$\dot{A} \equiv \dot{S} + \dot{H} = \Pi - B. \tag{9}$$

The sum of the bank's change in reserves and change in loans to the private sector is equal to its profits (from private sector loans) minus the additional credit to the state firm. If profits from private sector loans equal or exceed the additional credits to the state firm, then the bank has funds that can be added to reserves or loaned the private sector, and the relation is sustainable over time. The profits from the private sector can then continue financing the losses of the state sector.

From equations (1), (2), and (4) we obtain

$$\dot{A} \equiv \dot{S} + \dot{H} = rH - (iZ + wL + R - E) = rH - \theta. \tag{10}$$

Since the firm is making losses, we have here $\theta > 0$. From equation (7), we know that

$$\dot{H} = 0 \text{ or } \dot{S} = 0. \tag{11}$$

This provides the picture set out in Figure 3.1.

The system is thus sustainable if at time $t = 0$

$$H_0 > \theta/r, \tag{12}$$

that is,

$$rH_0 > wL - E + R + iZ, \tag{13}$$

where

$$wL - E + R = V - rD \equiv \tilde{V}.$$

Hence we have the sustainability condition

$$\tilde{V} < rH_0 - iZ. \tag{14}$$

That is, the loss of the firm net of interest liabilities needs to be smaller than the profit of the bank net of book profits (given by rD), if the firm and the bank are to remain viable.

The private sector has a critical role. If at time 0 there is a sufficiently large private sector that can generate profitable lending opportunities for the bank, ongoing financing of the state firm can be sustained. If the private sector is growing but remains for

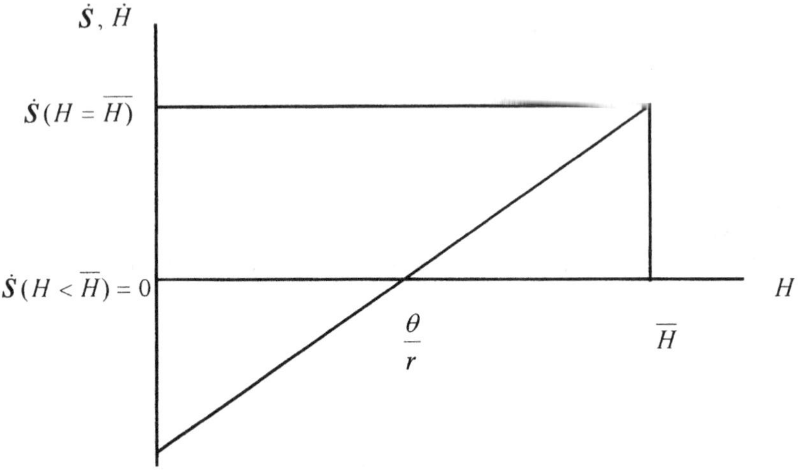

Figure 3.1.

the most part fragmented and self-financed in the informal economy, the bank and the state firm with it are on the road to failure.

Let us now consider the term R. The larger the rents R are, the greater the need for bank financing in any period (if the firm's revenues remain unchanged). Equivalently, then, the greater is R, the greater is the loss V, and the greater the likelihood that the viability condition (14) will not be satisfied.

Consider, in particular, circumstances where our model places the bank and the firm on a path to failure. Then progress along the path to ruin is hastened, the larger is R. From the perspective of the firm, R is a discretionary loss. A popular term for R is "milking the firm."

What are the considerations that enter into the choice of R? Increases in R increase bank financing needs. Whereas the system may be viable with R at zero or small, a sufficiently large R chosen over time can switch the regime from sustainable to nonsustainable. The bank and the firm together fail, because of the discretionary "losses" entailed in the path for the rent R over time. Time horizon considerations are clearly important. A long time horizon is conducive to keeping the bank and firm on a sustainable path. A short time horizon increases the values of R chosen, and can switch the path from sustainability to collapse.

If the stream of rents is contestable, a point of entry is provided for the theory of rent seeking. Losses are incurred as resources are allocated to contesting and defending the rents. Thus, high values of R can not only switch the path from sustainable to nonsustainable, but also introduce additional social costs because of higher prizes in rent-seeking contests.

There are some interesting extensions. Suppose that two (or more) state firms are sustained by credits from the same state bank. For each firm there are streams of rents R that are discretionary variables. If the rent streams are chosen independently by the firms, the circumstances describe the strategic behavior of a prisoners' dilemma. The persons extracting rents from each firm have an incentive to extract as much as possible before the impending collapse. The noncooperative equilibrium can again switch the path from sustainable to nonsustainable and hasten collapse, compared with a cooperative equilibrium. There is an evident similarity to the common-resource access problem. Here people are "fishing," but the "fish stock" is being replenished by bank credit. If they could cooperate to keep the supply of fish sustainable, they could fish for longer (perhaps forever). Of course, the fish pond is always in danger of privatization. That also decreases time horizons and increases R, again endogenously hastening collapse.

We come now to the final part of the process. The condition for sustainability is usually not satisfied, in particular because of the adverse incentives regarding R. The system persists on an unstable path, but before collapse takes place, bailout measures are introduced. At this point, the government takes over the liabilities – which means that the liabilities are transferred to the taxpayer, either via a special bond issue, or by the setting up of a state fund that takes over the liabilities. Or as in Russia domestic equity-for-debt swaps may take place with the banks. The final redistribution then occurs, with the creation and allocation of accumulated liabilities and new assets. Released from the past, the state banks can be restructured, and privatization can be contemplated (with some remaining problems; see Kapoor 1996).

THE PRIVATE BANKS

We have focused in the preceding sections on the state banks, with their nexus to the state sector. The banking systems of the transition economies have been, of course, expanded by the entry of private banks that do not bring with them the burden of past relationships. Such banks can start afresh with the advantage of no adverse historical attachments. Yet the private banks have in general also not fared well. In different countries, banks have failed, and depositors have lost their money.

Regulation of banks has therefore proved ineffective, or has been inadequate in warding off failure. While under socialism, regulation of economic activity, including the "banks," had been all-embracing, the transition in many dimensions moved the scope of regulation to the opposite extreme of anarchy (or what Abel and Bonin [1990] described as "state desertion"). Markets, of course, do not require regulation unless an acceptable case for market failure is made, and it is shown that regulation will not be subject to "capture" (capture theories and related viewpoints cast suspicion on the merits of government regulation, and suggest that regulation may not always be in the public interest). Regulation of banking systems has, however, well-founded justifications in moral hazard, adverse selection, and associated incentives of bankers to take unwarranted risks with depositors' money. Yet although the hand of government is called for, bank regulation has not been effective in the transition economies, and the new private banks, which as part of the new private sector are looked to as part of the means of successful transition, have often contributed to the problems of transition.

The conditions in which banks have been obliged to function in the transition have, of course, been extraordinarily difficult. In addition to weak economies, many of the basic requisites of sound banking have been lacking, including reputation. Reputation, of both the bank and the borrower, is an important element of banking. Established borrower-lender relationships reduce transactions costs. These relationships are established over time. They are paradoxically present between the state banks and the state enterprises, which makes the transactions costs there lower and facilitates the types of activities that we have already described. In the early days of transition, however, neither borrowers nor banks in the new private sector have established reputations.

Because the banks and bankers are unknown, it is difficult for the public to know whom to believe when offers of interest payments on deposits are made. The public may believe that higher returns reflect the superior efficiency of the bank and not greater risk.

Trust is necessary when money passes from depositors to the financial intermediary. The depositor relies on the bank to be prudent in spreading risk among prospective borrowers. Under conditions where trust has traditionally been low, the banks hold out a hope of honesty and competency in the activity of risk spreading. The past state savings bank is a model. The bank was extremely safe. The state owned the bank and did not default, thus protecting (nominal) savings. The trust is, of course, eroded when banks fail.

The banks are encumbered in the absence of reputations of the prospective borrowers who appear before them – and also by limitations on available collateral. This can consist of some privatized land and property that private individuals have acquired by restitution or "small" privatization, and also motor vehicles. Goods traded or the machinery bought can itself be collateral, but banks prefer some degree of self-participation in finance. Beyond the problem of finding appropriate collateral, the recourse available to the banks in the face of default of borrowers is time-consuming and inefficient. By the time a court judgment can be obtained, the debtor can be long gone, or the company that engaged in the transaction nonexistent.

The problems of collateral and enforcement increase the transactions costs of the banking system, and combine with the absence of established reputation of new borrowers to make lending highly risky. The high interest rates that compensate for the high transactions costs and risk further compound the banking system's difficulties, via adverse selection. That is, the high interest rates that the banks are compelled to charge are inefficient in excluding low-risk profitable lending opportunities, while the borrowers who are willing to pay the high interest rates are those with the more risky projects. It is precisely for this reason that banks ration credit rather than lending via the market to the highest bidder.

Banks in transition countries also confront norms of honesty that are below the levels generally encountered in the more developed market economies. For example, the same collateral may be used in different loans with different banks, letters of credit may be forged, companies may cease to exist after they have received bank loans. The transactions costs of banks are thereby further increased: for example, banks have responded by setting up their own private bonded warehouses to ensure that collateral in the form of imported goods is not used more than once. Appropriate bankruptcy laws can reduce incentives for deception by borrowers (see, e.g., Scheepens 1995), but such laws are often difficult to enforce in the transition. The likelihood of loss because of dishonest behavior supplements problems of moral hazard and adverse selection (where the problem is not dishonesty but inappropriate incentives).

Additional difficulties confront the banks in finding and keeping competent credit officers who are able to analyze business plans and can distinguish proposals that are more likely to succeed from those that are likely to fail – and who will not grant undue privileges in making credit-allocation decisions.

Thus while banking can be a difficult business under the favorable conditions of the developed market economies, conditions in the transition are considerably more difficult. The problems are compounded if the bankers themselves choose to make insider loans for personal benefit (i.e., not insider lending based on asymmetric information; see Rajan 1992). In Russia banks have been set up for this very purpose; the so-called pocket banks are owned by the enterprises that are the principal borrowers (see World Bank 1993). Here enters an addition to our model. If the banks are to survive, they must find sources for the ever increasing credits to the enterprises, and such a source is depositors' money from setting up their own bank.

Since outcomes can "naturally" be unsatisfactory in banking without illegal appropriation, it can be difficult to distinguish bad luck from incompetence or outright theft. Yet in some cases the indications are quite clear that the problems have derived not from borrowers walking away with depositors' money, but from the bankers themselves taking advantage of their insider positions to appropriate depositors' money.

Being a banker in some transition economies can itself be a personally risky activity. The occupational hazards are particularly great in Russia where the probability of violent death for bankers has been the highest among all occupations.

CONCLUDING OBSERVATIONS

The financial system is the basis of a market economy. Financial intermediation permits savers to spread risk and provides investors with access to resources. Under socialism there were no (nor could there in principle be) capital markets and no commercial banks. Since learning is not spontaneous, adjustments have been required in perceptions and understanding when, in the transition, people have confronted the new conceptions of private borrowing and the discretionary disposition by banks of the public's funds.

For the state banks, the situation that our model has described has for the most part passed in most countries. The liabilities have been nationalized, and the assets privatized. For the private banks, as well as for resuscitated state banks, the question is whether the maintenance of a Western-style market-based financial system is feasible in the near future.

Where major banks have failed, the public's cynicism regarding the market has been justified. The Communists told the people that markets exploit, and bank failures have provided justification in people's minds for this position (as have the pyramid schemes). In banking the ex ante prospects of success of the market regime could, however, not have been too great. For what is an honest banker to do in an economic regime where it was difficult to know whom one was dealing with, where loans and conditions of finance can be coerced, where death threats are credible, and where behavioral norms are not conducive to the development of long-term relationships based on mutual trust? If honest bankers encounter difficulties, and receive nothing for their efforts, the incentives are present for a banker to contemplate opportunism and dishonesty. The bank will still fail, but the banker will at least derive some benefit. Informational ambiguities will make it unclear whether an honest banker has honestly failed, or whether a dishonest banker has dishonestly failed.

How to "reform" this situation is a challenge of some magnitude. Of course, Western banks do not necessarily provide good role models. The U.S. savings and loan industry required a $150 billion bailout (see White 1991). In Japan at the end of March 1996, the twenty-one largest banks had made provisions for $86 billion of bad debts, and the equivalent of the savings and loan industry (*jusen*) was the proposed beneficiary of a bailout of over $6.5 billion. In the U.S. savings and loan case, there have been numerous ambiguities in personal proprietary associated with the failures. For Japan, we have the observation that: "Thanks to stories of reckless lending and, in some cases, corruption, bankers in Japan are now widely seen as sharp-suited gamblers rather than sober-suited financiers" ("Survey of International Banking," *Economist*, 27 April 1996). There are numerous other examples. In 1995 Crédit Lyonnais in France transferred FFr 135 billion of worthless "assets" to a new state company. In Scandinavia governments have spent in the neighborhood of 3 to 4 percent of GDP in recent years in bailing out failed banks. Other countries (the Bank of Crete, the Bank of Naples) add their experiences to the list.

We not wish to end on an unduly pessimistic note. The banking system is, however, very special in that people entrust their money to others from whom they assume prudence and honesty. Depositors also rely on regulatory authorities to oversee the activities of bankers to protect the public interest. Yet in economies where time horizons are short and where the characteristics of prudence, honesty, and regulation in the public interest are not always fully present, conditions for the functioning of the banking system are difficult. In the course of time, as norms of behavior and conceptions of responsibility change, as economic growth progresses, and as the recommendations noted at the beginning of this chapter are adopted and seriously implemented, banking in the transition economies will become a less precarious activity, for the banks and for their depositors.

REFERENCES

Abel, Istvan, and John Bonin. 1990. "State descrtion in the Transforming Economies: The Economic Black Hole." Paper presented at the annual meetings of the ASIA, Washington, D.C.

Bogetić, Željko, and Arye L. Hillman. 1995. Financing Government in the Transition: Bulgaria, the Political Economy of Tax Policies, Tax Bases, and Tax Evasion." World Bank, Washington D.C.

Bonin, John, Kálmán Mizsei, and Paul Wachtel. 1996. "Toward Market-Oriented Banking for the Economies in Transition: A Summary of Policy Recommendations." Institute for EastWest Studies, Prague.

Bonin, John, and Istvan Szekely. 1994. *The Development and Reform of Financial Systems in Central and Eastern Europe.* Cornwall: Edward Elgar.

Buch, Claudia M. 1995. "Bank Behavior and Bad Loans: Implications for Reforms in Eastern Europe." Kiel Working Papers, Kiel Institute for World Economics.

Coricelli, Fabrizio, and Alfredo Thorne. 1992. "Dealing with Enterprises' Bad Loans." *Economics of Transition* 1: 112–15.

Fama, Eugene. 1985. "What's Different about Banks?" *Journal of Monetary Economics* 15: 29–40.

Gelb, Alan, Arye L. Hillman, and Heinrich W. Ursprung. 1996. "Rents and the Transition." World Development Report Background Paper, World Bank, Washington D.C. Reprint as "Rents as Distractions: Why the Exit from Transition Is Prolonged." In Nicolas Baltas, George Demopoulos, and Joseph Hassid (eds.), *Economic Interdependence and Cooperation in Europe.* Springer Verlag.

Hillman, Arye L. 1994. "The Transition from Socialism: An Overview from a Political Economy Perspective." *European Journal of Political Economy.* 10: 191–225.

Kapoor, Michael. 1996. "Are Banks Ready (to Privatize)?" *Business Central Europe*, Economist Group (February): 7–11.

Nitzan, Shmuel. 1994. "Modeling Rent-Seeking Contests." *European Journal of Political Economy* 10: 41–60.

Rajan, Raghuram. 1992. "Insiders and Outsiders: The Choice between Informed and Arms-Length Debt." *Journal of Finance* 47: 1367–1400.

Roldos, Jorge, and Kenneth Kletzer. 1996. "The Role of Credit Markets in a Transition Economy with Incomplete Information." Working Paper no. 96/18, International Monetary Fund, Washington, D.C.

Scheepens, Joris P. J. F. 1995. "Bankruptcy Litigation and Optimal Debt Contracts." *European Journal of Political Economy* 11: 535–56.

Udell, Gregory F., and Paul Wachtel. 1994. "Financial System Design for Formerly Planned Economies: Defining the Issues." Leonard N. Stern School of Business, New York University.

White, Lawrence J. 1991. *The S and L Debacle.* Oxford: Oxford University Press.

World Bank. 1993. "Russia: The Banking System in Transition." Report no. 11818-RU. Washington, D.C.

CHAPTER 4

Financing Transition: Investing in Enterprises during Macroeconomic Transition

Willem H. Buiter, Ricardo Lago, and Hélène Rey

Macroeconomic stability can be viewed as a classic pure public (intermediate) good, both *nonrival*[1] and *nonexcludable*.[2] Macroeconomic stability boosts the quantity and quality of investment. In turn, productive investment is one of the key determinants of economic growth and rising living standards. The provision of macroeconomic stability is a natural responsibility of the government.

Macroeconomic instability often manifests itself through outright inflationary financing or else through a rising public debt–GDP ratio that is not matched by a rising capacity for generating future public (primary) budget surpluses necessary to repay that debt. There is a growing body of empirical evidence (and some recent theoretical research) on the existence of a close link between macroeconomic stability and economic growth (see, e.g., Fischer 1991, 1993; Barro 1995; Easterly 1996; and Bruno and Easterly 1996).

In the economies of Eastern Europe and the former Soviet Union (FSU), the swift and wide-ranging price liberalization measures with which transition was started and the initial monetary overhang inherited from the central-planning era caused an initial big spike in the rate of inflation. Some countries, like the former Czechoslovakia, Croatia, Hungary, Poland, Slovenia, and the Baltics were indeed able, through restrictive macroeconomic policies, to prevent what was fundamentally a one-off shock from turning into a process of high inflation. Others were less successful

[1] A good or service is "nonrival" if its use by one agent does not affect its availability to other agents (i.e., if the marginal cost of making it available to additional agents is zero).

[2] A good or service is "nonexcludable" if it is prohibitively costly to restrict access to it.

and perpetuated high inflation for several years. In the advanced countries, though, not everything was solved in one blow. Some of the countries successful in disinflation soon confronted unfolding disequilibria in the current account of the balance of payments that translated partly into buildup of private and/or public external debt. By 1997, thirteen out of the twenty-six borrowing countries of the European Bank for Reconstruction and Development (EBRD) were running a current-account deficit of 7 percent of GDP or higher. Russia was the main exception, still showing a current account surplus at the time. This increasing dependence on foreign savings led to fragile macroeconomic frameworks and eventual currency crises as that of the Czech Republic in 1997. Further, even in economies that have consistently reduced inflation and so far managed to steer though the external disequilibria – like Poland and Hungary – economic transformation has brought about continued reaccommodation of relative prices, changes in the general economic environment, and occasional banking crises. Needless to say, initial conditions varied widely across countries and influenced subsequent developments.[3]

Macroeconomic stability is also a critical prerequisite for effective enterprise decision making and performance. Technology and skills (including managerial ability and entrepreneurial flair) are clearly essential ingredients for good enterprise performance, but the macroeconomic environment surrounding the enterprise is no less relevant. Comparable investments and enterprises perform very differently in countries with differing macroeconomic and regulatory policies. If these policies provide stable signals and support low transaction costs, the quality of enterprise decisions, and thus the odds of success, improve.

Some authors have looked at the firm as a "nexus of contracts," both contracts internal to the organization of the firm itself (i.e., implicit or explicit contracts and practices involving management

[3] The former Czechoslovakia already had a tradition of fiscal conservatism while others like the former Yugoslavia had experienced high inflation for over a decade and yet others like the countries of the FSU and Bulgaria showed pervasive repressed inflation – manifested in shortages and an acute monetary overhang. On the external debt front, most countries of the region – with the exceptions of Bulgaria, the former Yugoslav republics, Hungary, Poland, and Russia – started their transitions virtually free from foreign debt. Of the heavily indebted countries only Hungary continued to honor its external debt commitments.

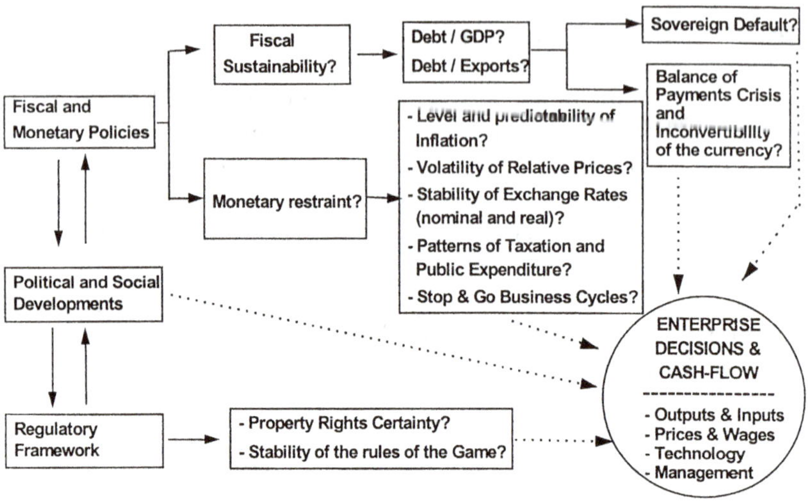

Figure 4.1. Environment surrounding enterprise decisions and cash flows.

and labor and other stakeholders in the firm, including equity owners and creditors), and contracts between the firm and external agents such as trade unions, suppliers, customers, local and national government agencies, and private interest groups with which the firm interacts in the marketplace or through nonmarket networks and modes of interaction.[4] The macroeconomic framework – encompassing inflation, taxation, public spending, stability of domestic and international relative prices, convertibility, and other elements – is a factor of fundamental importance for negotiating, interpreting, complying with, and enforcing contracts. Generally, the more stable the macroeconomic framework, the lower the transaction costs for the firm. Figure 4.1 provides a bird's eye view of how the macroeconomic environment conditions enterprise performance.

Further, the macroeconomic environment interacts with the market structure and the regulatory and tax regimes to influence the behavior and performance of enterprises. For example, a system of collective bargaining that would function well in a low-inflation framework, could lead to adversarial relations between

[4] See Coase 1937.

labor and management if inflation becomes high and unstable – the reason being that the latter creates uncertainty about the real value of the wage contract. Likewise, volatile inflation undermines the stability of the regulatory and tax frameworks. Indeed, as illustrated here, swings in inflation cause drastic changes in effective rates of taxation on capital or on "true" corporate income, even with an unchanged tax code. This means that the ranking of after-tax rates of return of a collection of investment projects is altered as the inflation rate changes, leading to inefficient allocation of resources and adding riskiness to enterprise and investor decisions.

This brings us to the central theme of the chapter: if transition involves a rapidly evolving macroeconomic environment, and this has fundamental effects on enterprise performance, then transition must have central implications for the financial structure of the firm, on the one hand, and for the behavior and performance of investors, including banks, on the other. In other words, macroeconomic conditions change during transition, hence influencing the enterprise; in turn, enterprise outcomes condition the performance of the enterprise's creditors (banks) and its residual claimants (shareholders).

In this respect, several relevant questions include inter alia the following. What are the relative roles of debt versus equity financing at different stages of transition? Would financial investors be more keen on investing in existing assets or in greenfield new ventures? What should be the comparative roles of securities markets and the banking sector in financing during transition? How do mutual and investment funds compare with commercial banks as vehicles for savings at different stages of transition?

These questions are very relevant for policy makers, in particular ministries of finance and central banks, which need to know how to balance the allocation of their – inevitably scarce – public management resources between the institutional development of securities markets (stock exchanges, brokers, securities commission, etc.) and the development of commercial banks (prudential regulations, banking supervision, etc.). Should this development be sequential – first banks, then securities markets or vice versa – or simultaneous? This chapter represents a first attempt to provide some tentative answers to these important questions.

The chapter is organized as follows. In the first section, the two main sources of macroeconomic instability, threats to the solvency of the state and to the net worth of the financial sector, are discussed. In the next section, a cursory review of the determinants of successful enterprise performance are presented. Special focus is given to the effects of macroeconomic distortions. The third section focuses quantitatively on the link between enterprise performance and the macroeconomic environment. The results and implications of some simulation studies are reviewed. These simulations compare the financial returns across countries on three stylized investment projects actually financed by the EBRD – two operating in the internationally exposed sector (an exporting enterprise and an import-competing enterprise) and the other in the nontraded sector, that is the local market, sheltered from international competition. The three projects are technically identical and the enterprises have identical gearing ratios across countries, but the macroeconomic environment faced by the firms differs from country to country. We also emphasize the distinction between so-called greenfield investments and investments in preexisting assets. In the final section, we draw the main implications for enterprise financing, investors' preferences regarding debt versus equity, and the relative roles of banking intermediaries and securities markets during transition.

SOURCES OF MACROECONOMIC INSTABILITY

Solvency of the State

Macroeconomic shocks can originate abroad or at home and within the public sector or the private sector. Macroeconomic management affects the transmission, amplification, or dampening of shocks, wherever they may originate. Yet it is fair to say that serious and persistent macroeconomic instability is most often[5] a reflection of the problems faced by the state in achieving a sustainable noninflationary fiscal and financial position.[6]

Resources for servicing the outstanding domestic and foreign

[5] A (global) systemic failure like the Great Depression is an obvious exception, although even there, government action or inaction at the very least aggravated the situation.

[6] The state in this context encompasses the central and local governments, the central bank, and the public enterprises.

debt must ultimately come from two sources: primary budget surpluses (i.e., current noninterest revenues in excess of current noninterest outlays) and seigniorage (the resources appropriated by the state through the printing of money by the central bank). Monetary growth sufficiently in excess of the growth rate of real productive capacity will sooner or later result in inflation: seigniorage turns into the inflation tax. The amount of real resources that governments obtain through the inflation tax is limited: as the rate of inflation rises, the private sector substitutes for domestic money by shifting into domestic and foreign assets (hard currencies) that are better hedges against inflation – thus, as the *inflation tax rate* increases, the *inflation tax base* decreases. For example, in Russia the share of foreign-currency deposits in the banking sector increased from 20 percent in December 1991 to 50 percent in March 1993. As inflation rises beyond a threshold, the inflation tax base – the monetary base as a proportion of GDP – declines more than proportionally. The result is that real revenues from inflation decline as the inflation rate explodes.

Inflation has other effects on the public finances as well. First there is the so-called Olivera-Tanzi effect according to which real tax revenues may decline with high rates of inflation, as taxpayers delay the settlement of tax liabilities. Since tax liabilities are generally not indexed to inflation or subject to an enforceable interest rate, delaying payment may reduce the real value of payments in a dramatic manner. A similar phenomenon occurs with the payment of electricity and water tariffs owed to public utilities. Indeed, if monthly inflation jumps from, say, 10 to 20 percent and the average tax (or tariff) collection lag is six months, the taxpayer can nearly halve her real burden by settling taxes on the last day of the semester. In an attempt to protect tax revenues from inflationary erosion, the Russian authorities established in 1992 a system of monthly advance payments for both the value-added tax (VAT) and the profit tax. However, even this system failed to deliver the targeted revenues due to increased tax loopholes, avoidance, and evasion. By 1997, fiscal revenues were running at about half the level agreed under the International Monetary Fund (IMF) program.

There can also be effects on taxes going in the opposite direction. As the Polish example shows, under conditions of reasonable compliance and moderate collection lags, historical cost accounting meant that taxable enterprise profits greatly overstated true profits during the high-inflation episode of 1990. When inflation subsided in 1991, both accounting profits and enterprise tax receipts collapsed (see Schaffer 1992).

Insolvency of the state can push countries to the verge of hyperinflation. Examples are Russia in 1992 and Armenia, Georgia, the Ukraine, and Turkmenistan in 1993. The consequences are devastating, when, at last, the deterioration of the fiscal situation can no longer be denied or ignored. The policy measures governments actually tend to resort to, frequently with the naive intent of forestalling the worst, often turn out to be extremely painful for households and firms. The state is often tempted to increase its *arrears* to the private sector, thus creating cash-flow problems for private suppliers and undermining the credibility of the state as the arbiter of contract disputes and the enforcer of the rule of law in economic affairs. Another emergency measure to cut (or, at any rate, to postpone) spending is *sequestration* (the withholding by the ministry of finance of previously authorized funds from the spending departments). This has been practiced extensively in the Russian Federation, Ukraine, and other economies during the period 1993–97. Emergency taxes are introduced, often in an arbitrary and haphazard manner, without much thought as to their administration or as regards their incentive and distributional effects.

Convertibility restrictions and multiple exchange rates are frequently reimposed (as in Uzbekistan in 1996–97), damaging international trade and financial transactions, in a (vain) attempt to make scarce foreign exchange go further. Attempts to suppress the symptoms of a real scarcity of loanable funds lead to interest rate ceilings well below the equilibrium level of interest rates and to the administrative allocation of funds at highly subsidized rates to politically favored borrowers. It is clear that all this cannot have but negative effects on the performance of the enterprises and their creditors.

Solvency of Financial Institutions

The financial troubles of enterprises transmit and manifest themselves first as illiquidity and often later as insolvency of their creditors – in transition economies, other enterprises, and banks.

Government assistance to recapitalize banks as their nonperforming loans to ailing borrowers pile up (or to settle interenterprise arrears owed to viable firms) puts further strain on already tight state budgets.

Stabilization itself, even in the absence of significant structural change, is often associated with a buildup of bad loans. This is because, as shown in Figure 4.2, successful disinflation tends to lead, initially, to very high and volatile ex post real (and/or foreign currency equivalent) interest rates on local currency loans.

Clearly, *high and volatile real rates* are apt to cause financial distress to debtors. High real deposit rates, reflecting the risk premium that needs to be paid to depositors to compensate for the risk of exchange rate devaluation and/or default of the deposit-taking institutions, mirror the high real lending rates charged by these to make up for potential losses stemming from the odds of borrower bankruptcy. Both the stabilization program and the risk of its failure contribute to these risk premiums. High nominal rates alone – even if real rates were low – can cause cash-flow problems because debtors are forced into accelerated and premature amortization, in real terms, of their debt, whenever they are not able to add to their borrowing an amount equal to the reduction in the real value of their domestic currency debt due to inflation.

Further to stabilization, *structural transformation* exposes creditors to severe counterparty risk as some debtors are faced unexpectedly with adverse developments beyond their control. As key relative prices change, as new competitors erode monopoly profits, as new markets emerge and old ones vanish, previously creditworthy borrowers may become insolvent. All of these stresses and strains are, of course, present, qualitatively, even in an economy that does not suffer macroeconomic disequilibria (i.e., Slovenia 1994–97): in principle, macroeconomic balance can be consistent in a dynamic, evolving economic system, with a considerable amount of microeconomic flux at the sectoral and individual firm levels.

It is during the *transition from plan to market*, a process involving macroeconomic stabilization and structural adjustment on an unprecedented scale, that the problems and risks facing enterprises are most acute. This is obviously true as regards the backlog

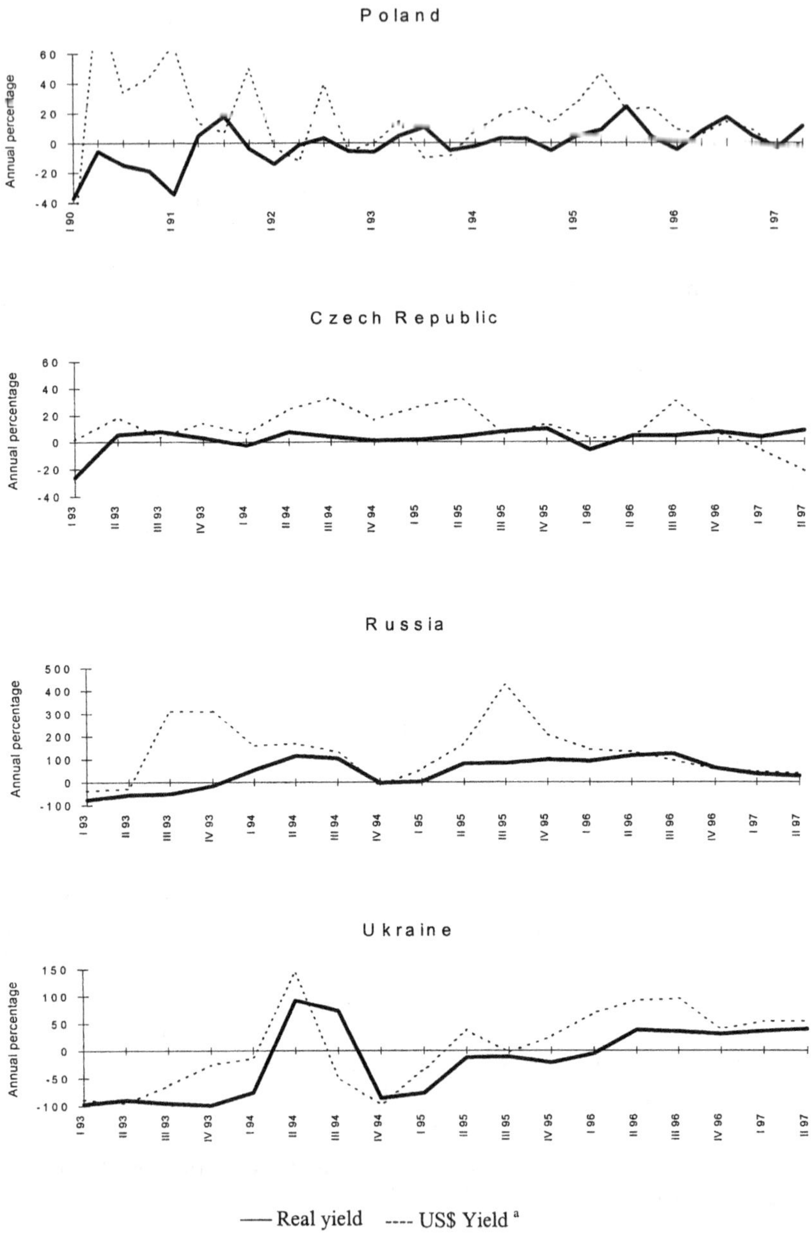

Figure 4.2. Real ex post interest rates on local currency loans. *Note*: Prime lending rates on local currency loans converted into US$ rates equivalent by discounting for the actual devaluation (revaluation) of the local currency occurred during the period.

of loans incurred during the prereform era (the so-called balance sheet or *stock problem*). It remains true also for new loans now that reform appears to be here to stay (the *flow problem*). Even competent Western bankers would have little evidence on which to base their assessment of the creditworthiness of loan applicants. Few potential borrowers have much of a track record or credit history, and for those which do, the past is likely to be a poor guide to the future: what made for enterprise success under central planning may bear little relationship to what is required for effective enterprise performance in a market regime – even less when the market structure is rapidly evolving and its dynamics bears a high degree of unmeasurable uncertainty. Thus, the *flow problem* of financial intermediation concerns the difficulty encountered by banks (and other lenders) in discriminating between good and bad risks when extending new loans. To compound the problem, *oversight* of banks by the monetary authorities is initially weak and *judiciary procedures* to repossess collateral are typically cumbersome. Real-estate markets and property registries are underdeveloped and the legal and institutional framework for securing liens (including mortgages) is severely restrictive. Secured transactions in movable property are rare and costly. All this adds greatly both to the cost of starting up a new business and to the cost of doing business.

The result of these deficiencies is recurrent banking failures. Like any bailout by the state, *recapitalization of banks* – or clearance of interenterprise arrears – can give rise to *moral hazard* (why engage in costly appraisal of borrowers if losses will be made up by the silent public partner with the deep pockets?) and *adverse selection* (the selection of investments that are excessively risky from a social point of view, because the bank gets the positive returns in the good outcomes while the state picks up the tab in the bad ones). Deposit insurance further encourages lending on excessively risky projects as the banks don't have to worry about bank runs by depositors fearful of bank default. When the banks in question are private, both moral hazard and adverse selection can be reduced by ensuring that the existing owners of the bank lose all their equity before any public sector money goes in. An idea of the burden to the public treasury of the bad loan problem is given by the experience of Hungary where some banks have been recapitalized in one way or another every year since 1990.

The total injection of public funds from 1992 to 1997 amounts to well in excess of 10 percent of 1997 GDP.[7]

The flow of *funds from the state budget to enterprises* is often intermediated through the banking sector. If the government bails out insolvent enterprises or banks directly through subsidies, this increases the conventionally measured budget deficit. If instead it instructs the central bank to provide subsidized credit to the enterprise, the subsidy element – the difference between the market rate and the subsidized rate times the amount of the loan – would, in principle, show up in the so-called *quasi-fiscal deficit* of the central bank. A calculation by de Melo, Denizer, and Gelb (1996) of the contribution of the quasi-fiscal deficit to the total "true" state budget imbalance is provided in Table 4.1. For countries in the early stages of transition, the quasi-fiscal deficit reached at some point as much as four times the conventional fiscal deficit and, indeed, made the overall public sector imbalance become as high as 40 percent of GDP (Kazakhstan 1992) or 33 percent of GDP (Belarus 1992). As these levels were far beyond the maximum sustainable long-run ratio of the inflation tax to GDP, they threatened to precipitate countries onto a hyperinflationary path.

Even harder to estimate than the quasi-fiscal deficit of the central bank is what we shall call the deferred (contingent) fiscal deficit. Instead of providing enterprises with explicitly subsidized loans, the central bank could lend to them at market rates, that is, without any explicit subsidy element being provided ex ante. Nevertheless both parties to the loan may be perfectly aware that in due course the contractual debt service payments will not be enforced (wholly or partly). What appears to be a loan on market terms is in fact a capital grant.[8] Rather than engaging in any "lending" to the enterprise sector itself, the central bank could encourage commercial banks to do the lending, with the central bank (implicitly) guaranteeing the loans. If this "guarantee" is

[7] Note that this happened in an advanced transition country like Hungary, which has a banking code guided by Basle-like adequacy ratios and better bank oversight standards than most other transition countries. Of course, the American savings and loan crisis and others elsewhere remind us that large-scale financial shambles are by no means confined to developing countries and transition economies.

[8] The grant could be contingent, with full servicing of the debt only waved under specified uncertain circumstances. Option pricing methods would have to be used to value such contingent claims on the government.

Table 4.1. *Fiscal and quasi-fiscal deficits for selected countries: 1992–93 (% of GDP)*

	Fiscal deficits		Central bank implicit subsidy[a]		Total budget deficits	
	1992	1993	1992	1993	1992	1993
Advanced transition[a]						
Czech Republic	0.5	−0.6	0.3	0.8	0.8	0.2
Slovakia	13.1	7.6	0.3	1.7	13.4	9.3
Intermediate transition						
Bulgaria	5.0	11.1	1.3	0.8	6.3	11.9
Estonia	0.5	1.4	—	0.2	—	1.6
Romania	5.5	1.0	5.9	3.9	11.4	4.9
Early transition						
Kazakhstan	7.3	1.2	32.7	—	40.0	—
Belarus	6.4	9.4	26.5	9.3	32.9	18.7
Turkmenistan	10.1	3.6	12.5	21.2	22.6	24.8
Uzbekistan	10.2	8.4	13.1	18.5	23.3	26.9

Notes: Quasi-fiscal deficit defined in a narrow sense because it excludes foreign exchange and other losses. Implicit subsidies from the central bank to commercial banks and economy due to difference between the central bank refinancing rate and inflation. Annual figures are averages of quarterly figures.
[a] The other countries of advanced transition, like Hungary and Poland, appeared to show relatively low central bank interest rate subsidies in those years.
Sources: de Melo, Denizer, and Gelb 1996.

called, the central bank would be bailing out a commercial bank, which got into trouble because it bailed out a nonviable state enterprise. Until the crisis hits, the deferred fiscal deficit would be hidden in the balance sheets (in the form of nonperforming loans) of the commercial bank sector.

Financial institutions, both banks and nonbanks, can be sources of acute financial instability when inadequate regulation and supervision encourages fraudulent behavior on a large scale. Extreme examples are the *pyramid schemes* that have operated and collapsed in Russia, Romania, Bulgaria, and, most recently and spectacularly, in Albania. Pyramid schemes are (de facto) deposit-taking institutions or investment funds that promise depositors or investors above-market interest rates – often way above market. They may succeed, temporarily, in paying these high rates of interest to earlier depositors, from the deposits of later investors.[9] They do not pay these high rates out of the proceeds from investing earlier deposits in productive assets or financial instruments yielding high rates of return. Indeed, pyramid schemes tend to have no (or just a very limited amount of) conventionally defined assets on their balance sheet at all. Their main "implicit asset" is their ability to attract future depositors with the promise of above-market rates of return. Any deposit-taking scheme promising an average rate of return in excess of the underlying growth rate of the real economy is likely to be fraudulent and doomed to collapse. In Albania, the value of the funds deposited in these pyramid schemes, including accrued interest, has been reported by some observers to have amounted to nearly 60 percent of annual GDP by the time these schemes began to collapse late in 1996 and early in 1997. Fraud on this scale can bring down governments, as in Albania in 1996.

MACROECONOMIC CONDITIONS AS A DETERMINANT OF ENTERPRISE DECISION MAKING AND INVESTMENT PERFORMANCE

Sources of Differential Enterprise Investment Performance

Economy-wide conditions influence enterprise performance in three ways: through the quantity and quality of the endowment of factors of production in each country; through the country's market structure and the regulatory and tax environment; and

[9] Pyramid schemes or Ponzi schemes are bound to collapse faster, the more the average real rate of return they offer exceeds the natural rate of growth of the real economy. Assume the real value of each individual depositor's investment in the pyramid fund is constant. Then the long-run average real rate of return on the fund cannot exceed the long-run population growth rate. If the real value of each individual depositor's investment in the pyramid fund grows at the same rate as productivity in the economy as a whole, then the long-run average real rate of return on the fund cannot exceed the sum of the long-run population growth rate and the long-run growth rate of productivity, that is, the natural rate of growth. An unfunded, pay-as-you-go (balanced budget) social security retirement scheme, where contributions by the working young are paid out in full each period to the retired population, is an example of a viable pyramid scheme. With per capita contributions constant in real terms, the rate of return on this scheme is the "biological rate of interest," that is, the rate of growth of population. With per capita contributions growing at the same rate as productivity, the rate of return on this scheme is the natural rate of growth of the economy.

through the stability of the domestic (and the international) macroeconomic environment.

Most transition economies are characterized by a serious imbalance between the availability of *physical capital*, including infrastructure, which is often obsolete, and of *human capital*, which tends to be relatively skilled and abundant. While some of the skills specific to the market service sectors (accounting, auditing, financial expertise, marketing, market-minded public administration, etc.) are now in short supply, any shortages in these areas can be remedied earlier and more easily than the shortfall in modern physical plant and equipment. Raising the capital formation rate will have the hoped-for productivity effects if it can be allocated to their most productive uses. Thus, the development of the domestic financial markets should be a top priority for policy makers.

Enterprise performance is influenced by the *regulatory framework* and the structure of product and input markets. Opening up the economy to external competition is the most effective way of exposing internationally tradable sectors – including most of industry, agriculture, and the natural resource sectors – to the efficiency-enhancing spur of world competition. In the sheltered sectors – not subject to international competition – which include services (transportation, wholesale and retail trade, utilities, etc.), government action is required to remove barriers to entry imposed by incumbents trying to increase and/or protect their margins and rents.

The very least any government should do to promote transition is to respect the important "negative list" of things it should not do. The key "don't" is the injunction not to get in the way of legitimate private initiative through excessive and intrusive regulation, entry-restricting licensing requirements, competition-distorting subsidies, or a punitive, arbitrary, and unpredictable tax code. More "positive" interventions include the provision of the public good of macroeconomic stability, that is, of a stable measure of value; the enforcement of private property rights and the rule of law; and the creation of a stable institutional framework for regulation and taxation.

Two aspects of the tax structure faced by enterprises are critical. The first is the quality of the design of the rules – in terms of neutrality, universality, and fairness. The second is the predictability of the rules over time. Enterprises may (up to a point) be able to live with an "imperfect" tax or regulatory system, as long as its incidence and enforcement are systematic, predictable, and stable. Governments that ceaselessly design and redesign tax rules impose costly and avoidable uncertainty on investment firms and markets.

The *macroeconomic environment interacts with the regulatory and tax environments* to influence the behavior of enterprises. For instance, the negotiation of and compliance with any contract that would function well in a low-inflation environment can be wholly dysfunctional under high and volatile inflation. The latter creates uncertainty about the real value of any pecuniary contract. Also, the duration of price, wage, and financial contracts tends to shorten with higher inflation and spurious costs in time and effort go into adversarial bargaining sessions.

Another example of how *macroeconomic instability undermines the effectiveness of the regulatory and fiscal framework* is given by the sharp changes introduced by inflation in the *effective rates of taxation* (ERT) on capital.[10] The ERT model can be used to illustrate these effects. First, for a specific investment project, the ERT model generates a multiperiod cash flow, on the assumption of a constant general price level (zero inflation). The internal rate of return (IRR) before taxes or subsidies is calculated for this cash flow. Then the entire relevant set of tax and subsidy policies appropriate to the project is imposed (profit taxes, depreciation allowances, interest deductibility, investment tax credits, tax holidays, dividend taxes, carry over of losses, etc.) on this cash flow. The before-tax cash flow is assumed to be independent of these taxes and subsidies (indeed a strong but inescapable assumption!). The after-tax IRR is then calculated. The ERT is defined as the difference between the before-tax and after-tax IRR's, expressed as a percentage of the before-tax IRR.

The exercise is then repeated for some positive rate of inflation. The before-tax real cash flow is also assumed to be independent of the rate of inflation. The distortionary effects of inflation come from the fact that the real value of taxes and subsidies will vary with the rate of inflation. The after-tax IRR on the project is

[10] For a more detailed explanation of the concept of the ERT, see European Bank for Reconstruction and Development 1993, 50–51.

Table 4.2. *Effective rates of taxation (ERT) with the tax code of Hungary* (%)

	No collection lags: Debt-to-equity ratio		Collection lag 6 months Debt-to-equity ratio	
Annual inflation	0	0.5	0	0.5
Baseline 0%	38	36	38	36
1994 actual 21%	43	38	39	34
1995 actual 28%	44[a]	38	39	33[b]

[a] Highest.
[b] Lowest.

therefore different with positive inflation from what it was with zero inflation. This difference in the after-tax IRR's is the effect of inflation on the effective rate of taxation.

An illustration of how the ERT for a given project investment – in fact, one financed by the EBRD – varies depending on the country's tax code and inflation rate is provided in Tables 4.2, 4.3, and 4.4.[11] These tables also contain sensitivity analyses of the ERT to inflation, to variations in the debt-equity ratio, and to tax collection lags for the tax codes of several countries. As shown, the ERT on capital for the project using Russia's tax code can be as low as 10 percent and as high as 77 percent. A similar range of variation results across countries. The ERT of the identical project fluctuates from 19 percent in Russia 1994 (if one assumes a collection lag of six months) and 87 percent in Ukraine 1994 (no collection lags). Not surprisingly, the country in which the project in question was indeed successfully carried out (Hungary) is where the ERT displays the narrowest range of variation under the different assumptions, between a low of 33 percent and a high of 44 percent.

[11] The country simulations are based on a successful private sector project cofinanced by the EBRD in Hungary. The calculations were performed by means of a variant of the software "Measuring Effective Taxation of Enterprises" (Dunn and Pellecchio 1990). The information on the specific conventions to calculate tax returns in each country was obtained from the booklet "Taxation in Eastern Europe, 1995" (Deloitte, Touche Tohmatsu International 1995). These conventions include: whether historical cost or replacement cost accounting is used to cost-out input inventories and depreciation allowances; whether interest on debt is deductible from taxable profits; whether or not distributed dividends are subject to taxation; whether losses can be carried over and for how many years.

Table 4.3. *ERT with the tax code of Russia* (%)

	No collection lags: Debt-to-equity ratio		Collection lag 6 months: Debt-to-equity ratio	
Annual inflation	0	0.5	0	0.5
Baseline 0%	32	32	32	32
1994 actual 203%	53	34	29	19
1992 actual 2318%	77[a]	51	14	10[b]

[a] Highest.
[b] Lowest.

Table 4.4. *Cross country comparisons of ERT* (%)

		Collection lag (months)	
Country	1994 annual inflation	0	6
Bulgaria	122	55	36
Czech Republic	10	−51	49
Hungary	21	38	34
Poland	30	47	41
Russia	203	34	19
Romania	62	61	47
Slovak Republic	12	42	40
Slovenia	18	41	37
Ukraine	401	87	37

Notes: The calculations assume a debt-to-equity ratio of 0.5 and full interest deductibility from taxable income for all countries in the table.

Note that these are not tax rates on profits but rather effective rates of taxation on capital as defined earlier – that is, 44 percent means that the before-tax IRR exceeds the after-tax IRR by 44 percent of the before-tax IRR. These examples bear out that the real burden imposed by a given tax code clearly is not inflation-neutral. As inflation changes, the ERT is subject to countervailing forces that do not cancel out. On the one hand, the historic cost accounting of depreciation allowances and input inventories (first in–first out, or FIFO accounting) tends to overstate taxable profits when inflation is high. On the other hand, collection lags and the deductibility from taxable profits of the nominal interest on the debt tend to reduce the tax burden on the firm.

Clearly, the sensitivity of effective rates of taxation to changes in the inflation rate, particularly when inflation is high, complicates the already difficult task – faced by bankers/lenders in transition countries – of screening out good and bad projects and/or borrowers. A specific borrower may be a better credit than another one at low inflation rates but worse at high ones. This example alone illustrates vividly the screening problem facing bankers and illustrates how difficult "sound banking" is during transition.

Macroeconomic Distortions

It is a robust empirical finding that high inflation is associated with (1) highly variable and uncertain inflation and (2) high relative price variability and unpredictability. High inflation produces a distortion of market signals and results in a worsening of coordination among economic agents' decisions. In extreme cases it severely impairs the proper functioning of a decentralized market economy. Unanticipated inflation in addition redistributes real resources from holders of nominally denominated local currency debt instruments toward the issuers of such instruments. With imperfect indexation of tax brackets, benefits, and wage contracts, further arbitrary redistributions of wealth and income occur. All these rather than the esoteric "shoe leather" and "menu costs" of fully anticipated inflation constitute the true social cost of inflation.[12]

Inflation is often the visible, monetary manifestation of unresolved social conflict about public spending and its financing. The resolution of such "wars of attrition" is a highly uncertain process. Both high inflation, and the anticipation of (eventual) fiscal and monetary corrections to control it, increase the uncertainty of the economic environment within which firms make production, employment, and investment decisions. Future fiscal measures and realignment of key prices will affect business profitability. Fiscal

[12] "Shoe leather" refers to frequent trips to the bank so that as little money as possible needs to be held in one's pocket; "menu costs" refers to the frequent relabeling of prices in restaurants, shops, etc.

retrenchment tends to be associated with a cyclical decline in economic activity, employment, and real wages and with a nominal and real depreciation of the currency.[13]

Stability of macroeconomic policy appears to be a much more important spur to private investment than reductions in statutory tax rates and interest rates of the magnitude that are commonly experienced.[14] The generous tax holidays enacted in the Ukraine during the period of hyperinflation and turmoil (1993–94) – including a constitutional provision whereby tax benefits could not be repealed by future legislation – were completely ineffective in attracting foreign investment.[15] Pindyck and Solimano (1993) arrive at the result that the volatility of the returns to capital has a depressing effect on investment and that this effect is greater for developing countries than for industrial economies. Further, they find that – after trying a range of indices of political and economic instability as explanatory variables – only inflation seems to be clearly and robustly correlated with the volatility of the return on investments.

Investment involves the commitment of resources today in anticipation of future, uncertain returns.[16] Recent firm-level empirical evidence for the United States suggests that an increase in uncertainty depresses investment (see Leahy and Whited 1996). Likewise, the empirical evidence surveyed by Pindyck and Solimano (1993) also suggests that investment is more likely to be delayed and depressed in the aftermath of stabilization in high-inflation countries. This wait-and-see attitude has been dubbed the "option value of waiting" (see Dornbusch 1990). Only when sufficient commitment to the reform process is shown and a track

[13] Real depreciation of the currency means a decrease of the relative price of nontraded goods to traded goods.

[14] See Pindyck and Solimano 1993.

[15] Needless to say that this provision was indeed repealed under a new constitution, in 1996. Cumulative FDI per capita to Ukraine during 1989–94 was only US$9 versus an average of US$44 for the region and a maximum of US$671 for Hungary.

[16] The option to invest is a call option that arises from the expandability of the capital stock, while the option to disinvest is a put option that arises from the reversibility of investment. The call option reduces the firm's incentive to invest, while the put option increases the incentives to invest. The call option is extinguished by investment and the put option is acquired by investing. Since the values of both options rise with uncertainty and the two options have opposing effects on the incentive to invest, the net effect of uncertainty is ambiguous. See Abel, Dixit, Eberly, and Pindyck 1995 and Dixit and Pindyck 1994.

record is established does private investment resume strongly. This may also account for the fact that foreign direct investment (FDI) in the region has been meager so far (particularly in the FSU) and heavily concentrated in the core of Central European countries (the Visegrad four) plus Slovenia and Estonia. In 1996, total FDI in the twenty-six countries of operation of EBRD reached just US$12 billion, a figure less than half the figure for Latin America in the same year.

Short-termism in contracts can be an individually rational response to instability. In addition, private markets most often do not fully index the capital value of long-term outstanding debt but do fully index short-term interest rates. In this borrowing environment loans become inevitably very short term. The long-term financing of investment may be impossible; borrowers are faced continuously with the problem of rolling over their debt, and the risk of a credit crunch is ever present. The shortening of wage contracts – particularly those subject to backward-looking indexation to inflation – creates further upward pressure on the inflation rate.[17] High inflation also diverts resources toward privately profitable but socially unproductive activities such as hyperactive treasury management and rent seeking. Typically, the financial and public relations managers of enterprises become more senior and better paid than the production, research and development, and design managers.

The underlying problem generating macroeconomic instability is the unsustainability of fiscal and financial policies. Occasionally, governments are able to "repress" inflation for a while by borrowing heavily, mostly from abroad. For a given budget deficit, governments often confront a short-run trade-off between monetary financing and external borrowing (i.e., a trade-off between lower inflation and a higher deficit in the current account of the balance of payments).[18] As the public debt builds up, however, this strategy eventually leads to a foreign exchange crisis and subsequent high inflation. Enterprise decisions – predicated upon the relative prices and rules prevailing prior to the crisis – may have translated

[17] Assume that annual inflation is running at 100% and wages are fully adjusted for past inflation every twelve months. If the indexation period were halved to every six months, the inflation rate would have to increase sufficiently to prevent average monthly real wages from rising sharply. See Pazos 1990.

[18] See Corden 1990.

into production processes that are no longer financially viable at the postcrisis relative price configuration.

THE EFFECTS OF THE MACROECONOMIC ENVIRONMENT ON ENTERPRISE PERFORMANCE AND FINANCING

Simulations of the Financial Performance of Investments in Three Stylized Enterprises across Countries in Transition: The Framework

In order to analyze the financial performance of enterprises (or more precisely, the returns to investing in enterprises) across different macroeconomic environments, the researcher would ideally like to be able to observe the behavior, during a given period, of "identical" enterprises across a group of countries with different macroeconomic environments. A practical alternative consists in simulating the performance of a common enterprise (or a bundle of them), using the actual historical observations on the key macroeconomic variables for each of the countries. This is the approach of this section. The exercise can be put as follows: an investor (henceforth the *Fund/Bank*) is assumed to be interested in the ECU returns to financing "identical enterprises" in four groups of countries in transition with very different macroeconomic environments. The countries are the Czech Republic, Hungary, and Poland (group 1), Romania (group 2), Ukraine (group 3), and Russia (group 4). We refer to the first three groups as advanced, intermediate, and early transition countries respectively. Russia represents a special category in between early and intermediate transition.

An enterprise is narrowly defined here as a production technology (linking output with fixed coefficients to intermediate inputs, labor, and capital services) and a financial structure (comprising equity and debt). The period of analysis is 1990 to 1994. The first enterprise is referred to as the "exportable," because it manufactures chocolate for exports. The second – referred to as the "import-competing" – is modeled on a bottle manufacturer catering to the domestic market. The third enterprise – the "nontradable" – is a firm providing cargo-transportation services in the national market.

The *microstructure* (the input-output coefficients of the three enterprises, the tax ratios on capital, the local- and foreign-currency debt-gearing ratios, the depreciation rates) are assumed equal for the four groups of countries. By contrast, the *macro-structure* (the prices of importables, exportables, and non-tradables, wages, inflation, devaluation, etc.) is different for each group.

The investor is looking into both "greenfield" investments (characterized by a common country-independent price of capital) and investments in already existing assets (which can involve discounts on the price of capital in the riskier countries). The investments can take the form of loans and/or equity; in turn the loans can be made in either hard currency (ECUs) or the local currency of the investee country (i.e., rubles in Russia). Also, the investments are assumed to pursue a pure financial return rather than control of the firm, and are small enough to be taken as marginal, meaning that they do not alter the debt or equity to capital-gearing ratios of the firm (existing prior to the investment).

The model used to calculate the results discussed here is briefly described in the appendix. The reader can find a more thorough explanation of the design of the model and the sources of data in Buiter, Lago, and Rey 1997.

The Results: Risk and Return of Individual Investments across Countries

Greenfield Investments

First we look at the statistical distribution of a (small) equity investment in a greenfield enterprise (in Figure 4.3, we show the results for the enterprise producing the exportable good) across each of the transition stages: advanced, intermediate, and early. Note that the horizontal axis gives the annual return to the equity investment plus the resale value of the undepreciated part of the capital stock. Thus, 1.37 means a return of 37 percent on the ECU invested. While we are aware that the distribution of annual equity returns tends to follow a log-normal distribution – that is, the lower tail is bounded at zero (a return of −100%), in the worst-case scenario – we assume only for the sake of a clearer graphical illustration that the mean and variance obtained in each of the simulations corresponds to a normal distribution.

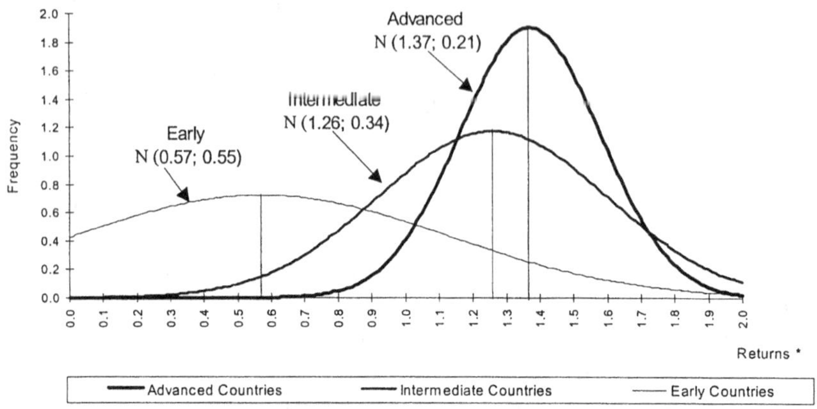

Figure 4.3. Distribution of equity returns to an individual greenfield investment in different countries (exportable good).

As the chart indicates, the equity invested performs uniformly better – it has a higher mean (1.37, i.e., a return of 37%) and a lower standard deviation (0.21) – in the advanced countries than in the intermediate ones. Similarly, the statistical distribution of returns to equity in the intermediate countries dominates that of the early transition ones. The former shows expected returns of 1.26 (or 26%) with a standard deviation of 0.34 while the latter shows expected losses of 0.57 (or −43%) and a standard deviation of 0.55. In other words, the less mature (more incipient) the transition stage, the lower the expected (mean) returns and the flatter or riskier becomes the frequency distribution. Results are not any different for the other two firms: those producing the import substitution and the nontradable goods as Appendix Tables 4.A.2 and 4.A.3 illustrate. Hence, investors should be inclined to invest greenfield in countries of advanced transition. The intuition is that with the price of capital (cost of the investment) equal in each of the three groups of countries, the higher macroeconomic stability of the advanced countries will represent better prospects, less volatility, and trouble doing business in these countries; thus, the superior and safer returns. Ceteris paribus, given the choice of setting up a brand-new chocolate factory – at the same cost of investment – in either Poland or Ukraine, the investor will certainly prefer Poland.

Lankes and Venables (1996) link greenfield investments to the control mode. Wholly owned subsidiaries of foreign firms are more likely to be greenfield investments and greenfield investments are more likely to occur when foreign investors want complete control of the entire production process of the company. This motive is especially powerful when there is strong emphasis on the quality of the product.[19] Here we provide an alternative view, based on the influence of macroeconomic conditions on microeconomic performance, where greenfield investments tend to be optimal in the countries that are more advanced on the transition path.

Debt versus Equity

Having selected the advanced countries, should the investor consider providing debt rather than equity? The answer can be found by comparing the distribution of debt returns to that of equity as provided in the Appendix Table 4.A.2. The *local-currency* debt returns display a lower mean (1.18 vs. 1.37) but also lower standard deviation (0.11 vs. 0.21). The *ECU* debt returns show an even lower mean (1.06) and are virtually riskless in this example. The choice of the instrument will therefore depend on the attitude toward risk of the investor; whether she would be willing to trade off returns for risk: a lower return at less risk. (Note in Appendix Table 4.A.2 that for the import substitution and the nontradable cases, the returns on local-currency debt exceed the returns on equity and at the same risk. Hence, in these two cases debt dominates equity). It is also clear that debt becomes less attractive relative to equity at earlier stages of transition since not only does the distribution of equity returns shift to the left (providing a lower expected average return) but it also has "fatter tails" with a higher probability attached to very bad outcomes. This means that as the probability of a full loss on the equity invested increases, the debt becomes riskier: more downside risk without any upside compensation. In sum, in the case of an individual greenfield investment, investors should always prefer investing in countries

[19] The Lankes-Venables (1996) survey shows that the proportion of greenfield investments in their group 1 (Czech Republic, Hungary) is 38% whereas it is only 32% in their group 2 and 30% in their group 3, which corroborates our results (their groups have been ranked using EBRD's transition indicators).

of advanced transition. In general, it appears that some risk-averse investors may also consider debt instruments.

Investments in Existing Assets

Although investors are in general not interested in greenfield enterprises in early transition countries, what about existing enterprises? If the assets (existing factories, natural resources, etc.) of a country or group of countries do not succeed in pricing themselves into the investors' portfolios at face value, there will always exist a sufficient discount for which these assets will become attractive. That indeed is a central message of this chapter: if a country has a highly unfavorable macroeconomic environment, it will pay for it through high discounts on the prices of its existing immobile assets.

The least-advanced countries on the transition path have the highest discounts on the price of their "sunk" capital. Therefore, the less advanced on the transition path, the bigger the incentive for investing in existing assets, ceteris paribus. But here ceteris paribus truly does mean holding a lot of other things constant. The existing capital in which the *Fund/Bank* can invest is often obsolete, depending on the countries and the sectors. In the Pissarides, Singer, and Svejnar (1996) survey, managers in Bulgaria and Russia complain that "capital is old" and claim that this obsolescence is one of the most binding constraints they face. Therefore, we make two assumptions regarding existing assets (enterprises). First, we proxy the magnitude of the existing asset price discount by the deviation of the country's current exchange rate from an estimate of the purchasing power parity (PPP) exchange rate. Second, while the assumption that productivity levels are the same across countries in the initial period may be suitable for greenfield investments, it is highly questionable when we turn to investments in existing assets. We therefore make a correction for the relative levels of productivity across countries in the initial period. We take average economy-wide $PPP GDP per employee to estimate the relative productivity levels of each country at the beginning of the period.

Under these circumstances, as Figure 4.4 shows, equity investments in early (and intermediate) countries may become attractive to investors because although the riskiness of these investments continues to be higher than that for advanced coun-

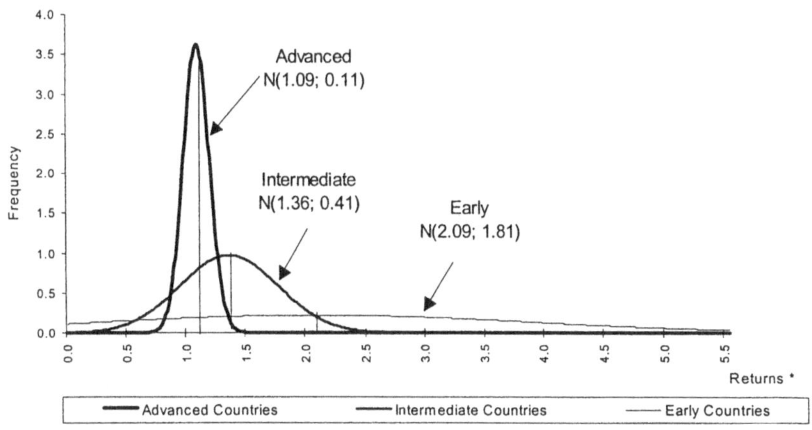

Figure 4.4. Distribution of equity returns to an individual investment in existing assets in different countries: (import substitution good). *Note*: 1.37 means an annual return of 37% [(1.37 − 1) × 100] and 0.57 means an annual return of −43% [(0.57 − 1) × 100].

tries, the expected returns also become much higher. The distribution depicted in Figure 4.4 portrays a mean of 2.09 (a return of 109%) at a risk of 1.81 for the import substitution enterprise, in the early transition group, both higher than the respective parameters for the intermediate countries. The same occurs when comparing the risk-return profile of the intermediate countries vis-à-vis the advanced ones. In other words, as investors move toward earlier transition countries in the search for discounted existing assets they face a rational choice of higher returns at the price of a higher risk.

If risk-taking investors wish to invest in existing assets in earlier transition countries, should they consider investing in debt instead of equity? The answer is no! Again, the "fat tails" of the distribution of returns to an investment in early transition countries, portrayed in Figure 4.4, signifies that a debt investment would bear close-to-equity downside risk with no upside payoff. In other words, if things go well the investor recovers principal and interest, if things go wrong the investor loses it all; and because of the "fat tails," the probability of losing it all is significant. Under these circumstances, rational investors should always prefer equity to debt.

The Results: Optimal Portfolios across Countries and Sectors

In this section, we analyze the portfolio choice of the *Fund/Bank* when confronted with the possibility of investing in debt and/or equity across countries and sectors. The reader should be aware that we assume that the "portfolio manager" has full knowledge of the expected returns of each instrument (debt or equity) in every one of the three enterprises for each of the four groups of countries. Further, she is also assumed to know the relevant variance-covariance matrix among all possible investments. These are "big ifs." As the aphorism goes: hindsight is 20/20. (This strong, heroic assumption of full information yields the implausible result of obtaining even risk-free portfolios in Figures 4.5 and 4.7).

Here comes into play Frank Knight's (1921) distinction between *risk* (a situation where the possible collections of outcomes and their probabilities are known) and *uncertainty* (where either are unknown). When dealing with countries in transition – a process of unprecedented systemic transformation from socialism into capitalism – the real world is indeed one of extreme uncertainty in Knight's terms. In consequence the numerical estimates arrived at here need to be taken with extreme caution. Hence, the qualitative conclusions rather than the quantitative results are of relevance.

In this section, we consider that the *Fund/Bank* can invest across sectors and countries in either greenfield or existing assets but not in both simultaneously. The algorithm utilized calculates the efficient portfolio composition (by instrument and group of countries) that minimizes risk for increasing levels of mean returns.

Greenfield Portfolios

The mean-variance efficient frontier is presented in Figure 4.5. As predicted by portfolio theory, it displays a convex shape whereby a higher mean can be obtained at the cost of higher risk, at decreasing returns. Figure 4.6 shows how the efficient portfolios quickly converge to 100 percent in equities – for reasonably small standard deviations of 0.006 upward – invested mostly and increasingly in the group of countries of advanced transition. Two lessons can be drawn. First, as noted in the previous section, when

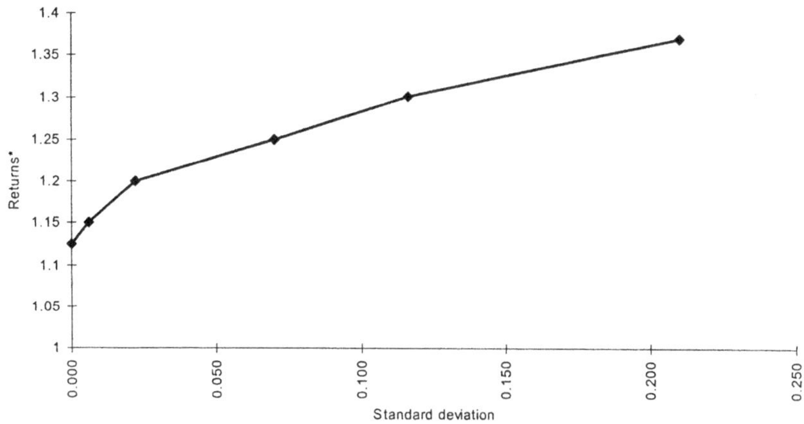

Figure 4.5. Mean efficient portfolios of greenfield investments across sectors and countries. *Note*: For returns, 1.37 means an annual return of 37% [(1.37 − 1) × 100] and 0.57 means an annual return of −43% [(0.57 − 1) × 100].

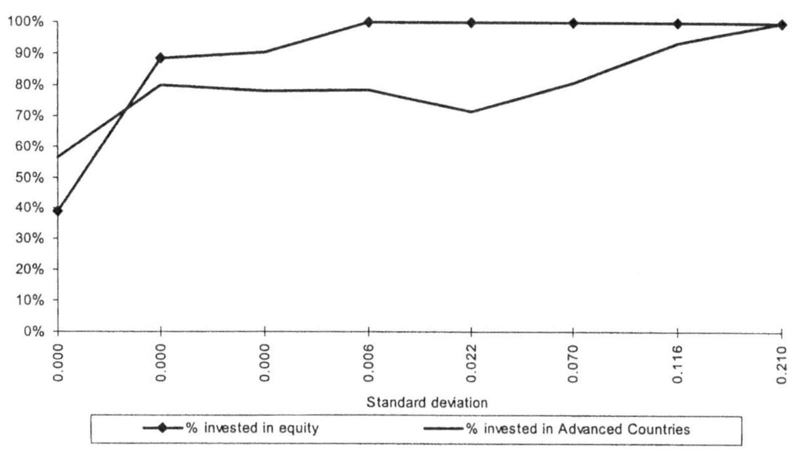

Figure 4.6. Composition, by instrument and country, of efficient portfolios in greenfield investments.

investing in a greenfield venture, advanced transition countries dominate. Second, the optimal portfolio looks more like that of a *Fund* (a portfolio of equity) rather than a *Bank* (a portfolio of loans) even at relatively low levels of riskiness. Indeed, if a *Bank* faces very high real interest rates in raising savings and term

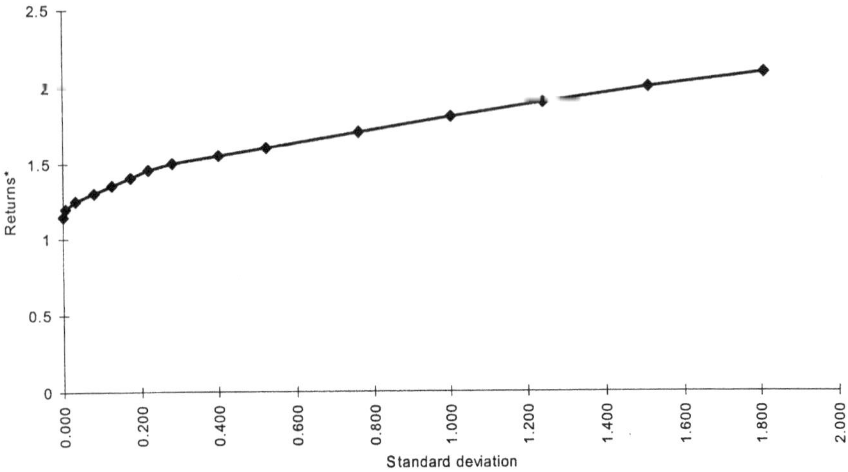

Figure 4.7. Mean-variance efficient portfolios of investments in existing assets across sectors and countries. *Note*: For returns, 1.37 means an annual return of 37% [(1.37 − 1) × 100] and 0.57 means an annual return of −43% [(0.57 − 1) × 100].

deposits – as Figure 4.2 showed – it appears that investing mostly in loans may not even be a profitable business. Of course, one can think of increasing sufficiently the spreads on lending rates; however, it is known that very high real rates would lead to both adverse selection of borrowers and even insolvency of otherwise financially viable debtors. The process of recurrent banking failures (and/or bailouts) in most countries in transition could be seen as providing some further empirical support, ceteris paribus, for this result. Bank lending does not appear to be, in general, a very profitable business during transition, particularly at the early stages.

Portfolio of Existing Assets
The mean-variance efficient frontier is depicted in Figure 4.7. Again, the portfolio soon collapses into 100 percent of equity investments, for standard deviations of 0.007 or above. In this case, by contrast, investments in advanced countries are only preferred for lower and intermediate levels of risk (standard devia-

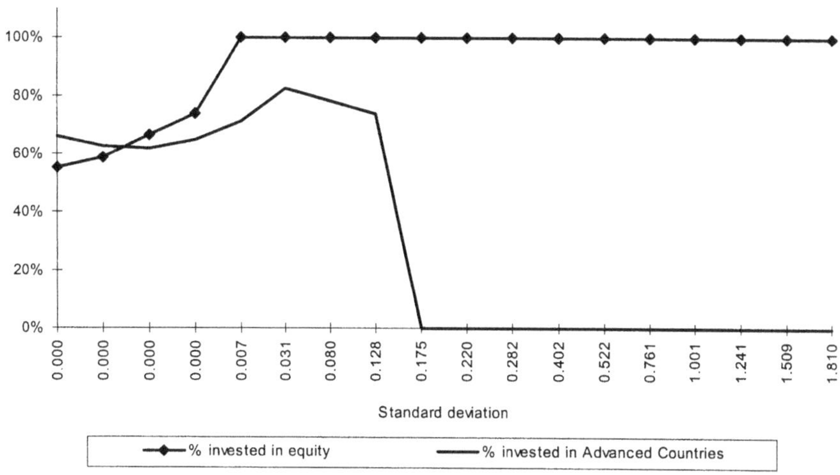

Figure 4.8. Composition, by instrument and country, of efficient portfolios of investments in existing assets.

tions of 0.128 or below); those investors (typically fewer) with a more relaxed attitude toward risk would prefer to look into heavily discounted assets in countries of earlier transition (Figure 4.8). Once more, the portfolio looks more like that of a *Fund* rather than a *Bank*.

IMPLICATIONS AND MAIN CONCLUSIONS

The analysis confirms the powerful influence of the macroeconomic environment on the performance of enterprises and investments. Kaufmann (1991) reaches the same conclusion in his review of a sample of over 1,300 investment projects financed by the World Bank and the International Finance Corporation (IFC) over the last half century (Table 4.5).

This theory is further corroborated by the fact that the countries in transition that have managed to achieve a more stable macroeconomy have also been able to attract larger flows of FDI. Figure 4.9 illustrates this positive, strong correlation by plotting the cumulative FDI per capita by country, during 1989–94, against

Table 4.5. *Economic returns of World Bank and IFC projects under different macroeconomic distortions (rates of return in %)*

Policy distortion index	All projects	Public projects	Private projects
Fiscal deficit[a]			
High (8% or more)	13.4	13.7	10.7
Low (less than 4%)	17.8	18.1	14.3
Trade restrictiveness			
High	13.2	13.6	9.5
Low	19.0	19.3	17.1
Foreign exchange premium			
High (200% or more)	8.2	7.2	*
Low (less than 20%)	17.7	18.0	15.2
Real interest rate			
Negative	15.0	15.4	11.0
Positive	17.3	17.5	15.6

Notes: Insufficient number of observations (less than 10) to make inferences.
[a]Percentage of GDP.
Source: World Bank 1991, 82. Data originate in Kaufmann 1991.

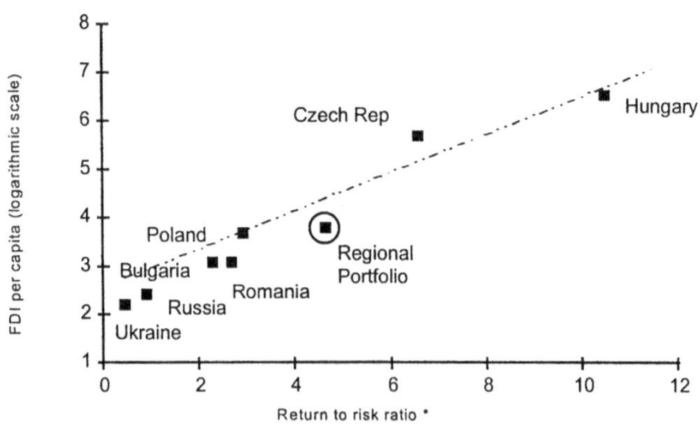

Figure 4.9. Correlation between foreign direct investment and countries return/risk. *Note*: Return to risk ratio as measured by the ratio of the mean return over the standard deviation of each portfolio.

the ratio of the average return over the standard deviation for each country's portfolio.[20]

The huge dispersion of returns to investments in countries of early and intermediate transition may constrain the bankability of these investments through debt instruments. In fact, loan financing can become close to equity risk without upside potential.[21] The recurrent banking failures registered by countries in transition so far – at a high cost for depositors, the public budget, or macroeconomic stability – support this view. By contrast, as we have illustrated in the simulations presented in this chapter, portfolios of equities across sectors and, furthermore, across sectors and countries seem to average out good returns and to diversify risks efficiently. It should be noted, however, that in practice exercising minority shareholders' rights in transition economies is by no means easy, as it is difficult to ascertain that one's own funds are not lost to a fraudulent securities transaction.

The implication may well be that in the early stages of transition, governments should place special emphasis on the development of the capital market – through the building up of effective stock exchanges and related institutions such as securities commission, independent registrars, safe custodians, and secure settlements – so that the stock exchange could serve as the primary vehicle for investment financing. Under this rationale, commercial banks should initially specialize in enhancing the economy's payments system by concentrating predominantly on demand deposits subject to high-reserve requirements. This approach could be particularly relevant for countries that follow a mass privatization model, which inevitably brings about a proliferation of privatization/investment (mutual) funds. Following this somewhat "provocative" logic, only when countries had progressed in their transition beyond a threshold of macroeconomic stability and

[20] The means and variances of country return used in Figure 4.3 are from a different (albeit similar in spirit) simulation study than the one considered in the preceding section. Unlike the simulations of the previous section, those generating Figure 4.3 include a direct, inflation tax–like adverse effect of inflation on enterprise performance. For details see Buiter and Lago 1996. Note that a proper measure of risk would not be based on the variance, but rather on the covariance of country returns with the returns available elsewhere.

[21] The interest rate on loans would have to be priced at high levels, which can cause financial distress for otherwise creditworthy borrowers and/or adverse selection.

structural reform, would long-term deposit taking and financing by commercial banks make sense.

The idea is indeed, tantamount to restating Henry Simons's (1936) equally "provocative" prescription for financial and monetary stability: "Demand-deposit banking would be confined to the warehousing and transferring of actual currency. Savings banks would be transformed into strictly mutual institutions or investment trusts."[22]

APPENDIX

The Model: Financial Performance of the Three Stylized Investments across Countries in Transition

This appendix draws on Buiter et al. 1997. Notation is as follows: x denotes the export sector, m the import substitution sector, n the nontraded sector, and l labor. The gross return, measured in ECU, on one ECU invested in the equity of industry j, denoted θ_j, $j = x, m, n$ can be written as in equations (1), (2), and (3).[23] We assume each enterprise is wound up at the end of the period and that the undepreciated part of the capital stock is sold. We also assume that the rate of inflation of capital goods prices is the same as the general domestic rate of inflation. p_{k_j} is the domestic currency price of a unit of capital in sector j; π_j is the net output per unit of capital in sector j; α_{ij} is the amount of input i used per unit of capital in the production of good j; $i = x, m, n, l$; $j = x, m, n$; p_x is the domestic currency price of exports; p_m is the domestic currency price of imports; p_n is the domestic currency price of nontraded goods and w is the money wage; i is the domestic one-period contractual nominal interest rate; ψ is the domestic rate of inflation; i^* is the foreign one-period contractual nominal rate of interest; δ_j is the proportional rate of depreciation of capital in sector j; γ is the proportional rate of depreciation of the nominal spot exchange rate; τ_j is the tax per unit of capital in sector j; d_j is the ratio of domestic currency debt to capital in sector j and d_j^* the ratio of foreign currency debt to capital in sector j.

[22] Simons 1936, 16.

[23] Strictly speaking, with limited liability, the rate of return to equity in sector j is max $\{0, \theta j\}$. Our simulations allow for this, but we omitted it in the text to avoid unnecessary clutter.

$$\theta_x = \left(\frac{1}{1 - d_x - d_x^*}\right) \left(\begin{array}{l} \frac{1}{p_{k_x}}[p_x\pi_x - p_m\alpha_{mx} - p_n\alpha_{nx} - w\alpha_{lx} - \tau_x] \\ -\left[(1 + i^*)d_x^* + \left(\frac{1 + i}{1 + \gamma}\right)d_x\right] + (1 - \delta_x)\left(\frac{1 + \psi}{1 + \gamma}\right) \end{array}\right) \tag{1}$$

$$\theta_m = \left(\frac{1}{1 - d_m - d_m^*}\right) \left(\begin{array}{l} \frac{1}{p_{k_m}}[-p_x\alpha_{xm} + p_m\pi_m - p_n\alpha_{nm} - w\alpha_{lm} - \tau_m] \\ -\left[(1 + i^*)d_m^* + \left(\frac{1 + i}{1 + \gamma}\right)d_m\right] + (1 - \delta_m)\left(\frac{1 + \psi}{1 + \gamma}\right) \end{array}\right) \tag{2}$$

$$\theta_n = \left(\frac{1}{1 - d_n - d_n^*}\right) \left(\begin{array}{l} \frac{1}{p_{k_n}}[-p_x\alpha_{mn} - p_m\alpha_{mn} + p_n\pi_n - w\alpha_{\ln} - \tau_n] \\ -\left[(1 + i^*)d_n^* + \left(\frac{1 + i}{1 + \gamma}\right)d_n\right] + (1 - \delta_n)\left(\frac{1 + \psi}{1 + \gamma}\right) \end{array}\right) \tag{3}$$

Let z_j be the resources (per ECU worth of capital) available first for servicing debt and then for paying out to shareholders in sector j. For instance, in the export sector,

$$z_x = \frac{1}{p_{k_x}}[p_x\pi_x - p_m\alpha_{mx} - p_n\alpha_{nx} - w\alpha_{lx} - \tau_x] + (1 - \delta_n)\left(\frac{1 + \psi}{1 + \gamma}\right)$$

Assume domestic currency debt and ECU debt are of equal seniority. With an uncertain earnings stream, default becomes a possibility and the return on a loan becomes potentially risky. The (gross) rate of return on a domestic currency-denominated loan to sector j, $1 + \tilde{i}_j$, is given by

$$
\begin{aligned}
1+\tilde{i}_j &= 1+i && \text{if} \quad z_j \geq \left(\frac{1+i}{1+\gamma}\right)d_j + (1+i^*)d_j^* \\
&= (1+i)\left(\frac{z_j}{\left(\frac{1+i}{1+\gamma}\right)d_j + (1+i^*)d_j^*}\right) && \text{if} \quad 0 \leq z_j \leq \left(\frac{1+i}{1+\gamma}\right)d_j + (1+i^*)d_j^* \\
&= 0 && \text{if} \quad z_j \leq 0
\end{aligned} \tag{4}
$$

The gross rate of return on an ECU loan to sector j, $1 + \tilde{i}_j$, is given by

$$
\begin{aligned}
1+\tilde{i}_j^* &= 1+i^* && \text{if} \quad z_j \geq \left(\frac{1+i}{1+\gamma}\right)d_j + (1+i^*)d_j^* \\
&= (1+i^*)\left(\frac{z_j}{\left(\frac{1+i}{1+\gamma}\right)d_j + (1+i^*)d_j^*}\right) && \text{if} \quad 0 \leq z_j \leq \left(\frac{1+i}{1+\gamma}\right)d_j + (1+i^*)d_j^* \\
&= 0 && \text{if} \quad z_j \leq 0
\end{aligned} \tag{5}
$$

In what follows we focus on the computation of the mean-variance efficient frontier, the set of portfolios with the lowest variance of returns for any given mean return. The *Fund/Bank* can invest in either equity participations or domestic currency and ECU loans. Either investment is considered marginal (i.e., does not alter the firms leverage ratios). The *Fund/Bank* can not engage in short sales of equity nor can it invest more than its capital (the *Fund*) or a leveraged multiple of it (the *Bank*).

We simulate the behavior of three sector-specific investment projects in the historical economic environments of the six transition countries – classified in four groups – between 1990 and 1994, interpreting the sample moments as estimates of the (conditional) means, variances, and covariances of mean-variance portfolio analysis. We first focus on "greenfield investments" so that the price of capital is identical across sectors and countries: $p_{k_{x_i}} = p_{k_{m_i}} = p_{k_{n_i}} = 1$ for all countries.

For our greenfield calculations, we assume that during the first period productivity levels in a given industry are the same in all

Table 4A.1. *Input-output coefficients*

Input-output	Export firm	Importable firm	Nontradable firm
Export		0	0
Import	62.4		0.1
Nontraded	2.5	11.2	
Labor	17.1	3.8	10.4

countries. Productivity levels for countries and sectors in subsequent periods are derived endogenously for the remaining periods, using both directly available and indirectly derived productivity growth data. We then discuss the case of investment in existing assets that can trade at a discount or premium.

Input-output coefficients (measured as quantity of input per unit of capital) were extracted from the operating accounts and the balance sheets of enterprises in three specific EBRD projects, as presented in their respective investment reports (Table 4A.1). The projects considered are a chocolate producer for the export sector, a bottle manufacturer for the import-competing sector, and a transportation company for the nontraded sector. They have no claim to generality but are roughly consistent with the findings of Lankes and Venables (1996) who state that in their sample export supply projects are "import intensive" and "skilled labour intensive," the labor bill accounting for 24 percent of the costs. These coefficients are assumed constant over the period of time considered (1990–94).

Gearing ratios of approximately 18 percent for both domestic and foreign currency loans, tax rates of 10 percent, and depreciation rates of 6 percent reflect the average ratios provided in the respective EBRD investment reports.

Returns on Greenfield Investments

We now estimate returns on greenfield investments. In Tables 4A.2 and 4A.3 we provide the mean and standard deviation of the returns to equity and debt in each of the three sectors for the countries of advanced transition (group 1) and early transition (group 3). The contractual interest rates on foreign currency loans

Table 4A.2. *Group 1 (advanced transition)*

	Expected return	Standard deviation
θ_x	1.37	0.21
θ_m	1.09	0.11
θ_n	1.14	0.11
$(1 + \tilde{i}_x)(1 + \gamma)^{-1}$	1.18	0.11
$(1 + \tilde{i}_m)(1 + \gamma)^{-1}$	1.18	0.11
$(1 + \tilde{i}_n)(1 + \gamma)^{-1}$	1.18	0.11
$1 + \tilde{i}^*_x$	1.06	0.01
$1 + \tilde{i}^*_m$	1.06	0.01
$1 + \tilde{i}^*_n$	1.06	0.01

Table 4A.3. *Group 3 (early transition)*

	Expected return	Standard deviation
θ_x	0.57	0.55
θ_m	0.85	0.73
θ_n	0.67	0.58
$(1 + \tilde{i}_x)(1 + \gamma)^{-1}$	0.36	0.49
$(1 + \tilde{i}_m)(1 + \gamma)^{-1}$	0.36	0.49
$(1 + \tilde{i}_n)(1 + \gamma)^{-1}$	0.36	0.49
$1 + \tilde{i}^*_x$	0.73	0.63
$1 + \tilde{i}^*_m$	0.73	0.63
$1 + \tilde{i}^*_n$	0.73	0.63

are LIBOR + 150 for group 1, LIBOR + 300 for groups 2 and 4, LIBOR + 450 for group 3. Contractual interest rates on domestic currency loans are domestic bank loan rates as provided by the International Financial Statistics (IFS) of the IMF. Gearing ratios, taxes, input-output coefficients, and initial productivity levels are assumed the same for all sectors and all countries. Returns differ because of different relative prices and wages, different productivity levels, interest rates, inflation rates, and exchange rate movements. They are thus determined by the interaction of the same microstructure and different macroeconomic conditions.

The returns show that in group 1 there is no default on any of the loans. In group 2 (not shown) there is no default on loans (although the ECU returns on local currency loans are very poor due to very strong exchange rate depreciation). In group 3 there are defaults on loans and equity[24] in the import-competing and nontraded good sectors. In group 4 (Russia), there are some defaults on loans and equity in the three sectors.

From these results, we can see that individual greenfield investments in groups 1 and 2 generally dominate investments in groups 3 and 4. *Greenfield investments have higher returns in countries that are in a more advanced stage of transition.* Nevertheless, returns differ widely by sector. Loans are obviously risky, either because of default risk (in countries of groups 3 and 4) or because of currency risk.

Optimal Portfolios of Greenfield Investments

The data on domestic interest rates are obviously not excessively reliable. When we look for the mean-variance efficient portfolios, we will therefore limit ourselves to equity and foreign currency loans. We show only the nondominated part of the mean-variance-efficient frontier (Table 4A.4). Columns 1 and 2 give the expected return and the standard deviation of the portfolio. In column 3, we show the proportion of the optimal portfolio held in equity and in the other columns we present the respective contributions of the four groups of countries to the optimal portfolio.

Investments in Existing Assets

We now try to allow for the fact that existing assets can sell at a discount in countries with unfavorable (macro)economic conditions – that is, we allow the price of capital p_{K_j} to differ across countries. Our estimate of the magnitude of the existing asset price discount is based on the deviation of the country's exchange rate from the measure of its PPP exchange rate for 1993 as estimated by the Organization for Economic Cooperation and Development (OECD) (Table 4A.5). No intraindustry differences in the discounts on these assets is allowed for.

[24] "Default" on equity simply means that the net rate of return is negative, or the gross rate of return θ_i is less than 1.

Table 4A.4. *Mean-variance efficient portfolios of greenfield investments*

Mean returns	Standard deviation	% equity	Group 1	Group 2	Group 3	Group 4
1.075	0.000	39.0	56.3	32.6	0.0	1.0
1.10	0.000	88.3	79.7	17.0	2.5	0.7
1.125	0.000	90.2	78.1	19.7	1.4	0.7
1.15	0.006	100.0	78.4	21.5	0.0	0.0
1.20	0.022	100.0	71.3	19.2	0.0	0.0
1.25	0.070	100.0	80.7	6.4	0.0	0.0
1.30	0.116	100.0	93.5	2.5	0.0	0.0
1.37	0.210	100.0	100.0	0.0	0.0	0.0

Table 4A.5. *Price of capital with respect to Group 1*

Group	Comparative price level (%)
2	64.8
3	37.4
4	54.8

Returns on Investments in Existing Assets

The means and standard deviations of returns on equity investments and loans in the three industries for groups 2 and 3 are given below in Tables 4A.6 to 4A.7. Since group 1 is our benchmark, returns are the same as for greenfield investments. Investing in existing assets has an impact on the relative profitability ranking of the investments: the high expected return on equity in the export sector for greenfield investments in group 2 was linked to the assumed high initial productivity level. With lower initial levels of productivity in the export sector of group 2, investments in the import-competing and nontraded sectors become relatively more profitable. For group 2, returns on loans are the same as for greenfield investments.

Contrary to the greenfield case, investing in equities in groups 3 and 4 by purchasing preexisting assets becomes very profitable (albeit also very risky) contrary to the case of greenfield investments.

Table 4A.6. *Group 2 (intermediate transition)*

	Expected return	Standard deviation
θ_x	0.72	0.43
θ_m	1.36	0.41
θ_n	1.48	0.50
$(1 + \tilde{i}_x)(1 + \gamma)^{-1}$	0.63	0.32
$(1 + \tilde{i}_n)(1 + \gamma)^{-1}$	0.63	0.32
$(1 + \tilde{i}_x)(1 + \gamma)^{-1}$	0.63	0.32
$1 + \tilde{i}_x$	1.07	0.01
$1 + \tilde{i}_m$	1.07	0.01
$1 + \tilde{i}_n$	1.07	0.01

Table 4A.7. *Group 3 (early transition)*

	Expected return	Standard deviation
θ_x	0.88	0.97
θ_m	2.09	1.81
θ_n	1.79	1.56
$(1 + \tilde{i}_x)(1 + \gamma)^{-1}$	0.36	0.49
$(1 + \tilde{i}_m)(1 + \gamma)^{-1}$	0.36	0.49
$(1 + \tilde{i}_n)(1 + \gamma)^{-1}$	0.36	0.49
$1 + \tilde{i}_x$	0.73	0.63
$1 + \tilde{i}_m$	0.73	0.63
$1 + \tilde{i}_n$	0.73	0.63

Optimal Portfolios of Existing Assets

Mean-variance efficient frontiers of portfolios of investments across sectors and across countries are shown in Table 4A.8. The specific numerical inputs and outputs of the exercise in this appendix are to be viewed as illustrative only. The data we used are highly unreliable; we had to make a number of heroic simplifying assumptions to get estimates of some of the variables we needed to apply our approach; and we could perform historical simulations only for a far too restricted number of periods. Nevertheless the framework we use seems to be useful to link the microeconomic performance of firms to their macroeconomic environ-

Table 4A.8. *Mean-variance efficient portfolios of investments in existing assets*

Mean returns	Standard deviation	% equity	Group 1	Group 2	Group 3	Group 4
1.075	0.000	55.3	66.3	26.7	3.8	3.2
1.10	0.000	58.5	62.8	30.5	2.7	3.9
1.125	0.000	66.6	61.9	31.3	1.9	4.8
1.15	0.000	73.8	64.6	29.3	1.6	4.5
1.20	0.007	100.0	71.2	24.0	0.0	4.7
1.25	0.031	100.0	82.5	17.5	0.0	0.0
1.30	0.080	100.0	78.1	21.8	0.0	0.0
1.35	0.128	100.0	73.7	26.3	0.0	0.0
1.40	0.175	100.0	0.0	85.0	0.0	15.0
1.45	0.220	100.0	0.0	85.2	0.0	14.8
1.50	0.282	100.0	0.0	82.4	1.8	15.8
1.55	0.402	100.0	0.0	72.6	9.8	17.6
1.60	0.522	100.0	0.0	62.8	17.8	19.3
1.70	0.761	100.0	0.0	43.3	33.8	22.8
1.80	1.001	100.0	0.0	23.8	49.8	26.4
1.90	1.241	100.0	0.0	4.2	65.8	29.9
2.00	1.509	100.0	0.0	0.0	83.6	16.4
2.09	1.810	100.0	0.0	0.0	100.0	0.0

ment and can be expected to give very interesting results when more and better data become available.

REFERENCES

Abel, A., A. Dixit, J. Eberly, and R. Pindyck. 1995. "Options, the Value of Capital and Investment." NBER Working Paper no. 5227, August.

Barro, R. 1995. "Inflation and Economic Growth." *Bank of England Quarterly Bulletin* (May): 166–76.

Bruno, M. 1993. *Crisis, Stabilisation and Economic Growth.* Oxford: Oxford University Press.

Bruno, M., and W. Easterly. 1996. "Inflation Crises and Long-Run Growth." NBER Working Paper no. 5290.

Buiter, Willem H., and Ricardo Lago. 1996. "Enterprises in Transition; Macroeconomic Influences on Enterprise Decision-Making and Performance." Mimeographed, EBRD, London, 23 June.

Buiter, Willem H., Ricardo Lago, and Hélčne Rey. 1997. "A Portfolio Approach to a Cross-Sectoral and Cross-National Investment

Strategy in Transition Economies." NBER Working Paper no. 5882.

Buiter, Willem H., Ricardo Lago, and Nicholas Stern. 1997. "Enterprise Performance and Macroeconomic Control." *Banca Nazionale del Lavoro Quarterly Review*. 200 (March): 1–22.

Coase, R. 1937. "The Nature of the Firm." *Economica*. 4 (November): 386–405.

Corden, W. M. 1990. "Macroeconomic Policy and Growth: Some lessons of Experience." In *Annual Conference on Development Economics*, 59–84. World Bank, Washington D.C.

de Melo, M., C. Denizer, and A. Gelb. 1996. "Patterns of Transition from Plan to Market." *World Bank Economic Review* 10, no. 3: 397–424.

Deloitte, Touche Tohmatsu International. 1995. "Taxation in Eastern Europe, 1995." London.

Dixit, A., and R. Pindyck. 1994. *Investment under Uncertainty*. Princeton, N.J.: Princeton University Press.

Dornbusch, R. 1990. "Policies to Move from Stabilization to Growth." In *Annual Conference on Development Economics*, 19–48. World Bank, Washington D.C.

Dunn, A., and A. Pellechio. 1990. "Analyzing Taxes on Business Income with the Marginal Effective Tax Rate Model." World Bank Discussion Paper no. 79, World Bank, Washington D.C.

Easterly, W. 1996. "When Is Stabilization Expansionary? Evidence from High Inflation." *Economic Policy* (1996): 67107.

European Bank for Reconstruction and Development. 1993. *Annual Economic Outlook*. London, September.

European Bank for Reconstruction and Economic Development. 1994. *Transition Report*. London, October.

European Bank for Reconstruction and Economic Development. 1995. *Transition Report*. London, October.

European Bank for Reconstruction and Economic Development. 1995. *Transition Report Update*. London, April.

Fischer, S. 1991. "Growth, Macroeconomics and Development." In *NBER Macroeconomics Annual* 6: 329–64. Cambridge, Mass.: MIT Press.

Fischer, S. 1993. "The Role of Macroeconomic Factors in Growth." *Journal of Monetary Economics* 32: 485–512.

Frydman, Roman, Cheryl Gray, and Andrzej Rapaczynski (eds.). 1996. *Corporate Governance in Central Europe and Russia*. Volume 1: *Banks, Funds and Foreign Investors*. Volume 2: *Insiders and the State*. Budapest: Central European University Press.

Kaufmann, D. 1991. "The Forgotten Rationale for Policy Reform: The Productivity of Investment Projects." Background paper for the *World Development Report 1991*. World Bank, Washington, D.C.

Knight, F. H. 1921. *Risk, Uncertainty, and Profit.* Boston: Houghton Mifflin.

Lankes, H. P., and T. Venables. 1996. "Foreign Direct Investment in Eastern Europe and the Former Soviet Union: Results from a Survey of Investors." Mimeographed, EBRD, London, April.

Leahy, J., and T. Whited. 1996. "The Effects of Uncertainty on Investment: Some Stylised Facts." *Journal of Money, Credit and Banking* 28, no. 1: 64–83.

Pazos, F. 1990. "Runaway Inflation: Experiences and Options." *Cepal Review*, no. 42 (December): 115–130.

Pindyck, R. S., and A. Solimano. 1993. "Economic Instability and Aggregate Investment." In *NBER Macroeconomics Annual*, 8: 259–303. Cambridge, Mass.: MIT Press.

Pissarides, F., J. Svejnar, and M. Singer. 1996. "Small and Medium-Sized Enterprises in Transition: Evidence from Bulgaria and Russia." Mimeographed, EBRD, London, April.

Schaffer, M. 1992. "The Enterprise Sector and the Emergence of the Polish Fiscal Crisis." Mimeographed, LSE, CEP.

Simons, H. C. 1936. "Rules versus Authorities in Monetary Policy." *Journal of Political Economy* 44, no. 1: 1–30.

World Bank. 1991. *World Development Report 1991*. Washington D.C.: World Bank.

PART II
Country Studies

CHAPTER 5

Banking Crises in the Baltic States: Causes, Solutions, and Lessons

Ardo H. Hansson and Triinu Tombak

In transforming a planned economy to a market basis, one sphere that requires particularly deep and difficult reforms is the banking sector. The banking systems and skills that had developed under central planning bear little resemblance to those which these countries now need. Banking regulation and supervision was irrelevant in the past, and had to be developed from scratch. The large degree of needed reforms, combined with the severe real and financial shocks faced by these economies, meant that much could go wrong and did go wrong in the banking sphere.

As other reforms progress, the relative importance of banking issues will grow. Commercial banks will still face difficulties and growing pains long after liberalization and privatization have been largely completed. The dominance of banks in the financial systems of economies in transition further increases the importance of these issues.

Reforms of the banking system can be divided into three main elements: planned "top-down" reforms (e.g., better regulation and supervision, legal reform, privatization, etc.); spontaneous "bottom-up" developments (e.g., new entry, mergers, etc.); and the occasional resolution of sudden and often violent banking crises.

All three elements have been particularly visible in the Baltic states of Estonia, Latvia, and Lithuania. As these countries emerged from a minimally reformed Soviet economic system, in which most decisions were made in Moscow, the extent of needed reforms and institution building was particularly large.[1] As in much of the former Soviet Union (FSU), and moreso than in

[1] This is in contrast to, say, Hungary, Poland, or former Yugoslavia, where significant market elements had been introduced earlier.

Central and Eastern Europe (CEE), the degree of bottom-up development of new banks has been extensive. Most importantly, all three countries have now faced large open-banking crises – Estonia in 1992 and Latvia and Lithuania in 1995. The sharpness of these crises helps to more clearly reveal the underlying causal factors as well as the main lessons from these experiences.[2] The differing influence of various factors in each of the crises also provides useful information on their comparative importance.

This chapter will focus on the nature of, reasons for, and key lessons from the Baltic banking crises. These issues will be discussed in several stages. A description of the major Baltic banking crises and the ways in which they were resolved is followed by discussions of the main factors behind these crises; the general lessons from these experiences for all economies in transition; and the near-term prospects for the Baltic banking systems, which stress the danger of complacency and the likelihood of continued problems. An appendix gives a brief overview of the recent evolution and reform of the Baltic banking systems, which can provide readers unfamiliar with the Baltic states a better context for understanding the Baltic banking crises.

BANKING CRISES IN THE BALTIC STATES

The major banking crises that have now hit all three of the Baltic States have presented their central banks with their greatest challenges. In this section, we broadly discuss how these crises evolved, leaving a discussion of the main reasons for the following section.

Estonia

Estonia was the first of the Baltic states to face a major banking crisis in late 1992, followed by a second smaller crisis in mid-1994. The first episode followed on the heels of Estonia's June 1992 introduction of its new national currency, the kroon. Soon thereafter, Estonian banks began to face rapidly growing delays in

[2] In contrast, banking crises in CEE have been smaller in magnitude and/or better hidden by more gradual reforms and/or extensive bank bailouts.

processing payments, which rose to about one month in November 1992 (Hansson 1995).

After attempts by the Bank of Estonia (BOE) to reduce this backlog through liquidity assistance had no visible impact, it responded with a bold decision to suspend the operations of Estonia's three largest commercial banks on 17 November 1992.[3] The problems of two of these banks – Union Baltic Bank (UBB) and the Northern Estonian Joint-Stock Bank (NEJSB) – were mainly linked to the freezing of their huge assets (about $76 million) in Moscow's Vneshekonombank (VEB), which rendered the banks both illiquid and insolvent.[4] The problems of Tartu Commercial bank (TCB) resulted from a host of shoddy banking practices (including connected lending), losses from foreign-exchange operations, and a weak loan portfolio, particularly a loan of EEK 73 million "guaranteed" by a major state enterprise which failed to be repaid.

This crisis was resolved in a very harsh way. The authorities closed and liquidated TCB with no rescue of depositors, who included many individuals. A liquidation commission was formed to auction the bank's assets, and depositors would be compensated only to the extent that the assets were recovered. So far, household depositors are thought to have recovered 50 percent of their money plus EEK 1,000 ($90) each, while enterprises have on average collected about 15 percent.

The UBB and NEJSB were merged and recapitalized by a combined reduction in liabilities and increase in assets. The former involved the forced exchange of remaining VEB-related deposits for equity claims on a separate BOE-managed "VEB Foundation," which would have the frozen VEB deposits as its sole assets. The fund's stated aim was to recover the maximal amount of these frozen moneys. The remaining capital shortfall was filled via a government bond issue.[5] This operation shared the burden of restructuring between some depositors, bank owners,

[3] The deposit liabilities of these banks together equaled about 40% of M2 (IMF 1993a).

[4] These deposits were created when the correspondent accounts of the NEB and UBB at VEB were credited with payments to Estonian exporters. When these banks were unable to access their VEB deposits, they initially paid exporters out of other resources, a strategy that could not be sustained indefinitely and which finally unravelled.

[5] For an extensive description of this operation and the whole crisis, see Hansson 1995.

and the government. The resulting state-owned Northern Estonian Bank (NEB) was also given temporary liquidity assistance by the BOE.[6]

The second smaller major banking crisis concerned the Estonian Social Bank (ESB), once Estonia's largest bank. ESB had acted as the government's main fiscal agent, and was also financing oil and metals trade. Citing a need to diversify risks, the government began to move some of its deposits to other banks in early 1994. This created liquidity problems and also revealed the bank to be insolvent, mainly as a result of extensive connected lending to small shell companies.

Surprisingly, the BOE initially treated the problem as one of illiquidity and provided loan assistance. When this failed to stem the outflow funds, it was forced to suspend the bank's activities in mid-August 1994. The BOE initially promised to liquidate the ESB, but later reopened it on 26 September with the support of more liquidity loans (the total of such assistance in August and September equaled 6 percent of base money [IMF 1995a]). This move turned out to be premature, as a full restructuring plan was not yet in place. The continued problems of the ESB then overwhelmed the small private Development Bank (DB), which had just bought a majority stake in the ESB.[7]

In the end, the authorities were forced to adopt a costly "classical" bailout of depositors (shareholders of the two banks did lose their investment). The banks were merged and refloated by declaring some BOE and government liabilities subsidiary to other claims, in effect turning government deposits and central bank reserves into equity. Even this move did not save the ESB, which was eventually turned into a loan recovery agency, which in turn was itself declared bankrupt on 26 August 1996.[8]

In 1995, the authorities hastily patched up a potential crisis in the NEB with an untransparent de facto bailout. In spring 1995, the BOE quietly provided the NEB with EEK 40 million of new capital to cover past losses. In August 1995, the authorities sold a

[6] Following this watershed, closing small banks became relatively easy for the BOE. When the Revalia and Narva Commercial Banks encountered difficulties arising from connected lending in 1993, they were closed and declared bankrupt. In both cases, creditors later sold the bulk of the balance sheet to a single buyer as the basis for a new commercial bank (Hansson 1995).

[7] The DB also suffered from connected lending and an overaggressive expansion strategy.

[8] *Eesti Paevaleht*, 27 August 1996. For more on this episode, see IMF 1995a.

one-sixth stake to the Union Bank of Estonia, and gave it control of the management of the bank. The shareholders then provided over EEK 200 million of 6-year guarantees, which could be called in an emergency – that is, fresh capital by any other name. This risky plan assumes that "turnaround management" will allow the bank to grow out of its difficulties, the size of which has yet to be determined by auditors.

Latvia

Until the end of 1994, overt problems in the Latvian banking system were limited to the revoking of licenses of some smaller banks. In 1994, five small and two medium-sized banks (Latvijas Tautas and TOP Banks) were declared insolvent (Fleming and Talley 1996). The major crisis evolved between February and May 1995. The bizarre 2 February arrest of two executives of midsized Lainbank, possibly related to feuds between rival commercial groups, hinted at banking problems and eroded public confidence. Another midsized bank, Latintrade, was suspended in late March.

The unexpected 17 March announcement that Baltija Bank (BB), the largest bank in the Baltics, would merge with Latvian Deposit Bank (LDB) and Center Bank, the sixth and eighth largest in Latvia, signaled a new serious turn of events.[9] BB held 30 percent of all deposits in Latvia, including 200,000 belonging to households. This move, which now appears as a last-ditch effort to stave off a collapse of all three banks, further increased public unease.

The next blow came from the release of, or failure to release, International Accounting Standards (IAS)-based financial statements for 1994 by 1 April 1995 (IMF 1995b), required as part of the Bank of Latvia's (BOL) program to strengthen prudential norms and improve accounting rules and auditing standards.[10] The emergence of previously hidden bad loans and foreign-exchange losses cut the recorded profits and capital of many banks. The fact

[9] LDB had ownership links to Center Bank and strong interbank links to BB. LDB had been a kind of national clearing center for many Latvian banks.

[10] Banks with over LVL 2 million of assets had to be audited by one of the "big six" firms. For more on the package of regulatory and supervisory improvements, see Paeglis 1996, Ross 1996, and Shteinbuka, Sniegs, and Kazaks 1995.

that two-thirds of banks reported losses for 1994 (IMF 1995b), and that BB and ten others had failed to meet the deadline for presenting financial statements (Paeglis 1996) increased public doubts about Latvian banks (Ross 1996).[11] As a result, the volume of resident and nonresident deposits in Latvian banks began to decrease gradually in the spring of 1995 (Ross 1996).

The BOL and some enterprises initially responded with liquidity support to major banks, including an LVL 2.7 million ($5 million) BOL loan to BB (Paeglis 1996). When the insolvency of BB became evident, the BOL ended this support. Yet, rather than immediately closing BB, it began negotiating with BB's managers and owners to devise a restructuring plan. While these negotiations dragged on, BB managers were able to strip the bank of some $260 million of assets (Fleming and Talley 1996). In particular, BB "sold" $160 million of its loan portfolio to Russia's Intertek Bank on 26 April, in exchange for Russian bonds, which may be worth only $48 million (*Baltic Observer*, 7 September 1996). Thus, delays in closing BB greatly increased the size of the hole in its balance sheet. BB was finally declared insolvent on 23 May, when its chairman and president were arrested and the BOL took over the management of the bank. In taking this step, the BOL cited not only insolvency, but also fraud and other criminal activities. LDB had already been closed on 29 April, while Center Bank and the tenth largest Olimpija Bank were closed in early June.

In the end, fifteen banks were suspended during the first seven months of 1995, including nine of those which had failed to present audited financial statements. These banks accounted for about $900 million, or 35–40 percent of banking system assets (Fleming and Talley 1996, Paeglis 1996), and 53 percent of household deposits (Ross 1996). The size of the hole of BB's balance sheet remains unclear pending the resolution of various legal claims and counterclaims.[12] Initial estimates were in the range of $320–380 million, or about 7–9 percent of Latvia's 1995 GDP (IMF 1995b, Fleming and Talley 1996, Paeglis 1996).

[11] BB had even refused to give its auditors full access to its documentation (Fleming and Talley 1996).

[12] The situation in BB was very confused. The bank initiated numerous claims to recover assets, many of which were in turn disputed. The confusion was fueled by missing or inadequate documentation to back the various claims, some of which were for very large sums, the resolution of which will greatly affect the amounts that can be recovered.

In early June, the Latvian authorities opted for a plan to resolve this crisis that combined closure of the failed banks with partial compensation of some deposits. The latter was to be financed by a reallocation of loans earlier received from the European Union (EU) and G-24, and by a new international bond issue. The roughly 500,000 depositors in the failed banks would receive up to LVL 500 ($950) in two stages; LVL 200 in the first year, and up to a further LVL 300 over the next three years (*Baltic Observer*, 21 September 1995). The total cost was estimated at LVL 53 million ($100 million). A harsher "market" approach, which would have placed a greater burden on depositors, was initially ruled out by approaching national elections, and a softer but more costly recapitalization by a tight budgetary situation.

The actual outcome was a bit different. All of the troubled banks were indeed closed. BB was declared insolvent in July 1995 and bankrupt in December 1995. The latter decision was appealed several times but finally confirmed in April 1996.[13] Yet because EU and G-24 monies were not made available for this purpose, while the proceeds of the August 1995 $40 million Eurobond issue were needed to fill a growing budgetary gap, the resources needed for the compensation program were not available. As of November, only 6,124 depositors had received a total of LVL 1.037 million ($2 million). The new government that took office on 21 December 1995 announced that the 1996 budget would not include further such compensations, suspending the program and leaving remaining depositors to collect their share of recoverable assets via bankruptcy. In the end, the crisis was resolved very much like the Estonian one of 1992, but more as a result of circumstance than of conscious design.

Lithuania

Lithuania was the last of the Baltic states to experience a major banking crisis. Until mid-1995, overt problems in its banking sector were limited to the failure and subsequent liquidation (mostly at Bank of Lithuania [BoL] initiative) of some small commercial

[13] The bankruptcy request taken up in the Economic Court on 24 November 1995 was successfully blocked by leading Baltija creditors and parliamentarians.

banks, beginning with Sekundes Bank at the end of 1993 (IMF 1995c).

More serious problems emerged in the summer of 1995, when two medium-sized banks ran into difficulties. Aurabank, then Lithuania's tenth largest and largely privately owned bank, faced a sudden liquidity crisis in June and was put under a de facto moratorium.[14] The authorities initially supported it with short-term liquidity assistance and by moving additional government deposits to the bank (Paeglis 1996). It was finally nationalized in December 1995, and later organized into the Property Bank, a bad-loan unit.

Vakaru Bank, then Lithuania's eighth largest and also privately owned, also experienced problems from the summer of 1995. In November, the government organized an extraordinary T-bill issue to raise LTL 30 million to cover its bad debts (Paeglis 1996). Vakaru was formally closed in December 1995, when an even larger crisis broke out after the leaking of a BoL investigation into the solvency of one bank prompted a gradual withdrawal of funds from banks.

This crisis erupted on 20–21 December 1995, when the BoL and government suspended the activities and arrested the directors of two private banks, the Lithuanian Joint-Stock Innovation Bank (LAIB) and Litimpeks Bank.[15] At the end of November 1995, they were the third and seventh largest banks in Lithuania, together controlling 19 percent of total banking assets (*Bank of Lithuania Monthly Bulletin*, 1996, 1). The portfolios of these banks (esp. LAIB) depended heavily on loans for fuel purchases by financially weak energy companies, including the Ignalina nuclear power plant and Mazeikiai oil refinery. This move came somewhat as a shock, since these banks were widely considered to be among the better ones. It came two weeks after they had agreed to merge to become the largest bank in Lithuania, and spurred an outflow from other banks. During the first two months of 1996, Lithuanian bank deposits fell by 9.5 percent and M2 by 12.2 percent (*Bank of Lithuania Monthly Bulletin*).

In taking this action, the authorities noted serious capital

[14] Paeglis 1996. This bank held negligible household funds (LTL 1.5 million), with most of its deposits belonging to the government and state agencies.

[15] The banks were closed to the public, and the only activity permitted was the collection of loans and other assets.

inadequacy resulting from a weak loan policy (including loans without collateral) and possible fraud. Both banks were also accused of having presented distorted figures to the central bank. As audits are still underway, the size of the hole in their balance sheets is unclear, but initial estimates put this in the range of LTL 420–560 million ($105–140 million) (Paeglis 1996).

The closure of these banks has been called both "decisive" (by the IMF) and "too late" (by a parliamentary commission) (Reuters, 7 February 1996). This step was indeed taken before the outflow had become massive (as in the case of Latvia's BB), and may thus have preempted a wider plundering of funds. Yet, as the weak capitalization of many Lithuanian banks had long been an open secret, others argued that the authorities had acted too slowly.

The ability of the authorities to resolve the crisis was severely constrained by the hasty moves of Lithuania's president and parliament to protect depositors in the two banks. On the day the crisis broke, the president promised that all deposits in these banks would be guaranteed (*Baltic Independent*, 12 January 1996). On 29 December, parliament passed an emergency partial deposit insurance law covering all banks (see the appendix). Other laws instituted full state guarantees for all creditors of LAIB and Litimpeks, mandated the rehabilitation of their operations by 1 February 1996, and allowed up to LTL 300 million of state guarantees on interbank lending.

On 28 January 1996, the authorities announced a sweeping restructuring plan worked out with World Bank and IMF assistance. This called for the merger of LAIB, Litimpeks, and Vakaru into one state-owned bank by 1 July 1996, which would then be recapitalized, restructured, and privatized by the end of 1997 (*Baltic Observer*, 1 February 1996). All deposits in the four crisis banks would be fully guaranteed, while Aurabank would be liquidated. Initial compensation (from unspecified budgetary resources) of up to LTL 1,000 ($250) per depositor was to begin on 1 February 1996, with remaining sums to be paid later (*Financial Times*, 30 January 1996). Household depositors would be the first to get their money back.[16]

[16] These payments began from 1 March 1996 for depositors with accounts having terms that ended before that date (*Baltic Independent*, 23 February 1996). By 19 March, 29,900 of the 52,000 individual depositors in the two banks had received up to LTL 1,000 (*Eesti P'Nevaleht*, 10 April 1996).

In addition, the plan called for the preemptive merger, recapitalization, and privatization of two large troubled banks, the Savings Bank and State Commercial Bank (SCB), and the continuation of a recapitalization and privatization program for the Agricultural Bank. The bad debts removed from the balance sheets of all seven banks would be shifted to a special loan recovery agency. Other banks would be given until May 1996 to meet new capital requirements, under the threat of liquidation (*Baltic Independent*, 2 February 1996).

The cost of the entire restructuring package was placed at a huge LTL 1.3 billion ($325 million), LTL 1.1 billion ($275 million) of which would come from 5–7 year interest-bearing domestic bonds (*Financial Times*, 30 January 1996; *Baltic Observer*, 1 February 1996). The rest would be borrowed from international financial institutions (IFIs), including about $50 million from the World Bank, or come from the budget (*Baltic Observer*, 1 February 1996).

Yet, before enacting this plan, and against the wishes of the IFIs, the authorities gave the banks a few months to prepare their own rescue packages, hoping that this would allow a less expensive resolution.[17] If realistic and acceptable plans were not proposed, the original plan would be enacted. As should have been expected, these insolvent banks proposed plans that had a central role for unconditional government loan guarantees (LTL 220 million in the case of LAIB and LTL 80 million for Litimpeks [*Baltic Securities Update*, February 1996]). Since such support amounts to an injection of fresh capital, it represents a partial bailout of shareholders, and should thus be unacceptable by any reasonable standards.

The actual resolution of the crisis evolved differently from the initial plan. On 21 May 1996, the prime minister announced that the government would nationalize LAIB to prepare a restructuring plan for parliament's approval. Depositors would get full access to their funds once the bank was rehabilitated (*OMRI Economic Digest*, 23 May 1996). This plan, along with a $125 million financing package to fund compensation of depositors by 1 November 1996, was approved by parliament on 18 June (*Baltic*

[17] The banks have persistently lobbied for permission to restore full operation, with support for this move also coming from some members of parliament.

Times, 20 June 1996). Litimpeks Bank was allowed to reopen on 10 June after raising additional capital on its own (*Baltic Times*, 13 June 1996). On 4 September 1996, the BOL began bankruptcy proceedings against Vakaru Bank, hoping that private investors would revive the bank through agreement with creditors (*Baltic Times*, 12 September 1996).

REASONS FOR THE BALTIC BANKING CRISES

Each of the Baltic banking crises was the combined result of several factors, with a different mix at play in each episode. This complicates the analyses of single crises, but also helps to identify the factors that have generally been most important. In this section, we discuss the reasons behind the Baltic banking crises. We first highlight the four which we believe to have been the most important, and then discuss six additional factors.

Major Reasons for the Baltic Banking Crises

The four key reasons for the recent banking crises in the Baltic states were unexpected changes in the macroeconomic environment; inadequate enforcement of existing prudential regulations; abuse by "insiders"; and reckless expansion of assets and/or credits. We discuss each factor in turn.

Unexpected Macroeconomic Changes

Unexpected changes in the macroeconomic environment refer to those changes which banks did not fully anticipate when forming their business strategies. These can in turn be divided into three subcategories. The first, a sudden tightening of domestic macroeconomic policies has been widely discussed in the literature on economic transition. In the period before concerted stabilization, banking became a lucrative and deceptively easy business. Highly negative real interest rates meant that most firms would have little trouble repaying credits. Debtors that did face difficulties could often get ad hoc government support to facilitate loan repayment. The ability of banks to tap cheap central bank credits, earn high incomes from foreign-exchange trading, and arbitrage between cash and noncash money created further profit opportunities.[18]

The onset of macroeconomic stabilization in 1992–93 created a very different environment, which many bankers failed to anticipate and adjust to. Real interest rates rose, reducing the ability of borrowers to repay their loans as originally agreed. Cuts in government subsidies further curtailed their ability to mask financial difficulties. Central bank credits became more expensive or (under the quasi–currency board monetary systems of Estonia and Lithuania) largely unavailable. Stable and unified exchange rates cut the profits from foreign-exchange trading.

This change was quickly felt in Estonia, where the first crisis broke out only 4–5 months after currency reform. Its impact was delayed in Latvia and Lithuania, partly as a result of weaker bankruptcy systems, which allowed the financial problems of firms to be hidden for longer periods, including by running up arrears to other creditors (e.g., suppliers, workers, and the tax authorities). The problems of Latvian banks were compounded by the long average maturities of deposit liabilities relative to those of loans (Shteinbuka et al. 1995). When stabilization finally led to a fall in nominal interest rates, interest income fell more rapidly than did interest expenditures.

A second related factor, less discussed in the transition literature, is a sudden curtailment of capital inflows. This was most crucial in the Latvian case. The rapid initial growth of Latvia's banking system had been fueled by capital inflows, the bulk of which probably came from Russia and other members of the Commonwealth of Independent States (CIS). In 1994, when the total liabilities of banks grew by 97 percent, those to nonresidents grew by a massive 337 percent in lats, and 386 percent in dollars.[19] In the CIS states, a combination of weak and restricted banks, low real interest rates, depreciating domestic currencies, and general instability led asset holders to seek better stores of value abroad.[20] As Latvia was nearby, had no capital controls, and actively sought foreign deposits, it became attractive to many CIS investors.

[18] For more discussion of the early banking environment, see the appendix.

[19] Published statistics do not break this down by source country.

[20] This is analogous to the often noted positive impact on capital flows to emerging markets of low interest rates in industrial countries.

The resulting inflow of capital may have encouraged banks to give riskier loans and increase their exposure to exchange risk (IMF 1995b). Their credit analysis could scarcely have been thorough. It also allowed banks to mask emerging problems, as existing depositors could easily be repaid from new inflows, even when the bank's assets were not performing. In the limit, it created fertile ground for Ponzi (pyramid) schemes, which can only be sustained by a continued inflow of new funds.

In the spring of 1995, Russia's modestly successful stabilization began to bite (Ross 1996). This created a different environment of higher real interest rates and a more stable ruble. Combined with a slight strengthening of some Russian banks and a general tightening of credit conditions, Russian investors had more incentive to repatriate some of their capital held in Latvia and other foreign countries. Liabilities of Latvian banks to nonresidents peaked in December 1994 and BOL net foreign assets one month later, curtailing the liquidity of banks that had relied on new inflows of money. Since depositors would now have to be repaid from loan proceeds, the underlying cash flow problems and bad debts were suddenly revealed.

This factor was also at play in Lithuania, albeit in a somewhat different way. The financial weakness of key Lithuanian enterprises, especially in the energy sector, was long concealed by the government's channeling of official credits to these firms. IMF (1995c) notes that during 1992–94, the government directed almost one-half of its foreign borrowing to finance primary energy inputs.[21] As the financial situation of these firms was getting worse rather than improving, the problems in the real sector could not be concealed for long, and eventually emerged in the form of bad loans.

The third macroeconomic factor, also infrequently discussed in other contexts, was the choice of policy mix. This worked through its impact on the level of real interest rates. In the short-run, tight financial policies usually force up nominal interest rates while cutting inflation. The resulting unanticipated rise in real interest rates reduces the ability of borrowers to repay loans as originally agreed, increasing the potential stock of bad loans.

[21] As Lithuania's official debt stood at $587 million at the end of 1994, this suggests that over $250 million may have gone for such purposes.

This factor appears to have been crucial in Latvia and Lithuania, where a mix of tight monetary policy, loose fiscal policy, and a weak exchange rate peg resulted in very high real (or dollar) interest rates. In Latvia, the growth of central bank net foreign assets (NFA) during 1993–95 was identical to that of base money. Thus, the BOL behaved somewhat like a currency board when viewed over this whole time span. In Lithuania, base money grew slightly less than NFA, meaning that net domestic assets actually fell. Holding other things constant, such tight monetary policy raised real interest rates.

These rates were further increased by a loose fiscal policy. In Latvia, this took the form of central government budget deficits ranging from 0.1 percent of GDP in 1993 to 3.8 percent of GDP in 1995. In Lithuania, it took the form not of open budget deficits, which stayed in the range of 1–2 percent of GDP, but of "quasi-fiscal" deficits. These are losses elsewhere in the economy, which will eventually have to be covered by the state budget. Examples include losses of state-owned enterprises and banks (SOEs and SOBs), which will lead to the future government recapitaliztion of these firms; government loans to enterprises, which will not be repaid as agreed; and the future need to cover loan guarantees, deposit insurance, and other contingent liabilities.[22]

Finally, the credibility of the pegs of the lats to the SDR and litas to the U.S. dollar were reduced either by the lack of a clear commitment to defend the peg at all costs (Latvia), or by the stipulation that one authority alone could change the exchange rate after mere "consultation" with another (Lithuania).[23] As capital mobility was high in both countries, the uncovered interest parity condition implied that a market expectations of devaluation would push domestic interest rates above foreign levels (Hansson and Sachs 1994).

The perceived weakness of the existing peg is most evident in BB's strategy of taking lats deposits and giving dollar loans, which led to a large open foreign exchange position (Hallagan 1995,

[22] For an extensive discussion of these problems in the Baltic states, see Hansson 1996.

[23] The original Lithuanian law allowed the government to change the peg in consultation with the BoL. Later, these responsibilities were reversed. Had Lithuania adopted, for example, a "double key" system, where the approval of both was required, the peg would have been more credible in the short-term.

Shteinbuka et al. 1995, Fleming and Talley 1996). This strategy was clearly based on expectations that the lats would be devalued, as evidenced by the high interest rates that BB paid for lats deposits relative to those on foreign currency deposits or loans. BB may have believed that its expectations would become self-fulfilling, since its "too big to fail" status would force the BOL to devalue in order to save it. Instead, the lats appreciated gradually from 0.595 LVL/USD at the end of 1993 to 0.548 LVL/USD one year later, resulting in large interest income and revaluation losses for BB. By early 1995, growing confidence in the exchange rate peg led to a drop in interest rates,[24] but by this time the damage had been done.

In contrast, Estonia chose a very different policy mix. Within the constraints of the currency board system, the BOE pursued a loose monetary policy. This included a sharp reduction in de facto minimum reserve requirements (IMF 1995a), additional reductions in the reserve requirement on household deposits at the Savings Bank, and the growth of BOE net domestic assets as a result of banking crises and other central bank losses. This was combined with a very tight fiscal policy, with the central government running consistent surpluses over the period 1990–95.[25] Finally, the stipulation in law that only parliament could devalue the kroon (which would be very difficult in practice) gave the exchange rate peg great short-term credibility. All of these factors worked to keep nominal interest rates very low, and real interest rates negative. As a result, borrowers were squeezed less, reducing the growth of bad loans.[26]

[24] The average interest rate on new 3–6 month credits fell from 68.3% in June 1994 to 36.7% in March 1995.

[25] In addition, quasi-fiscal deficits so far appear to have been smaller in Estonia than in the other two Baltic states (Hansson 1996).

[26] Negative real interest rates do, however, create a potential for greater risks in the future. In an environment in which negative rates are combined with large capital inflows and a recovering economy, granting loans can appear to be a deceptively easy business. This can cause Estonian bankers to become overly confident in their ability to avoid bad loans. Were these favorable conditions to end, for example, due to a capital outflow leading to a credit squeeze, and thus to higher interest rates and lower inflation rates, the volume of bad loans could grow rapidly. Even without such a shock, current rates of inflation will not be sustained indefinitely, meaning that adjustment to lower inflation rates is needed in any case. This requires Estonian bankers and bank regulators to anticipate a rise in future real interest rates and a slowdown in the growth of bank liabilities, and to make preemptively the required adjustments in macroeconomic assumptions, loan-loss reserves, and restrictions on bank lending practices.

Inadequate Enforcement of Existing Prudential Regulations

The second key factor behind all Baltic banking crises has been an inadequate enforcement of existing bank regulations.[27] Weak enforcement was the combined result of many factors, the most obvious being the small number and inexperience of supervisors. As all Baltic central banks had often been urged by the international financial institutions to increase the number of supervisors, and offered technical assistance to do so, their failure to take this advice could partly reflect an initial lack of appreciation for the importance of banking supervision.

In addition, Baltic supervisors apparently focused their efforts on small banks, but were more wary of tackling larger banks (this now appears to be changing in Latvia). This was a clear misallocation of resources, as most small banks held few household deposits and presented little systemic risk. The unwillingness of the regulatory authorities in economies in transition to bring larger banks into line appears to reflect the combined effect of four factors: a weak appreciation for the dangers of banks not fulfilling prudential regulations; a (usually unfounded) hope that existing problems will go away on their own, that banks will somehow grow out of their difficulties;[28] the strong political power of some bank owners and/or managers, including the support of some parliamentarians and officials for failed large banks;[29] or outright physical fear when banks had a criminal element.

The first factor must have been important in the first crises in each country, since the need to enforce strictly prudential regulations might not become clear until driven home by painful experiences. In subsequent episodes, when the lessons from the first banking crisis should have been learned, only the latter three factors can be explanations for the passivity of the regulatory authorities.

[27] Problems with the regulations themselves are discussed later.

[28] This sentiment may have been further fueled by the fear that allowing banking problems to come out into the open would lead to accusations that the authorities had failed in bank supervision.

[29] In Latvia and Lithuania, some parliamentarians took up the cause of the failed banks with unusual vigor, and lobbied for their quick reopening or against a formal declaration of bankruptcy; see *Baltic Independent*, 1 December 1995, for a description of such actions in the BB case. The less visible support of state officials for given bank owners or managers cannot be documented, but should not be ruled out in any country.

Moreover, the failure to take action against large banks is more likely to have been at the level of central bank management than of the supervisory staff, and not only because the latter lack the mandate to take such actions. It is unlikely that supervisors had been unaware of the problems in banks that later failed and had not reported these to senior management. In small countries like the Baltics, supervision is facilitated by the free flow of information within a banking community where "everyone knows everyone." In this setting, the location and nature of most major problems will hardly be a secret, even under weak accounting rules.[30] While such informal information alone cannot be the basis for taking action against a particular bank, it will point supervisors to the real problems.

Evidence of weak enforcement abounds. The IMF (1994) noted Estonia's need for better enforcement of regulations. The extensive connected lending that had taken place in the ESB was an open secret in the banking community, yet the ESB was allowed to continue operating until a crisis actually broke out. The weakness of management at the NEB, where a potential crisis was patched up in 1995, was also well known in the banking community, but neither the government as owner nor the BOE as regulator took early steps to remedy the situation.

In Latvia, the IMF (1995b) noted that "the progress achieved in introducing prudential regulations and in monitoring financial institutions has not always been matched by adequate enforcement." The unsustainability of BB's strategy of betting against the lats and aggressively expanding its balance sheet by attracting lats deposits with up to 90 percent interest rates (Hallagan 1995) must have been clear, but resulted in no sanctions. The failure to close BB as soon as problems emerged allowed the noted transfer of assets to Russia's Intertek Bank (Fleming and Talley 1996). Shteinbuka et al. (1995) argue that "while the appropriate regulations were in place, there were inadequate administrative means for enforcing them."[31] Paeglis (1996) argues that "commercial banks did not take the central bank's demands seriously." Subsequently, the BOL took part of the blame for the banking crisis,

[30] In contrast, banking supervisors in Russia face a much more daunting task, since each bank can more easily remain anonymous.

[31] They do, however, note that it is not clear whether many improvements were possible in practice, given the large number of banks that had to be supervised.

agreed that tighter supervision was needed to avoid a repeat, and took highly praised steps to improve supervision (Fleming and Talley 1996; *Baltic Independent*, 6 October 1995).

In Lithuania, the IMF (1994c) noted that "enforcement procedures are not yet well developed." Paeglis (1996) claims that the BoL has been "to a large extent neglecting its duties as the supervisor of commercial banks," noting that it had conducted no audits of banks between 1992 and November 1995. Later, the weak capital base if not insolvency of some banks was an open secret in the banking community. Ideally, the operation of at least the insolvent ones would have been quickly suspended. Instead, these banks were allowed to continue operating, further increasing the size of the hole in their balance sheets.

Other prudential regulations were also not enforced effectively. One owner of LAIB reportedly received loans of LTL 100 million ($25 million) (Paeglis 1996; *Baltic Observer*, 18 January 1996), while the bank's registered capital in October 1995 was only LTL 42 million. This was far in excess of limits on connected lending and exposure to a single borrower. In May 1996, the governor of the BOL announced that only three banks had met all performance criteria, while five banks did not satisfy a single one of them (*OMRI Economic Digest*, 23 May 1996).

Abuse by Insiders

The third major reason for Baltic banking crises was abuse by insiders, who include bank managers, bank owners, and the state. In many cases, owners, managers, and the state are the same or highly related, making it hard to separate the three.

Abuse by managers was facilitated by poor corporate governance of banks, which reduces the accountability of managers to owners. In some cases, supervision by owners was hampered by poorly worded bank statutes. Weak governance was probably most crucial in the SOBs, because in the early phase of economic transition the state can be very poor at supervising its own firms. Evidence is largely anecdotal and includes the failure to dismiss managers whose incompetence was widely known, the payment of high salaries, and the construction of opulent bank offices at a time when the balance sheets were already weak.

Much more important has been abuse by owners, usually in the form of connected lending. This grew out of the way in which many new commercial banks were formed with the explicit aim of crediting owners. In the ruble era, when interest rate ceilings led to an excess demand for loans, new shareholders were often attracted by promises of better access to credits. Owners were able to pressure those in management (who Bourke [1996] terms "powerless figureheads") into giving loans to their own poorly screened and very risky projects. This sometimes took the form of "distress borrowing" by firms that were clearly poor credit risks. Owners could often receive many times more resources in the form of loans than they had put in as equity.[32]

These factors were clearly at play in several Estonian bank failures (ESB, Revalia Bank, Narva Commercial Bank). In Latvia, the failed Kredo Bank supposedly issued 98 percent of its credits to one owner (*Baltic Independent*, 24 November 1995). The failed Latvian Credit Bank had issued 60 percent of credits to associated persons. Connected lending was also crucial in the collapse of BB (IMF 1995b). Of nineteen Latvian banks that had become insolvent, fourteen had exceeded limits on lending to owners (Paeglis 1996).

As noted already, connected lending was extensive at LAIB. The fact that the Ignalina nuclear power plant was both a major shareholder and recipient of loans at Litimpeks suggests similar problems there. Aurabank reportedly gave its largest shareholder LTL 45 million ($11.2 million) loan plus an unrestricted credit line (Paeglis 1996). Similar problems were rumored at Vakaru Bank.

Unfortunately, connected lending is very difficult to control in practice, as bank owners can easily hide behind several layers of offshore companies (Paeglis 1996). Formal legal definitions can be easy to circumvent, as a "related business partner" is nearly impossible to define unambiguously. Connected lending has also facilitated intentional bankruptcy (e.g., attracting as many deposits as possible with the intention of vanishing with these funds, often via an offshore firm) and outright fraud.

Finally, abuse by the state (or forced "public policy lending") was most prevalent in Lithuania. One reason was the government's ownership stake in major banks, which gave it direct leverage over their lending decisions – that is, led to "official connected

[32] See Shteinbuka et al. 1995 for a good discussion of the motivations of some Latvian bank owners.

lending." This was most evident in the energy sector, where price controls forced firms to sell their output at below cost. The financing of these losses through large explicit subsidies was ruled out by a tight state budget. Thus, low energy prices could only be sustained by providing funds in the form of loans. Yet, a loan to a money-losing borrower does not inject fresh capital, but simply keeps it liquid. When this loan is given with few if any conditions, the borrower is likely to be further decapitalized.

The IMF (1995c) notes that the Agricultural Bank extended credit partly under direction of the parliament and government. The Savings Bank and Agricultural Bank have reportedly each given the state energy company $20 million of loans on favorable terms (*Baltic Times*, 16 May 1996).[33] Most strikingly, a December 1994 BoL decision to waive the reserve requirement for the Agricultural Bank for three months so that it could extend a $12.5 million loan to the energy sector (IMF 1995c) could only lead to deeper banking problems down the road.

The state can even pressure banks in which it does not hold shares to give commercially unjustified loans. All banks will try to keep good relations with the authorities, not only because of their regulatory clout, but because they are potentially large customers, for example, through the current accounts of ministries and state agencies: the privately owned LAIB was a major lender to the Ignalina power plant and Mazeikiai oil refinery.[34]

Reckless Expansion

The final major reason for the Baltic crises was the reckless expansion of bank assets and/or loans. Any bank will have a maximum rate at which it can safely expand, beyond which loan evaluation begins to suffer and internal controls begin to fray. Such expansion is especially dangerous when fueled by liabilities attracted by above-market interest rates. As this constraint is on the ability to absorb a rapid flow of new loans, the fact that the Baltics began from a low stock of credits relative to GDP is not relevant.

The growth rate of nominal and real bank balance sheets during a calendar year is shown in Table 5.1, with the real rate of growth

[33] For example, in November 1995, the Mazeikiai refinery borrowed a $4 million from the Savings Bank to finance purchases of crude oil (*Baltic Observer*, 23 November 1995).

[34] An alternative interpretation is that such lending was not urged by the government, but done under the presumption that these borrowers would be "too big to fail" and thus be bailed out by the state.

Table 5.1. *Growth of commercial bank assets in the Baltic states*

	1993	1994	1995
Nominal growth rate of bank assets			
Estonia	33.5	57.6	47.5
Latvia	53.3	96.8	−27.9
Lithuania	—	74.9	8.1
Real growth rate of bank assets			
Estonia	−1.6	11.2	14.4
Latvia	15.6	55.8	−41.4
Lithuania	—	20.6	−20.2

Sources: Central bank statistics, IMF International Financial Statistics. Latvian figures for 1993 are annualized rates based on data for the last 11 months.

expressed relative to the consumer price index (CPI). Had 1992 data been available, they would have shown a large decline in real assets as a result of inflation. The key figure to note is the massive 55.8 percent real growth of bank assets in Latvia in 1994, immediately before its 1995 banking crisis, which was followed by an equally sharp decline. In a setting where the economy was stagnant, the 1994 tempo was hardly sustainable.[35]

These aggregate figures hide the even faster growth of new banks, which increased their share of total assets from 23 percent at the end of 1992 to 89 percent two years later (Fleming and Talley 1996). For example, BB increased its assets from $25 million in January 1993 to $242 million in January 1994 (a real annual growth rate of over 600%!) and then to almost $500 million by early 1995 (a further real increase of about 60%) (Fleming and Talley 1996). In Lithuania, the growth of the new LAIB into one of the largest banks suggests a similar rapid tempo.

Other Factors Leading to Banking Crises

Six other factors were of more modest importance in the Baltic banking crises. Most are well understood and discussed in other

[35] BOL governor Repse later agreed that "banks developed too fast" (*Baltic Observer*, 5 October 1995).

settings. Although we discuss these in the past tense, most remain important today. The first is the impact of market reforms on the fortunes of individual enterprises. Reforms not only faced firms with hard budget constraints, but also led to a very different structure of relative prices and other incentives than under central planning. Some firms that had been profitable under the old system would now be unviable and unable to service their debts on the agreed terms. This particularly concerned energy-intensive producers, which suffered from a move to world market prices for fuels.

The importance of this factor was diminished in the FSU by the near hyperinflation of the early 1990s. This led to a de facto restructuring of all domestic currency-denominated debts, and meant that the portfolio of an average bank would soon be dominated by fresh loans rather than ones given in the past. It is likely to be more important in, for example, Hungary or ex-Czechoslovakia, where low inflation preserved the real value of old debts.[36]

The second such factor is an inadequate legal and regulatory framework. Understandably, early banking laws in the Baltics were weak or incomplete. Prudential regulations were limited or vaguely worded. Licensing requirements were minimal, meaning that persons who were unfit to be bankers were able to enter this sector. Supervisors were limited in their ability to change control of an existing bank, remove bank managers, fine banks, give cease-and-desist orders, or close or liquidate a bank that failed to meet existing regulations. Limits on banks' investments in real estate and equities were weak or nonexistent. The resistance of individual banks and banking associations to the needed tighter limits slowed their adoption (Bourke 1996).

For example, Estonia's first banking law only stated vaguely that "the BOE implements control of the debts of banks to foreign creditors in accordance with Estonian law." It placed no limits on the allowed exposure to a single debtor. This allowed UBB and

[36] One exception was the terms-of-trade shock resulting from increases in Russian raw materials prices, which occurred after Baltic stabilization had taken hold. When the prices of these goods were kept artificially low, their export through Baltic harbors offered extremely high rates of return for traders. If banks that financed such operations did not understand the temporary profitability of this trade, they could be left holding many bad loans. Some banks were highly exposed to such firms, and suffered accordingly.

NEJSB to accumulate huge exposures to VEB without sanctions. In the end, deposits of these banks in VEB totaled $76 million, compared with their combined share capital of a mere $1 million (Hansson 1995).

Latvia's May 1992 commercial bank law was a six-page-long "bare-bones first effort" to provide a legal framework for banking (Fleming and Talley 1996). It did not specify any prudential regulations, but merely allowed the BOL to establish these (World Bank 1993b). Until late 1994, Latvia had no restrictions on open foreign-exchange positions (Ross 1996). Lithuania's first commercial bank law did not allow the BoL to remove managers of banks without the approval of the owners.

In addition, the lack of proper land and collateral registries allowed borrowers to pledge the same assets several times (*Baltic Observer*, 14 September 1995), meaning that apparently secured lending was really unsecured. This increased the possibilities for fraud and the risks faced by banks in providing loans (Shteinbuka et al. 1995).

The third source of problems was weak accounting laws and auditing requirements, particularly concerning loan-loss provisioning. The ability of banks to roll over problem loans concealed their true solvency and created a false picture of health. Bank profits and thus net worth were overstated. When the hidden problems finally emerged, especially through improved accounting and auditing, the resulting erosion of profits and capital was unexpected. When large, these changes could transform a seemingly solvent bank into an apparently insolvent one. Thus, these changes did not cause crises, but simply brought them forward in time. Other difficult accounting issues include the possible fictiveness of capital (i.e., buying shares with funds borrowed from the same or another bank), and the treatment of guarantees and other contingent liabilities.[37]

The role of these factors is evident in Latvia and Lithuania. In Latvia, the BOL decision to require banks with total assets of over LVL 2 million to be audited by one of the "big six" firms revealed the weak state of BB and other banks. In Lithuania, new loan classification and provisioning rules were introduced in April 1994. In that year, the BoL instructed all except three banks to

[37] For a discussion of such ficticious capital in the BB case, see Paeglis 1996.

build up reserves in anticipation of dealing with bad loans, rather than pay out dividends (in 1993, most paid dividends) (IMF 1995c). The resulting cut in profits and capital may have hit (previously excessive) public faith in the banking system.

The fourth such reason is weak and inexperienced bank management. As some of the banking skills (e.g., credit analysis and liquidity and risk management) required in a free-market environment must be learned partly by trial and error, some of the resulting mistakes were unavoidable. Others reflect missed opportunities. For example, many lending decisions at Estonia's TCB appear to have been made at the whim of the managing director, without using even the limited credit analysis skills that were available. In all three countries, some loans have been given without collateral, or with illiquid collateral, which has little value outside its existing use. Some banks had poor internal controls, spent more on building opulent premises than on creating solid loan departments, and gave loans with poor or absent documentation.[38]

A fifth reason was moral hazard. Banks could lend to patently weak enterprises, for example, in the energy or agroprocessing sectors, on the presumption that the state would be forced to come to their rescue. Even when no explicit deposit insurance was available, depositors might have placed funds in obviously weak banks presuming that these would be bailed out. Finally, some banks may have even counted on having their equity compensated – they believed that the government would recapitalize them without a dilution of existing equity claims. All of this fueled reckless banking behavior.

In a few episodes (e.g., ESB and Aurabank), a sixth and final reason was the sudden removal of government deposits. These withdrawals were motivated by the rational desire to protect the value of deposits in cases where the government may have caught wind of impending problems. Yet, a rapid withdrawal could have brought the inevitable crisis forward by increasing short-term liquidity problems. In these episodes, the failure of the supervisors to have closed these banks earlier was more to blame than the government actions, which only revealed the underlying problems.

[38] For instance, some banks issue guarantees that were unrecorded, or had falsified signatures.

LESSONS FROM THE BALTIC BANKING CRISES

The concrete episodes and causal factors we have described provide many lessons for reducing the risk of banking crises in economies in transition, as well as for managing and resolving these. In this section, we draw out the most important of these lessons.

Banking Crises Are a Highly Likely Outcome of Economic Transformation

Most economies in transition that have made good progress in stabilization have now experienced serious banking difficulties. Some have emerged as open crises, while others have been at least temporarily resolved by overt or hidden bailouts. The regularity of such problems in the "second phase" of economic transformation suggests that, in one form or another, they are highly likely if not inevitable.

The link with transition is not so much through the direct channel of structural change – that is, the changing fortunes of individual borrowers. Some of the more spectacular collapses in the Baltics were not in the former SOBs, which would be most burdened by the legacy of the past, but in new commercial banks (TCB, BB, LAIB, etc.), which had started with a clean slate and could choose among potential clients.

The main impact of transition was the temporary vacuum that it produced in the form of an initially inadequate legal, institutional, and knowledge basis for banking in a market economy. Bankers could not hope to understand or predict a change in macroeconomic conditions they had never experienced before, or to learn quickly the credit analysis skills needed in the new setting. Well-functioning laws took time to be put in place. The practical skills of supervision could not be learned overnight. Many of the needed changes would only be prompted by a serious crisis, which clearly showed their importance and thus spurred action. Yet, postponing stabilization or legal and institutional reform in the name of delaying banking crises was not a serious option either. In such a vacuum, much could go wrong.

Though almost inevitable, banking crises are not entirely negative. They do have high direct costs in terms of lost income and output. Before the banking crisis, the Latvian economy had been expected to grow by 4–5 percent in 1995. Instead, it shrank by 1.6 percent, and will barely begin recovering in 1996. Yet, crises are also opportune moments to strengthen financial discipline, to bolster the reputation of the authorities as tough players, to weed out high-risk banks, and to spur serious real restructuring. When well handled, large crises can consolidate rather than derail stabilization and reforms. The 1992–93 banking crisis was in many ways a positive turning point for the Estonian economy. Latvia also appears to be emerging with a smaller but stronger banking sector and growing confidence in the stability of the economy, as revealed by sharply dropping nominal interest rates.

Lessons for Minimizing the Risk and Size of Banking Crises

Yet, while crises of some form will occur, their number and severity can be reduced by proper preventive steps. We focus on ten key lessons for minimizing the risk and size of banking crises.

1. Very rapid real growth of bank assets or loans is often not healthy, but rather a sign of reckless lending and thus of potential future crises. Fast growth of the banking sector can lead to a boom-and-bust cycle of high profits and major losses, which is less optimal than a slower but more sustainable growth of banking assets. Put differently, growing intermediation should not always be encouraged or applauded. When excessive growth is general – that is, visible in the consolidated balance sheet of commercial banks – the central bank can use aggregate instruments (higher minimal reserve requirements or capital adequacy and liquidity ratios) to slow the rate of credit expansion. When restricted to a few banks, and especially when fueled by payment of very high interest rates on liabilities, the reaction (beginning with moral suasion and ending with sanctions) should come from bank supervisors.

2. In a related way, large foreign capital inflows can increase the likelihood of banking crises. These have several positive elements (e.g., as a sign of confidence in the economy, greater access to financing for needed projects, etc.), but also increase the fragility of the banks that intermediate them.[39] At best, large net inflows into banks will help to conceal their true level of bad loans.

[39] For a theoretical analysis of some of these dangers, see Goldfajn and Valdes 1995.

At worst, they can facilitate Ponzi schemes. The resulting depression of real interest rates will create a feeling of overconfidence among bankers and supervisors by making banking look deceptively easy. Large capital inflows can also lead to real exchange rate appreciation, which erodes the competitiveness of past borrowers. Preemptive efforts to slow capital inflows can thus reduce the risk of future disturbances.

3. Problems can emerge even where quantitative indicators show that all is fine. A given bank's expansion can be highly dependent on the joint continuation of several trends, such as rapid growth of liabilities, low real interest rates, and sustained economic growth.[40] When one of these elements moves differently than expected, even by a small amount, the bank's whole strategy can unravel. Because the true health of banks can be much poorer than standard ratios indicate,[41] bank supervisors must rely on more qualitative information.

4. The mix of macroeconomic policies can influence the risk and size of banking crises. A combination of loose fiscal policy, tight monetary policy, and a weak exchange rate peg is a recipe for very high real interest rates. Enterprises that had received loans on the basis of lower assumed rates would face difficulties in repaying these debts. Moving toward tighter fiscal policies and more credibly stable exchange rates, possibly in combination with a bit looser monetary policy, can help bring high real interest rates down to manageable levels.[42]

5. An overly liberal regulatory environment is very dangerous. In the early phase of transition, banks that are given too much freedom of action will be prone to abuse this, if not consciously then out of inexperience. Therefore, standard prudential norms should be very tight, and possibly tighter than those in developed

[40] For example, the Estonian Social Bank relied on the government keeping the bulk of its current accounts there, while Baltija Bank's strategy depended upon a near-term devaluation of the lats.

[41] Right before its collapse, the ESB appeared to be in compliance with most of the standard prudential ratios. In 1994, BB reported large profits and net worth. LAIB was thought to be one of the better banks in Lithuania. In addition, the fact that only 2 percent of the assets of the failed Latintrade bank have so far been recovered indicates the large potential gap between apparent and real solvency.

[42] In Latvia, interest rates on government T-bills have dropped sharply from March 1996. One explanation is that a reduction in the budget deficit relative to 1995 has cut the government's need to borrow money, reducing the supply of bonds and lowering interest rates.

market economies. This holds especially when weak accounting laws lead to an overstatement of the net worth of banks. Tight limits on the value of equity and real estate in total assets, and on the degree of connected lending are particularly important. Laws should give supervisors intermediate instruments between doing nothing and closing the bank.

6. A central bank that appreciates the need for stronger supervision can improve its effectiveness with a few relatively easy steps. More supervisors can be hired and trained.[43] The focus of supervisory efforts can shift from small banks toward the larger ones that really matter. A focus on outliers (e.g., banks with unusual interest rate policies or rapid growth rates), or on unusual merger proposals involving large banks, will often point supervisors to where the main problems lie.

7. More important than improved laws, regulations, and supervision is a willingness of the central bank management to enforce existing regulations and take action against banks that are not in compliance. Put differently, the main bottleneck is often not weaknesses in existing laws or a lack of information about where problems lie, but an unwillingness or fear to enforce existing limits on the basis of available information. Again, taking action against small banks is relatively unimportant, and no indication of real resolve. What really matters is how medium- and large-scale banks are treated.

8. Abuse by insiders is an important source of banking problems, albeit one difficult to control. Better corporate governance cannot simply be imposed, although boards of directors of SOBs can be improved by better selection and compensation. Connected lending can be relatively easily concealed. One possible solution is to allow regulators to act on the basis of more qualitative information, as connected lending can be fairly obvious yet hard to prove. Tighter limits on the ability of "offshore" companies to own stakes in banks, as in recent changes to the Latvian banking law, could limit one of the prime channels for connected lending.

9. The government should not abuse commercial banks for political goals, especially by urging them to lend to insolvent SOEs. Such lending will solve a short-term financial problem, but at the expense of greater problems in the future.

[43] In many cases, technical assistance for facilitating this will already be on offer.

10. Privatization is not a sufficient condition for creating more prudent commercial banks. In the Baltics, some of the most severe crises occurred in largely private banks (TCB, BB, LAIB, etc.), while the until recently state-owned Unibank acted relatively prudently.[44] Before good laws and effective supervision are finally established, the proclivity of private owners to abuse their banks can be as great as the ineffectiveness of state-owners in managing theirs. If banks perceive the authorities to be weak, they will act imprudently regardless of who their owners are.

Lessons for Handling Banking Crises Once They Have Broken Out

As no two banking crises are alike, the lessons for handling these are far less general. The ideal strategy depends on the specific circumstances, particularly on the degree of systemic risk and interbank exposure. Still, at the risk of excessive generalization, we present seven more robust lessons.

1. Once serious problems emerge, it is important to act quickly. Otherwise, the cost of their eventual resolution can grow rapidly. Insiders or market participants who sense an impending crisis will have very different incentives than normally. In some cases, they will try a "double or nothing" strategy to save the bank with a single very risky deal that would rescue the bank if it were to pay off, but further deepen problems if it failed (e.g., at Estonia's TCB and Revalia Bank). Alternatively, if the bank seems doomed to failure, insiders will have incentives to strip assets, harming the interests of other creditors and/or shareholders (e.g., at Latvia's BB). Also, a closed bank should never be opened before its solvency and liquidity have been clearly restored. If players understand that a reopened bank is not viable in the medium run, they will try to withdraw their money at once, spurring a new crisis.[45]

2. When a bank's problems reflect insolvency, these cannot be solved by central bank lending or the transferring of government deposits. The initial treatment of many of the described episodes

[44] Just as many counterexamples can be found – for example, the poorly managed state-owned NEB compared to the innovative new private Estonian banks.

[45] Such behavior was evident at the ESB, and would be likely to occur if the closed Lithuanian banks were allowed to reopen before having clearly been recapitalized.

as liquidity crises merely increased the final cost to the state. Such actions are effectively bailouts of well-connected creditors with public funds. If liquidity ("lender of last resort") assistance is provided, this should go to other banks that might face a temporary run on deposits, rather than to the insolvent banks.

3. When a crisis occurs in the early stages of a banking sector's development, the option of liquidating rather than rehabilitating banks should be strongly considered. The way in which authorities react to the first major crisis will greatly affect their reputation as "tough" or "soft." If a soft resolution leads depositors or bank owners to believe that they will again be rescued, the costs of resolving future crises will grow. The softer authorities have been in the past, the more painful will be the resolution of new crises, but also the more there is to gain from taking a stand and strengthening their reputation.[46] Liquidation in Estonia in 1992–93 and Latvia in 1995–96 left those countries with more conservative and potentially stronger banks.

4. The slow pace of bank privatization in economies in transition also argues in favor of liquidation, as this avoids the renationalization of failed banks. Clients of liquidated banks will slowly move to other banks, some of which are private. Rehabilitation plans that call for a rapid divestiture of the resulting state stake may be too optimistic, not only because privatization will be slow, but also because the market value of the bank can shrink further (if not disappear) while under state management.

5. Rehabilitation should be considered only when there is a clear systemic risk. If undertaken, it should always be conditional, and at a minimum involve the ousting of existing management and shareholders.

6. Restructuring plans presented by owners of insolvent banks are rarely credible, as they usually involve a de facto government bailout of the same shareholders who led the bank into its problems.[47] Such plans should only be considered if they involve no government guarantees and will obviously restore solvency.

[46] For this reason, Bank of Latvia governor Repse was critical of Lithuania's proposed resolution of its banking crisis. He warned that the "lack of decisive action" on the part of the Lithuanian government could lead to a deeper crisis later in the year, and that "such policies allow bankers to feel that they can do as they wish" (*Baltic Independent*, 23 February 1996).

[47] This is seen in the recent proposals in Lithuania, which all call for large state loan guarantees, which are little more than unconditionally provided fresh capital.

7. Attempts to resolve crises by merging bad banks with good banks are extremely risky, especially when this involves central bank pressure on the good bank. Such moves can easily be followed by the collapse of the merged bank, either because of a fall in public confidence (a "contamination effect") or because of the weak capital adequacy in the merged bank.[48]

APPENDIX: DEVELOPMENT OF THE BALTIC BANKING SYSTEMS

The overall development of the Baltic banking systems has been influenced by numerous factors. This appendix outlines the main trends in each country, most of which are qualitatively quite similar.

Starting Conditions

The banking system of the late central-planning period was unsuited to market conditions. It was effectively monopolized by a single "monobank" (Gosbank in the USSR), while a market economy requires competition among several banks. The "monobank" was also more of a state accounting agency for monitoring the fulfillment of production and investment plans than a real bank. Once the central plan foresaw a given transaction, the "monobank" had to passively finance it. For this reason, it did not make independent lending decisions or face real risks, and thus failed to develop the human and organizational capital required in the new market setting.

Two-Tier System

The first step needed to move the banking system toward a market basis was the replacement of this "monobank" with a "two-tier" system comprised of a single central bank and many competing commercial banks. In the Baltics and other Soviet republics, this process began in 1987–88 with the separation from Gosbank of five specialized banks: the Bank of Industry and Construction

[48] A strong bank might wish to acquire a bank with negative net worth if it is perceived to have good "intangible" value, such as a large client base or branch network. As such intangibles are likely to pay off only in the future, they should be viewed as illiquid assets, and are thus of no value in fending off short-term liquidity problems.

(Promstroibank), the Savings Bank (Sberbank), the Housing and Social Bank (Zhilsotsbank), the Agricultural Bank (Agroprombank), and the Foreign Trade Bank (Vneshekonombank, or VEB). Estonia, Latvia, and Lithuania later "nationalized" the local branches of these banks – that is, brought them under local jurisdiction.[49]

These five banks, which initially continued their former specialization, formed the core of the new commercial banking sector. Each state later restructured these in slightly different ways. Each preserved an independent Savings Bank, which continued to focus on taking household deposits, but which was gradually relieved of its earlier 100 percent reserve requirement.[50] As the assets of these banks were frozen in Moscow, all had to be recapitalized either via an explicit transfer of new assets (Estonia and Latvia) or by an open-ended state guarantee (Lithuania) (IMF 1994c).

The remaining four banks were treated differently. In Estonia, the bankrupt branch of VEB was merged with the new Bank of Estonia (BOE) in 1990. In 1991, the previously nationalized Bank of Industry and Construction was split into two parallel entities, one that took over most past assets and liabilities, and the other that started as a new commercial bank.[51] The Housing and Social Bank was reorganized into the Estonian Social Bank, which mainly served central and local governments. Most branches of the old Agricultural Bank, which had become the Estonian Land Bank, became independent regional banks in May 1992. At the beginning of 1993, ten of these were reintegrated to form the Union Bank of Estonia.

Latvia adopted a different approach.[52] In May 1992, it merged the forty-five branches of the "nationalized" ex-Soviet banks (except the Savings Bank) into the Bank of Latvia (BOL). Later, nine were sold to commercial banks and fifteen were consolidated into eight banks and sold via share offerings. At the end of 1993, the remaining twenty-one branches were merged as the new state-owned Universal Bank of Latvia (Unibank) (Fleming and Talley

[49] For example, Lithuania did this via a parliamentary resolution in October 1990.

[50] In some cases, the Savings Bank was taken over by the central bank (Estonia) and in others by the government.

[51] World Bank 1993a. The latter gradually pulled over most customers of the old bank. The former became a hollow shell, and was formally liquidated in October 1993 (Hirvensalo 1994).

[52] For a good discussion of its strengths and weaknesses, see Fleming and Talley 1996.

1996). Unibank and the Latvian Savings Bank were restructured in April 1994 by the replacement of their nonperforming loans with long-term government bonds.

Lithuania's approach was an intermediate one. In January 1991, the new Bank of Lithuania (BoL) absorbed the local branches of the Social Bank and the Industry and Construction Bank. In mid-1992, it absorbed the bankrupt local VEB branch, leaving the Agricultural Bank as an independent state-owned bank.

A second step in the creation of a "two-tier" system was the reestablishment of central (national) banks. The BOE was reestablished in December 1989, the Bank of Lithuania in February 1990, and the Bank of Latvia in July 1990. Before the restoration of state independence in August 1991, these institutions had little power compared with the local Gosbank branch, which controlled the processing of payments. They focused on preparing the introduction of national currencies and the legal groundwork for independence.

The role of the new national banks was enhanced by their postindependence takeover of the local Gosbank branches. They had also inherited some commercial functions by absorbing local ex-Soviet banks, and became true central banks only after devolving these functions. This was completed in Estonia in May 1992 with the formation of the North Estonian Joint-Stock Bank (NEJSB). The Bank of Lithuania spun off its commercial functions gradually. In late 1991, three of its branches became independent banks (IMF 1993b). This process was completed in September 1992 with the merger of the remaining commercial functions of the BoL into the new State Commercial Bank of Lithuania (SCB). The devolution of the forty-five commercial branches initially merged with the Bank of Latvia was completed with the formation of Unibank.

Legal Reform

Legal reform was needed to make laws governing banking consistent with a market economy. The Soviet law of November 1989 that granted the Baltic republics some economic autonomy also extended to the banking system. The parts of the law concerning banking resembled the All-Union legislation under preparation at the time, but adopted at a later date. Yet, as Moscow did not relinquish all authority over the Baltic banking systems, the period before independence became a legal muddle in which two separate authorities both tried to impose different banking laws.

Estonia began its own legal reforms by passing a semi-market-based banking law covering both central and commercial banks in December 1989. The May 1993 Law on the Bank of Estonia formalized the independence of the BOE from the government. A new Law on Credit Institutions was approved in December 1994.

In Latvia, the reform of banking laws began with the adoption of new commercial and central banking laws in May 1992. Following the banking crisis of 1995, the Saeima approved a new Law on Financial Institutions in October 1995. This tightened prudential ratios (especially limits on foreign exchange exposure and loans extended to owners and major clients) established procedures for bank bankruptcy and gave the BOL greater enforcement powers for supervising the banking system (Shteinbuka et al. 1995, Paeglis 1996).

The reform of Lithuania's banking laws began in July 1992 with the Commercial Bank Act. In December 1994, the Bank of Lithuania Law and the Commercial Banking Law were adopted.

New Entry

In the Baltic states, new commercial banks were first established in 1988. Many were "pocket banks" formed by state enterprises and/or cooperatives to provide for their own banking needs. Others were private and focused on raising deposits to lend to owners, or on gradually evolving into universal banks. Some even grew out of branches of state-owned banks (SOBs) that had become independent.[53] Most were small and earned much of their income from foreign-exchange trading. They did minimal lending, usually only at short maturities of less than three months. Far less than one-half of these entities became full-fledged banks, with the rest remaining little more than foreign-exchange traders or "pocket banks."

New entry led to a sharp rise in the number of licensed banks. In December 1988, Tartu Commercial Bank (TCB) became the first

[53] For example, the Revalia Bank and Narva Commercial Bank broke away from the Estonian Social Bank, while Aurabank broke away from the SCB of Lithuania.

new commercial bank in Estonia. The number of Estonian banks rose to twelve by mid-1991 and to a peak of 42 at the end of 1992. The first two commercial banks in Latvia were founded in 1988. After an additional four were established in 1989, the number increased to a very high sixty-three by the end of 1993 (Shteinbuka et al. 1995). In March 1993, the Latvian government also revived the Mortgage and Land Bank (MLB) (which had existed during the interwar period of independence) as a state commercial bank. The first new Lithuanian commercial bank was registered in January 1989. The total number of operating banks rose to twenty by December 1991, and to twenty-eight (including three SOBs) by early 1994.

This rapid new entry was the combined result of several factors. First, high inflation had eroded the real value of the minimal capital needed to start a bank. In Estonia, this had fallen to only about $40,000 in mid-1992 (Hansson 1995). Second, limited licensing requirements placed few other barriers to entry into this sector. Third, the formation of a bank gave owners access to cheap Gosbank credits, with interest rates far below the inflation rate.[54] Fourth, a depreciating ruble and a large cash shortage-induced gap between cash and noncash exchange rates made foreign-exchange trading highly profitable. Finally, a good location to work as a financial intermediary between CIS countries and the West also increased the potential profitability of Baltic banks.

Because this number of banks was clearly far too high, this fast growth would be followed by an equally rapid process of consolidation.

Privatization

As in most economies in transition, the privatization of Baltic banks has progressed very slowly, and foreign banks have until recently shown little interest in participating. Initially, privatization took a largely uncontrolled "spontaneous" form, facilitated by the unclear legal environment and weak capacity of the state to enforce existing laws. Some branches of the SOBs simply broke away and were quietly privatized. In other instances, managers of

[54] In 1992, the annual rate of growth of the consumer price index was 953% in Estonia, 959% in Latvia, and 1,163% in Lithuania, while Gosbank credits were usually available at double-digit annual rates.

SOBs would first form a new private bank and then lure away its better customers (often using the physical assets of the SOB). The agricultural, industrial, and housing banks in Estonia, as well as the three large Lithuanian SOBs were all partially "spontaneously" privatized.[55] Only Latvia was able to strictly limit the degree of spontaneous bank privatization.

In contrast, conscious top-down privatization has been rare and slow. This has involved the sale of new shares and/or existing stakes. In Estonia, it began in June 1993, when the BOE expanded the capital of the Savings Bank (where it was the sole owner), and sold the resulting one-third share to a local Estonian bank. In June 1995, a 31 percent increase in the bank's share capital was sold to the European Bank for Reconstruction and Development (EBRD). These moves, combined with further bottom-up privatization, reduced the state share in the Savings Bank to 24.06 percent as of December 1995. More recently, a one-sixth stake in the NEB was sold to a major Estonian commercial bank. All of these sales have occurred in an ad hoc way without a coherent, well-conceived privatization strategy.

In Latvia, top-down privatization has been better organized but also slow. In December 1992, the Saeima entrusted bank privatization to a multiagency committee. A four-stage privatization program of the biggest state-owned bank (Unibank) began in 1995. In the first stage, Unibank's share capital was increased by LVL 2.5 million out of retained profits and reserves. The second stage, in which 50.001 percent of shares were sold to the public, clients, and employees for privatization certificates, began in May 1995. The third stage, completed in May 1996, saw a further LVL 6 million increase in share capital to LVL 19.9 million ($40 million), of which the EBRD took LVL 4.5 million and Swedfund took LVL 1.5 million.[56] In the final stage, the remaining state shares will be sold through the Riga Stock Exchange (IMF 1995b). Progress in selling stakes in the Latvian Savings Bank and

[55] In Lithuania, the "self-privatization" of 49% of the shares of these banks was written into their charters. More recently, the "renegade" board of Estonia's troubled, state-owned North Estonian Bank (NEB) tried to sell part of the bank without prior government approval. In January 1995, it proposed to increase share capital from 43 to 88 million EEK, and sell these shares to five major clients of the bank. The government quickly declared this to be against existing privatization laws and stopped the transaction.

[56] *Baltic Times*, 16 May. As a result, the state stake was diluted to 35%.

Table 5A.1. *Total banking assets and M2 as a share of GDP, 1993–95*

	1991	1993	1994	1995
Assets/GDP				
Estonia		20.9	26.8	29.5
Latvia		27.7	40.9	43.6
Lithuania		22.5	—	28.8
M2/GDP				
Estonia	67	18.9	21.8	22.8
Latvia	52	22.9	30.0	28.0
Lithuania	39	14.5 (Q4)	13.1	21.6

Sources: 1991 figures are estimated by the World Bank, others are from the national statistical agencies and central banks.

MLB has been slow, with the latter unlikely to be sold before 1998.

In Lithuania, there is only a vague commitment to top-down privatization as a long-term goal. No specific plans have been elaborated for the sale of the remaining state stakes in three state-controlled banks (IMF 1995c), although several proposals have been discussed.

An important opposite trend has been renationalization resulting from the reversion to state ownership of problem banks. In early 1993, two major banks were involved in Estonia's first banking crisis – the largely private Union Baltic Bank and the state-owned NEJSB were recapitalized and merged into a fully state-owned bank. In 1994, the failed (by that time largely privately owned) Estonian Social Bank reverted to state ownership in the same fashion. If the recent Lithuanian banking crisis is resolved as initially planned, the bulk of that country's banking sector will also return to state hands.

Size and Structure of the Banking Sector

The Baltic banking sectors vary in size relative to their economies. In Table 5A.1, we present the evolution of two such measures – total assets of commercial banks and M2, both expressed as a share of GDP. The figures are midyear stocks relative to annual GDP.[57]

The higher levels of assets and M2 in Latvia reflect the greater role of nonresident deposits in that country. The ratios of M2/GDP compare with levels of around 15 percent in Russia, 31 percent in Poland, and 74 percent in the Czech Republic (World Bank). Their size is inversely related to the degree of past inflation.[58] The effect of inflation is seen by comparing the later figures with the 1991 levels. In many developed countries, the ratio of M2 to GDP is over 100 percent.

The market structure that lies behind these aggregates is the combined result of new entry, restructuring, mergers, privatization, renationalization, and liquidation. One indicator of this structure is the number of banks. In Estonia, this has fallen from a high of forty-two at the end of 1992 to twenty-two at the end of 1993 to sixteen in January 1996. The number of licensed Latvian banks has fallen sharply from a high of sixty-three at the end of 1993 to fifty-five at the end of 1994 (Ross 1996) and thirty-seven at the end of 1995.[59] In January 1996, the Lithuanian banking sector consisted of twelve operating banks, down from twenty-seven only one year before.

Consolidation was a combined result of bank failures and mergers. The former resulted from factors discussed here. The latter reflects a conscious policy decision of central banks and was spurred by phased increases in minimal capital requirements. Estonia increased its minimal bank share capital from EEK 0.5 million ($0.4 million) to EEK 6 million in January 1994, EEK 15 million in April 1995, and EEK 25 million ($2 million) in April 1996 (IMF 1994a).[60] An especially high barrier was a BOE requirement that by 1 January 1996, all banks must have their own

[57] This presents the most accurate picture in a high-inflation environment, where the comparison of end-year figures with full-year flows would lead to an overstatement of the ratio. In Lithuania, 1993 figures for M2 are for the fourth quarter, as midyear figures are not available.

[58] High inflation would sharply cut real money demand and wipe out any "monetary overhang" that had been accumulated in the past. Following such an episode, the rebuilding of real balances and other components of the money supply can only occur gradually over time.

[59] Of these thirty-seven banks, only sixteen had general licenses which allowed the taking of household deposits.

[60] The Law on Credit Institutions envisions a phased increase in minimum share capital to the current EU level of ECU 5 million (about EEK 75 million) by January 2000.

funds (including reserves and retained profits) of at least EEK 50 million ($4 million).[61]

Latvia raised the minimal share capital to establish a new bank from LVL 0.1 million to LVL 2 million ($4 million) in December 1994. Existing banks were given until April 1996 to raise share capital to LVL 1 million ($2 million) (with five banks failing to reach this threshold), and a further two years to raise it to LVL 2 million.

Lithuania increased minimal share capital to LTL 10 million ($2.5 million) on 1 July 1995 (six banks failed to meet these requirements). It plans further increases to LTL 20 million ($4 million) by 1 January 1997, with a target of ECU 5 million (ca. LTL 26.5 million) by January 1998.

A second measure of a banking sector's structure is its concentration, which has gradually increased through the closure of small banks. At the end of 1995, the share of the five largest banks in total bank assets was 74.6 percent in Estonia, 56.8 percent in Latvia, and 70.7 percent (including frozen banks) in Lithuania. Thus, Estonia now has the most concentrated banking system and Latvia the least concentrated.

In Estonia, three of the five largest banks (Union Bank, Savings Bank, and NEB) have grown out of the old SOBs (only partially in the case of NEB), while two (Hansabank and Tallinna Bank) are new banks. Of these, one is majority state-owned (NEB), one with a large minority state stake (Savings Bank) and three almost entirely private. In September 1995, the state still held 18 percent of the total share capital of banks (10% via the BOE, 5% via the government, and 3% via state-owned enterprises, or SOEs).

In Latvia, two of the five largest banks (Unibank and Savings Bank) have grown out of the old SOBs, while three (Parex, Riga Commercial Bank, and Rietimu Bank) are new. Of these five, one is majority state-owned (Savings Bank), one has a significant minority state stake (Unibank), and three are almost entirely private. Overall, Latvia appears to have the highest share of private ownership of banks in the Baltics.

In Lithuania, three of the five largest banks (Agricultural Bank, SCB, and Savings Bank) grew out of the old SOBs, while two

[61] This threshold is to rise further to EEK 75 million by the beginning of 1998.

(Lithuanian Joint-Stock Innovation Bank and Vilniaus Bank) are new banks. Three of these five remain majority state-owned, while two have up to now had largely private ownership.[62] Again, the resolution of the recent banking crisis may raise the share of state ownership through renationalization.

Full foreign ownership of banks is limited to Finland's Merita and Ukraine's INKO (in Estonia) and France's Société Generale and Russia's Latvian Business Bank (in Latvia). The EBRD, Swedfund, Finnfund, and Germany's DEG have minority stakes in the "investment banks" of each country, and the first two have also bought similar stakes in some privatized banks. Ownership by Russian capital has clearly been important in Latvia but is hard to measure. Recent offers of new shares by Estonian banks have also brought in new portfolio owners from abroad.

The structure of the Estonian and Latvian banking sectors most closely resembles that of Russia, in that new private banks have developed rapidly and left the old SOBs with a fairly small market share. In contrast, the Lithuanian banking sector resembles those of many CEE countries, where the old SOBs (often privatized by now) continue to dominate.

Deposit Insurance

Until the end of 1995, formal deposit insurance in the Baltics was restricted to a clause in the Lithuanian Civil Code guaranteeing deposits in banks with majority state ownership. In all three countries, there is a strongly presumed implicit guarantee on household deposits in the savings banks. A formal general deposit insurance law (offering limited coverage to all depositors) has been tabled in Estonia and is being considered in Latvia. In the midst of the recent crisis in Lithuania, the Seimas hastily passed emergency deposit insurance legislation giving full guarantees to depositors in two large failed banks, and 80 percent coverage of litas-denominated household deposits up to LTL 5,000 ($1,250) in all banks (Paeglis 1996). The degree of implicit deposit insurance in Estonia and Latvia has varied from case to case, all the way from zero to full compensation.

[62] The direct state stake in LAIB was only 0.4% (*Eesti Päevaleht*, 10 April 1996).

REFERENCES

Bourke, Michael J. 1996. "The Banking Crisis in Latvia and Lithuania – The Real Lessons." *Baltic Observer*, 25 January, 12.

Fleming, Alex, and Samuel Talley. 1996. "The Latvian Banking Crisis: Lessons Learned." World Bank Policy Research Paper no. 1590, April, World Bank, Washington, D.C.

Goldfajn, Ilan, and Rodrigo O. Valdes 1995. "Balance of Payment Crises and Capital Flows: The Role of Liquidity." Brandeis University, Waltham, Mass., August.

Hallagan, William. 1995. "Big Bang Banking Reform: The Latvian Experience." Washington State University, Pullman, July.

Hansson, Ardo H. 1995. "Reforming the Banking System in Estonia." In Jacek Rostowski (ed.), *Banking Reform in Central Europe and the Former Soviet Union*, 142–65. Budapest: Central European University Press.

Hansson, Ardo H. 1996. "Hidden State-Sector Losses and Fiscal Pressures in Transition Economies: Examples from the Baltic States." Mimeographed, World Bank, Washington, D.C., February.

Hansson, Ardo H., and Jeffrey D. Sachs. 1994. "Monetary Institutions and Credible Stabilization: A Comparison of Experiences in the Baltics." Prepared for the conference on Central Banks in Eastern Europe and the Newly Independent States, University of Chicago Law School, April.

Hirvensalo, Inkeri. 1994. "Banking Reform in Estonia." *Review of Economies in Transition*, Bank of Finland, no. 8: 75–95.

International Monetary Fund. 1993a. "Latvia." *IMF Economic Reviews* no. 6 (June).

International Monetary Fund. 1993b. "Lithuania." *IMF Economic Reviews* no. 7 (June).

International Monetary Fund. 1994a. "Estonia." *IMF Economic Reviews* no. 7 (August).

International Monetary Fund. 1994b. "Latvia." *IMF Economic Reviews* no. 10 (November).

International Monetary Fund. 1994c. "Lithuania." *IMF Economic Reviews* no. 6 (August).

International Monetary Fund. 1995a. "Republic of Estonia – Recent Economic Developments." *IMF Staff Country Report* no. 95/40 (May).

International Monetary Fund. 1995b. "Latvia – Recent Economic Developments." *IMF Staff Country Report* no. 95/125 (December).

International Monetary Fund. 1995c. "Republic of Lithuania – Recent Economic Developments." *IMF Staff Country Report* no. 95/28 (August).

Paeglis, Imants. 1996 "Troubling Bank Failures in Latvia and Lithuania." *Transition* 2, no. 10: 14–17.

Ross, Tanel. 1996. "Latvian Banking Crisis: Background, Solutions, Consequences." *Baltic Review* (Spring): 10–11.

Shteinbuka, Inna, Edgars Sniegs, and Martıns Kazaks. 1995. "Factors and Consequences of the Banking Crisis in Latvia." *Bulletin of the Ministry of Finance of the Republic of Latvia*, no. 2: 6–17.

World Bank. 1993a. *Estonia: The Transition to a Market Economy.* Washington, D.C.: World Bank.

World Bank. 1993b. *Latvia: The Transition to a Market Economy.* Washington, D.C.: World Bank.

CHAPTER 6

Monetary and Exchange Rate Policy, Capital Inflows, and the Structure of the Banking System in Croatia

Velimir Šonje, Evan Kraft, and Thomas Dorsey

Although heavily affected by war, Croatia has undertaken fundamental macroeconomic reforms since achieving independence in 1991. High inflation was brought under control in late 1993 by an exchange-rate-based stabilization program, and inflation has been kept to an average annual level of 1.2 percent in the three years since stabilization. This is the lowest level among transition countries (Figure 6.1). Reform of monetary instruments, current-account convertibility, and fiscal consolidation were part of the stabilization effort. However, imperfect financial markets faced strong capital inflows. The associated current-account deficit complicates maintenance of stabilization in the long run.

Competitive forces are at work to address the shortcomings of the financial system, but each source of competition has its own limitations. Entry into Croatian banking has been extensive, but most of these new banks are still quite small. Bank rehabilitation has been progressing slowly and lagged behind macroeconomic stabilization. Foreign banks have hesitated to enter the Croatian market, in part due to local and regional security risk.

Croatia has continued to experience a very high interest rate spread between average bank deposit and lending rates (about 20% on average) nearly three years after reducing inflation to no more than industrial country levels. (See Figure 6.2.) The purpose of this chapter is to analyze recent Croatian experience regarding the evolving structure of the banking system with a particular focus on the influence of late bank restructuring and weak competition on interest rates. We also try to establish a link between microeconomic structural considerations, and macroeconomic monetary considerations. A set of regressions on a cross section of Croatian banks attempts to determine the extent to which individual banks' characteristics can explain

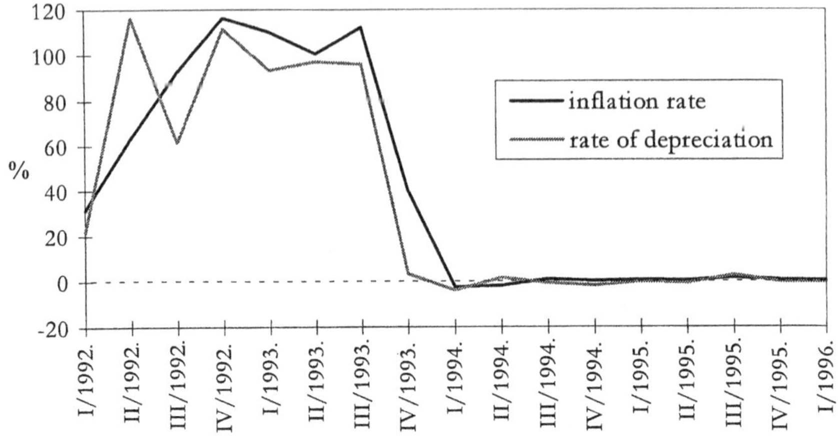

Figure 6.1. Inflation rate and rate of depreciation of HRK/DEM exchange rate (quarterly).

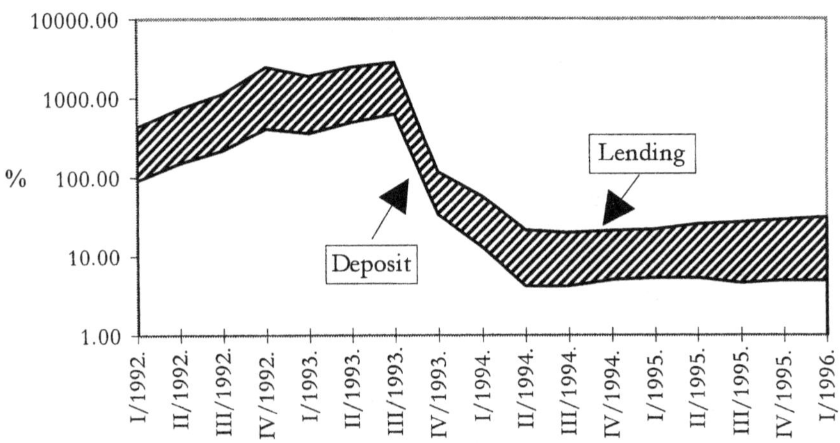

Figure 6.2. Interest rates of DMBs (on a yearly basis, quarterly averages).

interest rate spreads and other key features of bank performance. We present findings supporting the thesis that the Croatian banking system is characterized by weak competition that allows banks to pass costs onto clients in the form of higher spreads and that macroeconomic policy tools are likely to have little long-term impact on these spreads absent structural change in the banking system. We show that when the first best solution (microeconomic structural reform) is absent, and when faced with strong capital inflows requiring sterilization, the second best solution (macroeconomic, i.e., monetary) is to manage liquidity by increasing both the rate of reserve requirements and the rate of remuneration.

The first part of the chapter presents background information on the Croatian macroeconomic environment, its stabilization program, and the structure of the banking system relevant to these two different approaches to examining banking system performance. The next part presents the microeconomic, cross-section analysis of banking system cost and profit ratios. Specifically, a series of cross-section regressions on data for individual banks assess the determinants of spreads, administrative and overhead costs, and profitability, using as independent variables original and current ownership status, scale variables, and proxies for competitive conditions. The third part takes the macroeconomic approach, developing an autoregressive econometric model to examine the determinants of overall interest rate spreads in the banking system. The model seeks to identify the effects of the exchange rate, reserve requirements, rate of remuneration on reserves, and the real money supply on aggregate spreads. The last part attempts to draw some conclusions from both sets of empirical estimates. The evidence suggests that any attempt to lower spreads by expansionary monetary policy may only jeopardize the achievements of the stabilization effort and that only structural measures to control costs in banking, including bank rehabilitation, would be likely to lower spreads in Croatia.

THE CROATIAN ECONOMY, STABILIZATION PROGRAM, AND BANKING MARKET STRUCTURE

Despite long experience with two-tier banking in former Yugoslavia, banks acted as a less direct substitute for Soviet-type central planning from the 1960s through the late 1980s. Large national and local oligopolies were the most important founders of the banks, and the most important clients. Negative real interest rates served as a vehicle for the redistribution of depositors' (mainly households') savings to investment projects decided upon in the political arena.

There was little effective competition among banks. The structure of the banking market reflected the politically determined economic structure of the time. Croatia had two nationwide banks and eighteen regional banks before 1989. All were owned by groups of socially owned enterprises that were also the major borrowers. In 1989–90, banks were refounded as joint-stock companies owned by these founders, but initially this proved just a legal change with little economic impact in most cases. Bank shares were nonmarketable, lending to related parties remained a widespread habit, and consequently it was not a surprise when international auditors reported huge potential losses at the beginning of the 1990s.

The war associated with the breakup of the former Yugoslavia complicated the problem further. The Croatian government had neither the funds nor the organizational resources to undertake a credible bank rehabilitation process during hard times. In any case, bank rehabilitation was prevented by high inflation until the stabilization program of October 1993. Bank rehabilitation legislation came in spring 1994, and the Agency for Bank Rehabilitation began operations in late 1995, two years after the successful stabilization of exchange rate and prices.

Although thirty-two new domestic banks entered the market in the 1990–95 period, they were small and only beginning to compete with older and larger banks in the retail banking market. Old banks have kept their close links with old, privatized, and unprivatized enterprises, and have kept the deposits of enterprises as well as the bulk of household deposits. Enterprises have not moved their deposits, because that could endanger getting loans – such enterprises would have great difficulty qualifying for loans from new banks that use commercial lending criteria. New banks do not have the branch network needed to compete for retail deposits and have mainly offered credit to largely underserved new enterprises. Their lending has been funded from capital or nondeposit borrowing. Bankers mention the high reserve requirements of the National Bank of Croatia (NBC), ranging as high as 41 percent at the end of 1995, as a reason to avoid seeking deposits.

Notwithstanding these difficulties, there were three other processes going on that likely enhanced competition and soundness in the banking system: reform of central banking and banking

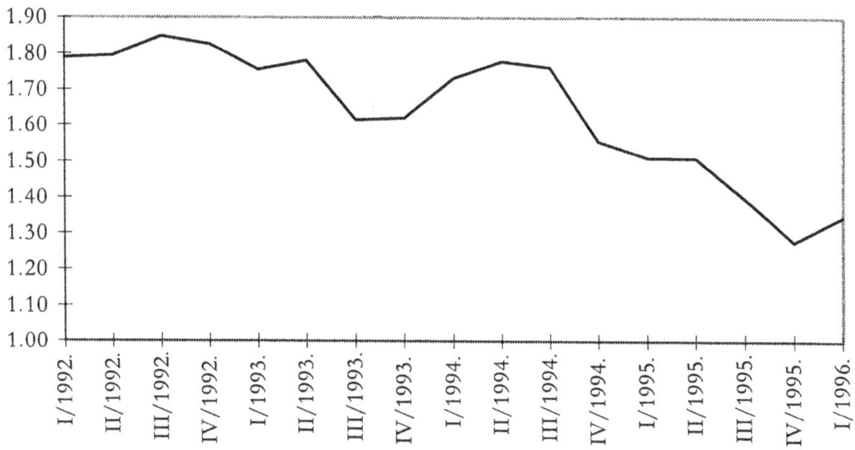

Figure 6.3. Money multiplier M1/M0 (quarterly averages).

regulation and supervision, macroeconomic stabilization, and privatization. We discuss these in turn.

Prior to the announcement of the stabilization program in October 1993, the NBC changed its operating procedures. The instruments of quotas and selective rediscounting, perhaps the centerpieces of monetary policy under the old regime, were gradually phased out. The automatic right to draw on required reserves was removed. NBC foreign-exchange purchase auctions soon became the main means of injecting liquidity into the economy, and elimination of the automatic right to draw on required reserves made it possible to sterilize excess liquidity created by foreign exchange intervention. Figures 6.3 and 6.4 clearly point to the fact that both the money multiplier and net domestic assets of the central bank declined significantly prior to stabilization, especially in the third quarter of 1993.

Moreover, a significant one-shot drop in the money multiplier occurred in the quarter prior to stabilization due to the first big increase in the required reserve ratio. The reserve requirement rose from 13 percent in April to 29.5 percent in September 1993. The decline in real money was so sharp in the prestabilization period that the current U.S. dollar amount of the NBC's international reserves exceeded the current U.S. dollar amount of M1 at the beginning of stabilization (Figure 6.5). Fiscal policy was also

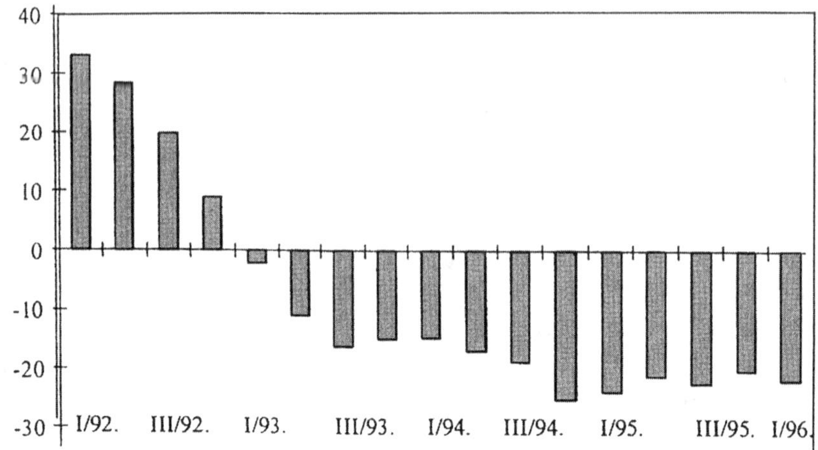

Figure 6.4. NBC's net domestic assets (million HRK, January 1992 prices, quarterly averages).

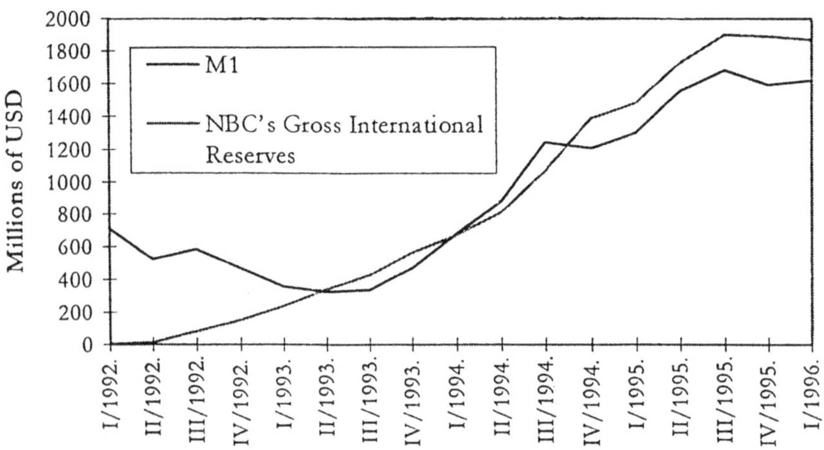

Figure 6.5. Money supply (M1) and NBC's gross international reserves (quarterly averages).

tightened; the budget was brought into approximate balance in 1993 and government borrowing from the NBC and the banking system in general was sharply curtailed. Hence monetary and fiscal policy set the basis for successful stabilization.

In October 1993, internal convertibility of the domestic cur-

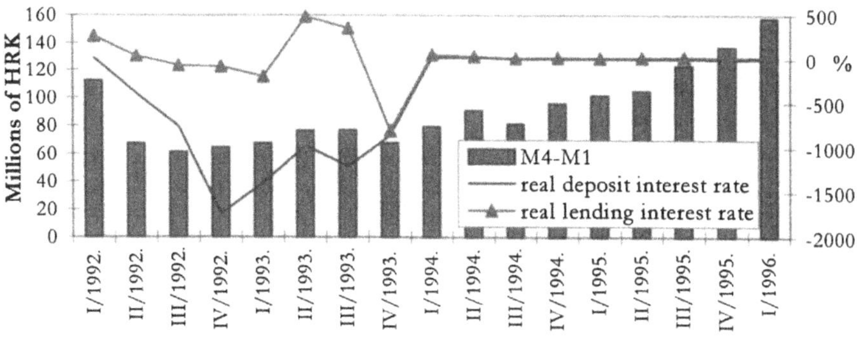

Figure 6.6. M4-M1 (January 1992 prices, quarterly averages) and real interest rates of DMBs (on a yearly basis, quarterly averages). *Note*: Real (M4-M1) is a good proxy for real capital inflows because large part of it is kept at foreign exchange deposits, which increased mainly due to repatriation of savings held abroad and due to withdrawals of foreign exchange cash from "matrices."

rency was introduced, and a credible exchange rate announcement was made. Once the foreign-exchange market was liberalized, the exchange rate started to appreciate in nominal terms due to a break in expectations and due to tight monetary policy in the months preceding stabilization. The November 1993 inflation figures showed spectacular success.

Thereafter, monetary policy remained restrictive in the sense that the NBC allowed further nominal appreciation of the exchange rate. When dangerous pressures toward significant short-run depreciation occurred at the end of the third quarter of 1995, the NBC again reacted with significant sterilization. A sharp one-shot drop in the money multiplier occurred once again in the last quarter of 1995. The money and foreign-exchange markets stabilized without a significant loss of international reserves, showing the NBC's strong commitment to sound monetary management.

The change in the monetary policy regime toward sterilized intervention actually began with the increases in reserve requirements in late spring 1993. This is the period when lending interest rates became positive in real terms (ex post) and capital inflows began (Figure 6.6). After stabilization of the exchange rate and prices, inflows speeded up. Extremely high real interest rates occurred during the quarter of stabilization and the quarter thereafter. They fell to a minimum (at a still high level) in the third quarter of 1994, and then started to rise again. Interest rate spreads behaved similarly.

It is tempting to conclude that the behavior of interest rates is closely related to monetary policy. One may speculate that, if the NBC had been less "restrictive," the lending interest rate and spread might be lower, with positive impact on real growth in the poststabilization period. This line of reasoning implicitly assumes that there is a stable Keynesian monetary transmission mechanism that works through flexible, market-sensitive interest rates. But there are a number of reasons to believe that such mechanisms do not exist in Croatia.

First, four big problem state-owned banks became constant users of money market funds after stabilization, showing no signs of change in their liquidity position. Daily minuses in their gyro accounts were covered by borrowings on the overnight money market. With nowhere else to turn, the problem banks were ready to pay high interest rates for overnight funds. Their demand for money market funds was in fact interest rate inelastic. Rehabilitation of these banks was discussed, because nonperforming assets had been estimated at 20 percent of total assets, but the implementation of the program was delayed until 1995 for the smallest of the four, and until mid-1996 for the second and third largest. The largest bank began rehabilitation at the end of 1996. Thus, even the first practical steps toward bank rehabilitation lagged two and a half years after macroeconomic stabilization.

Second, market concentration was high, and showed no signs of significant change: the two largest banks still controlled 54.7 percent of total assets in 1995.

Third, strong growth in all monetary aggregates, including bank credits, did not induce a drop in interest rates after mid-1994. Money growth was due to foreign-exchange inflows, reflected mainly in the extremely rapid growth of households' foreign exchange deposits, which, throughout the whole period, comprised 45 to 60 percent of M4. So, the foreign-exchange position of domestic commercial banks was systematically open, and this made them particularly sensitive to current and expected exchange rate changes.

The size of the interest spread, its significant variability after stabilization, and the fact that bad state-owned banks in Croatia had lower lending interest rates and spreads than good

Table 6.1. *Banking system assets by ownership and region, end 1991 through end 1995 (in %) share of assets*

	1991	1992	1993	1994	1995
State	62.1	67.0	65.0	62.3	58.9
New private	2.1	3.5	3.8	7.7	10.0
Mixed/privatized	35.8	29.5	31.2	30.2	31.3
National	55.0	55.3	59.2	54.7	54.7
Regional	42.9	42.7	38.2	40.5	38.5
Zagreb	2.1	2.0	2.6	5.9	7.8

Table 6.2. *Number of banks by ownership and region, end 1991 through end 1995*

	1991	1992	1993	1994	1995
State	13	17	17	18	18
New private	8	13	18	24	27
Mixed/privatized	8	8	8	8	8
National	2	2	2	2	2
Regional	20	25	28	31	33
Zagreb	7	11	13	17	18
Total	29	38	43	50	53

banks call for a close investigation of the supply side of the credit markets.

Tables 6.1 and 6.2 show the share of the banking system assets classified by type of bank ownership and regional competition conditions. Three categories of ownership are employed in the tables. "New private" banks are those private banks established since 1989 with a private ownership structure; "mixed/privatized" banks are those older banks with mixed but (by the end of 1994) majority private ownership structures; and "state" banks are those older banks the majority of the shares of which are owned by majority-state enterprises. Problems with classification arise because, as noted already, the banks from the old regime were owned by groups of socially owned enterprises. This ownership structure initially remained intact during the privatization process.

It was gradually changed through sales of new bank shares to household or other buyers, and through the ongoing process of enterprise privatization. We define mixed/privatized banks as those banks majority-owned by new private firms, fully privatized firms, majority privatized firms, or private individuals as of the end of 1994. In our tables, there is no change in the composition of mixed banks over time; the same eight banks contribute to the "mixed" data for all years. Changes in the share of this group over time reflect only the relative performace of these eight banks and not changes in the composition of the group as banks move from "state" to "mixed" categories.

The regional categories also require some explanation. Each regional bank competes primarily only with the two national banks and does not compete significantly with other regional banks or Zagreb-based banks other than two national banks. New entry has changed this situation to some degree, but the new entrants have been heavily concentrated in Zagreb, the largest market in Croatia, with between one-fourth and one-fifth of the country's population.

COMPETITION AND EFFICIENCY IN THE CROATIAN BANKING SECTOR

There are competing influences in the relationship between profitability, interest rate spreads, growth, and overhead cost structure on one hand and ownership, age, competitive environment, and scale on the other hand. The nature of bank ownership structures might be expected to be particularly important. New private banks might be expected to perform better than old, state-owned banks. This superior performance might be thought of as having a variety of causes; the new banks would not be burdened by an existing portfolio of suspect loans inherited from the former regime. Their private ownership would establish incentives that would make it less likely that they would engage in money-losing new lending for political reasons or reasons related to moral hazard inherent in their ownership structure. They would also be expected to avoid excessive overhead costs in the form of overstaffing, excessive wages, or real-estate or other "empire-building" activities divorced from profitable banking. Older banks that have been privatized might be thought of as an intermediate case, performing better than old, majority state-owned banks because of the improved incentives associated with the transformed ownership but less well than new private banks. On this basis, we elaborate three hypotheses about the new private banks.

The first hypothesis describes the new or private banks as "lean and mean." Support for this hypothesis would provide evidence that new private or privatized banks have higher profits, lower interest rate spreads, and lower overhead-to-assets ratios. Conversely, the hypothesis suggests that older and majority-state-owned banks might be expected to be relatively unprofitable, exhibit higher spreads, and have higher overhead cost ratios under this hypothesis. This is arguably the mainstream stereotype of banks (or other economic enterprises) in transition economies: the old regime is characterized by bloat and inefficiency for which cost control and aggressive pricing brought about through privatization and new private entry are the remedy.

A second hypothesis would have it that new private banks (but not necessarily privatized banks) are exploiting a niche to engage in what might be characterized as "cream skimming" – taking the most profitable customers on both the deposit and lending sides of the balance sheets by providing higher quality services (and therefore incurring higher costs). These banks might also be expected to be relatively profitable, but, unlike banks under the first hypothesis, they might be expected to have higher interest rate spreads and perhaps modest growth rates reflecting the preference for high rates of return over aggressive expansion. This hypothesis would be consistent with the view that existing bank ownership links have channeled excessive credit to bank shareholders while pushing otherwise creditworthy customers to the margins of the banking system where they would face higher rates due to greater competition for funds. Support for this hypothesis would be finding evidence that new or private banks have higher profits, and relatively high interest rate spreads.

A third hypothesis, closely related to the "cream skimming" hypothesis, is that the new private banks behave as "aggressive full-service banks" also taking the most profitable customers on both the deposit and lending sides of the balance sheets by providing higher quality (and therefore incurring higher costs). These banks might also be expected to be relatively profitable, but they might be expected to have higher overhead-cost-to-assets ratios. Unlike banks under the cream-skimming hypothesis, however, they would be expected to have lower interest rate spreads

Table 6.3. *Capital and employee productivity (in thousands HRK, end 1994)*

	Average assets per bank	Capital asset ratio (%)	Assets per employee	Personel expense/ assets (%)	Reserves/ gross loans (%)
New private	237,359	49	3,099	2.28	7.82
Privatized	2,747,445	17	2,759	2.22	9.01
State	2,279,218	16	2,935	1.71	11.76
All banks	1,226,108	23	3,003	2.09	10.37

and high rate-of-asset growth reflecting the preference for aggressive expansion over high rates of return. Such banks might typically be foreign banks (largely absent from Croatia in 1995) or domestic banks seeking low-risk foreign or domestic "blue-chip" clients. This hypothesis would be supported by finding that new or private banks had higher profits, higher overhead-to-assets ratios, and relatively low interest rate spreads.

To begin studying these hypotheses, we show the average size of the banks and several other characteristics of banks in the various sectors in Table 6.3 (end of 1994 data). New private banks are on the order of one-tenth the size of state and mixed banks respectively. Capital among new banks of all sorts is remarkably high. We will see below that capital to a great extent plays the role of deposits for these banks. Old banks – whether privatized/mixed or state-owned – have much lower levels of capital adequacy. Note that capital adequacy levels in general seem acceptable, even for the old state banks, although, at least for the worst banks, potential loan losses may in fact exceed existing capital.

Efficiency measurement in banking is a complicated issue. Costs and inputs can be measured and compared to assets (as is done later), but quality of services is harder to measure. For example, Berger, Kashyip, and Scalise (1995) found that noninterest expenses relative to assets were rising in the United States in recent years as a result of increased competition and inovation. What is described here as efficiency refers to a narrow cost-efficiency concept – that is, it does not account for service quality.

Two personnel-based measures of banking overhead costs are assets per employee and personnel cost relative to assets. Data

Table 6.4. *Banking system cost/asset ratios and interest rate spreads by market type, age, and ownership in 1995 (in %)*

Type	Noninterest expense/assets	Administrative costs/assets	Achieved interest rate spreads
State	8.3	4.7	6.6
New Private	9.0	4.7	10.8
Mixed/privatized	8.3	4.7	8.7
National	4.7	2.4	3.6
Regional	8.4	4.6	7.6
Zagreb	9.4	5.2	7.8

from 1994 on both employee productivity measures appear in Table 6.3. The evidence is mixed; new private and mixed banks have lower costs by the assets-per-employee measure but state banks have lower cost by the personnel-costs-to-assets measure. It seems that the new private banks tend to pay higher wages, possibly to attract experienced personnel away from older banks or to provide greater employee incentives.

Data on broader cost measures appear in Table 6.4. All ownership categories have almost identical ratios of administrative cost to assets while new private banks have slightly higher ratios of total noninterest cost to asset than state or privatized banks. One item that does stand out in Table 6.4 is the much lower administrative and noninterest cost ratios of the two national banks (one privatized and one still in state ownership). These data point to the fact that special attention should be given to the problem of economies of scale.

There are marked differences between various classes of banks in terms of interest rates and achieved interest rate spreads. It may be seen in Table 6.4 that national banks have much lower interest rate spreads than either regional or Zagreb banks and that new private banks have higher spreads than state banks with privatized banks falling in between. Table 6.5 presents data on interest income, interest rates, and profitability. Data show that new private banks and new mixed banks held an advantage in net interest income as a ratio of total income. New private and privatized banks tend to charge higher interest rates on short-term loans. The structure of profitability is largely consistent with the interest

Table 6.5. *1994 interest and return on assets indicators (in %)*

Type	Short-term loan rates	Return on capital	Return on assets
State	21.13	−18.83	−1.45
New private	24.34	5.10	1.28
Privatized	18.33	7.41	0.68
All banks	21.73	−5.48	−0.57

rate levels. Both new private and privatized banks are profitable by all measures. New private banks are the most profitable by the return-on-assets measure, but are less profitable by the return-on-capital measure due to the high capital holdings of new private banks.

These high capital holdings are partially explained by initial difficulties in developing a retail deposit base. Opening up a branch network requires large initial investment in both equipment and personnel. Furthermore, the short-run opportunity cost of such a business strategy during 1995 was high. In the short run, it was more profitable for the new capital-rich banks to lend through the interbank money market than to invest in branch networks.

The descriptive statistics introduced here suggest that the new private banks can be said to be engaged in "cream skimming" (the second hypothesis discussed earlier) – taking the most profitable customers on both the deposits and lending side of the balance sheets by providing higher-quality services (and therefore incurring higher costs and charging higher interest rates). However, it is important to control for scale economies and regional effects systematically, so we ran a series of cross-section regressions to test the hypotheses and to shed light on competitive conditions in the Croatian banking market.

The results of the regressions, based on data for forty-eight banks, further support the "cream-skimming" hypothesis. First, the return-on-assets ratio was regressed on the logarithm of total assets to capture the effect of economies of scale, the ratio of deposits to total assets (to capture the effect of dependence on borrowed resources), and dummy variables for local banks based in Zagreb, new private banks, and privatized/mixed banks

Table 6.6. *Determinants of profitability*

	Dependent variable: Profits/assets (t-statistics in parentheses)	
Constant	0.0032	0.030
	(0.68)	(1.65)
Natural log of assets	0.0003	
	(0.08)	
Deposits/assets	−0.046	−0.034
	(−1.35)	(−1.28)
New private	0.015	0.020
	(1.25)	(1.95)*
Privatized	0.018	0.015
	(1.29)	(1.07)
Zagreb	0.013	
	(1.05)	

Notes: F(2,42) = 0.5595.
* Indicates statistical significance at the 5% level.

(Table 6.6). The restriction was statistically insignificant (as measured by the F-statistic) and the new private dummy variable became positive and significant (by conventional t-statistic measures) while the privatized dummy variable remained positive but fell short of the traditional t-statistic levels for statistical significance.

These regressions indicate that private banks, particularly new private banks, are more profitable than state banks, when scale effects and the influence of deposit-to-asset ratios are taken into account. Two features of the "insignificant" variables are worthy of note. First, the dummy variable for Zagreb, although of a low level of significance, has an unexpected sign. Rather than suppressing profits, the more intensely competitive Zagreb market appears to be associated, albeit weakly, with higher profits. The second feature worth noting is the economic significance of the coefficients on these new private and privatized dummy variables. The dummy on new private banks suggests an additional profit effect for new private banks equal to 2.0 percent of assets, almost exactly the size of the mean profit to assets ratio for all banks (2.1%). The estimated profit effects for privatized banks (1.5%)

Table 6.7. *Determinants of noninterest and administrative expenses*

	Dependent variable: Noninterest expenses/assets		Dependent variable: Administrative expenses/assets	
Constant	0.244	0.247	0.165	0.155
	(4.00)**	(5.46)**	(5.06)**	(5.58)**
Log assets	−0.015	−0.015	−0.011	−0.011
	(−3.31)**	(−3.36)**	(−3.86)**	(−4.17)**
Deposits/assets	0.036	0.058	0.041	0.054
	(0.84)	(1.63)	(1.71)	(2.47)**
New private	0.012		−0.010	
	(0.88)		(−1.18)	
Privatized	−0.001		0.001	
	(−0.07)		(0.11)	
Zagreb	0.012		0.013	
	(0.80)		(1.47)	

Notes: F(3,42) = 0.543 for noninterest expense to assets ratio. F(3,42) = 0.885 for administrative expense to assets ratio.
** Indicates statistical significance at the 1% level.

are also large in economic terms. This suggests that the low statistical significance may be more the result of low sample size rather than small economic effect.

The second result shown in Table 6.7 takes two input efficiency measures as dependent variables and shows significant economies of scale via the negative coefficient on log assets. These results tend not to support the idea that new private banks or more competitive banking markets will reduce costs in the Croatian case or that older or state-owned banks are suffering from bloated overhead costs. The new entrants may be more efficient in the sense that they are providing a higher level of service with the same cost ratios as other banks. However, it does not seem to be the case that the new private or privatized banks are providing lower-cost banking services once the influences of scale and dependence upon deposits are taken into account.

The third set of results is based on interest rate spreads as the dependent variable (Table 6.8). It suggests that regional variable does not have much explanatory power, while economies of scale are only marginally significant. However, the size of the coefficient on noninterest expenses from the restricted regression suggests

Table 6.8. *Determinants of interest rate spreads*

	Dependent variable: Interest rate spread (t-statistics in parentheses)	
Constant	−0.080	−0.008
	(−1.12)	(−0.53)
Log assets	0.0049	
	(1.02)	
Noninterest expenses/assets	0.938	0.893
	(5.64**)	(6.02**)
New private	0.025	0.025
	(1.64)	(1.89*)
Privatized	0.025	0.023
	(1.39)	(1.30)
Zagreb	0.019	
	(1.22)	

Notes: F(2,42) = 1.48.
* Indicates statistical significance at the 5% level.
** Indicates statistical significance at the 1% level.

that more than 89 percent of these costs are passed on to customers in the form of lower deposit rates or higher credit rates.

The fourth set of econometric results synthesizes the previous considerations. On the basis of the results in Tables 6.6–6.8, and because of the correlation between capital (capital adequacy and/or capital asset ratio) and interest spread (which was also reflected in the significance of the new private dummy), we created a single index that synthesizes the following variables (in order of factor loadings): capital adequacy, whether the bank was founded after 1990, loan-to-deposit ratio, total assets (negative sign), and administrative costs over assets. We call this factor a "new" factor. Factor analysis also created an index that synthesised assets per employee and administrative costs over assets (negative sign). We call this second factor an "efficiency" factor, since its two main components show the efficient use of assets and low administrative costs. We used the two factors as independent variables in the regression shown in Table 6.9.

Croatian private banks, particularly new private banks, are more profitable, faster growing, and have higher spreads than banks remaining in state hands. There are strong diseconomies of

Table 6.9. *Determinants of interest rate spreads*

	Dependent variable: Interest rate spread (t-statistics in parenthesis)
Constant	17.29
	(36.47)**
New factor	2.81
	(2.44)**
Efficiency factor	−0.994
	(−0.87)

Notes: Adjusted R-squared: 0.35.
** Indicates statistical significance at the 1% level.

scale that fall heavily on the new private banks because they tend to be smaller than other banks.

This "cream-skimming" strategy was made possible by the high interest spread available to the new private and privatized/mixed banks, and especially by the opportunity to lend in the interbank market at high rates and low risk. And the presence of "cream-skimming" possibilities allowed new banks to survive, and even to be profitable, despite internal inefficiencies. So, the long delay in bank rehabilitation did not only negatively affect bad banks, it affected smaller and better banks too, because it weakened pressures pushing banks to develop long-term competitive strategies. After all, reduction in interest rate spreads does not seem likely to be the direct, near term result of new entry by new private banks.

MACROECONOMIC DETERMINANTS OF AGGREGATE INTEREST RATE SPREAD

Linking Micro to Macro

In this section, we use our findings from the second part of the chapter to justify assumptions and to test hypotheses about the behavior of aggregate interest rates and the aggregate interest rate spread. The purpose is to estimate an aggregate interest spread equation that rests upon our microeconomic findings.

Essentially we found that the banking system is characterized by very weak competition. Hence we assume the system to be a monopoly, and start from a stylized version of the aggregate flow of profits equation

$$Pkn = il(Akn - \mathrm{r}Dkn, E)(Akn - \mathrm{r}Dkn) + idcbrDkn + ilfcEAfc - idDkn - idfcEDfc. \quad (1)$$

P is profits, i stands for the nominal interest rate, A is interest earning assets, D is deposits, E is the current market exchange rate, and r is the rate of reserve requirements, while subscripts l and d are used to distinguish between lending and deposit interest rates, and superscripts kn and fc are used to denote kuna and foreign currency amounts. Hence, for example, il is the interest rate on domestic currency credits.

The equation states that profits equal earnings on domestic credits, interest on reserves, and interest on foreign-exchange assets minus interest paid on domestic and foreign-exchange deposits respectively. The stock supply of domestic currency credits is given by the difference between total domestic currency assets and assets that are deposited at the central bank on an obligatory basis (the term in parentheses). The central bank pays a rate of remuneration $idcb$ on these funds. Banks control the lending rate on credits in domestic currency, while commercial banks' deposit rates as well as the lending rate on foreign assets are assumed to be given exogenously. The interest rate on credits in domestic currency depends both on the amount of credits and on the nominal exchange rate. The latter is the mechanism that commercial banks use to protect the real value of their stocks and flows in an environment with a long inflation history.

First we check for the possible effect of exchange rate depreciation on the lending rate under the assumption that the banking system as a whole maximizes monopolistic profits:

$$P/E = Lkn(il/E) + ilfcAfc - idfcDfc = 0, \quad (2)$$

where $Lkn = Akn - rDkn$, or:

$$il/E = (idfcDfc - ilfcAfc)/Lkn. \quad (3)$$

The impact of the exchange rate on the lending interest rate depends on the extent of currency mismatch and the relationship between foreign-currency deposit interest rates and foreign-currency asset interest rates. Equation (3) implies that banks transmit all exogenous exchange rate shocks to clients (in the form of higher lending rates in domestic currency – that is, higher spreads – if deposit rates are given) depending on the structure of the balance sheet and interest rates.

Obviously, the sign of the right-hand side of equation (3) may vary from country to country and from period to period. Indeed, the derivative can easily be unstable; this seems to be the case in Croatia, as we will show.

It is important to point out that this effect is the result of changes in marginal cost to the banks, rather than a capital or balance-sheet revaluation effect. The latter effect would be only a one-time change, and would not affect equilibrium. In other words, given an excess of foreign-exchange liabilities relative to assets, a devaluation can create a capital loss, but this capital loss would not affect interest rates since these would already have been set so as to maximize revenue. Only if the devaluation affects marginal costs – for example, by changing the local currency costs of raising new foreign-exchange deposits – could it affect interest rates.

Second, we check for the impact of the rate of reserve requirements:

$$il/r = (il - idcb)/(Dkn/Lkn). \qquad (4)$$

As long as the lending rate on domestic credits is higher than the rate the central bank pays on banks' deposits (i.e., as long as the opportunity cost of holding reserves is positive), which is the case in reality, expression (4) is positive.

Finally, note that the first derivative of the domestic-currency interest rate over domestic assets is negative as long as both variables are positive, which is the case in reality.

Estimation Results

The monthly interest rate spread equation is estimated for the poststabilization period (1994 onward). The dependent variable is calculated on the basis of the interest rates that banks charge on new loans extended and deposits collected within a month. These figures are based on weighted averages of lending and deposit interest rates of Croatian commercial banks. The spread variable is the difference between the lending and deposit rate, calculated on the basis of interest rates on domestic currency loans and deposits only.

The list of explanatory variable candidates is given by the foregoing theoretical discussion. The first independent variable is the exchange rate versus the deutschemark (E). The end-month exchange rate is used. We use the DM exchange rate because mark-denominated or indexed assets and liabilities dominated the foreign part of banking system's balance sheet. The second variable is the rate of reserve requirements (r). In fact, this is the rate of overall obligatory reserve requirements, because two instruments of compulsory sterilization have been used in Croatia: standard reserve requirements and obligatory NBC bills. The overall rate is the weighted average of the two rates. Hence, the third explanatory variable, the rate of remuneration (*rem*), represents the weighted average of the rates of remuneration on two instruments. The fourth explanatory variable is real money ($m1$). This is taken as a proxy for bank assets.

Initial regression trials systematically exhibited strong first-order autocorrelation, so we proceeded to use AR(1) models estimated by the Cochrane-Orcutt procedure. Originally, three variables were defined in terms of rates (spread, remuneration, obligatory reserves) and two in terms of levels (nominal exchange rate and real money). Hence, in the AR(1) model, the first difference of the natural logs of the exchange rate and real money were used.

In doing the estimation, we were aware of the fact that in the few months immediately following the announcement of the stabilization program in October 1993, the variability of both the dependent and independent variables was much higher than it would be later, due to changes in the monetary and exchange rate policy regime. For example, real interest rates jumped to more than 50 percent a month after the announcement, when the exchange rate appreciated in nominal terms, and prices stabilized. From January 1994 onward expectations started to consolidate, since the program gained longer-run credibility, but movements were still erratic. In addition to this, the government experimented with a tax on lending interest rates, which was abolished in spring 1994.

A further element was commercial bankers' reluctance to appreciate the exchange rate. They expected that the central bank would buy any excess supply of foreign exchange at the prevailing exchange rate. On the other hand, the central bank was reluctant to intervene immediately because it was afraid of overextending the money supply at the beginning of the program and because it wanted to show its commitment to the floating exchange rate regime. So, there were diverging expectations between the central bank and commercial banks, which caused both rigidity and erratic reactions of money and exchange rate in the first six months after the announcement. At the very beginning of the program the system was out of equilibrium: either the exchange rate had to appreciate further or the money supply had to grow faster. Nothing happened and inertia was present both in money and exchange rate level for a few months. When agents adapted their expectations and learned how to behave in the new regime, adjustment started from both sides.

Therefore, it was not a surprise that regressions that encompassed months at the very beginning of stabilization exhibited bad results. Shortening the estimation period by one month from the beginning of the period starting in October 1993 initially gave very different estimates in different regressions. In "earlier" regressions encompassing initial observations, all variables changed signs and significance at least once. However, stable estimates occurred in equations starting from April 1994 and later equations (starting from May and so forth). This family of results has the following in common: changes in real money and nominal exchange rate do not explain the interest rate spread, and the rate of reserve requirements as well as the rate of remuneration have strong and expected impacts on the interest rate spread (positive and negative respectively). Hence we present in Table 6.10 results from the monthly equation for the period from April 1994 to August 1996 in equations (1) and (2). Equation (3) is for the period from December 1993 onward in order to show how strong initial variations of the exchange rate out of equilibrium affected the estimation results in an economically meaningless way.

The results show clearly that the exchange rate and real money did not contribute to the explanation of the interest rate spread after spring 1994. Problems with the exchange rate influence are expected both on the basis of theory and on the basis of the fact that from spring 1994 onward the exchange rate was very stable, so that pressures coming from the foreign-exchange market are reflected in variations of monetary variables – money, reserve

Table 6.10. *Determinants of aggregate interest rate spread, 1994–96*

	Dependent variable: Difference between kuna lending and deposit rates (t-statistics in parenthesis):		
	April 1994–August 1996		December 1993–August 1996
	(1)	(2)	(3)
spread t-1	0.6667	0.6786	0.6180
	(4.271)**	(4.739)**	(5.023)**
r t	0.3099	0.3065	0.2304
	(3.532)**	(3.701)**	(1.054)
rem t-1	−0.8776	−0.8815	−0.3643
	(−2.211)*	(−2.342)*	(−0.385)
DlnEt	8.1863		−194.183
	(0.234)		(−2.928)**
Dlnmlt	0.7913		0.5689
	(0.211)		(0.049)
R2adj.	0.868	0.887	0.723
Durbin's h-statistic	−0.317	−0.312	0.172
F-statistic	47.054	101.510	22.624

* Indicates statistical significance at the 5% level.
** Indicates statistical significance at the 1% level.

requirements, rate of remuneration, and interest rates – rather than through the exchange rate.

The absence of a role for real money is somewhat more surprising. It can be explained by both the nature of the monetary transmission mechanism and the structure of the banking system. Bad banks and their clients generated interest rate inelastic demand for credits, so that the central bank could not influence money-market interest rate movements downward. Money was created exclusively by foreign-exchange-market interventions, so that only banks with excess foreign reserves participated in the money creation mechanism in the first step. Generally, these were good banks.

On the other hand, sterilization of excess domestic liquidity was mainly done by increasing reserve requirements for all agents in financial intermediation. Sterilization affected the whole system, money creation was transmitted mainly through a few banks, and interest rates were inelastic. Expansionary monetary policy that increased real money in the short run had no influence on the aggregate spread. It could only jeopardize stabilization efforts by inducing exchange rate depreciation and/or inflation. These relationships are not modeled explicitly, but we believe that such developments would have had significant social costs.

The policy of sterilizing excess liquidity by raising the reserve requirement was legitimate, especially in light of the strong impact of the rate of remuneration. Besides allowing successful macroeconomic control in a system with underdeveloped indirect monetary policy instruments, this policy probably produced microeconomic benefits. Since banks were burdened with bad loans and bank restructuring/privatization was lagging behind macroeconomic reforms, the policy of simultaneously increasing the rates of reserve requirements and remuneration prevented overextension of new doubtful loans, while giving back a fair return to banks – the monthly rate of remuneration on kuna deposits at the central bank in most of 1995 and 1996 was 2 to 3 percent higher than the interest rate the banks paid on kuna deposits. Without this sterilization, managers in the bad banks would have had more funds at their disposal without any of the constraints that would have come from the rehabilitation program. Extension of new bad loans would have implied different types of social costs in terms of higher inflation and higher future fiscal costs of bank rehabilitation.

Hence the policy of increasing the reserve requirement and the rate of remuneration simultaneously minimized the probability of macroeconomic failure and prevented banking failures from getting worse. In addition to that, it minimized the size of the spread in a given financial environment.

In general, in an economy with a fiscal surplus, the central bank can remunerate more than the market deposit rate, up to the market lending rate, so that there would be no opportunity costs for banks and no impact on the spread at the margin. However, such a solution can imply social costs via the higher taxation needed for a stronger fiscal stance (in an extreme version, this would imply the ministry of finance covering the central bank's loss). And it raises the following question: wouldn't it be wiser to spend fiscal revenues directly on bank rehabilitation, which can change the behavior of the banks, than to remunerate reserve assets at a higher rate? Undoubtedly, the answer is yes, but still the policy is viable if the funds needed for credible rehabilitation are greater than funds available for remuneration, and/or if the credible institutional framework for bank rehabilitation has not been set up yet. Generally, such a monetary policy stance in a given financial environment appears to be the second best solution as long as the first best solution (credible bank restructuring) is not producing the expected results, or has not begun yet due to political, financial, or other real-world constraints.

The parameters from the second equation (Table 6.10) imply that the effect of a percentage point increase of the rate of reserve requirements can be offset by a 0.348 percentage point increase in the rate of remuneration. What the National Bank of Croatia actually did from mid-1994 to the end of 1995 was to raise the rate of reserve requirements by 12.3 percentage points and the rate of remuneration by 2 percentage points. The liquidity flow from higher remuneration on reserves was not strong enough to make the policy neutral, but a simple calculation based on estimated equation (2) suggests that the impact of the central bank's sterilization policy on the spread did not exceed 2 percentage points. The actual increase in spreads was much higher, around 10 percentage points, implying that this large increase can be predominantly explained by exogenous shocks and inertial factors. Both have to do with structural factors analyzed at the microeconomic level and expectations, outside the direct scope of influence of monetary authorities.

CONCLUSION

Croatian experience shows that it is possible to have a long period of stable exchange rate and prices even if bank rehabilitation lags behind other reforms. Nonetheless, credible, rapid rehabilitation should be done as early as possible during the course of the program, because rehabilitation is perhaps the most effective device to eliminate the effects of past and present financial market imperfections. In Croatia, these imperfections went far beyond the burden of nonperforming loans from the old system: they included high market concentration, a new burden of nonperforming loans due to improper risk valuations, regional barriers to competition, war risk, the legacies of the failure of past rehabilitations, and the low interest rate elasticity of the demand for credits and money market funds.

Our investigations showed a low degree of competition and great differences in interest rate policies among banks. The interest rate spreads of individual banks appeared to be positively correlated to capital adequacy ratios and noninterest expenses, and negatively correlated to the age and size of the bank. Excessive administrative costs in the banking industry were passed onto clients in the form of higher spreads. The banking system was trapped in a kind of a "bad equilibrium" with few incentives to enhance competition. Numerous new and small private banks did not enhance competition pressures because they operated below efficient scale and used capital instead of deposits as a prime source of funds. Our microeconomic findings suggest that only structural measures that can help control costs in banking, including bank rehabilitation, would be likely to lower spreads in Croatia.

If bank rehabilitation lags behind macroeconomic stabilization in this type of financial system, and capital inflows are strong, monetary authorities can choose the second best solution in order to preserve stability gains. It appears that (partly) sterilized foreign-exchange interventions, implemented by raising reserve requirements and remuneration, eventually combined with nominal exchange rate appreciation, are the best policy as long as the banking system is still fragile and indirect policy instruments still underdeveloped.

The macroeconomic estimation results point to the fact that monetary expansion itself exhibits no influence on interest rate spread. They also indicate that there is nothing to gain from monetary expansion in terms of interest rates, and there is a lot to lose in terms of stability. Since there were no developed market (indirect) instruments of monetary policy, increasing obligatory reserves was the most effective way to control the money supply. It diminished the future social costs of bank rehabilitation because it took excess reserves from the hands of the managers of bad banks, and it probably limited the future social costs of inflation.

On the other hand, this second best policy imposed new costs because raising reserve requirements increased the interest rate spread. However, these costs were partly offset by higher remuneration of reserves. As long as higher remuneration is covered by the central bank's profits, the social gain is straightforward. If this policy implies fiscal coverage of central bank's losses, the result is not so clear, because it implies a dominant role of the budget over the central bank, regardless of the legislative framework, and this may have bad effects in the long run.

APPENDIX

Table 6A.1. *Factor loadings*

	Factor 1 "new"	Factor 2 "efficiency"
Capital adequacy	0.89	0.21
Founded 1990 or after	0.82	—
Loans/deposits	0.67	0.41
Total assets	−0.57	—
Assets per employee	—	0.82
Administrative costs/assets	0.48	−0.73

Unit Root Tests

Having in mind the dynamics of variables in the poststabilization period, we limited our efforts to testing if variables in levels are I(1). If no higher order integration order is expected, then the most powerful statistical test is the Sargan Barghava test. The critical value of the statistic at 1 percent significance level is 1.081. Results are shown in Table 6A.2.

Table 6A.2. *Unit root tests*

	Constant		t-test		CRDW	
Variable	Level	First difference	Level	First difference	Level	First difference
Spread	19.575	−1.552	8.125	−1.256	0.259	1.536
ln(M1/M0)	0.429	−0.011	16.586	−1.119	0.149	2.228
ln(HRK/DEM)	5.910	−0.004	1,291.783	−0.893	0.782	1.711
ln(M1/P)	8.751	0.041	148.785	2.785	0.073	1.100
rr	32.814	−0.183	27.304	−0.221	0.440	2.044

REFERENCES

Anušic, Zoran, Zeljko Rohatinski, and Velimir Šonje. 1995. *A Road to Low Inflation*. Zagreb: Government of the Republic of Croatia.

Berger, Allen M., Anil K. Kashyip, and Joseph M. Scalise. 1995. "The Transformation of the US Banking Industry: What a Long Strange Trip It's Been." *Brookings Papers on Economic Activity* 2(1995): 55–218.

Ize, Alain. 1996. "Capital Inflows in the Baltic Countries, Russia and Other Countries of the Former Soviet Union: Monetary and Prudential Issues." IMF Working Paper 96/22, International Monetary Fund, Washington D.C.

Kraft, Evan. 1995. "Crisis, Reform and Restructuring: Banking in the Transition in Slovenia and Croatia." *Privredna Kretanja i Ekonomska Politika* (April): 15–57.

Kraft, Evan. 1996. "Towards a Market-Oriented Banking System in Croatia: The Roles of Entry, Competition, Privatization and Rehabilitation." Paper prepared for the 4th EACES Conference, Grenoble, 12–14 September.

McKinnon, Ronald. 1991. *The Order of Economic Liberalization*. Baltimore: John Hopkins Press.

McKinnon, Ronald, and Huw Pill. 1995. "Credible Liberalizations and International Capital Flows: The 'Over-Borrowing Syndrome.' Mimeographed, Stanford University, Stanford, Calif.

Rostowki, Jacek. 1995. "The Banking System, Credit and the Real Sector in Transition Economies." In Jacek Rostowski (ed.), *Banking Reform in Central Europe and the Former Soviet Union*. Budapest: Central European University Press.

Schranz, Mary S. 1993. "Takeovers Improve Firm Performance: Evidence from the Banking Industry." *Journal of Political Economy*.

Škreb, Marko. 1994. "Banking in Transition: The Case of Croatia." National Bank of Croatia, Zagreb.

Šonje, Velimir, and Marko Škreb. 1995. "Exchange Rate and Prices in a Stabilization Programme: The Case of Croatia." Paper presented at the First Dubrovnik Conference on Economies in Transition, June.

Wheelock, David C., and Paul W. Wilson. 1995. "Explaining Bank Failures: Deposit Insurance, Regulation, and Efficiency." *Review of Economics and Statistics*.

CHAPTER 7

Monetary and Financial Market Reform in Transition Economies: The Special Case of China

Robert A. Mundell

Is China a "transition country"? The answer is no, if by transition country is meant one that is converting from the rule of a communist party to a democracy. The answer is yes, however, if what is meant is the transformation of an economy from monopoly state socialism toward decentralized entrepreneurial capitalism. If China has traveled a smaller distance down the road to political transition than its counterparts in Eurasia,[1] it has in many respects made an even greater transformation on the economic front. If it is incorrect therefore to call China a transition country, it is undeniable that it is a transition economy.

China stands out as a special case among transition economies for several reasons. In the first place, not under the thumb of the Soviet Union, it was able to begin its economic transition more than a decade earlier than the Eurasian economies. A second difference is that it entered its economic transition as a primarily agricultural economy, starting from a much lower level of economic development than countries in Eurasia. A third difference lay in its transition strategy, which emphasized reform by sectors – sequential incrementalism – rather than gradualism or shock therapy. A fourth difference is that its growth strategy focused on the creation of free economic zones, the promotion of the international sector, and strong encouragement of foreign investment. A fifth difference is that it resisted the temptation to use the money-inflation tax as a source of finance and has instead made strong efforts through central bank policy and monetary reform to keep inflation under control.

The contrast of China's inflation and growth experience with

[1] Throughout this chapter I use the terms "Eurasia" and "Eurasian countries" to refer to the countries of Eastern Europe and the former Soviet Union.

that of Eurasia is remarkable. Whereas inflation in China was kept within reasonable limits, the Eurasian transition countries have inflated at levels that in some cases have reached five digits. While growth in China has been setting all-time records, the Eurasian economies have experienced superdecline. The mistake in the Eurasian countries was to let government output collapse before the preconditions had been laid for the monetary stability, deregulation, and tax reform needed for the expansion of private output, leaving in its wake unemployment and massive output contractions. In a few of the countries, by 1993, the contractions had ended and recovery had begun; nevertheless, by the end of 1995, not a single Eurasian country had recovered its pretransition level of GDP![2] The transition in the Eurasian countries has been a debacle of the first magnitude.

China is unique in that it is a developing country, a transition economy, and an Asian "dragon" rolled into one. What makes China's situation of exceptional importance is its potential as a world superpower and the enormous economic potential of its vast active population, coupled with the starring role of stunning growth in its high-tech coastal provinces.[3] Growing at an average rate of 9.2 percent since 1978, and at 12.1 percent over 1992 to 1995, China has set new growth records. Even more remarkable has been China's trade, with exports rising fourteenfold, from $10 billion in 1978 (0.8 percent of world exports) to $148.8 billion in 1995 (almost 3.5 percent of world exports).[4] International reserves in 1996 topped $75 billion.

Like most growth "miracles," China's has been associated with the shift of labor from low-productivity agriculture to high-productivity industry, combined with rapid urbanization, absorption of foreign technology, and a favorable age distribution of the labor force. The period of supergrowth ends when bottlenecks appear. A typical bottleneck is the supply of labor. But in China this is a long way off. Two-thirds of the labor force is still in agriculture

[2] See my essay "Inflation and Growth in the Transition Countries," in M. Guitian and R. Mundell (eds.), *Inflation and Growth in China* (Washington, D.C.: International Monetary Fund, 1996).

[3] Parts of this section are taken from my introduction to the *Inflation and Growth* volume referred to in note 2.

[4] Joint ventures accounted for almost 40% of foreign trade in 1995 (*China Daily* 15, no. 4516 (13 January 1996): 1. In 1995 foreign investment amounted to $35 billion and China's trade surplus was nearly $20 billion.

and there are more than 150 million surplus workers in the countryside. China will run out of water before it runs out of people.

The supply of capital could become a bottleneck unless saving keeps up. But in China, saving, spurred by the household sector, has increased from 30 percent of GDP in 1978 to 40 percent in 1994. The population policy, limiting families to one child, deprived adults of their traditional social security system and forced households to save. Partly in response, household saving soared from 18.6 percent of total savings in 1978 to 71.5 percent in 1993 with no signs of abating in recent years. Moreover, technology-intensive capital is available from abroad with direct investment of $28 billion in 1994 and $37 billion in 1995. This has fed the booming capital-intensive export-oriented coastal regions to which Deng Xiaoping had given his blessing in his 1992 tour of Southern China.

This is not to say that supergrowth can be taken for granted or will continue indefinitely. Neglect of important sectors of the Chinese economy has created bottlenecks in communication, energy, transportation, and financial management. These key industries are exclusively reserved for the public sector.[5] A major problem exists with the structure and efficiency of state enterprises. By contrast to the booming private sector, which grew at an annual average rate of 38.5 percent from 1990 to 1994, the state sector expanded only 7.1 percent over the same period. The share of industrial output accounted for by state enterprises has fallen from 80.7 percent in 1978 to less than 40 percent in 1995.

The solvency of state-owned enterprises, more than half of which make losses, presents a major problem. Instead of losses forcing cost-cutting adjustments or bankruptcies, the typical state-owned enterprise has been kept in business with infusions of credit from the banking system. As a consequence, debts of state-owned firms have mounted, building up a chain of interfirm indebtedness.[6] A major stumbling block to reform of the state

[5] A major priority of the Chinese government is said to be to maintain ownership of the firms in the "vital" industries such as telecommunications, steel, electric utilities, and transportation. These firms number less than 1,000, out of a total of 74,066 firms (1992), so there is enormous scope for privatization.

[6] Firm indebtedness can be broken into (a) intrafirm debts, mainly debts to workers' pension funds; (b) interfirm debts; and (c) firm-bank debts. An attempt to resolve the debt-chain problem in the early 1990s did not work out because firms used new central bank funds primarily for repayment of intrafirm debt, essentially repayment of debts to pension funds.

enterprises has come from managers and workers with vested interests in the security of their jobs and pensions.

In the early years of the reform era, agriculture, liberalized in the early 1980s when the commune system was replaced with the household responsibility system, was the showpiece of China's reform strategy and it resulted in a grain surplus, albeit temporary. But since 1985 infrastructure in the rural sector has been neglected and production has stagnated. When, in 1993, inflationary expectations increased, farmers hoarded grain, and market supplies fell. The tropismatic response of the authorities was to blame speculators and reimpose some price controls. Recently, the government has reemphasized agricultural reform and put an increase in grain production high on its agenda.

Equally important has been the need for reform and modernization of China's financial system. Prior to 1978 (and still today), the People's Bank of China (PBC) was the dominant financial institution, handling most of the performing transactions of the country; the Bank of China (BOC) and the People's Construction Bank of China (PCBC) operated as special departments within the PBC.[7] After 1978 reforms were implemented and these banks, by 1983, had become specialized banks under the PBC, a two-tier banking system was established for the first time in a socialist country, and the PBC became a genuine (but not independent) central bank. In 1993 further steps were taken to lodge control of the money supply in the hands of the PBC, to finance budget deficits with issues of short- and long-term bonds instead of PBC overdrafts, and to establish a clear-cut distinction between "policy lending" and "commercial lending." Policy lending includes loans for investment to infrastructure projects, to loss-making state-owned enterprises (SOEs), for the alleviation of poverty, to subsidized sectors such as education and health, and for power and transport facilities that have been designated national priorities.

Many of these reforms were confirmed in the monetary law passed on 18 March 1995, the first monetary law since the founding of the People's Republic. This law confirmed the role of the

[7] For a recent review of China's financial reforms, see H. Merhran, M. Quintyn, T. Nordman, and B. Laurens, "Monetary and Exchange System Reforms in China: An Experiment in Gradualism," IMF Occasional Paper no. 141 (International Monetary Fund, Washington, D.C., September 1996).

PBC as the sole monetary authority in China and outlined its functions, powers, and responsibilities. The law was the outcome of a long debate on the subject that had begun sixteen years before the law came into effect and which drew on international experiences and advice from the International Monetary Fund.[8]

Two basic issues were left open in connection with the goals of monetary policy. One of them was the subject of intensive debate. In an important policy document it had been stated that "stability of the value of the currency is the central bank's main objective." However, in a document issued by the State Council, growth was also mentioned: "The ultimate objective of the central bank's monetary policy is to maintain the stability of the value of the currency so as to promote economic growth." A version of this latter objective came out in the new monetary law, which states that "The aim of the monetary policy is to maintain the stability of the value of currency and thereby promote economic growth." This phrase provides some discretion to the authorities, although it is acknowledged that if the law is interpreted correctly, monetary policy will not be used to promote growth if it is at the expense of stability of the currency.

But what does "stability of the currency" mean? It could refer to stability of the money supply (or its rate of growth), stability of the price level, or stability of the exchange rate. If China had a stable currency in terms of other currencies, there would be no room for an independent policy with respect to the price level or the money supply. On more than one occasion China has had to confront conflicts between internal and external stability and its choice of exchange system is closely tied up with the interpretation of its new monetary law.

The significance of the new law will only be understood in the light of China's past experiences and progress in the modernization and reform of its financial system. The following pages will therefore review key aspects of China's financial economy, touching on such subjects as inflation and growth experience; monetary deepening; the relation between government credit and investment; interpretation of the targets of China's monetary policy;

[8] See the discussion in Wenkai Yang, "Significance of China's New Monetary Law," in Manuel Guitian and Robert Mundell (eds.), *Inflation and Growth in China* (Washington, D.C.: International Monetary Fund, 1996), 284–86.

and the international aspects of China's financial position and prospective policies, especially taking into account Hong Kong's integration after 1 July 1997.

INFLATION, GROWTH, AND RESERVES

When the Communist Party set up a new government on the mainland in 1949, it lacked organized sources of revenue and, like most revolutionary governments, turned to the printing press. The result was a sharp hyperinflation that necessitated a 10,000:1 currency reform in 1952. Since that time, or at least until the 1980s, inflation ceased to be a problem for China. From 1953 to 1984, inflation in China was lower even than in the most stable Western countries.

In the early period, from 1953 to 1959, inflation averaged about 1.5 percent; this corresponded to an average (but erratic) recorded growth rate of 10.7 percent for the period. Over the next three years, during the famine of the "Great Leap Forward," output fell by one-third and prices rose 24 percent. But for the next decade the price level actually declined at an average rate of 1.5 percent, almost restoring the prefamine price level, while growth averaged 10 percent. In the following years from 1973 to 1984, when Western countries were experiencing two-digit inflation rates in the wake of the breakdown of the international monetary system, prices rose only by an average of 1.5 percent, while growth was maintained at a respectable 7.7 percent.

It should not be overlooked, of course, that general price controls existed in the years before the mid-1980s. Measured price changes under a system of price controls does not accurately reflect the "true" rate of inflation, due to price repression. Over this early period, China's economy was characterized by excess demand, shortages, and a monetary overhang. With the lifting of price controls, therefore, prices would increase even in the absence of additional monetary expansion. For this reason, comparison of recent inflation with that of earlier decades is not strictly valid.

The year 1985, however, saw an important change in the inflation situation. In that year, several prices were liberalized at a time when credit was expanding rapidly. For the three years 1985–87, prices rose at an average of 7.4 percent while the money supply

Table 7.1. *Inflation, growth, money, and the exchange rate, 1985–97*

	1985	1986	1987	1988	1989	1990	1991	1992	1993	1994	1995	1996	1997
Growth	12.9	8.9	11.6	11.3	4.1	3.8	9.20	14.2	13.5	12.7	10.5	9.7	8.8
Inflation	12.0	6.5	7.2	18.7	18.3	3.1	3.5	6.3	14.6	24.2	16.9	8.3	2.8
Nom GDP	23.1	13.6	16.7	24.5	13.7	10.5	14.2	20.7	28.8	33.6	25.1	17.4	10.2
Money	23.2	27.9	18.5	20.0	6.3	20.1	28.2	30.3	21.8	28.5	18.8	19.8	27.0
Exchange rate Yuan/$	2.94	3.45	3.72	3.72	3.77	4.78	5.32	5.51	5.76	8.62	8.35	8.31	8.28

was rising on the average at 23.2 percent. The two following years were more alarming. When further decontrol measures were implemented in 1988, prices soared by 18.5 percent in 1988 and 17.8 percent in 1989. Two years of back-to-back inflation of more than 15 percent created a sense of panic and the beginning of a run on bank deposits.[9]

Forced to act, the government tightened monetary conditions, reduced investment, scrapped further decontrols, and postponed the projected elimination of the two-tier pricing system. The money supply expanded by only 6.3 percent in 1989 and investment increased by only 1.2 percent in 1990. In response to these measures the economy responded sharply; inflation came down to 1.4 percent in 1990 and 5.1 percent in 1991. The inflationary scare of 1988 and 1989 was calmed and macroeconomic balance was restored. The disinflation measures, however, had a high cost in terms of economic growth. From its extraordinary average of 11.5 percent over 1983 to 1988, growth plummeted to 4.3 percent in 1989 and 3.9 percent in 1990. See Table 7.1.

Costly as the recession was in terms of growth, it brought in its train an important change in the macroeconomy. For the first time, firms in the new China had difficulty selling outputs and had to compete for markets by lowering prices. The slowdown thus had the salutary effect of ending the era of the shortage economy and introducing a better framework for macroeconomic stability.

Recovery came in 1991. Investment grew by 18.8 percent and GDP growth recovered to 8.0 percent. The expansion continued

[9] See Gang Yi, *Money, Banking, and Financial Markets in China* (Boulder, Colo.: Westview Press, 1994), 198–99.

at an even more rapid rate in 1992 and 1993 with investment increasing by over 28 and 22 percent. The economy heated up with growth in 1992 and 1993 at the heady rates of 13.6 and 13.4 percent respectively. The economy was once again locked in its supergrowth mode.

Once again, the resumption of supergrowth brought a cost in terms of inflation. After two years of an inflation rate averaging less than 5 percent, it increased in subsequent years to 6.4 percent in 1992 and then to 14.7 percent in 1993. Rapid investment was again being financed by the banking system. The money supply expanded by 20.1 percent in 1990, 28.2 percent in 1991, 30.3 percent in 1992, but then fell back to 21.6 percent in 1993.

The year 1994 began with a dramatic change in the exchange rate. On 1 January 1994, China announced steps to unify its exchange rate and establish "conditional" current-account convertibility. At the same time it raised the renminbi price of the dollar from 5.8 Yuan = \$1 to 8.4 Yuan = \$1, a devaluation of almost 45 percent. This devaluation, achieved in moving to what was announced as a floating system (but in reality was a quasi-fixed rate system), was a boon to export markets and helped to bolster export-led growth.

Devaluation also, however, ignited new inflationary pressures. Prices of international goods rose directly, and other prices rose as a consequence of the balance-of-payments surplus that expanded the reserve base of the monetary system. Driven largely by central bank purchases of foreign-exchange reserves, the money supply expanded by over 30 percent in 1994 and consumer prices shot up to an alarming 24.1 percent rate.

Again, the government had to take corrective action. It was not initially obvious, however, what steps were necessary. There were two points of view that the monetary authorities had to consider. On the one hand, insofar as the exchange rate change undervalued the renminbi, it could be argued that the rise in prices was a once-for-all "price spike" applying to traded goods; the inflationary potential of the undervalued renminbi would be largely dissipated by the rise in prices that took place in 1994; according to this view, inflation would subside of its own accord even without a change in current monetary policy as the surplus in the balance of payments was being brought under control. On the other hand, the danger was more serious if the extraordinary rise in prices in 1994 carried with it the threat that it would raise inflationary expectations, bring about a resumption of hoarding and another flight from money, or if it were accommodated by further credit expansion. Because the inflation risk seemed more urgent, the authorities decided to tighten. Credit expansion was reduced and investment was curtailed; the money supply, which had increased by 30.4 percent in 1994 was held to 24.6 percent in 1995.

The three major inflation indexes turned down in 1995. For 1995,[10] the rate of increase of consumer prices had been reduced from 24.2 percent in 1994 to 16.9 percent in 1995; similarly, the increase in the retail price index had come down from 21.7 percent in 1994 to 14.8 percent in 1995; and the increase in the GDP deflator had fallen from 19.5 to 13.5 percent. Growth fell, but only slightly, to 10.5 percent. In 1996, price increases had returned to the single-digit pattern and in 1997 had fallen below 3 percent. The stabilization policy was therefore an outstanding success.

China's promising economic prospects in the world of Asian and world finance make its exchange rate policy a matter of exceptional importance. The renminbi had been held in the range of Y 1.5–2.5 = $1 for three decades before the 1980s. After 1985, when the dollar depreciated against other major currencies, the renminbi started to depreciate against the dollar, the latter reaching an average of Y 3.7 in 1987, Y 4.7 in 1989, Y 5.8 in 1993, Y 8.6 in 1994, Y 8.3 at the end of 1995, and has remained around that range thoughout 1996 and 1997. The problem for macroeconomic management in the future is to coordinate monetary, fiscal, and exchange rate policy to prevent rising costs from generating the syndrome of overvaluation.

What level of external reserves does China need? There is no scientific way of determining an "optimal" level of reserves. It is related to the exchange system and the adjustment mechanism. If a country has a fixed exchange rate and allows the balance of payments to determine its monetary policy (as in a currency board arrangement), there will be confidence in the ability of the system to withstand shocks and fewer reserves will be necessary; at the same time the fixed exchange rate will provide an anchor around which other policies revolve and expectations about future policy can be formed. If, on the other hand, a country fixes the exchange

[10] The monthly inflation rate actually reached a peak in October 1994.

rate while it at the same time pursues a monetary policy unconnected with the balance of payments, it puts itself on a collision course with stability and there is no feasible level of reserves that can save it from disaster. Fixed exchange rate systems survive only if monetary policy is endogenous.

There was a time when a country might be content with reserve levels equal to about a quarter of annual imports. This level sufficed in the Bretton Woods era before 1971. But with the extreme degree of volatility associated with flexible exchange rates today, required reserves are much larger. Nevertheless, for most countries they have proved to be hopelessly inadequate,[11] as the fiascos in Mexico in 1994–95, and in East Asia in 1997 and 1998 made abundantly clear. A major part of the problem of course is that these countries had pseudofixed exchange rates – that is, they fixed the exchange rate without dedicating monetary policy to balance-of-payments equilibrium. This weakness made them sitting ducks for speculators in recent years, and many of the countries had to have recourse to massive bailouts from the International Monetary Fund (IMF) and the international community at the expense of their policy sovereignty.

The loss of policy sovereignty needs to be emphasized. National foreign exchange and gold reserves are needed as a cushion against contingencies and to defend a country's exchange rate, protect it against speculative attacks, and maintain confidence in the government's ability to carry out its economic strategy. But reserves are also a symbol of a nation's power and independence. In the absence of ample international reserves, a nation subjected to speculative attack would have to borrow from the credit markets, other governments, or the IMF, in the process accepting conditions that are not compatible with other objectives. The typical medicine for a country forced to draw upon the IMF involves tight money, tax increases, and cuts in government spending, measures that in some cases are necessary but in others undermine growth prospects. In the case of China, with its two-digit growth rates, a cessation of growth is particularly

[11] In 1996, imports and reserves, expressed in billions of dollars, and the ratio of reserves to imports, expressed in percentages, were as follows: for Thailand, 73.5 and 25.9 (35.2%); for Korea, 150.3 and 23.1 (15.4%); for Malaysia 78.4 and 18.2 (23.2%); for Indonesia 42.9 and 12.4 (28.9%); for Singapore 131.3 and 53.2 (40.5%); for China 138.9 and 73.0 (52.6%); and for Japan 349.2 and 144.2 (41.3%). Source: *IMF International Financial Statistics Yearbook* (1996).

costly. Only a mismanaged economy needs to draw upon the IMF.

In order to avoid the ramifications of indebtedness to the IMF, it would be desirable for China to build up a substantial portfolio of international reserves. In the case of China a figure for reserves (including the reserves of Hong Kong) of $200 billion would not be excessive, bearing in mind that the opportunity cost of these reserves, if invested in liquid short-term assets, is relatively small for the insurance and independence they provide. Once the desired level of reserves is reached, automatic reinvestment of the earnings would result in a growth of reserves at a rate equal to the interest rate.

Another consideration relates to the composition of reserves. Most of China's reserves are in dollars, as they should be, given the status of the dollar as the world's most important currency and the exchange rate policy of the Chinese monetary authorities, which has been directed mainly at holding the yuan-dollar rate. In the course of building up to a larger total level of reserves, however, it would be desirable to diversify China's reserve portfolio into yen, marks (or, later, euros), and even gold. International currency reserves have the defect (from the standpoint of the holder) that they are subject to political manipulation and may be blocked in the event of international disturbances. The time to diversify, of course, is not when the yen is high, but when it is near the bottom of its cycle. Such diversification should be achieved in the course of accumulating additional reserves rather than in switching out of existing holdings.

China has much to gain from further movements toward financial liberalization. In 1994 China took a big step to current account convertibility and unification of the exchange rate. Further steps in the direction of full convertibility of the renminbi and greater liberalization have been facilitated by the strong (but weakening) external payments position and bulging foreign exchange reserves. It once appeared that China's goal of full convertibility by the year 2000 could be achieved one or two years before that date. The Asian currency crisis have made even that date unlikely. When complete current-account convertibility is achieved, however, it should probably be associated with another devaluation designed to maintain the momentum of the export boom, especially if China has to cope with competitive devaluations as a result of the financial crisis in several other East Asian countries. In the meantime, China's best policy stance is to consolidate the gains on the inflation front and keep the inflation rate to low single-digit levels.

MONETARY DEEPENING

China has been a dual economy in the sense that some sectors were monetized while others were not. To investigate this phenomenon, we shall find it convenient to relate different measures of money to nominal GNP. The different measures of money are currency in circulation, M0; the latter plus demand deposits, M1; and the latter plus savings and time deposits, M2. The ratio of M0 to Y will be called M0 liquidity; the ratio of M1 to GNP, M1 liquidity; and the ratio of M2 to GNP, M2 liquidity. The second column in Table 7.2 shows that currency outside banks, as a proportion of national income, quadrupled between 1952 and 1990, a clear sign of the rapid spread of the cash economy. Since 1990, I have used GDP rather than national income as the deflator, and the trend continues until 1993. In 1993, however, the upward trend came to an end and in the following two years currency as a share of GDP declined. If we assume the downward trend is sustained, what can have caused the reversal of trend?

One explanation is that the downward trend reflects an upsurge in inflationary expectations. If that were true, it would mean that, with the reduction in the inflation rate, the upward trend in the currency liquidity ratio would be resumed. If increased inflationary expectations were the reason, however, we should expect similar changes in the other liquidity ratios.[12] But M1 liquidity was more or less unchanged while M2 liquidity soared. For this reason, the inflationary expectations hypothesis does not seem to be the likely explanation.

An alternative explanation is that monetization of the currency component of the economy has been satiated and that the role of currency as an inferior asset has begun to set in. Remember Marshall McLuhan's definition of money as "the poor man's credit card." Of the three categories of liquidity, M2 has the

[12] Inflation could be expected to affect the liquidity ratios in the same direction unless interest rates on M2 liquidity, or convenience benefits on M1 liquidity were altered.

Table 7.2. *Liquidity ratios in China: 1952–95(%)*

Year	M0 liquidity		M1 liquidity		M2 liquidity	
1952	4.7		15.7		17.2	
1953	5.6		14.3		16.1	
1954	5.5		15.6		17.7	
1955	5.1		16.0		18.5	
1956	6.5		16.8		19.8	
1957	5.8		17.9		21.8	
1958	6.1		23.0		28.0	
1959	6.1		26.5		32.1	
1960	7.9		28.1		33.5	
1961	12.6		38.6		44.2	
1962	11.5		42.8		47.2	
1963	9.0		39.1		43.7	
1964	6.9		32.5		37.3	
1965	6.5		31.2		35.9	
1966	6.8		31.1		35.7	
1967	8.2		37.4		42.3	
1968	9.5		41.6		47.1	
1969	8.5		36.1		40.8	
1970	6.4		29.7		33.8	
1971	6.6		30.1		34.4	
1972	7.1		30.4		35.3	
1973	7.2		32.3		37.5	
1974	7.5		34.1		39.9	
1975	7.3		34.7		40.7	
1976	8.4		38.1		44.7	
1977	7.4		35.0		41.9	
1978	7.0		31.5		38.5	
1979	8.0		35.1		43.5	
1980	9.4		39.1		50.0	
1981	10.1		43.4		56.7	
1982	10.3		45.0		60.8	
1983	11.2		46.1		64.9	
1984	14.0		51.9		73.4	
1985	14.0		46.3		69.3	
1986	15.4		50.9		79.3	
1987	15.5		49.0		81.9	
1988	18.1		46.6		78.9	
1989	17.9		44.0		83.2	
1990	18.5	14.9[a]	47.8	39.6[a]	96.7	83.0[a]
1991	19.7	15.7	52.4	44.5	108.9	92.1
1992	21.7	18.0	56.9	48.8	115.6	101.2
1993		18.6		45.2		95.4
1994		16.6		49.0		106.8
1995		15.0		48.8		115.8

[a] Alternative series for 1990–95 from *IMF International Financial Statistics* (May 1996).

Sources: Original data from *Almanac of China's Finance and Banking; Statistical Yearbook of China*; and *Statistical Abstract of China*; see Gang Yi, *Money, Banking and Financial Markets in China* (Boulder, Colo.: Westview Press, 1994), table 4.2.

Table 7.3 *Liquidity ratios in several countries and various years (%)*

Country	M0 liquidity		M1 liquidity		M2 liquidity	
China 1954	5.5		15.6		17.7	
China 1964	6.1		32.5		37.3	
China 1974	7.5		34.1		39.9	
China 1984	14.0		51.9		73.4	
China 1992	21.7	18.0[a]	56.9	48.8[a]	115.6	101.2[a]
China 1994		16.6		49.0		106.8
China 1995		15.0		48.8		115.8
Japan 1954	7.5		25.8		58.4	
Japan 1994	9.0		32.3		113.8	
Korea 1974	5.4		12.7		32.8	
Korea 1994	4.3		10.6		43.6	
Singapore 1974	10.5		22.9		55.4	
Singapore 1994	8.9		22.2		89.2	
Philippines 1994	5.6		9.5		45.8	
Thailand 1994	4.3		20.4		167.0	
Malaysia 1994	8.5		30.3		89.2	
Indonesia 1992	4.4		11.1		45.8	
United States 1974	4.7		19.7		62.9	
United States 1994	5.4		18.3		59.8	
Czech Republic 1994	8.1		38.9		80.9	
Slovenia 1994	2.6		7.8		34.6	

[a] GDP deflator; earlier figures for China use national income as deflator.
Sources: *IMF International Financial Statistics,* various years.

highest income elasticity of demand for money and M0 the lowest.

China's cash liquidity ratio has probably peaked and is now tending downward. Nevertheless, it is astonishingly high by international standards. Table 7.3 presents liquidity ratios for various countries in various years at various states of development. China's cash ratio is far higher than all the other countries. What is the explanation?

The answer is the primitive nature of the payments system in China. Most payments are made in cash; checking accounts in renminbi are rare. M1 has little independent meaning in China as distinct from M2. A major banking reform is required before China's financial institutions can be brought up to modern standards.

The growth in M2 liquidity in China is remarkable. At the end of 1995 it was 115 percent of GDP. As incomes have risen, savings

Table 7.4. *Ratio of reserves to money + quasi money*

Year	Reserves/(M + OM)	Year	Reserves/(M + OM)
1985	67.9	1991	40.9
1986	44.5	1992	37.5
1987	39.1	1993	37.9
1988	38.2	1994	36.7
1989	40.8	1995	34.2
1990	42.0	1996	

Sources: *IMF International Financial Statistics*, various years.

Table 7.5. *The monetary deepening criterion: Ratio of reserve money to "total" money, 30 countries, 1993 or 1994 (%)*

Country	Ratio	Country	Ratio
China 1994	36.7	U.K. 1993	3.9
Malaysia 1994	22.5	Canada 1994	6.3
Singapore 1994	17.3	France 1993	6.9
Mongolia 1994	33.1	United States 1994	10.3
Pakistan 1994	40.2	Germany 1994	14.6
Korea 1994	18.2	Spain 1994	15.9
Bangladesh 1994	30.0	Portugal 1994	24.7
Sri Lanka 1994	36.3	Czech Rep. 1994	26.9
Thailand 1994	11.6	Poland 1994	28.3
Phillippines 1994	25.9	Egypt 1994	32.1
Bhutan 1994	53.0	Argentina 1993	33.3
Nepal 1993	41.5	Colombia 1994	45.4
Israel 1994	18.3	Romania 1994	45.8
Ghana 1994	40.0	Mali 1994	71.5
India 1993	32.4	Chad 1994	80.0

Sources: *IMF International Financial Statistics Yearbook* (1995).

have increased and time deposits have been a major component of savings. This partly reflects lack of alternative outlets to savings in capital markets. An important consequence is that the ratio of reserve to "total" money, as measured by the sum of money and quasi money, has declined precipitously. As Table 7.4 shows, it fell in half from 1985 to 1995.

Nevertheless the ratio of reserves to "total" money is much higher in China than in most other countries. Table 7.5 presents some data on monetary deepening for thirty countries, where monetary deepening is measured by the ratios of reserve money to "total" money (again, as defined by money plus quasi money). By inspection it can be seen that the most advanced countries all have low ratios of reserve money to "total" money, whereas the least-developed countries have high ratios. For example, all the advanced countries have lower reserve ratios than China and so do most of the more advanced countries in Asia. In other words there is a general presumption that reserve ratios are in inverse relation to economic development.

Table 7.6 presents more information about income levels and monetary deepening. It ranks 115 countries according to 1995 per capita income, measured in U.S. dollars at then current exchange rates, and relates this data to the monetary-deepening relation, the ratio of reserve money to money plus quasi money. The inverse correlation between per capita income and the ratio of reserve money to total money is readily apparent. The 26 richest countries – from Switzerland down to Spain – all had reserve ratios of 21 percent or lower. On the other hand, the 26 poorest countries – from Ethiopia at the bottom to Lesotho – all had reserve ratios over 30 percent.

GOVERNMENT CREDIT AND INFLATIONARY FINANCE

Inflations have always been associated with government budget deficits. During wartime, governments bite off more than they can chew. They can't pay for wars with taxes because the citizens would revolt. So they pay for wars by printing money, what economists generally call the inflation tax. Because, however, seigniorage can be extracted even without inflation, it should more generally be called the money tax.

Governments have a budget constraint. They have to finance expenditures in one of three ways: taxation, borrowing, and monetary finance. The choice of financial method depends partly on the level of financial development and the stability of the financial system. Some governments can finance expenditures by issuing debt because there is confidence that the government will repay the debt and there is confidence in the currency in which the debt is denominated. International investors look at both country default risk and at currency risk.

Table 7.6. *Income per capita and monetary deepening criterion: Ratio of reserve money to money plus quasi money, 1994*

Rank by GDP/N	Country	Population 1995 (est.)	GDP per capita, US$, 1995	Reserve money/ money + Q-money, 1994
1	Switzerland	7.0	35,329	8.8
2	Japan	125.0	32,496	8.5
3	Denmark	5.2	28,331	12.0
4	United States	263.0	27,122	10.3
5	United Arab Emirates	1.2	25,722	19.3[a]
6	Norway	4.3	24,431	8.1[a]
7	Sweden	8.8	24,012	13.7[b]
8	Germany	81.6	23,809	14.6
9	Austria	8.1	23,552	10.5
10	Hong Kong	6.2	23,117	n/a
11	Kuwait	1.8	22,863	7.3
12	France	58.1	22,377	6.9[a]
13	Singapore	3.0	21,303	17.3
14	Canada	29.5	21,280	6.3
15	Netherlands	15.4	19,965	12.0
16	Belgium	10.1	19,703	13.7[b]
17	Iceland	0.3	19,128	9.3
18	Australia	18.0	18,708	8.5
19	Italy	57.3	18,486	21.0[a]
20	Finland	5.1	18,282	17.5
21	United Kingdom	58.0	17,473	3.9[a]
22	Israel	5.4	14,874	18.3
23	New Zealand	3.5	14,516	2.4[a]
24	Taiwan	21.4	13,625	12.9
25	Ireland	3.6	13,419	13.9[a]
26	Spain	39.2	11,661	15.9
27	Cyprus	0.8	10,909	25.0
28	Iraq	20.1	9,676	40.1
29	Korea	45.0	9,202	18.2
30	Barbados	0.3	8,734	16.5
31	Argentina	35.0	8,601	33.3[a]
32	Oman	2.0	8,294	21.2
33	Bahrain	0.6	7,660	12.9
34	Portugal	9.9	7,342	24.7
35	Greece	10.5	7,291	27.6[a]
36	Malta	0.4	6,951	35.3
37	Seychelles	0.1	6,950	51.7
38	Saudi Arabia	18.0	6,594	26.9[b]
39	Uruguay	3.2	5,314	34.7
40	Mexico	95.0	5,237	12.9

Table 7.6. (*cont.*)

Rank by GDP/N	Country	Population 1995 (est.)	GDP per capita, US$, 1995	Reserve money/ money + Q-money, 1994
41	Malaysia	20.1	4,164	22.5
42	Gabon	1.1	3,596	32.4
43	Grenada	0.1	3,548	20.2
44	Chile	14.0	3,493	86.1
45	Trinidad and Tobago	1.3	3,340	24.4
46	Hungary	10.3	3,274	59.0
47	Botswana	1.5	3,206	44.7
48	Syria	14.1	2,995	62.8[b]
49	Mauritius	1.1	2,993	19.4
50	South Africa	41.0	2,969	11.7[b]
51	Panama	2.6	2,811	46.5[c]
52	Venezuela	22.0	2,783	22.6
53	Brazil	165.0	2,734	13.5[a]
54	Thailand	60.3	2,559	11.6
55	Costa Rica	3.1	2,548	49.2
56	Algeria	28.0	2,429	34.2
57	Paraguay	4.8	2,371	41.3
58	Turkey	63.0	2,297	24.5
59	Fiji		2,165	15.0
60	Jamaica	2.6	2,067	37.4
61	Colombia	35.0	1,901	45.4
62	Peru	23.5	1,828	35,9
63	Tunisia	8.9	1,717	23.0
64	Cameroon	13.1	1,571	26.3
65	Cape Verde Island	0.4	1,444	61.5
66	Congo	2.6	1,391	50.6
67	Ecuador	11.4	1,389	44.8[b]
68	Guatemala	10.5	1,338	28.9
69	Vanuatu	0.2	1,318	11.6
70	El Salvador	5.6	1,318	34.6
71	Papua N. Guinea	4.2	1,204	10.8[a]
72	Morocco	27.1	1,154	29.7
73	Iran	61.0	1,120	41.3[a]
74	Swaziland	0.9	1,092	22.3
75	Jordan	5.5	1,067	51.6
76	Bolivia	8.5	962	20.8
77	Dominican Republic	8.0	931	44.9
78	Philippines	68.5	898	25.9
79	Côte d'Ivoire	14.2	839	35.8
80	Senegal	8.3	834	38.6
81	Indonesia	195.2	789	12.7[b]
82	Liberia	5.1	755	68.9

Table 7.6. (*cont.*)

Rank by GDP/N	Country	Population 1995 (est.)	GDP per capita, US$, 1995	Reserve money/ money + Q-money, 1994
83	Zimbabwe	11.5	698	30.7
84	St. Lucia	0.1	661	19.0
85	Egypt	59.1	654	32.1
86	Honduras	5.9	639	27.6
87	Haiti	7.2	554	63.7[a]
88	Benin	5.5	494	48.8
89	Togo	4.0	487	30.5
90	Lesotho	2.0	470	18.3
91	China	1210.0	450	36.7
92	Burkina Faso	10.0	405	64.3
93	Comoros	0.6	404	38.1
94	Central African Republic	3.4	403	86.8
95	Mauritania	2.2	394	72.2
96	Pakistan	130.0	381	40.2
97	Ghana	17.5	365	40.2
98	Sierra Leone	4.5	348	53.1
99	India	950.0	324	32.4[a]
100	Madagascar	14.5	309	37.1
101	Mali	10.8	300	71.5
102	Niger	8.6	273	56.6
103	Nigeria	110.0	253	42.1[b]
104	Sudan	29.8	251	51.7
105	Bangladesh	120.0	242	30.0
106	Malawi	10.0	233	42.7
107	Somalia	9.2	202	42.8[b]
108	Rwanda	7.9	199	41.7[a]
109	Kenya	30.0	188	33.5[a]
110	Burundi	6.3	184	38.4[b]
111	Zambia	9.5	179	52.0[b]
112	Nepal	21.6	156	41.5[a]
113	Mozambique	17.5	72	98.7[d]
114	Zaire	43.5	70	43.7
115	Ethiopia	60.0	52	58.0

[a] 1993.
[b] Various earlier years.
[c] Ratio of foreign assets to deposit money + quasi money.
[d] 1991. Figures for reserve money and money + quasi money approximated from IFS data.

Sources: WEFA's *Rankings of the World's Economies by Size* (1994) for GDP per capita; *IMF International Financial Statistics Yearbook* (1994) for reserve ratios.

The United States can finance its large deficit, equal to about 2 percent of its GDP, by issuing bonds. This is because (1) the United States government has no history of default, so creditors expect to be repaid; and (2) there is confidence in dollar-denominated government bonds; there is little ground for expectation that the United States is about to embark on an inflationary course. Similarly, there is confidence in the government bonds of Japan, Germany, and Switzerland because there is confidence in their currencies. The same is true of France and the United Kingdom, but not to quite the same extent; the public thinks the currencies of these countries might depreciate and so they have to pay a higher interest rate to cover a higher currency risk. As we go down the line we come to Italy and Spain, who have to pay high interest rates because there is not too much confidence in the abilities of the governments to get its deficit under control, and avoid monetization of the debt and currency depreciation.

Nevertheless, these countries all have the ability to borrow both domestically and internationally in their own currencies. But the currencies of most countries of the world are not like this. Countries with histories of inflation and currency depreciation, or governments that have a penchant for inflation, will not be able to borrow in national currencies. These countries will have to borrow in foreign currencies, creating the risk that the domestic currency obligations will be higher if the foreign currency appreciates. But any kind of borrowing reaches a limit sooner or later. The higher a country's debt, the higher the country risk and the less likely that a country can borrow even in foreign currency at reasonable interest rates. A country's credit rating is very carefully watched by the international financial community, and this fact exerts a certain discipline on a country's macroeconomic policies. Every country wants to maintain the confidence of the international financial community.

Nevertheless, for many countries, there is no confidence in government bonds. The countries with very low domestic public debt – GDP ratios are nearly all countries with too much inflation. No one will buy the government bonds without high interest rates to cover inflation risk, and the government cannot afford to pay high interest rates. The public thinks the inflation rate will be higher than the government says it will be so market agreement is not possible. There are no long-term bonds in countries with significant – and variable – inflation rates.

Countries that do not have a well-developed bond market have recourse to inflationary finance – printing money. How much money to print, or let the banking system create, is one of the hardest policy choices a government, or its central bank, must make. No one wants to say that countries should not create money. Society needs money, as a medium of exchange and unit of account. It has a productivity. A scarcity of money sacrifices output. But too much money leads to inflation. How to strike the balance?

The answer is not easy. The difficulty lies in this solemn fact: the government determines how much money is in existence, but the public determines its real value. If people have more money than they want to hold, they will spend it and prices will rise. If they have less money than they want to hold, they will sell goods and the price level, if it is flexible, will fall.

The public's demand for money is real demand. The government determines how much money is in existence, but the people determine how much it is worth! People normally try to keep a fraction of their income in the form of money balances; they need more at high price levels than at a lower price levels. Experience shows that in the aggregate people try to hold about a quarter of their income in the form of money balances. This means that the velocity of turnover of money is four. Put another way, a velocity of four means that income is four times the money supply.

But velocity is not a constant. It will itself depend on the expected cost of holding money. If people expect money to depreciate, they will keep a smaller proportion of their income in the form of money and velocity will be correspondingly higher. Far from being a fanciful concept, this is an economic reality. Forty years ago, my colleague at Columbia, Phillip Cagan, studied several hyperinflations and established a clear-cut relation between velocity and inflation. The higher the inflation rate the higher the velocity.[13]

[13] More exactly, Cagan demonstrated that the real demand for money is negatively related to his measure of the expected in rate of inflation; with unchanged output, this implies a positive relationship between velocity and expected inflation. See P. Cagan, "The Monetary Dynamics of Hyper inflation," in M. Friedman (ed.), *Studies in the Quantity Theory of Money* (Chicago: University of Chicago Press, 1958), 25–117.

Now let us go back to the money tax idea. The government can finance part of its spending by printing money. This is a legitimate function up to a point. For example, if the private sector is saving and investing and the economy is growing, the public will demand more money to keep the ratio of money and income the same. This means that there is a noninflationary budget deficit that can be financed by money creation.

But if the government has a larger deficit than this noninflationary budget deficit, the public will get more money than they want to hold at constant prices, so prices will rise. The rising prices, if continued, will induce the public to expect inflation, and so what will they do? They will react to it by lowering their real-money balances, and velocity will rise.

This rise in velocity – which means a flight from money to goods – will by itself produce a rise in the price level even without additional money. It lowers the base of the inflation tax and makes deficit financing more expensive in terms of its inflation cost. Government needs to know how much spending it can finance by money creation without causing inflation, and also the inflation cost of additional spending over and above this amount. Three decades ago, I made a model putting these things together in order to study the efficacy of inflationary finance as a means of increasing the growth rate.[14]

To keep things simple, I will make it a "bare-bones" model, eliminating qualifications that can be considered later. Let g be the budget deficit, expressed as a fraction of GDP, written as PO, that is financed by money creation. Let central bank money be R (for reserves) and let M be the money supply; and let $R = \alpha M$ be the relationship between central bank money and the money supply, α being the reserve ratio. Then $g = G/PO$. But $G = dR/dt = \alpha dM/dt$, so $g = \alpha(1/PO)\, dM/dt = \alpha M/PO\, (1/M)dM/dt$. If we write $\rho = (1/M)dM/dt$, we have $\rho = gv/\alpha$, where $v = PO/M$, the income velocity of money. This relationship

$$\rho = vg/\alpha$$

shows that the budget deficit financed by money is proportionate to the rate of monetary expansion. The higher the money-financed

[14] R. A. Mundell, "Growth, Stability and Inflationary Finance," *Journal of Political Economy* 73 (April 1965): 97–109.

deficit, and the lower the reserve fraction, the higher the rate of monetary expansion.

There is now, however, another relationship that comes from people's behavior with respect to money balances. As the quantity theory of money shows

$$MV = PO.$$

Put dynamically, the sum of the rate of growth of money, ρ, and velocity equals the sum of the rates of inflation, π, and growth, λ, that is,

$$\rho = (1/v)dv/dt = \pi + \lambda.$$

Let us assume, tentatively, that velocity is constant, so that we can write this equation more simply as follows:

$$\rho = \pi + \lambda$$

Now we are making progress! Because ρ also equals

$$\rho = vg/\alpha,$$

we have

$$\pi + \lambda = vg/\alpha$$

or

$$\pi = \frac{vg}{\alpha} - \lambda.$$

This equation shows us the rate of inflation will be higher, the higher is income velocity, the lower is the reserve ratio, the higher is the budget deficit, and the lower the rate of economic growth. For example, suppose the ratio of income to money, velocity, is 4, the reserve ratio is 0.5, and the rate of growth is 0.10 = 10 percent. Then the rate of inflation will be

$$\pi = 8g - 0.10.$$

Thus, if the budget deficit is 0.05 = 5% of GDP, the rate of inflation will be

$$\pi = 8 \times 0.05 - 0.10 = 0.30 \text{ or } 30\%\text{t}.$$

If the budget deficit is 0.12, as it is in many countries of the former Soviet Union, the rate of inflation would be 86 percent!

$$\pi = 8 \times 0.12 - 0.10 = 0.86 = 86\%.$$

Thus far we have not taken into account the observed fact that velocity depends on the rate of inflation (more exactly, expected inflation). To take that into account, let us go back to our formula

$$\pi = vg/\alpha - \lambda$$

and treat v, not as a constant, but a variable function of the rate of inflation, $v(\pi)$. We need to know the velocity function. Fortunately, there has been some study of this question. One approach is to approximate the velocity function by a linear relationship, as follows:

$$v = v^* + \eta\pi,$$

where v^* is the velocity at zero inflation. In the Chinese context, let us pull a rabbit out of a hat and put numerical values to this velocity function, writing it in the form

$$v = 2 + 4\pi,$$

where the rate of inflation π is measured as a fraction, that is, 0.2 equals 20 percent. In this schedule, if inflation is zero, velocity is (as it is in China) 2, but it doubles to 4 at 50 percent inflation, and rises to 6 at 100 percent inflation and to 8 at 150 percent inflation. Although velocity may not rise rapidly enough under this relationship at high rates of inflation, it is a good approximation for ranges below, say 80 percent, which is more than sufficient for the case of China.

Now, from the equation

$$\pi = vg/\alpha - \lambda$$

we get, after inserting the velocity inflation function,

$$\pi = (v^* + \eta\pi)g/\alpha - \lambda$$

$$\pi = \frac{v^* g - \alpha\lambda}{\alpha - \eta g}.$$

Taking our assumed values for the velocity function, and inserting them into this equation, that is, $v^* = 2$ and $\eta = 4$, and assuming that the reserve ratio $\alpha = 0.5$, we get a revised relation between the budget deficit and the inflation rate, that is,

$$\pi = \frac{2g - 0.5\lambda}{0.5 - 4g}.$$

Let us forecast China's growth rate at 10 percent for 1995, slightly lower than last year but nevertheless remarkable by international standards. In that case we have

$$\pi = \frac{2g - 0.5}{0.5 - 0.4g}.$$

If the budget deficit is 5 percent, that is, $g = 0.05$, the rate of inflation, $\pi = 16\ 2/3\%$.

If the budget deficit is 8 percent, that is, $g = 0.08$, the rate of inflation, $\pi = 61.1\%$.

If the budget deficit is 10 percent, that is, $g = 0.10$, the rate of inflation, $\pi = 150\%$.

MONEY-FINANCED GROWTH

So far, we have not given much attention to growth. What determines the rate of growth? How is the government budget deficit related to the rate of growth? What is the relation between inflation and growth? These are issues that are relevant.

First, to the determinants of the growth rate. Growth depends on the increase in productive resources and on technology. The simplest, but still a very useful theory of growth, is that which can be derived from the ratio of output to capital, $O = \phi K$, where ϕ is the average productivity of capital. In conjunction with this equation, we have the relation between saving and output, that is, $S = sO$, where s is the propensity to save. Saving, which equals investment (I) determines the growth of the capital stock so that we can write $sO = I = dK/dt$. On the other hand, we know that $dO/dt = \phi\ dK/dt$. By eliminating dK/dt we arrive at the result $(1/O)dO/dt = \lambda = s\phi$, the relation made famous by Roy Harrod and Evsey Domar. We can insert this relation into the foregoing inflation-growth relation, that is, into

$$\pi = \frac{v^* g - \alpha\lambda}{\alpha - \eta g}$$

to get

$$\pi = \frac{v^* g - \alpha s\phi}{\alpha - \eta g}.$$

If we assume the output-capital ratio is 0.25 (implying a capital-output ratio of 4), and the saving rate is 0.4 (which is just about China's rate), we would arrive at a growth rate of 10 percent.

Up until now, we have assumed that the government deficit is spent entirely on consumption, with no spillover effects on the capital stock. It is now time to make some allowance for government capital formation. Government investment adds something to the growth rate. In the extreme case where the entire deficit is devoted to capital formation, the government contribution to the growth rate will be $g\phi$ and the total growth rate will be $(g + s)\phi$. To lend more precision, let γ be the fraction of the deficit spending that goes into investment. Then the growth rate will be $\lambda = (\gamma g + s)\phi$. When this relation is inserted into the inflation equation, we get

$$\pi = \frac{v^* g - \alpha(s + \gamma g)\phi}{\alpha - \eta g}$$

or

$$\pi = \frac{g\,(v^* - \alpha\gamma\phi) - \alpha s\phi}{\alpha - \eta g}.$$

It can be seen that the existence of government investment ($\gamma > 0$) introduces a factor that results in a lower rate of inflation and a higher rate of growth than would exist if the deficit spending were entirely allocated to consumption.

In China, it is especially important to allow for changes in the degree of monetization. This factor can be taken into account by assuming that the demand for money is proportionate, not to money income, but to the proportion of the economy that is monetized. Differentiation of the quantity equation then results in

$$\rho = \pi + \lambda + \mu,$$

where μ is the rate of increase in monetization.

If this new equation is substituted into the other equations, we arrive at a corrected criterion for the inflation rate:

$$\pi = \frac{g\,(v^* - \alpha\gamma\phi) - \alpha s\phi - \alpha\mu}{\alpha - \eta g},$$

from which it can be seen that the monetization factor reduces the inflation rate from what it would have been in its absence.[15]

INFLATION SEMIELASTICITIES

When Cagan studied several postwar hyperinflations, he was able to estimate the expected negative relationship between real money demand and the inflation rate (put another way, velocity rises with expected inflation);[16] Maurice Allais did related work. This is an important factor in the theory of money because the level of real-money balances is the base of the inflation tax. The proceeds from raising the inflation tax reach a maximum when the elasticity of demand for real-money balances is equal to -1.

Why is this relation so important? The answer: monetary targeting depends on it. If money demand varies with inflation, the quantity theory of money (another feather in the cap of ancient China!) in its simple version no longer holds. If money demand changes with the expected rate of inflation, monetary targeting would not work very well. Small changes in expectations could lead to substantial changes in prices.

Some economists think the case for money targeting can be saved even if velocity changes with inflation, provided these changes are predictable – that is, provided Cagan-type money demand functions are stable. Many economists have therefore examined the money-inflation (or, because the nominal interest rate incorporates an inflation premium, the money–interest rate relationship) relationship for several countries, including that for China. The IMF has recently estimated income elasticities and inflation semielasticities of demand for currency, money, and "broad money" for China for the period 1983–93; however, the

15 Further development of this formula would require a consideration of a number of additional factors such as the following: (1) government investment may have a different productivity than private investment; (2) inflation may alter saving and private growth; (3) budget deficits to finance SOE investment may have a different productivity from that needed to finance increments to social capital; (4) allowance should be made for an open economy with net capital imports; (5) the inflation rate has been assumed to be known and constant whereas it actually may be uncertain and variable; (6) the reserve ratio may not be constant; (7) the public's expectations of inflation will be affected by exchange rate expectations; and (8) in an open economy, with a fixed exchange rate, monetary policy will be constrained by the requirements of balance-of-payments equilibrium.

16 Cagan, "The Monetary Dynamics of Hyperinflation."

Table 7.7. *Income elasticities and inflation semielasticities of demand for money in China, 1983–93*

	Currency	Narrow money	Broad money
Income elasticities			
1983–88	1.9	1.5	1.8
1989–93	1.7	1.5	1.6
Inflation semielasticities			
1983–88	−1.2	−1.5	−2.2
1989–93	−1.0	−0.9	−1.5

Sources: "Economic Reform in China: A New Phase," IMF Occasional Paper 114 (International Monetary Fund, Washington, D.C., November 1994), appendix IV, 66–77.

IMF economists found it better to break the series into two parts, 1983–88 and 1989–93. The results are shown in Table 7.7. Note that the income elasticities are all between 1.5 and 2 and the inflation semielasticities are between −1 and −2. An inflation semielasticity of −1.5 means that an increase in the inflation rate of 10 percentage points will reduce real-money balances (or increase velocity at constant output) by 15 percent. Revenue from the inflation tax would reach a maximum at 66 2/3 percent.

The most important targets of monetary policy are a stable and growing economy. But these targets are, to some extent, distinct. Monetary policy cannot achieve both of them at the same time. Many if not most economists believe that price stability is one of the best ways in which monetary policy can contribute to a stable and growing economy. It is sometimes true, of course, that, in the short run, easing credit can spur output and restricting credit can reduce growth. But if inflation increases substantially, and must eventually be stopped before confidence breaks down, the price paid in terms of growth and employment will be much higher than if inflation had not been allowed to break out in the first place. Monetary policy has a clear comparative advantage in achieving price stability.

On the other hand, other factors are more efficient at achieving a high growth rate. The best ways for the government to contribute to high and sustainable economic growth, apart from a stable and predictable monetary environment, are for the government to ensure (1) free markets; (2) a legal system to enforce property rights in the private and public sectors; (3) a predictable, enforceable, and equitable pattern of taxes that do not interfere with incentives for producing, selling, and inventing; (4) real interest rates sufficiently positive to promote high savings; (5) access to unrestricted financial markets by both investors and savers; (6) a public sector that provides necessary infrastructure, especially roads and communications networks; (7) an efficient and accessible education system that ensures a high percentage of well-trained high school graduates and college graduates sufficient to enable the human resources for an increasingly hi-tech services sector; and (8) a clear delineation of property rights in all sectors to ensure the most efficient utilization and optimal investment in land, the environment, and human resources. Working on these factors is the best way to ensure sustainable economic growth.

CHINA'S MONETARY POLICY

With the foregoing factors in mind, it is time to get back to factors determining China's monetary policies. It is first important to monitor the rate of monetary expansion. Even in countries that are growing rapidly, as in Japan during its "Sudden Economic Rise" in the period 1955–70, Japan's rate of monetary expansion was in the range of 14–26 percent. When monetary expansion reaches 25 percent, it is much too high. The Chinese target for 1995 of 20–23 percent for M1 and 23–25 percent for M2 may be too high, but it has the merit that it brought the rate down from actual money expansion rates in 1994 and 1993.

Monetary targeting is not by itself a sufficiently fine instrument for controlling monetary policy. There are a number of difficulties: (1) most central banks do not have fight control over short-run changes in the money supply; (2) targets for monetary expansion will be treated skeptically by the public (central banks usually overshoot their monetary targets except during recessionary periods); and (3) fixing the rate of monetary expansion, even if possible, would not stabilize prices and might involve severe shifts in the exchange rate. For these reasons, and without denying the

Table 7.8. *Growth of output, investment, prices, and money: China*

	1984	1985	1986	1987	1988	1989	1990	1991	1992	1993	1994	1995
GDP	14.6	12.9	8.5	11.1	11.2	4.3	3.9	8.0	13.61	13.4	11.8	10.0
INV	22.7	27.3	13.3	14.7	10.4	−15.5	1.2	18.8	28.3	22.0	3.3[a]	
CPI	2.7	11.9	7.0	8.8	20.7	16.3	3.1	3.4	6.4	14.7	24.1	20.0
M0			24.0	15.0	22.7	24.3	30.1	25.7	18.0	27.1	37.0	20.5
M1	21.4	32.7	18.3	26.4	24.7	7.8	13.4	25.5	31.6	27.9	24.5	20–23
M2	21.4	40.4	89.2	30.7	25.8	16.3	26.2	29.1	28.8	25.7	56.1	23–25

[a] Fixed assets investment increased 27.8% in 1994 (People's Bank of China, *China Financial Outlook '94*, p. 89) in nominal terms, and the figure of 3.3% real growth results from subtracting from this figure the increase in the CPI; this is obviously an underestimate to the extent that the CPI increased more than the relative investment deflator.

Sources: *IMF International Financial Statistics Yearbook* (1995); *China Economic Outlook* '95, People's Bank of China, (May 1995); and "Economic Reform in China," IMF Occasional Paper, (International Monetary Fund, Washington D.C., November 1994).

importance of monitoring money growth, it is necessary to pay attention to other instruments of monetary policy as well.

For example, the severe Chinese growth recession of 1989–90 was associated with a severe drop in the growth rate of M1 and M2 in 1989. It would have been desirable to avoid the growth recession and the drops in M1 and M2 growth; but M_0 actually rose substantially in both recession years, indicating that the monetary slowdown was an effect of the growth recession, not a cause (see Table 7.8). More probably the cause of the 1989–90 slowdown was the sharp drop in real investment. Investment, which ranges between 35 and 40 percent of GDP, is a strategic decision variable in China's economy. After expanding in real terms at rates in the range of 10 to 15 percent of GDP, real investment suddenly fell by 15.5 percent in 1989, and barely achieved positive growth in 1990. It seems likely, therefore, that accelerator effects widening the swings in investment and multiplier effects spread the slowdown to the rest of the economy. The large difference between growth rate of reserve money on the one hand and of M1 and M2 on the other indicates a sharp change in the reserve ratio and the banking multiplier.

Commitment to a monetary target is not in the long run compatible with a fixed-exchange rate. This is because the foreign-exchange operations needed to keep the exchange rate fixed themselves affect the reserve base. The money base can be increased by expanding assets in only four ways: foreign assets;

Table 7.9. *PBC asset structure billions of Yuan (end of period)*

Asset type	1988	1989	1990	1991	1992	1993	1994	1995
Foreign	28.2	40.5	82.1	140.0	133.0	146.0	445.1	667.0
Central government	57.7	68.5	80.1	106.8	124.1	158.3	168.8	158.3
Other dom.	32.9	38.2	46.4	52.3	73.5	95.5	72.8	68.0
Deposit money banks	336.4	421.0	509.1	591.8	678.0	962.6	1,045.1	1,151.0
Res mon	398.4	491.1	638.7	793.1	922.8	1,254.0	1,721.8	2,076.0

Sources: *IMF International Financial Statistics*, various years; and *China Financial Outlook '95*, p. 91.

claims on government; claims on other domestic transactors; and claims on deposit money banks. Table 7.9 shows the PBC asset structure for recent years. Notice that in 1988 the bulk of PBC assets comprised loans to the deposit money banks. This would remain true throughout the period. However, by the end of 1995, foreign assets had become much more important. At the end of 1993, foreign assets "backed" only 11.6 percent of the money base; at the end of 1994, the figure had surged to 25.9 percent; and by the end of 1995, it had risen further to 32.1. Increased foreign-exchange backing for the renminbi has become an increasingly important feature of the Chinese banking structure.

The increasing international structure of the reserve assets is a function of China's balance of payments surplus that has developed in the past two years. Prior to 1 January 1994, the official exchange rate of the renminbi was adjusted according to movements in the value of a basket of internationally traded currencies. After that date, the People's Bank of China quotes the midpoint rate against the dollar on the basis of the previous day's prevailing rate in the interbank foreign exchange market. Licensed commercial banks quote their transactions rates within the floating margins set by the People's Bank. The devaluation that accompanied the reform more than compensated for the removal of a wide range of controls and left the renminbi undervalued.

Table 7.10 presents the percentage changes in the reserve assets and the composition of these changes. Note first the uneven growth of the money base, and the changing composition of

Table 7.10. *Composition of increase and percentage changes in reserve assets (%)*

Asset type	1988	1989	1990	1991	1992	1993	1994	1995
Foreign[a]	3.4	13.3	28.2	37.6	−5.4	3.9	69.6	62.6
Deposit money banks[a]	94.1	91.1	59.6	53.4	66.5	85.9	17.8	29.9
Res mon[b]	25.2	23.3	30.1	24.2	16.4	35.9	37.6	20.6

[a] Percentage of reserve expansion accounted for by expansion of foreign assets, and deposit money bank assets.
[b] Percentage increase in reserve assets.
Sources: *IMF International Financial Statistics* (January and April 1995); and *China Financial Outlook '95*, p. 91.

increases in the base. The big upsurge of the money base in 1993 came about as a result of the expansion – a tripling – of loans to the commercial banks, presumably to finance the budget deficit. On the other hand, a continuation of this credit to the Deposit Money Banks in 1994 would have caused an unacceptable price acceleration due to the expansion of the reserve base arising from the balance-of-payments surplus.

The problem of budget deficits has usually been the major culprit in creating monetary stability, insofar as nonindependent central banks are compelled to finance the budget deficit. In China, the PBC is not required to finance government deficits, but it may be pressured into lending to state-owned banks, which in turn lend to government. Indirectly, therefore, inflationary finance, while indirect, is still a threat. The problem in most transition economies in Eastern Europe and the former Soviet Union is steadily declining revenue from SOEs. In China subsidies to loss-making SOEs remain a factor in the budget deficit, while tax revenues from profitable SOEs have been a declining source of revenue as a proportion of GDP. China has been able to avoid the huge deficits that have confronted other transition economies, but the problem of loss-making SOEs will get worse rather than better as they become decreasingly competitive. For this reason the next two or three years are crucial ones.

The renminbi had been held in the range of Y 1.5–2.5 = $1 for three decades before the 1980s. After 1985, when the dollar depreciated against other major currencies, the renminbi started to depreciate against the dollar, the latter reaching an average of Y 3.7 in 1987, Y 4.7 in 1989, Y 5.8 in 1993, and Y 8.6 in 1994. It is true that the renminbi appreciated somewhat over the course of 1994, the dollar falling from Y 8.7 at the beginning of the year to Y 8.4 at the end, continuing its rise slowly into April 1995. But with a rate of inflation of 24 percent in 1994 and 15 percent in 1995, much of the undervaluation of the renminbi has been dissipated.

PRICE STABILITY AS A TARGET

Most economists believe that price stability is one of the best ways in which monetary policy can contribute to a stable and growing economy. It is sometimes true, of course, that, in the short run, easing credit can spur output and restricting credit can reduce growth. But if inflation increases substantially, and must eventually be stopped before confidence breaks down, the price paid in terms of growth and employment will be much higher than if inflation had not been allowed to break out in the first place. Monetary policy has a clear comparative advantage in achieving price stability.[17]

If it is agreed that the main objective of monetary policy is price stability, there is by no means a general consensus on how best to achieve it. This is perhaps not surprising because all countries are not in the same position. A monetary policy that is valid for the United States may not be valid for Mexico, Canada, or Argentina. What is valid for Japan many not be correct for South Korea or Taiwan. What is valid for Germany may not be valid for Austria or the Netherlands. Every country faces a different situation.

One possibility is to fix the exchange rate to a large country that

[17] A government that focuses on price stability cannot obviously at the same time maximize revenue from the inflation tax! However, it is easily shown that a government that maximizes revenue from the inflation tax has carried inflation beyond the optimum. Even under "pure" inflation where inflation is completely predictable and constant, and all prices move in the same proportion, there is a pure welfare cost of inflationary finance. This means that an inflation rate that maximized government revenue from the inflation tax would be above the inflation rate that maximized economic welfare. But the main welfare costs from inflation arise from the fact that, rather than being predictable or constant, inflation is uncertain and variable. The price system is, inter alia, a mechanism for transmitting information about scarcity relationships. Inflation undermines the ability of the price system to fulfill its task as relative prices change, not only because of changes in scarcity relationships but because of different speeds of reaction to inflation. Distortions of consumption and investment lower the return to capital and make investment less productive.

has a low rate of inflation. In this case monetary policy must be governed, at least in part, by the balance of payments as it would be in an automatic system. When the balance of payments is in surplus, the central bank must intervene in the foreign-exchange market to prevent its currency from appreciating; this automatically increases the supply of bank reserves and leads to increased spending, thus reducing the surplus. On the other hand, when the balance of payments is in deficit, the central bank must intervene to prevent its currency from depreciating, reducing bank reserves and tightening credit and reducing spending, leading to a reduction in the deficit.

Another possibility is to try to fix the rate of monetary expansion. The difficulty with that policy is that the central bank does not directly control the rate of monetary expansion. To a large extent it controls the money base, but the ratio between the money base (and the banking multiplier) is not fixed. Even if the rate of monetary expansion is fixed, the rate of inflation and the exchange rate may fluctuate erratically.

Yet a third possibility is to target the rate of inflation itself, easing or tightening as the rate of inflation steps above or below its target level. The difficulty with that policy is that there are substantial lags in the effect of monetary policy, and targeting rates of change may exaggerate swings in the inflation rate and exchange rate.

For many countries a fixed exchange rate represents the best way to import the scarcity relationships of an efficient foreign country. It also promotes financial efficiency and monetary integration. Under a well-working system of fixed exchange rates, relative prices and interest rates in the home country have to be the same (except for trade impediments) as those in the rest of the world. The money supply becomes endogenous, rising and falling with surpluses in the balance of payments. A fixed exchange rate system becomes, for many countries, the best means of achieving the inflation rate of the foreign-currency area.

With an inflationary system, however, a country that pegged its exchange rate would soon be forced off its peg as it lost competitiveness. Suppose, for example, that a country has a rate of inflation that is, say, 10 percent above its currency partner, a situation like that which has prevailed recently in China. That country might initially set its exchange rate (the price of foreign currency)

20 percent above its purchasing-power-parity equilibrium, undervaluing its own currency by a corresponding amount. After one year, the currency would be undervalued by only 10 percent; after two years, it would be at its equilibrium value; and after three years it would be overvalued by 10 percent. Theoretically, it could devalue by 20 percent every two years, existing half the time with an undervalued currency and the other half, overvalued.

The problem with that system is that the public has a memory. Think of the prospect of a 20 percent gain a week before the devaluation! The annualized rate of return on speculation would be 20 × 55 = 1,100 percent. Long before the devaluation occurred speculators would anticipate the event and outward capital flight speculation would provoke a crisis. Shades of Mexico 1994–95! Shades of Britain, September 1992, when a week before Britain was forced off its DM peg, the speculator George Soros borrowed almost UK £5 billion for a week, invested them in marks and schillings, and made a cool $1 billion after the pound depreciated by 20 percent.

To mitigate this problem, some economists think a country should devalue more frequently – devalue once a year by 10 percent instead of once every two years by 20 percent, or even more frequently. Some countries have tried the experiment with a daily devaluation planned and published in a schedule in advance. It amounts to convertibility at a depreciating exchange rate. In Latin America this experiment was called the tablita system. I would judge it a noble experiment that failed. I would not recommend it to China or any other country because it does not generate credibility that the system will be maintained and therefore leads to a premium in domestic interest rates that goes far beyond the normal devaluation premium.

What I have said here about the exchange rate and purchasing-power parity does not mean that I think market interest rates are driven by purchasing-power parity. But purchasing-power parity is by no means irrelevant. It is a long-run relationship. For example, the purchasing-power parities of currencies like the Austrian schilling and German mark are about the same because the schilling has been fixed to the mark for several years and prices have had time to adjust.

The exchange rate is one of the most important prices in any country. The more open a country, the more important the exchange rate is in its monetary policy. In a very small open economy, international prices dominate and so the exchange rate determines the domestic price level. There is a connection also in a more closed economy but it is not so large or so immediate.

There is another relationship. The smaller the economy, the more open it is likely to be. In a small economy like Luxembourg, for example, exports constitute about 70 percent of GDP; in an entrepôt economy like Hong Kong, exports are 200 percent of GDP. But in large economies like the United States or Japan, exports are closer to 10 percent of GDP. Most countries fall between these two extremes.

There is a basic guideline that follows from these relationships. Small, open economies will find a regime of fixed exchange rates to be the most attractive system, if they can find a suitable reference currency to fix. A satisfactory reference currency should be the currency of a large country with a satisfactory inflation rate. Because the country is small, it can unilaterally fix its exchange rate without disturbing the effectiveness of the monetary policy of its partner.

The fact that a system of fixed exchange rates has proved to be acceptable for a small country does not mean that it is inappropriate for a large country; fixing the exchange rate can also be a good policy for a large country. But when an economy is large, it can no longer be said that its fixing policy will not alter the effectiveness of the monetary policy of the partner country. There is an asymmetry between large and small countries.

The asymmetry can be understood by considering the differences between, say, Canada fixing its currency to the U.S. dollar, and the United States fixing its currency to the Canadian dollar. Alternatively, consider the same experiment between Germany and Austria. The large country could completely dominate the monetary policy of the smaller country.

The more countries are in a fixed exchange rate area (called a "currency area") the more beneficial it is to be a member of it. For any given rate of inflation, the larger the currency area the more "shockproof" it will be. A large currency area like the United States, for example, with its $7 trillion GDP, could withstand billions of dollars of capital inflows and outflows without being destabilized; but a small currency area would be rocked by even small shocks. In this sense currencies, like countries, gain strength by alliances.

Because of this interdependence, a country must take into consideration, before adopting an exchange rate policy, the condition of the international monetary system. It is unnecessary, except in passing, to mention the systems before the end of World War II. Bimetallism ruled the world up to 1870; this was followed by the gold standard from 1870 to 1914, followed by an interwar period of considerable chaos until the formation of an international monetary system based on the U.S. dollar, anchored to gold, since 1934 and confirmed at Bretton Woods in 1944.

The postwar period that lasted from the end of the war to 1971 was a period of growth and monetary stability. The major countries all had fixed exchange rates to the U.S. dollar, which, alone, was convertible into gold. The period 1950–71 was a period of rapid growth, fixed exchange rates, and monetary stability.

Not so the following period. The dollar lost its gold anchor, and the rest of the world abandoned its dollar anchor. Monetary discipline weakened and inflation broke out all over the world. Countries moved to flexible exchange rates. The 1970s was a decade of great inflation, certainly the most inflationary decade ever in a period of comparative peace.

But many countries abhorred flexible exchange rates. Instead, they sought alternatives. Europe formed a kind of monetary system on its own, essentially dominated by the German mark. Many countries fixed their currencies to the dollar.

The 1980s brought about a correction to the inflationary 1970s. Under President Ronald Reagan and the influence of supply-side economics, price stability was restored in the U.S. economy, and the Reagan-Bush expansion lasted for seven years, from 1982 to 1990. The dollar appreciated in the first half of the decade and depreciated in the last half, while stability was being gradually restored. In the middle of 1990, the United States went into a nine-month recession, but the expansion that started in the spring of 1991 has continued through 1996. The Reagan-Bush-Clinton expansion in the United States from 1983 to 1996 (decline occurred in only one year, 1990), in which 32 million jobs were created, is perhaps the most remarkable expansion in the history of the world. The dollar stabilized in the 1990s, and the inflation rate has been held to 3 percent.

Meanwhile, Japan, now the second largest economy in the world, has found its yen being used increasingly in international transactions. Of the three largest economies, the United States represents about 22 percent of the world economy; Japan, about 13 percent; and Germany, about 8 percent. The international monetary system is now a multiple-currency system with the dollar setting the tone for the world economy, but the mark and yen have been rising as important regional currencies and even global currencies.

CURRENCY AREAS AND FINANCIAL MARKETS

It would make life simpler for other smaller countries if the three monetary leaders fixed exchange rates and agreed on a common rate of inflation for the core of the world economy. The gain from such a large currency area would be substantial. However, it is not likely to happen in the near future. The size of the U.S. economy makes it less open than the others, so that its exchange rate (more exactly, the vector of exchange rates) is not as important a policy variable as it is in more open economies. Any initiative for fixing exchange rates will not come from the United States. Germany, and possibly Japan, may have an interest in stabilizing exchange rates, but not at the potential U.S. inflation rate. Another factor is important. Europe, with its commitment to monetary union, has little interest in an international monetary reform that would make its own monetary union unnecessary. The upshot is that there is little prospect in the next decade for an international monetary reform that would stabilize the major exchange rates. Other countries will therefore have to cope with a world in which there are at least three currency blocs.

Meanwhile, the rest of the world, in the absence of a fixed rate bloc among the three leading countries, has some compensation in that, should a country choose to fix its currency, it has a choice of major currency partners. Inflation preferences play a role in choosing which (if any) of the three currencies to fix. Germany can be expected to have the lowest inflation rate, say 1 percent; Japan would come next, with 2–3 percent; and the United States third, with 3–4 percent. By this criterion, most of the developing countries, hard put to prevent depreciation against the dollar, would be better off with a peg to the dollar rather than to one of the two currencies scheduled to appreciate against the dollar. The very factors that weaken the power of the United States – its budget and trade deficits – make it a more attractive anchor for the developing and transition economies.

There are other considerations. One is size. As the largest economy, the United States is the most shock-resistant. This stability is reinforced by the greater diversification of the United States, balanced with its manufacturing, service, and important agricultural sector. The U.S. basket of commodities is closer to the world consumption basket than are the commodity baskets of Japan or Germany, and the diversification of the U.S. economy provides added stability to the U.S. dollar as an anchor currency.

Another consideration is communication, a factor that is very important for the capital market. The language of Frankfurt is German; of Tokyo, Japanese; of New York, English. This gives New York an advantage in a world where English is the major second language. However, Tokyo is closer to China and that is a factor that would give Japan an edge as a currency partner were it not complicated by historical and political factors.

Every country is in a different position. To repeat, the exchange rate policy that is optimal for Austria and the Netherlands is not necessarily optimal for India or China. Austria and the Netherlands have chosen to fix their currencies firmly (but not irrevocably) to the deutschemark, relying on the monetary leadership of the Bundesbank. This is clearly the best policy for a relatively small country near to a large and stable neighbor.

Notice that fixing the rate does not just mean buying and selling DMs for schillings or guilders; it also means allowing purchases and sales of foreign exchange to alter the money base, just as if Austria and the Netherlands were monetary provinces of Germany. In other words, that successful policy means giving up monetary independence. There is some room, in a growing economy, for domestic credit expansion, but not to the extent that it prevents the adjustment mechanism from working. A fixed exchange rate means that a country has to give up monetary independence, but it nevertheless gains the objectives of price stability, which should be, for most countries, the goal of monetary policy. Austria and the Netherlands also gain the essential advantages of a large monetary area and Germany's inflation rate; Germany also benefits from its wider monetary area. If current plans for

European Monetary Union go through, a greater monetary area will develop in the next few years in Europe that would benefit all of the countries in that region

The success of the currencies of Austria and the Netherlands, vis-à-vis the DM, based on the combination of a fixed exchange rate and a monetary policy that backs that up, is analogous to, but not quite so strict as, Hong Kong's policy. Hong Kong fixes 1 U.S. dollar at HK 7.8. When the designated banks buy U.S. $100, they supply HK 780 to the market; and when they sell U.S. $100, they take away HK 780 from the market. Hong Kong's monetary policy ensures monetary equilibrium in the sense that the public always gets the quantity of HK dollars it wants to hold.

The policy also ensures balance-of-payments equilibrium. Just as the state of New York solves any balance-of-payments disequilibrium with automatic money flows, so does Hong Kong. If Hong Kong has a deficit due to excess spending, the reduction in money balances would soon curb expenditure and eliminate the deficit; and when there is a surplus due to, say, booming exports, the influx of money would increase spending and bring the balance of payments back into equilibrium.

An important question is the rate of inflation under a currency board. The rate of inflation at home will depend on the inflation rate of the "reference country"producing the currency to which the home currency is pegged. Because Hong Kong's currency is fixed to the U.S. dollar, Hong Kong will have a price level relative to the United States that is compatible with equilibrium in its balance of payments. With qualifications, it can be said that Hong Kong will eventually get the rate of inflation of the United States.

The qualifications, however, are important. In the first place, the common inflation rate of a currency board refers to the change in prices of a common price index. If the consumer price index (CPI) of the home country had different weights than the CPI of the reference country, changes in relative prices within the commodity baskets would mean different "measured inflation" rates. Another qualification refers to entry conditions. If a country adopts a currency board system, it may enter the arrangement at an exchange rate that undervalues or overvalues the home currency. If the home currency is initially undervalued, domestic inflation will exceed the foreign inflation rate until the price level and the *real* exchange rate have been adjusted to the equilibrium level; similarly, if the home currency is initially overvalued, domestic inflation will have to be lower than the foreign inflation rate until the real exchange rate has been brought back into equilibrium. This fact will be less important the longer the currency board has been in operation.

A third factor relates to differential productivity changes. A change in the relative costs of producing domestic (nontraded) and international (traded) goods means that the *real* exchange rate will have to change. If the nominal exchange rate is fixed, as it is under a currency board regime, the price level will have to adapt. Specifically, if there are productivity increases in the production of international goods relative to those in the production of domestic goods, the nominal price of domestic goods will have to rise. There is some evidence that this process has been at work in making Hong Kong's consumer price index rise at a faster rate than that in the United States.

Currency boards are of course not a new phenomena. They have existed for centuries. One of the earliest was the currency board established in Mauritius in 1849. They were widely used in the British colonies before World War I.[18] Currency boards have been seen to be a way in which a country can gain the monetary stability of a larger partner without completely sacrificing seigniorage.

Hong Kong had currency boards for several years before and after World War II with the Hong Kong dollar fixed to the pound sterling. Since 1972, it has related its currency to the U.S. dollar, and since 1983 with a currency board system, with the U.S. dollar fixed at HK $7.8. By this means Hong Kong has managed to become one of the most prosperous economies in Asia and an important center of the international capital market.

The currency board arrangements of Hong Kong could well be imitated by some other countries. If Mexico had a currency board arrangement in 1994, it would not have succumbed to the policy mistakes it made in December and magnified in January and February 1995. Argentina weathered the "tequila effect" because it had a convertibility law that makes the central bank act much like a currency board. The fact that Argentina was able to

[18] For a recent discussion of currency boards, see Steve H. Hanke, Lars Jonung, and Kurt Schuler, *Russian Currency and Finance: A Currency Board Approach to Reform* (London: Routledge, 1993).

weather the storm, despite a massive run on the banking system, builds up confidence that it will be able to maintain it in the future. For the first time since the 1920s (when Argentina had an earlier currency board), Argentina has managed to achieve monetary stability.

Which countries should be adopted as the reference currency? We have already discussed the situation in Europe. For the economic neighbors of the United States – Canada, Mexico, Brazil, Argentina, and so on – it is natural to elect the dollar as the reference currency if they choose, or are able to fix at all.

The situation in Asia is more complicated. From the standpoint of its powerful economy, Japan is an economic superpower. It also has a supply of savings that enables it to export capital at an astonishing rate. Japan is not only the largest creditor in the world, it is the largest creditor known in the history of the world. Its net creditor position has now U.S. $1 trillion, almost 25 percent of its GDP; this sum is invested in all the continents but especially in Southeast Asia.

At the present time, the largest financial center (measured by stock market capitalization) is New York. That is followed by Tokyo, which is currently about two-thirds the size of New York. Tokyo is followed by London, which is about a quarter the size of New York. London is followed by Frankfurt, which is one-tenth that of New York. The Asian markets then enter the picture, starting with Hong Kong, which is 5.6 percent of New York. In 1995 Hong Kong capitalization was $276 billion, Taipei was $236 billion; Sydney, $207 billion; Kuala Lumpur, $191 billion; Seoul, $183 billion; Singapore, $150 billion, Bangkok, $124 billion; Bombay, $93 billion; Jakarta, $48 billion; Manila, $45 billion; China, $38 billion; and Karachi; $11 billion. The combined Asian market (excluding Tokyo) amounts to $1,602 billion, about equal to London and Frankfurt combined, and about a third of the New York market.

For geographical and other considerations, a strong financial center is likely to develop in Asia outside Tokyo. The natural place is China, clearly the country that has the least-developed financial market relative to its GDP at current exchange rates and even more at purchasing-power-parity exchange rates. Hong Kong is already an important financial center and, as far as international finance is concerned, has recently become larger than Tokyo.

On 1 July 1997, China absorbed the Hong Kong colony but with a commitment to let it keep its economic system for fifty years. This event cannot fail to have far-reaching implications for the Asian economy. An immensely prosperous island-city-state, with a GDP over $100 billion, and exports that in 1996 reached $200 billion, Hong Kong will add tremendous potential human and financial capital to China and will provide a model for what much of the rest of China can achieve in the long run. The example of Hong Kong's financial system is bound to accelerate the modernization and reform of China's financial sector. Its exchange rate history also provides some valuable lessons.

China will find it in its interest to make the mainland more like Hong Kong rather than vice versa. This is also true for its monetary and exchange rate system. A fixed exchange rate solution for China would enable it to converge toward Hong Kong's inflation rate and pave the way for additional monetary reforms in China: (1) the achievement of convertibility on both current and capital account; (2) fixed exchange rates with the Hong Kong and U.S. dollars; and, finally, when China's financial system has matured to Hong Kong's level, monetary union with Hong Kong.

A fixed exchange rate policy for China presupposes a reference currency. At the present time the natural choice of reference currency is the U.S. dollar. However, the yen is the second most important currency in the world and fluctuations in the yen-dollar are disturbing to China and Hong Kong (and the rest of Asia). As Europe moves toward its own continental monetary union, the opportunity presents itself for greater monetary integration among the main Pacific countries; as Japan has recently increased its profile in the monetary arrangements in the Pacific, so should China. It would be in China's interest to move toward a more active role in international monetary affairs, and in particular to work toward an Asian currency area based on fixed exchange rates among the U.S. dollar, the Japanese yen, and the currency that emerges from the integration of the Chinese renminbi and the Hong Kong dollar.

At the annual meeting of the IMF and World Bank in Hong Kong in September 1997, Japan proposed the creation of an Asian fund for addressing the financial problems of the countries in the region. Provided the fund was multilateral and revolving, so that it did not become an alternative instrument for long-term aid, it could also become a forum for intraregional discussions in Southeast Asia. Some kind of monetary regionalism in the area is inevitable and it is natural that Japan, which is the world's second largest economy and its largest creditor, would play a leading role with China in this venture. Although the idea got short shrift from the IMF and the U.S. Treasury), which saw it as a potential challenge to its own leadership position, the idea will undoubtedly surface again in a different form as its usefulness – indeed inevitability – becomes more apparent.

In the long run, with complete integration between the Hong Kong dollar and the renminbi, a fully convertible joint currency, and Hong Kong's advanced banking system, legal structure, and bilingual community, China will emerge as a dominant economy in Asia.

CHAPTER 8

The Financial Sector and High Interest Rates: Lessons from Slovenia

Velimir Bole

In October 1991, Slovenia launched its new currency. High inflation was immediately attacked by drawing money out of the economy. Stabilization policy was implemented with restrictive monetary policy and fiscal policy of a balanced budget. Stabilization policy went hand in hand with a restructuring of the real and financial sectors and permanent sterilization efforts. In addition to a wholesale reshaping of the economy, a voucher system of privatization was introduced.

Stabilization resulted in a steady calming inflation. By the end of 1995, it had dropped to around 0.7 percent per month. The economy started to pick up; after the first two years of stabilization, it started to grow at around 4 percent per year. The economy ran high surpluses in current account till 1995; afterward current account balance became negligible. Foreign-exchange reserves increased even more because of significant inflows of foreign capital. The policy makers were mostly concerned by pressure from costs of wages and interest rates; those costs were high permanently.[1] Wages increased over 29 percent in real terms (GDP only 12%) to 1996, while interest rates started to fall from the level of around 15 percent for real lending interest rates only after the first half of 1994.

Stubbornly high real interest rates are known in other stabilization episodes.[2] In Chile, for example, interest rates soared in real terms to over 48 percent per year during the financial liberalization period; in Israel, the marginal real interest rate attained over 35 percent, on average, during the first two years of stabilization. Rocketing of real interest rates was especially pro-

[1] See details in Bole 1995.

[2] See, for example, Bruno and Meridor 1991, Ortiz 1991, Corbo and de Melo 1985.

nounced in the economies where stabilization was combined with massive deregulation and the opening of the financial sector.[3] There are also well-documented episodes of significant sterilized foreign exchange intervention; they usually resulted in increased instability in the financial sector and upward pressure on real interest rates.[4]

Two main groups of factors influencing interest rates in the poststabilization period have to be mentioned. The first group comprises factors related to the way stabilization is managed, with its credibility and fundamentals. The second group includes those factors which influence the quality of financial intermediation – the efficiency of the financial sector.

From high-interest-rate episodes in developing countries there are plenty of possible messages or guidelines on how to reduce the significant long-term increase in interest rates when stabilization and financial restructuring take place. Using such guidelines, this chapter will try to answer the question, What were (and are) the factors that pushed real interest rates in Slovenia so high and for so long in the period after stabilization and restructuring began? Particular attention will be given to factors influencing real interest rates through inefficiencies in the financial sector.

The chapter is structured as follows. First, the dynamics of interest rates after 1991 is documented. Second, evidence on the possible effects of monetary and fiscal policies on interest rates is presented. The third section tackles the scale of financial repression in Slovenia; likely consequences of the banks' rehabilitation and regulator's capital requirements are also studied. Probably the most important lesson is presented in the fourth section, which documents that in the stabilization period specific market structure of the loanable funds intermediation considerably increased real interest rates. Policy consequences are also discussed.

DYNAMICS OF INTEREST RATES AFTER STABILIZATION STARTED

In Slovenia, interest rates were also indexed before declaring monetary independence (October 1991). Every month, interest rates were formally adjusted for the rate of indexation. The only

[3] See Corbo and de Melo 1985 or McKinnon 1990.
[4] See, for example, Calvo, Leiderman, and Reinhart 1993.

exception was interest rates on sight deposits, which were not fully indexed. Till May 1995 the rate of indexation was equal to the rate of inflation of the previous month; after that date, moving averages of inflation rates in previous months were used as an indexation rate.

Because of indexation, the "real part" of interest rates was formally the policy target after 1991.[5] The "real part" of interest rates should have shown actual opportunity costs of the instrument. In setting the "real part" of interest rates, the policy of commercial banks was explicitly given. Therefore, the "real part" of interest rates was not changed automatically but according to the decision of individual banks.

In Figure 8.1 monthly nominal interest rates and the "real part" of interest rates are presented for several instruments (short- and long-term credits, sight and time deposits, and money market funds).[6] Obviously, because of indexation, nominal interest rates were strongly correlated. It is worth stressing that deposit and lending interest rates for firms in the business sector did not depend on the sector of production to which they belonged.

Reducing interest rates in the first two years after stabilization was mainly the result of abating inflation. Only the "real part" of lending rates (and not deposit rates) has been reducing since the very beginning of the stabilization period (October 1991). Although the "real part" of lending rates dropped more significantly already in the first half of 1993 (a quarter after bank rehabilitation started), significant changes in the trend of the real lending interest rates started as late as the middle of 1994.

In the first year and a half after stabilization started, the "real part" of interest rates was significantly different from the actual (ex ante) real interest rates. Actually, backward indexation brought about higher, and especially much more volatile, (ex ante) real interest rates than were the "real part" of interest rates. Monthly nominal and real interest rates for short-term credits,

[5] In 1991, inflation was very high, over 21% per month, so indexation of interest rates was necessary to prevent the flight in foreign-exchange deposits. Memories of hyperinflation in 1989 (when Slovenia was still a part of Yugoslavia) were still deeply rooted. Even in 1995, banks were still reluctant to state interest rates only in nominal terms (without a monthly adjustment for the rate of inflation) although inflation had abated to only 0.7% per month.

[6] In what follows, the presented interest rates are, in principle, marginal interest rates; the opposite case will be noticed.

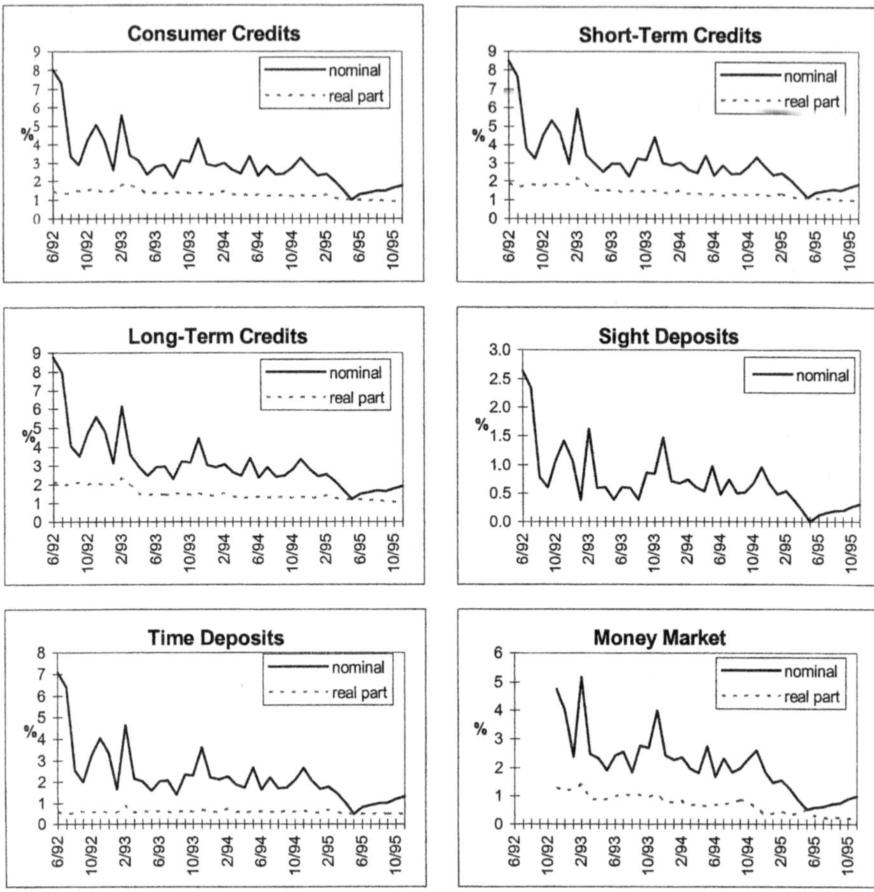

Figure 8.1. Nominal interest rates and "real part." *Source*: Bank of Slovenia, monthly bulletins.

sight deposits, and time deposits are shown on Figure 8.2. Monthly real interest rates and the "real part" of interest rates for short-term credits and time deposits are given in Figure 8.3.[7]

Figure 8.3 reveals that, periodically, very high real interest rates

[7] Estimates of real interest rates are from Bole 1996a. The (ex ante) real interest rates are estimated as suggested in Mishkin 1984 or Elliott 1977. Namely, ex post real interest rates are regressed on different nominal variables whose values are known at the time of supplying corresponding financial instrument. Estimated values are used as ex ante real interest rates.

in the first year and a half of stabilization were mainly the result of the backward indexation of interest rates. Namely, the "real part" of the interest rates was almost stable in the first year of stabilization – for credits, at less than 2 percent per month and for 90-day time deposits, at slightly over 0.5 percent per month. At the same time, (ex ante) real interest rates increased, peaking to 5 percent per month for credits and to 3.2 percent for time deposits. On average, differences were much smaller. In the first two years of stabilization, the difference between monthly real and the "real part" of interest rates was 0.12 of a percentage point for credits and 0.07 of percentage point for time deposits.

Because lower inflation than expected could push real interest rates up in a successful stabilization, price-indexed instruments are frequently proposed in such situations. Continuation of indexation after radical stabilization, however, is not desirable.[8] The Slovenian experience provides a clear lesson: if indexation is not ex post (using actual inflation rate), possible effects of indexation on real interest rates are still quite substantial.

Figure 8.2 shows clearly enough that, in Slovenia, the Fisher effect was small.[9] Namely, from the figure, it is obvious that nominal and real interest rates are highly correlated in dynamics (apparently not in levels).[10]

The decline of real interest rates intensified after the third quarter 1994 (see Figure 8.3). Until the beginning of 1996, real interest rates almost halved! Lending rates were reduced significantly more sharply than deposit rates, so that lending margin was also greatly reduced.

Since the first half of 1995, banks have started to set interest rates on some short-term instruments in nominal terms, without separating the "real part" and indexation rate. That happened in 1995 for the first time after four years.

HIGH INTEREST RATES AS A "SIDE PRODUCT" OF STABILIZATION

That the stabilization policy can induce a prolonged period of high real interest rates is hardly an unknown fact about the post-

[8] See Fischer 1991.

[9] Similar results are known also for some developed countries in Europe. See Mishkin 1984.

[10] For details, see Bole 1996a.

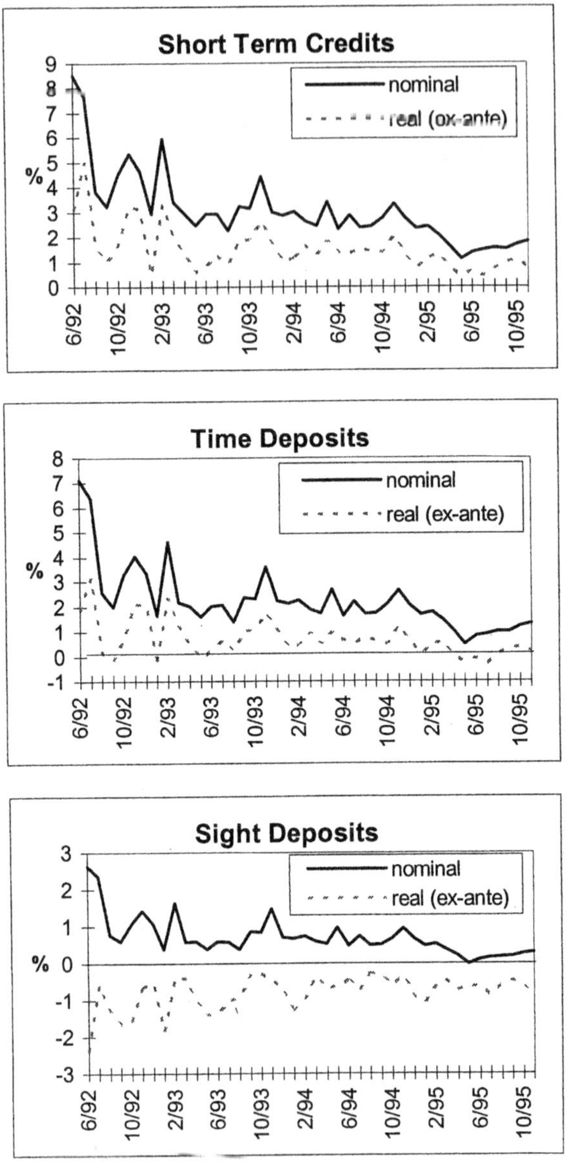

Figure 8.2. Nominal and (ex ante) real interest rates. *Sources*: Bank of Slovenia, monthly bulletins; Bole 1996a.

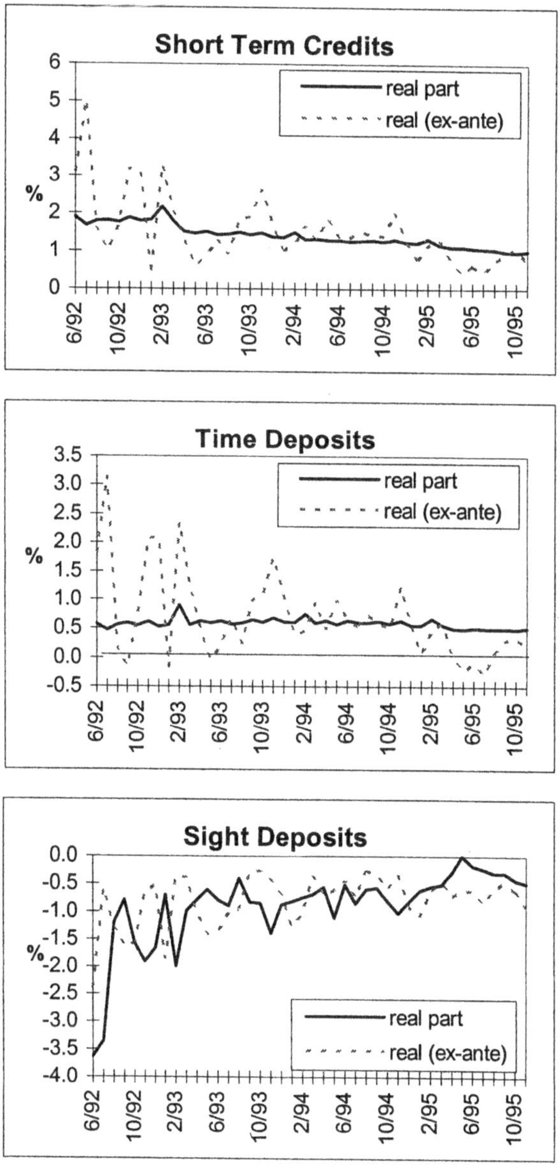

Figure 8.3. "Real part" and (ex ante) real interest rates. *Sources*: Bank of Slovenia, monthly bulletins; Bole 1996a.

stabilization period, and is even known to occur in successful episodes.[11] High real interest rates in the poststabilization period can stem from deliberately restrictive monetary policy. Besides, credibility (noncredibility) of stabilization can influence the difference between expected and actual inflation and, therefore, also real interest rates. High real interest rates can result also from the way monetary policy is used.[12]

Monetary Policy

In Slovenia, exogenous money and a floating exchange rate are two main pillars of monetary policy. The monetary rule used for determining target money includes also interest rate effect.[13] Therefore, it does not seem probable that deliberately tight monetary policy could cause prolonged high real interest rates. To demonstrate the stance of monetary policy, interest rates, money supply, and demand are illustrated in Figures 8.4, 8.5 and 8.6.

Broad money and total tolar credits, relative to total transactions (payments) of all nonbank sectors, are presented in Figure 8.4. Except seasonal peaks at the end of the year, broad money was increasing (against the volume of total transactions) rather smoothly after stabilization started. On average, the ratio of broad money over total transactions increased by 13 percent every year. Dynamics of the relative credits was almost the same as that of the relative broad money.

Figure 8.5 depicts growth rates of broad money (M2) and interest rates on ninety-day time deposits; growth rates of total credits (in tolars) and interest rates on credits are presented in Figure 8.6. Growth rates of broad money have been systematically greater than interest rates; on average, the difference was slightly greater than 1.7 percentage points per month (22 percentage points per year). Interest rates on credits were also systematically lower than growth rates of total credits; the average monthly difference was 1 percentage point (12 percentage points per year) from June 1992 to the end of 1995. After the end of 1994, growth

[11] See Bruno and Meridor 1991 for Israel and Ortiz 1991 for Mexico.
[12] See Bruno and Meridor 1991 and Fischer 1986. [13] See Bole 1995.

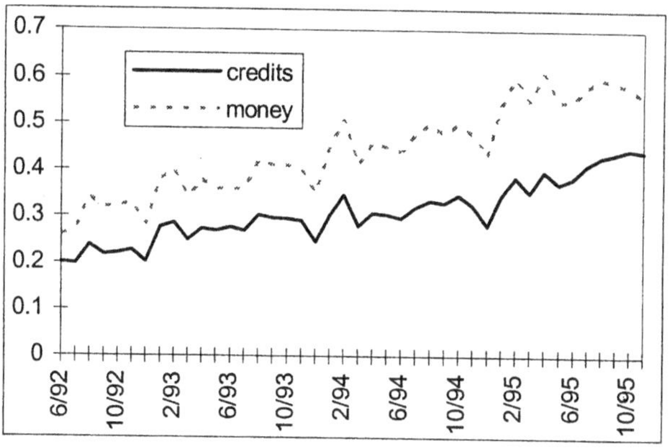

Figure 8.4. Tolar credits and broad money (per unit of transactions). *Sources*: Bank of Slovenia, monthly bulletin; and own calculations.

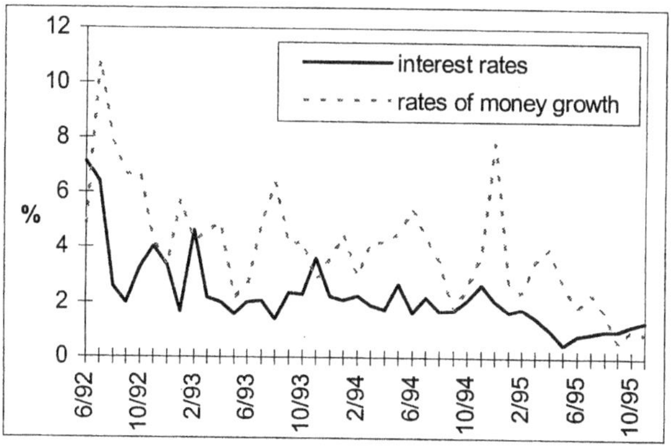

Figure 8.5. Broad money and interest rates. *Source*: Bank of Slovenia, monthly bulletins.

rates of credits were more than twice as high as corresponding interest rates.

In the successful stabilization episodes abroad, differences between interest rates and growth rates of credits and money were significantly smaller.[14]

[14] See, for example, Ortiz 1991 on Mexico and Bruno and Meridor 1991 on Israel.

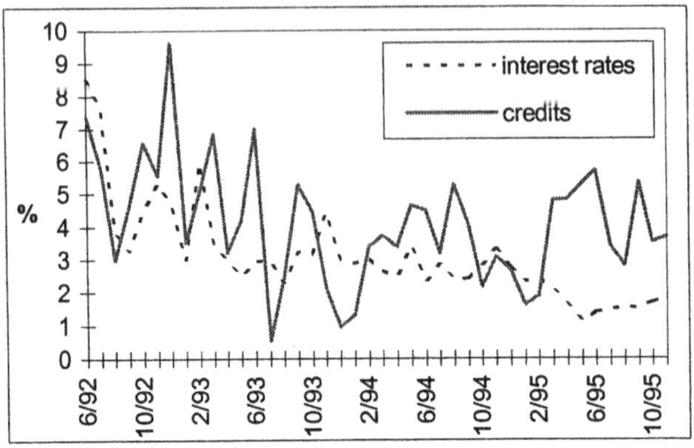

Figure 8.6. Growth of tolar credits and interest rates. *Source*: Bank of Slovenia, monthly bulletins.

Fiscal Policy

The ex post real interest rates are high in successful stabilization also because expected inflation is higher than actual. Therefore, the period of high real interest rates could also be shortened through increasing the credibility of the stabilization efforts. Because the fiscal balance explicitly shows how serious the government is with its stabilization measures, fiscal surplus (its overshooting) builds credibility of stabilization policy and therefore mitigates pressure on ex post real interest. Fiscal overshooting also reduces strains on real interest rates directly. Namely, curtailing government's domestic borrowing diminishes crowding out on the domestic capital market, and so also alleviates pressure on real interest rates.

In the next section, it is shown that, not only ex post, but also ex ante real interest rates were high in the first three years of stabilization. So, it seems that credibility of the government's efforts actually hasn't been so important. Table 8.1 presents some further evidence supporting the same conclusion about the credibility of the stabilization policy.

Obviously, fiscal policy has been on the side of stabilization since the beginning of stabilization. General government balance was almost negligible in the first four years of stabilization. Besides, the total interest-payment burden on the government did

Table 8.1. *Indicators of fiscal policy (% of GDP)*

	1992	1993	1994	1995
General government surplus (deficit)	0.3	0.3	−0.2	−0.0
Tax revenue	46.4	47.1	47.1	46.2
Government's interest payments	0.5	1.3	1.5	1.1
External public debt				9.0
Internal public debt				16.5[a]

[a] Estimated.
Sources: Bank of Slovenia, monthly bulletins.

not indicate any threat to the sustainability of the prevailing performance of balanced fiscal account.

It is worth stressing that, after 1992, the government collected through taxes around 46 to 47 percent of GDP, which is a high rate for much stronger economies. However, the share of taxes in GDP over 45 percent is still not exceptional among transitional economies or economies that have been successfully stabilized.[15]

In summary, there is hardly a piece of empirical evidence supporting the view that, in Slovenia, a prolonged period of high real interest rates stemmed from deliberately tight monetary policy, fiscal disorder, or noncredibility of the stabilization efforts.

INEFFICIENCIES OF THE FINANCIAL SECTOR AND HIGH INTEREST RATES

Beside effects of the stabilization policy itself, inefficiencies in the financial sector could also result in a prolonged period of high real interest rates.[16] "Classical" reasons for inefficient intermediation of loanable funds are overregulation of the financial sector – significant financial repression – and financial disorder in the time of high inflation. More recent cases from the Southern Cone, in Latin America, uncovered possible malfunctions of financial intermediation emanating from the "free-style" liberalization of the financial sector; those malfunctions could have even worse effects

[15] See Bruno and Meridor 1991. [16] See Fischer 1991.

on interest rates than a repressed (otherwise inefficient) financial sector.[17]

At the very beginning of stabilization, like other countries in transition, Slovenia started to restructure its financial sector to enable the intermediation of domestic loanable funds as well as the inflow of foreign capital. The evidence disproves that the malfunction of the financial sector in the stabilization period was the result of the restructuring financial sector, or even that inefficiencies resulted from actual financial repression! Because high real interest rates are among the most important consequences of (potential!) financial sector malfunctions, actual repression at the beginning of stabilization and the main development of the system of financial intermediation in the period of stabilization deserve closer examination.

Inefficiencies Stemming from Financial Repression

Was financial repression in Slovenia at the beginning of the 1990s high compared with that in other developing countries? Perhaps it was. But it was hardly an important obstacle for the efficient intermediation of loanable funds in the first four years of stabilization. In Tables 8.2 and 8.3, some indicators are given to illustrate this point.

Table 8.2 shows effective rates of reserve requirements, interest rates paid by the central bank (the Bank of Slovenia) on obligatory reserves, interest rates for the central bank liquidity credit (three days), inflation rate, and effective rates of (required) foreign-exchange minimum. There were no differences in reserve requirements rates for nonindexed tolar deposits, and deposits indexed with, respectively, inflation or foreign exchange rate.

Commercial banks in Slovenia also offer deposits in foreign exchange. In the first year of stabilization, the central bank imposed a "foreign-exchange minimum" to increase as much as possible the probability of servicing these deposits in the event of a foreign-exchange shortage or a run on foreign-exchange deposits. After 1992, when foreign-exchange reserves had already attained a high level, the foreign-exchange minimum was retained as a

[17] See McKinnon 1990 or Dijaz-Alejandro 1985.

Table 8.2. *Financial repression indicators*

	1992	1993	1994	1995
Obligatory reserves (effective rate)	10.6	7.7	7.0	7.5
Interest rates on obligatory reserves	1.0	1.0	1.0	1.0
Forex minimum (effective rate)[a]	80.7	63.7	63.9	68.5
Interest rates on BOS (3 days) liquidity credits	37.9	27.0	12.5	
Retail prices (rates of growth)	92.9	22.9	18.3	8.6

[a] Internal data of BOS.
Sources: Bank of Slovenia, monthly bulletins.

Table 8.3. *Indicators of asset quality*

	1992	1993	1994	1995
Normal (%)	75.0	81.1	86.1	89.9
Doubtful and loss (%)	17.3	7.6	5.6	4.0
Government inv. bonds (%) of total assets)	0.4	14.5	15.1	14.3

Sources: Bank of Slovenia, monthly bulletin, Bank of Slovenia, annual reports; and own calculations.

sterilization instrument – it mitigated effects of the inflow of foreign capital through the household sector. Because the inflow of foreign capital through the household sector was mainly very short term,[18] the foreign-exchange minimum was also used to insulate the domestic banking system from permanent instabilities of capital flows. Commercial banks could keep the foreign-exchange minimum in deposits abroad, in foreign-exchange bills of the central bank, in foreign currency, or in government bonds of OECD countries.

Except reserve requirements, there were no limitations on growth or structure of the banks' assets. Reserve requirements were drastically cut immediately after monetary cessation

[18] See Bole 1994. [19] See, for example, Leiderman and Bufman 1995.

of Slovenia. As is presented in Table 8.2, reserve requirements were, for the whole of the stabilization period, of the same order of magnitude as in developed Western economies. At the same time, the effective rate of reserve requirement was much lower than in some successfully stabilized and financially liberalized countries.[19]

Although the effective rate of the foreign-exchange minimum was higher than the reserve requirement rate, it restrained banks much less than increased marginal cash-deposit requirements usually used in economies facing a significant inflow of foreign capital.[20]

Other standard means of repressing the financial sector, known in developing countries,[21] were almost completely absent in Slovenia. From the very beginning of stabilization, there were no new directed credits for priority sectors of the economy, and no mandatory investments in different government funds or bonds.[22] Besides, lending interest rates depended only on the banks' own business policy, as there was no ceiling on interest rates.

In the first six months after stabilization started, a scarcity of foreign exchange and the complete suspension of the foreign financial support (in the time of secession) forced policy makers to control capital outflows and to ration foreign-exchange inflows for some priorities; that was the only domain of significant repressing of the financial (bank) intermediation in the stabilization period!

Effects of Financial Restructuring

Financial restructuring in Slovenia went hand in hand with thorough reshuffling of the institutional and incentive structure of the economy. Therefore, it is impossible to speak about the reform of the financial sector as being an isolated and coherent activity on its own. The financial sector was actually adjusted as and when problems appeared.

From the very declaration of monetary independence, efficiency of the financial sector was seriously hampered by a large

[20] See, for example, Calvo et al. 1993.

[21] See Leiderman and Bufman 1995.

[22] Such measures are quite common in developing countries. See Leiderman and Bufman 1995.

share of nonperforming credits and a huge volume of frozen foreign-exchange deposits (over 70% of households saving). The two biggest banks had the bulk of nonperforming credits in their balance sheets. Actually, at the time of launching a new currency ("tolar"), disorder and disablement of the financial sector in Slovenia were similar to the impairment of the financial sector at the end of unsuccessful liberalization experiments abroad.[23]

In Table 8.3, the percentage of (on and off balance) A assets[24] as well as the percentage of unrecoverable claims[25] are given. The impairment of the total banking sector is well illustrated by the fact that more than 17 percent of (on and off balance) assets were unrecoverable before bank rehabilitation started. An estimation of the marginal effects of unrecoverable claims on the lending margin cannot be made directly, due to lack of data. It is estimated, therefore, through evaluating the marginal effects of bank rehabilitation measures on interest rates.

In a later phase of stabilization (two years after starting), a third important deficiency in the financial system became apparent. Facing a fast increase in the inflow of foreign capital, banks were not able to intermediate it without causing significant swings in the foreign-exchange rate. Especially dangerous was the inflow of very short term capital through the household sector.[26] Instability of the foreign-exchange rate, triggered by capital inflows, also increased the correlation of default risks between different clients. The bulk of clients comprised exporters or suppliers of the export sector. So risks of their default were highly correlated. The macroeconomic instability, caused by the variability of the foreign-exchange rate, also induced moral hazard in banks and therefore pushed real interest up.[27]

Reducing banks' exposure to foreign-exchange risks by enforcing closed foreign-exchange positions would have further increased correlation of default risks of the banks' clients. Enforced closing of open positions would have increased foreign-exchange rate instability, particulary in the presence of short-term capital inflows. That is the reason why the central bank did not insist on

[23] See Dijaz-Alejandro 1985 or Corbo and de Melo 1985.
[24] In World Bank guidelines classified as "standard."
[25] In World Bank guidelines classified as "loss."
[26] See Bole 1994. [27] See McKinnon 1990.

closing open foreign-exchange positions in the first years of stabilization.

To eliminate the main causes of the financial sector inefficiency, bank rehabilitation started in 1993 in the two biggest banks. Nonperforming credits and off-balance claims were replaced by long-term government bonds. Management was changed. At the time of rehabilitation, both banks were put under the control of an existing government agency. Interest rates on government bonds were fixed. After nonperforming credits were replaced by governments bonds, the operative income cash flow of both banks became positive.

Besides direct bank rehabilitation, the government also restructured banks indirectly by restructuring the real sector. Some important firms (heavily burdened by loans) obtained government bonds (and became state-owned) to improve their financial position.[28] Firms used these bonds mostly for settling their debts to banks. So bank portfolios obtained government bonds instead of nonperforming credits.

The central bank also increased the minimal required capital for commercial banks; this minimal level of capital was mandatory for banks to be licensed for foreign-exchange transactions. The new minimal capital requirement, needed for getting a full license,[29] was set at DM 60 million. Increased minimum capital requirement would have to increase the robustness of banks facing volatile capital flows. It was expected that the increased minimum capital requirement would also accelerate bank mergers and therefore, over the long term, increase efficiency of financial intermediation.

The scale of direct and indirect rehabilitation measures is illustrated by the share of the long-term (investment) government bonds in total (on and off balance) assets of banks (see Table 8.3). Because the volume of performing assets increased considerably, it was expected that the lending margin would have to decrease.

In Table 8.4 results of a cross-section analysis of lending (gross) margins in 1993 and 1994 are provided. The lending margin is

[28] Number of employed was usually a "criteria" for getting government bonds. So the biggest chunk of bonds went for the restructuring of steel and shipping.

[29] To offer also foreign exchange deposits and to perform foreign-exchange payments.

Table 8.4. *Effects of financial restructuring on lending margin*

	1993	1994
const.	9.803 (5.6)	6.680 (3.9)
KAAK		−0.053 (−1.8)
DKAAK	−0.031 (−1.7)	−0.057 (−1.6)
STB	54.001 (1.5)	72.845 (2.2)
VLOB	−0.036 (−1.3)	−0.034 (−1.1)
KCDE	0.026 (0.5)	0.108 (1.5)
DKCDE		0.137 (1.8)
R^2	0.16	0.30

Notes: KAAK capital adequacy (in the previous year); DKAAK capital adequacy (increment); STB operative costs per unit of balance sheet; VLOB deposits per unit of balance sheet (in the previous year); KCDE unrecoverable claims (in the previous year); and DKCDE unrecoverable claims (increment).

defined as a difference between lending rate on short-term credits and deposit rate for time (thirty to ninety days) tolar deposits in December of respective years. Predetermined variables are capital adequacy at the end of the previous year, change of capital adequacy in the current year, operative costs per unit of the total balance sheet, share of nonperforming credits[30] at the end of the previous year, change of nonperforming credits in the current year, the ratio of total tolar deposits (sight and time), and the total balance sheet at the end of previous year.

Capital adequacy variables are included to embrace the effects of expected insolvency costs on the lending margin.[31] Namely, through indirect rehabilitation of banks and increasing of the minimum capital requirement, the expected insolvency costs would have had to decrease.[32]

Nonperforming credits are included in the equation to encompass the effect of the costs of writing off losses. To diminish the

[30] "Doubtful" and "loss" in World Bank classification. In what follows, term credits are used, while actually total (in and off balance) financial claims are used in estimation.

[31] See Baltensperger 1980.

[32] See a similar study for Japan in Okina and Sakuraba 1994.

pressure of the costs of writing off losses, profits have to increase as does the lending margin. As the actual rehabilitation of banks started by replacing nonperforming credits with government bonds,[33] both variables of nonperforming credits embrace effects of the necessary increase of profits to cover losses.

The ratio of tolar deposits and balance sheet is increasing as financial deepening gets under way. The increasing share of foreign-exchange deposits or interbank credits raise pressure of the costs of intermediation and therefore also lending margin. Thus, increasing financial deepening has to squeeze lending margin.

Regression functions are estimated for 1993 and 1994 because more recent data have not been available. Cross-section data of thirty banks are used in the estimation. The estimated regression coefficients and corresponding t-statistics are given in Table 8.4.

The statistical quality of the estimated regressions is approximately the same as in similar cross-section studies abroad.[34]

In 1993, only effect of changing capital adequacy is statistically significant (at 10%). Higher values of t-statistics also have variables of operative costs and tolar deposits. The capital adequacy variable has a negative sign. So banks with lower expected insolvency costs had, ceteris paribus, a smaller lending margin, in 1993.[35] A sign of operative cost and tolar deposit variables are expected: costs are pushing lending margin up, while tolar deposits squeeze the lending margin. But variables are not statistically significant.

The statistical quality of the estimated regression for 1994 is considerably higher than that for 1993. Except for tolar deposits and the share of nonperforming credits in the previous year (1993), variables are significant at 10 percent. All variables have the expected sign.

Capital adequacy variables significantly squeezed the lending margin in 1994. An increase of capital adequacy by 10 percent would have brought about a drop in the lending margin of 0.1 points.

[33] See similar specification in Okina and Sakuraba 1994.

[34] See Bernanke in Lown 1991, or Okina and Sakuraba 1994.

[35] In a study for Japan, capital adequacy is statistically significant while the change of capital adequacy is not. It has, however, a negative sign!

The coefficient of the change of nonperforming credits is statistically significant and positive. Banks with bigger drops of nonperforming credits, therefore, reduced lending margins more than other banks in 1994. A decrease of nonperforming credits share of 10 percent reduced the lending margin by 0.2 points in 1994.

In 1994, lending margin depended mostly on operative costs (per unit of balance sheet). Banks with 10 percent lower costs (per unit of balance sheet) than the average for the banking system had, on average, a 0.36 points lower lending margin in 1994.

In summary, presented empirical evidence does not support the view that financial inefficiencies stemming from overregulation (financial repression) were unduly large in the stabilization period. Two basic steps in the financial restructuring in the period of stabilization were bank rehabilitation and the increase in the minimum capital requirement. Both significantly contributed to a reduction in the lending margin already in the first year after implementing the process.

CHARACTERISTICS OF FINANCIAL INTERMEDIATION AND HIGH INTEREST RATES

At the beginning of stabilization, in 1991 and 1992, many firms were "distress borrowers": their demand for credits was inelastic on interest rates. Not only the restrictive stance of monetary and fiscal policy, but also the collapse of the market in former Yugoslavia[36] increased the number of "distress borrowers" considerably. The number of normal and doubtful and loss assets in Table 8.3 shows that, in 1992, around one-quarter of clients could not obtain credits on normal terms. Actually they had access only to the curb market. At the same time, interest rate elasticity of loanable funds supplied from the nonbanking financial sector (insurance companies, broker houses) and other firms active in curb market was very high.

Greater mobility of deposits (higher interest rate elasticity of supply of loanable funds) of a significant part of nonbanking sector increased uncertainty. Bigger enterprises from retail trade, especially gasoline trade, were among the most active suppliers of

[36] In the 1980s, Slovenian firms sold more than 30% in other parts of Yugoslavia.

mobile deposits. Banks didn't know what interest rate to bid because suppliers of funds for large (short-term) deposits were better informed. Interest rate uncertainty, due to such unstable large deposits, was exemplified by the behavior of smaller (new) banks which intermediated a considerable chunk of these deposits.

New, small banks were usually overcapitalized. Nevertheless, they were not able to increase considerably credits to firms from the real sector. Their marketing and knowledge of their potential clients were poor, international payments connections with correspondent banks were almost absent, and they were understaffed for appropriate monitoring. So their credit activity turned to safe clients (old, big banks) or to credits using mostly highly liquid collateral (credits to broker houses). To support their credit activity, they had to increase their market share in loanable funds through bidding very high deposit rates.[37] Small new banks attracted a greater part of unstable, large deposits than other banks. Collected excess funds were then offered to firms active on the capital market and on the interbank market at even higher interest rates. Debtors on the interbank market were usually big (old) banks, and especially banks with solvency problems. In Table 8.5, institutional structure of deposits is shown and also the scale of the interbank money market.

The central bank was unable to ease monetary policy to mitigate liquidity pressure because of still very high inflation and almost absent income policy. On the other hand, anchoring through exchange rate would make sterilization of the enormous inflow of foreign capital completely impossible. Through the household sector alone, flow of very short term foreign capital attained over 2 percent of GDP.[38] Therefore, in the case of foreign exchange anchoring, policy makers would be unable to prevent considerable real appreciation of the tolar, with well-known adverse consequences for longer-term performance of the economy.

Uncertainty on the deposit market, hand in hand with interest rate inelastic credit demand, pushed deposit interest rates up and, therefore, also lending rates.

[37] Overcapitalization increased their moral hazard when bidding deposit interest rates.
[38] See Bole 1994.

Table 8.5. *Indicators of deposit and money market*

	1992	1993	1994	1995
Deposits of households (% of total)	27	25	33	35
Deposits of business sector (% of total)	47	48	43	42
Deposits of nonbanking financial sector and government (% of total)	26	27	24	23
Interbank credits (less than 30 days; % of base money)	30.3	25.4	19.6	13.3

Sources: Bank of Slovenia, monthly bulletins.

High interest rate elasticity of the supply of loanable funds and low (or zero) elasticity of the demand for credits are two pillars of the theoretic model for a market of financial intermediation, which can explain a prolonged period of high interest rates in cases like Slovenia. In theory, it is a well-known fact that a market of financial intermediation has to be modeled as a double Bertrand market. More recent studies of such markets revealed that equilibrium prices on such a market can be far from intuition. What seems very important is the fact that "winner-take-all" competition for inputs (deposits) and price (interest rate) inelasticity on supply (credit) market implies Nash equilibrium (subgame-perfect) prices (interest rates), which are higher than Walrasian and with excess stock (of loanable funds).[39]

A simplified theoretical explanation of interest rate effects of uncertainty[40] is as follows. "Winner-take-all"-like competition on the deposit market considerably increases uncertainty of the banks. They don't know the interest rates bidded by other banks for deposits, while suppliers of loanable funds (for large deposits) do know that. At the same time, banks are aware that bank(s) with the highest bid would "take all" supplied funds (unstable deposits). They also know that, on the money market, other banks

[39] See Stahl 1988, Yanelle 1988, or Yanelle 1989.
[40] "Strategic uncertainty" in Yanelle 1989.

would have to borrow from "winners" and pay even higher interest rates!

Cross-section as well as time series empirical analysis confirms that in the Slovenian stabilization, interest elasticity of the demand for credits was really negligible and that mobility of deposits of "nonhousehold" sector was very high.[41]

The central bank attacked high real interest rates by trying to reduce uncertainty on the deposit market (interbank variability of interest rates).[42] The central bank started to penalize individual banks whenever their deposit interest rates exceeded average interest rates "too much." It did it through reducing permitted intermonth variability of obligatory reserve fulfillment for banks with deposit rates overshooting the band around average interest rates. Namely, in Slovenia normal fulfillment of obligatory reserves could vary from day to day. Only the monthly average matters. After 1994–96, in every quarter, the central bank reduced in advance the potential day-to-day variability of obligatory reserves (vault money, giro account, and "reserve" account) for all banks that overshot the band around the average of deposit interest rates (of all banks) in the previous quarter.

It is clearly illustrated in Figures 8.1, 8.2, and 8.3 that effects on lending rates were almost immediate. Already in the last quarter of 1994, the lending rates started to drop significantly in real terms. Through 1995–96 (in a one-year period) lending rates had already dropped over 30 percent.

After June 1995, commercial banks made an agreement on the highest possible deposit rates. Because this agreement eliminated (strategic) uncertainty on its own, the central bank placed its measures on hold. However, to make agreement credible (to prevent possible free-rider behavior) commercial banks authorized the central bank to supervise its fulfillment. Until June 1996

[41] See Bole 1996b. It is shown that growth of deposits from household and the "nonhousehold" sector Granger-causes interest rates, while feedback effects from interest rates are insignificant. The hypothesis that interest rates do not Granger-cause growth of short- and long-term credits can not be rejected! Empirical data also confirm that decrease of growth rates of household deposits increases interest rates, while decrease of growth rates of deposits from the "nonhousehold" sector reduces interest rates. On cross-section data correlation between share of "nonhousehold" deposits and deposit interest rates is very high and positive.

[42] Perhaps strong "moral suasion" applied by the Bank of Israel in May 1989 worked along the same lines. See Fisher 1991.

(in two years), real lending interest rates almost halved. In June 1996 the best (A) clients[43] could get short-term credit paying interest rates around 6.5 to 8 percent in real terms.

SUMMARY

In the stabilization period, real lending interest rates soared in Slovenia. Deposit rates were also very high.

High real interest rates prevailed over three years although empirical evidence does confirm that fiscal policy was in a stabilization track (budget was balanced) and that money supply was adjusted permanently according to economic activity, inflation, and interest rates.

It has also been demonstrated that inefficiencies stemming from a repressed financial sector were probably smaller than in other developing countries. The bank rehabilitation and the increase of banks' capital reduced lending margin significantly in the stabilization period.

The double Bertrand market structure of loanable funds intermediation is pinpointed as an important reason for a prolonged period of high real interest rates after stabilization started. The distress borrowing and high interbank mobility of the large unstable deposits were the crucial precondition for that. It is shown that successful policy measures, utilizing these results, were adopted.

REFERENCES

Baltensperger, E. 1980. "Alternative Approaches to the Theory of Banking Firm." *Journal of Monetary Economics* 6: 1–37.

Bernanke, B. S., and C. S. Lown. 1991. "The Credit Crunch." *Brookings Papers on Economic Activity* 2: 205–47.

Bole, V. 1994. "The Inflow of Capital through the Household Sector" (in Slovene). *Gospodarska Gibanja* 9: 23–42.

Bole, V. 1995. "Stabilization in Slovenia: from high inflation to excessive inflow of foreign capital." Paper presented at the first Dubrovnik Conference on Transition Economies. Working Papers 1995/1, Economic Institute at School of Law, Ljubljana.

[43] "Normal" in World Bank classification.

Bole, V. 1996a. "Interest Rates after 1992; Dynamics and Structure" (in Slovene). Working Papers 1996/1, Economic Institute at School of Law, Ljubljana.

Bole, V. 1996b. "The Market Structure of Financial Intermediation and High Interest Rates" (in Slovene). *Gospodarska Gibanja* (1996): 23–36.

Bruno, M., S. Fischer, E. Helpman, N. Liviatan, and L. R. Meridor. 1991. *Lessons of Economic Stabilization and Its Aftermath*. Cambridge, Mass.: MIT Press.

Bruno, M., and L. R. Meridor. 1991. "The Costly Transition from Stabilization to Sustainable Growth: Israel's Case." In Bruno et al. 1991, 241–77.

Calvo, G. A., L. Leiderman, and C. Reinhart. 1993. "The Capital Inflows Problem." IMF Papers on Policy Analysis and Assessment, International Monetary Fund, Washington, D.C.

Corbo, V., and J. de Melo. 1985. "Overview and Summary." *World Development* 13: 863–66.

Dijaz-Alejandro, C. 1985. "Good-bye Financial repression, Hello Financial Crash." *Journal of Development Economics* 19: 1–24.

Elliott, J. W. 1977. "Measuring the Expected Real Rate of Interest: An Exploration of Macroeconomic Alternatives." *American Economic Review* 67: 429–43.

Fischer, S. 1986. *Indexing, Inflation, and Economic Policy*. Cambridge, Mass.: MIT Press.

Fischer, S. 1991. "Panel Discussion: What's New Since Toledo?" In Bruno et al. 1991, 404–9.

Leiderman, L., and G. Bufman. 1995. "Financial Reform in Israel: A case of gradualism." In R. Dornbusch and Y. C. Park (eds.), *Financial Opening; Policy Lessons for Korea*, 295–322. International Centre for Economic Growth.

McKinnon, R. I. 1990. "Financial Liberalization in Retrospect: Interest Rate Policies in LDC's." In G. Ranis and T. P. Schultz (eds.), *The State of Development Economics: Progress and Perspectives*, 386–415. Cambridge: Basil Blackwell.

Mishkin, F. S. 1984. "The Real Interest Rate: A Multi-Country Empirical Study." *Canadian Journal of Economics* 17: 283–311.

Okina, K., and C. Sakuraba. 1994. "Bank Balance Sheet Adjustment and Interest Rate Policy in Japan." In *National Differences in Interest Rate Transmission*, 155–78. Basle: Bank for International Settlements.

Ortiz, G. 1991. "Mexico beyond the Debt Crisis: Toward Sustainable Growth with Price Stability." In Bruno et al. 1991, 283–322.

Stahl, D. 1988. "Bertrand Competition for Inputs and Walrasian Outcomes." *American Economic Review* 78: 189–201.

Yanelle, M. O. 1989. "The Strategic Analysis of Intermediation." *European Economic Review* 33: 294–301.

Yanelle, M. O. 1988. "On the Theory of Intermediation." Ph.D. dissertation, University of Bonn, Bonn.

CHAPTER 9

Bank Rehabilitation in Slovenia: With Emphasis on Nova Ljubljanska Banka

Franjo Štiblar

Rehabilitation of banks is one of the most important and complicated problems in economies in transition. Slovenia was among those countries which started with it relatively early in transition, parallel to rehabilitation of the enterprise sector. After three years positive results are evident, but the consolidation of the banking sector will not be finished until the rehabilitation of banks is terminated by a formal act of the central bank and privatization of rehabilitated banks completed.

This chapter describes Slovene experience with bank rehabilitation in general and the special case of Nova Ljubljanska Banka. After the Slovene banking sector is described, the chapter considers rehabilitation in general and then the experience of rehabilitation in the largest Slovene Bank – Nova Ljubljanska Banka.

BANKING SECTOR IN SLOVENIA: BASIC INFORMATION

In the 1990s, the Slovene banking sector is characterized by a relatively simple structure, autarchy (compared with banking in developed market economies), regional and market concentration (within the country), and, at the same time, the overbanking and overcapitalization of many existing banks. In detail, Bremec (1996) lists the following characteristics of the Slovene banking sector at the beginning of the 1990s:

lower efficiency than for enterprises in comparison with Western developed countries (lack of competition, entry is controlled),
high operating costs in comparison with competition abroad,
underdeveloped orientation to market of financial services,

underdeveloped risk management,
overbanking with regional concentration at the same time,
overcapitalization of banking sector,
lagging behind world trends in using modern information technology,
existence of contaminated bank loans and insufficient provisioning,
a need for rehabilitation of the majority of the banking sector on an unprecedented scale (over half of the banking system is in a very small monetary area) in comparison with experiences with bank restructuring in the West.

Normative dynamics in the banking field was intense in the past twenty years with new banking laws adopted in 1985 and 1989 (in the former Yugoslavia) and in 1991 (one of the constitutional laws). After 1991, deficiencies of the law and absence of regulation in several fields have been supplemented with several decrees and other normative acts.

All basic laws on banking, which are still valid today, were enacted in the package of "constitutional laws" on the day of proclamation of independence of Slovenia on 25 June 1991 (*Official Gazette of the Republic of Slovenia*, January 1991).

The Law on Banks and Savings Banks consists of general provisions and specific provisions on establishment of banks (very high minimum capital requirement), banking groups, the capital of banks, bank credit, liquidity and open position, deposit business, guarantees, management of banks, reporting internal control, supervision of banks, and business secrets. A special section is devoted to savings banks and other financial institutions. The banking regulation will be described in detail throughout the text.

Slovenia also enacted the Law on Prerehabilitation, Rehabilitation, Bankruptcy, and Liquidation of Banks as one of the constitutional laws in June 1991. One small savings bank was bankrupt in 1989 and one larger bank (1.7% of total banking assets) began bankruptcy procedures in July 1996. The law describes conditions and procedures under which the bank is put under Bank of Slovenia (BoS) auspices into one of the previously mentioned positions and out of regular business.

The Law on the Bank of Slovenia contains several provisions

related to banks, including the care for the liquidity of the banking system as one of its special tasks and the supervision of banks.

Under present banking legislation there is no special deposit insurance scheme either from the government or central bank or from the banks themselves in the form of a special deposits insurance association. As is well known, there is moral hazard in establishing such a deposit insurance scheme for banks.

New legislation on banking is in preparation, the process beginning in 1994, with the latest draft law produced in the middle of 1996. In the past, as we just noted, normative dynamics in the banking field was quite intensive, with new banking legislation adopted in 1985 and 1989 (in former Yugoslavia) and in 1991 (one of the constitutional laws). After 1991, deficiencies of the law and absence of regulation in several fields have been supplemented with several decrees and other normative acts. The new banking law should incorporate all these novelties. It comes more as a recognition and confirmation of the existing situation than as an introduction of wholly new solutions.

The draft version of the new banking law (May 1996) defines banking and financial services, financial organizations, and connected institutions in the introductory general articles. The second chapter has statutory provisions related to capital, shareholders, and banking organizations. The third chapter concerns licensing of banks. The next chapter outlines regulations of subsidiaries and branches of foreign banks in Slovenia, with the general view that branches (without their own capital and directly connected to head-office banks abroad) will be allowed, thus closing the gap to the European Union (EU) legislation. In the fifth chapter, the financial group is defined.

The sixth chapter contains prudential regulation including application of Bank for International Settlements (BIS) standards: 55 million DEM is defined as the minimum capital required for the full license, a requirement for a minimum 8 percent capital adequacy ratio. There are articles on risk assessment and provisioning, limiting nonbanking assets to 100 percent of a bank's capital and capital investment to other financial organizations to 60 percent of its capital, liquidity requirements, protection against different risks (currency, interest rate, maturity mismatch in balance sheet), connected persons, large exposure (over 10% of bank's capital), the maximum limit of large exposures to 800 percent of capital, and a 20 percent share as a limit to non-connected institutions.

The seventh chapter deals with protection of confidential information and chapter 8 with bank business reports. Chapters 9 and 10 deal with internal and external bank supervision. Chapter 11 defines measures available to the central bank related to supervisory report. Chapter 12 concerns the regulation of the deposit insurance scheme: 26,000 DEM as insured deposit, special reserves of banks in the amount of 0.1 percent of deposits from natural persons with the bank. Chapter 13 deals with bankruptcy and liquidation of banks; 14, with the regulation of Post Bank; 15, with the Banking Association; 16, with savings houses; 17, with savings-credit institutions for cooperatives; 18, with penal provisions; and 19, with transitory and final provisions. Most adaptation to the new law should be completed in one year, the remaining provisions until the end of the year 2000 or 2001.

Other laws also affect the banking sector, for instance the Law on Bank of Slovenia. Important among them is a newly prepared law on foreign financial operations that will include regulation of foreign direct investment (FDIs).

SLOVENE BANKING SECTOR IDENTITY CARD

The number of commercial banks increased from sixteen in the 1980s to thirty-four at maximum in 1994. In the middle of 1996 twenty-nine banks are operating with around 10,000 employees.

The size and the level of financial deepening of the Slovene economy is illustrated in Table 9.1. Financial deepening is taking place after independence, although the monetization of the Slovene economy remains under the level for developed market economies: velocity of M1 is still above ten, with international standards around five; total assets of the banking sector count for 70 percent of GDP, while in economies with a developed financial structure they are well above 100 percent.

While in the first years of independence the banking sector as a whole was undercapitalized (the world standard for capital multiplier is seventeen), after additional capitalization of the largest banks in rehabilitation and additional capitalization of small

Table 9.1. *Monetary aggregates and banking sector development, 1991–95*

	1991	1992	1993	1994	1995
GDP (current bio tolars)	1,017	1,435	1,844	2,198	2,502
GDP (million current USD)			14,170	18,600	19,230
End of period (billion tolar)					
M0				85	115
M1	39	81	116	170	204
M2	74	186	303	487	615
M3	137	314	513	733	940
M1/M0 = multiplier				1.35	2.00
GDP/M1 = velocity		12.5	12.5	10.8	10.8
A = banking assets	325	624	932	1,243	1,553
K = capital of banks	14	17	24	105	127
A/GDP = share	0.61	0.65	0.67	0.71	
A/K = capital multiplier	27	39	11.8	12.2	

Sources: Bank of Slovenia, monthly bulletins, and annual report (Ljubljana, 1996).

banks (fulfilling increasing minimum-required capital request) the banking sector became overcapitalized. It was the intention of the central bank this way primarily to protect banks from the volatility of external financial flows typical for a small open economy, but, at the same time, to decrease the number of banks to approximately half of present number (see monthly *Bulletin of BOS*, April 1996).

The money multiplier for M1 increased between 1994 and 1995, indicating a stronger role for the banking sector in its "secondary emission of money" compared with the BOS "primary emission," another indication of financial development.

The number of banks operating in Slovenia reached its peak in 1994 (Table 9.2). In mid-1996 they number thirty-two but really twenty-nine (if both old Ljubljanska Banka and old Kreditna Banka Maribor, which practically do not operate, and Bank Triglav, which is under bankruptcy, are excluded). The banks employ around 10,000 workers, which is less than 1 percent of the work force. The number of banks with full license is fifteen, but one of them has been under bankruptcy procedures since July 1996. Among them, seven are registered for both commercial and investment banking (one in bankruptcy procedure with

Table 9.2. *Development of the Slovene banking sector, 1991–96*

Years	Number of banks	Capital	Total assets: In billion SIT	Total assets: In million $	Total assets: As % of GDP
1991	26	63	327.3	5.8	
1992	30	103	628.0	6.4	62.0
1993	32	142	937.4	7.1	65.3
1994	33	173 (220)	1174.0	9.3	64.6
1995	31	212 (263)	1493.0	11.9	67.9
1996[a]	32	(270)	1710.0	12.4	

[a] As of May 1996.
Sources: Bank of Slovenia publications.

1.5 percent share in assets of the banking sector and ranked number 12 by the size of assets), two for commercial banking and dealing with securities, and six with full commercial banking license.

In the observation period total banking assets increased from around 60 to 70 percent of GDP indicating relatively poor financial structure, which, in fact is cleaned of doubtful assets. The number of savings institutions (houses) was reduced to seven controlled and nine altogether. In 1995 and for eight months of 1996 there was no license issued for a new bank or savings house.

After independence profitability of banks in Slovenia has constantly improved, going from losses for the system as a whole in 1992 to substantial earnings, although return on equity (ROE) and return on assets (ROA) remain still below international standards for the sector as a whole in 1995 (Table 9.3). Overcapitalization is indicated with low capital multiplier, which is rising constantly, albeit slowly.

Structural Characteristics of the Slovene Banking Sector

Structural characteristics are discussed at length in a study from 1994 (*Banking Newsletter*, 1995). They include relation of the banking sector with different economic sectors, regional structure, market concentration, and ownership structure. Here, some of these conclusions are only summarized.

Table 9.3. *Income statement of the banking sector in Slovenia, 1992–95 (in millions SIT)*

	1992	1993	1994	1995
Net interest	40,925	70,142	31,153	42,128
Net commissions	9,698	15,566	11,695	19,692
Net other income	−14,118	−14,297	13,000	19,320
Operating expenses	−16,261	−22,180	−36,828	−44,689
Depreciation	−2,296	−3,267	−3,330	−6,103
Net write-offs, provisions	−33,464	−45,626	−11,018	−15,180
Net income before taxes	−15,516	338	4,672	15,168
Average rates SIT/$	81.29	113.24	128.81	118.52
SIT/DEM	52.13	68.43	79.37	82.66
ROE (%)	−15.1	0.2	2.7	7.2
ROA (%)	−2.5	0.0	0.4	1.0
Assets/equity	6.1	6.6	6.9	7.0

Sources: Reply to EU Questionnaire, Government of the Republic Slovenia, July 1996.

Table 9.4. *Sectoral structure of Slovene banking sector balance sheet, 1993 (%)*

Sector	Assets	Liabilities
Enterprise	36	25
Household	7	32
Government and BOS	29	12
Domestic interbank market	12	14
Foreign interbank market	16	17

Sectoral Structure

In 1993 the balance sheet of the banking sector in Slovenia had a structure as shown in Table 9.4. Net creditors were households, net debtors were enterprises and government (plus BOS), with interbank market being quite equilibrated. Recently the share of credits to households started to increase and to enterprises to decrease so that mismatch in these two sectors' positions in banking balance sheets between credits given and deposits received decreased. Government and BOS retained their peculiar position of net debtors related to rehabilitation bonds issued.

Table 9.5. *Concentration of banking market: Shares of five largest banks (%)*

Country	Balance sum	Capital	Deposits	Credits
Slovenia				
August 1994	68	36	64	64
December 1995	59	(42)	54	62
Bulgaria 1992	67	50		
Czech Republic 1993		45		87
Poland 1992		44	39	25
Croatia 1993 (7 banks)	85	78		
Developed economies			53	

Sources: Vienna Institute for Comparative Studies, Vienna, various reports, *Economist*, 2 May 1992; for Slovenia: Reports to the Banking Association, 1994, 1995.

Regional Structure

According to detailed analysis made by Repanšek (1994), the Slovene bank services market was relatively closed in the middle of 1994 and the situation improved only slightly afterward. This is related to labor immobility, bad traffic connections, and some other factors. At that time six out of twelve Slovene regions were not opened to banks from other regions, and this changed only slightly as "domestic" banks now do not have a monopolistic but still have a dominant position in their regions. On the other hand, the capital city Ljubljana is the center of banking concentration with practically every larger bank having a branch or at least an office there.

Market Concentration

The structure of the banking sector, based on the size of individual banks, is relevant in both ends: upper end (the share of five largest banks), which indicates the level of concentration and monopolistic situation; and lower end, which indicates the dispersion of small banks, probably unable to sustain fierce competition in the market in the future because of the lack of economy of scale.

By international standards the over 70 percent share of the five largest banks in the country (Table 9.5) indicates overconcentration (Netherlands, for instance, among developed economies of normal size exceeds this number). In the upper end of concentration are Belgium and France; in the middle are Spain,

Great Britain, and Italy; at the lower end of concentration is Germany, where the share of deposits in the five largest banks does not exceed 20 percent.

Concentration in the Slovene banking sector is relatively strong, but still at the level similar to other economies in transition, and it is also decreasing. A similar conclusion was obtained by Repanšek (1994). He calculated the value around 1,500 for the usual index of concentration obtained as a sum of percentage shares of all existing banks in Slovenia. The range for this indicator is between 0 (if there is an infinitive number of banks with insignificant shares each) and 10,000 if there is only one bank (100% × 100%). The values of concentration coefficients of the Slovene banking sector from 1991 to 1995, respectively, are 2,800, 2,500, 1,800, 1,300, and 1,200.

At the lower end, the dispersion of banks in Slovenia is above optimal, which leads to overcapitalization (mentioned earlier) and substandard "productivity" as measured by balance sum/capital and balance sum/employees. Employees in banking represent around 0.5 percent of the Slovene population, compared with 1.1 percent in Germany or 0.3 percent in Hungary.

The largest bank in Slovenia, Nova Ljubljanska Banka, has currently 28 percent market share, followed by SKB with 12 percent and NKB Maribor with 11 percent. Four other banks have shares of 4 to 5 percent (Koper, Celje, A-banka, Kranj) and the remaining twenty-two banks together account only for one-third of the aggregate balance sheet.

Ownership and the Share of Foreign Capital in Banking Sector

Among twenty-nine banks twenty-seven are in private ownership; two are under rehabilitation (their rehabilitation was formally completed June 1997) and thus in state ownership. Foreign capital is present in fourteen banks, but predominantly in small banks, so that the share of foreign capital in total capital of the banking sector is less than 10 percent. Among banks with foreign capital, one bank is 100 percent owned by foreigners and five banks are in majority foreign ownership. The analysis of the competitive position of banks with foreign capital (Bremec 1996) shows that their active rates are above average for the banking system and their passive rates at the average (due to interbank agreement on the upper limit for passive banking interest rates). Results indicate that until now foreign banks did not contribute substantially to competitiveness in the market of banking services; they have larger margins and, surprisingly, they are not recognized by customers for better quality or a wider range of banking services.

Performance of Slovene Banks in 1995 and the First Half of 1996

The Slovene banking sector started the 1990s with losses, which called for its restructuring. Indicators of financial performance of banks in the early years of independence were calculated, for instance, by Kraft (1995), who also presented a comparison with the banking sector of Croatia.

In 1995, the banking sector performed relatively well and the real sector worse, which is different than in 1994, when losses in the banking sector were still significant compared with those in the real sector. In 1995, only three smaller banks suffered losses. Positive financial results of the banking sector helped the economy as a whole to produce a positive income statement in 1995 in the range of 1.2 percent of GDP. The enterprise sector suffered losses in aggregate, although they were much smaller than in previous years.

Results indicate that profitability of the banking sector was above the average of developed economies standards (Table 9.6), partly due to special laws favoring performance of the banking sector. This is true especially for banks in rehabilitation, which were among the best according to financial results. The overcapitalization is still strongly present, more in smaller new banks than in larger "old" banks.

Increasing the lower limit of founding capital up to approximately 60 million DEM for the full license did not lead to bank mergers, as desired by the BOS. Instead, actions were twofold: banks either increased founding capital to requested levels (regardless of the amount of banking business there is available and profits that can come out of it), or they opt for the less than full license (for instance, without possibility to collect foreign-exchange deposits). Thus, the number of banks remains high (twenty-nine, lower than the maximum thirty-four), but only fifteen of them have a full license for all businesses. Apparently increasing competitiveness and economic criteria of profit rather

Table 9.6. *Major financial indicators*

	Slovene banks in 1995	World standards
A = balance sum	1.552.889	
K1 = capital (1-tier)	127.430	
K2 = total capital (1 + 2-tier)	234.208	
P = profit before taxes	16.370	
P/K1	12.8%	10.4%
P/K2	7.0%	
P/A	1.0%	0.61%
A/K1	12.2	17 times
A/K2	6.7	
Real interest margin	2.6 p.p.	2.59 p.p.
Real realized active rate	6.1%	
Real realized passive rate	3.6%	
Operating costs/noninterest earnings	54%	
Operating costs/A	3.0%	3.04%

Sources: Bank of Slovenia data from bulletins and annual report (1996); world standards data from Bollenbacher 1992.

than administrative barriers will ultimately bring the number of banks to optimal level, taking into account the economy of scale. But that will take some more time, although the proposed new banking law, which would enable foreign banks to establish branches in Slovenia, could accelerate the process.

It is interesting that the real interest rate margin (in percentage points) is close to the world standard. Real active and passive interest rates actually paid are much lower than even prime rates on the active side, which are presently at 9 to 10 percent. This indicates the low collection share of interest and/or the worsening of the situation causing delays in interest payments by the Slovene enterprises in the second half of 1995.

Total operating costs compared with banking balance sum is for Slovenia, again, close to the world averages of 3 percent. The 54 percent coverage of operating costs with noninterest income is not enough, as the optimal solution for a solid bank is to cover all the costs with earnings from services and, at the same time, to retain its earnings from interest rate margins for expansion and provisioning.

At the end of June 1996 total assets of the banking system were 1,652 billion tolars SIT (18.3 billion DEM), average capital 232 billion SIT, profit before taxes 15.5 billion SIT (Svetina, NLB Internal Report, 1996). It means:

average ROE, 6.7%
average ROA, 0.9%
capital multiplier, 7.1
interest margin, 2.3%
costs/noninterest earnings, 55%
costs/average assets, 1.6%
costs per employee, 4.9 million SIT
average liquid assets/average total assets, 5%
credits/deposits, 81%
average total assets per employee, 162 million SIT

In the first half of 1996, the group of middle-sized banks increased their shares in the banking system: in credits to nonbanking sector by 4 percentage points, deposits from this sector by 5, and its balance sum by 5.

With inflation at 5.7 percent, in the first six months of 1996 the balance sum of the banking sector increased by 10 percent and banks' credits by 13 percent and deposits by 16 percent. Total profits earned were 14 billion SIT (155 million DEM). Balance sum/employee equaled 162 million SIT.

BANK REHABILITATION: SLOVENIA'S APPROACH

Slovenia's approach to bank rehabilitation is presented through some of the causes, the size of the problem, macroeconomic factors, the response from the state authorities and the techniques they used, the costs, and finally the lessons and achievements of Slovenia's program.

Models of Bank Rehabilitation

A socialist country in transition cannot ignore the issue of bad debts and linkages between financial restructuring of enterprises and banks. Simultaneous restructuring on both fronts seems to be a prerequisite for success in the transformation of the economy.

Once a decision on bank restructuring is made, the next question is whether it should be done directly by creditors and private owners after privatization (the Russian approach) or by the government. If after government intervention is chosen, in deference to the Simoneti-Kavalec scheme (1995, 12), three models are distinguished here.

1. Centralized approach (Hungary), which involves full recapitalization of troubled banks with interest-bearing government bonds, carving out bad debts and transferring them to a specially created restructuring agency MBFB (Hungarian Investment and Development Bank), leading to moral hazard problem, as banks registered all potentially bad debts and were not compelled to be prudent (especially after lack of consistent policy led to repeated carving out of newly emerging bad debts);
2. Decentralized approach (Poland), where banks are recapitalized sufficiently so that they are able to create adequate provisions for bad loans of enterprises and, at the same time, a mechanism is introduced that compels the banks to restructure enterprise-debtors themselves;
3. Centralized-decentralized approach (Spanish–United States model, adopted by Czech republic, Slovenia), where recapitalization with bonds (centralized approach) is not full, and, therefore, banks in rehabilitation are forced to do their part in the restructuring and in solving the problem of bad debts (decentralized part), which remain in their balances even after the swap of bad debts for government bonds occurred.

Each method has its advantages and disadvantages. The results show, however, that it is not good to wait with bank restructuring and also to leave it fully to private creditors or future owners. On the other hand, fully centralized government handling of bad debts leads to negative consequences of moral hazard problem (curing only consequences, not causes of the banking crisis). At the beginning of transition, international financial institutions (IFIs) supported and suggested the decentralized approach of the Polish type; more recently, however, they suggest also the Slovenian approach (to Croatia).

Table 9.7. *Bad loans in the banking sector (in millions SIT)*

All banks	1993	1994	1995
Bad loans	n/a	62,350	55,789
Bad loans/total assets	n/a	5.06%	3.58%
Bad assets, on and off balance	90,018	80,723	68,949
Bad assets/total assets	7.6%	5.6%	3.9%

Sources: EU Questionnaire, July 1996.

Bank Rehabilitation the Slovenian Way

The banking crisis started in Slovenia with transition (restructuring) and separation (loss of markets led to recession, plus severed monetary stance to liquidity problems and insolvency of enterprise sector) depression of the economy, which led to rapid deterioration of banks' loan portfolios. Other factors influencing the banking crisis in Slovenia were financial sector liberalization including freeing of interest rates and eased entry of new banks (domestic, less for the foreign). In 1992, thirteen out of twenty-six banks were affected with losses counting for more than 70 percent of total deposits. Over 30 percent of the total banking sector portfolio was nonperforming. The rehabilitation program started officially at the beginning of 1993.

At the independence in 1991 the share of bad in total banking assets was over 10 percent, the share of nonperforming bank credit portfolio over 30 percent. In three banks that were put under rehabilitation, it was above 40 percent. The share of bad loans in total assets decreased to only 3.58 percent and the share of total bad assets to 3.9 percent until end of 1995 (Table 9.7).

The "differentia specifica" of Slovenia's approach toward bank rehabilitation comprised two elements. First, in the decentralized-centralized approach, the government intervened directly into the banks with a swapping of bad assets of banks with state bonds, but not in the full amount (as in Hungary), thus preventing moral hazard and requesting self-rehabilitation efforts of banks under rehabilitation themselves. At the same time, it was not left to banks alone to intervene in a decentralized way (with some state support), as in the case of Poland. The second approach was gradual, different from other shock ("cold turkey") approaches. According to some information in the media, the World Bank actually endorsed the Slovene approach toward bank rehabilitation, proposing Croatian authorities choose the similar approach. Slovenia could not swap all of the banks' bad debts both due to fiscal (public debt burden) and monetary (potential money expansion) limitations. But, at the same time, a gradual approach forced banks to do their part and to restructure internally in due course.

It took three years to come close to completion of the rehabilitation of the two largest banks in Slovenia (plus bank number six, which was put under rehabilitation a year later and subsequently integrated into a second bank).

Legal-Institutional Framework

Among first acts of the Slovene government after the proclamation of independence was the adoption of the Law on Bank Rehabilitation in June 1991 and the establishment of the Bank Rehabilitation Agency (BRA) by decree in October 1991, subsequently modified by decrees in 1993.

The legal framework of the rehabilitation is provided by general financial and enterprise sector laws as well as a few specific laws, among them: the Law on Guarantee of Bonds issued by the Republic of Slovenia for bank rehabilitation; the Law on the Substitution of Banks' Claims against the National Bank of Yugoslavia (NBY) Deriving from Citizens' Frozen Currency Deposits with Bonds of the Republic of Slovenia; the Law on Slovenian Ironworks Rehabilitation; the Law on Covering Slovenian Claims against Iraq, Cuba, and Angola; as well as the Law on Claims against NBY and the Constitutional Law on Establishing Nova Ljubljanska Banka and Nova Kreditna Banka Maribor.

The main objectives of bank rehabilitation were to achieve (Dežclak 1995):

capital adequacy according to international standards,
positive cash flow and current operation income,
reduction of banking interest rate,
restoration of credibility in international financial markets, and
introduction of basic principles of prudential behavior by banks.

The usual procedure for the bank put in rehabilitation was:

- writing off of current losses,
- swapping bad assets for government bonds,
- transferring bad assets to BRA, and
- BRA engagement as temporary owner (supervisor) of banks delegated by decree from the Ministry of Finance (MOF).

Main policy responses to the bank crisis from the state included:

- stricter supervision by the Bank of Slovenia (BOS),
- prudential regulation, embodied in the new 1991 banking law,
- introduction of minimum capital levels (in absolute terms) and minimum capital adequacy rules,
- strict laws on credit provisioning,
- creation of a special bank rehabilitation agency (BRA), and
- improved coordination between state authorities (MOF, BOS, BRA) and banks.

Specific techniques used were:

- takeover of banks in rehabilitation by the state through the BRA,
- partial exchange of foreign exchange deposits in former National Bank of Yugoslavia and bad customer loans with BRA (later state) bonds, and
- temporary relaxation of supervision ratios for banks in rehabilitation, which ended in 1994.

The burden of losses was paid by former owners (shareholders) who had their shares replaced with the subordinated claims against BRA. Foreign-exchange deposits of customers in Slovenia were repaid, and the government issued bonds in the range of 1.8 billion DEM (parliament allowed for an upper limit of 2.2 billion). They will be repaid by the sale of rehabilitated banks.

In the process of rehabilitation the BRA adopted rules for its functioning. Among them were the Program for Rehabilitation of Banks, Criteria and Procedures for Approving Loans, Code of Ethical Behavior, and Directives on Solving Bad Assets. The BRA organizational structure includes a council of five members, headed by the minister of finance (including the governor of BOS and three ministers), a managerial board (five members), and a director. It has around thirty employees. The BRA is suppose to work in close relation with authorities (Ministry of Finance and

Table 9.8. *Classification of banks' credit exposures, 1993–95*

Credit exposure ratings	% of total credit exposure		
	1993	1994	1995
A	81	86	89
B	7	5.7	4.5
C	5	2.5	1.6
D	3	2.6	2.1
E	4	3.1	1.8

Sources: EU Questionnaire, July 1996.

the BOS) and with the Development Agency, responsible for restructuring of enterprises.

The Results

Rehabilitation Status for Slovene Banks

Based on decrees of the BOS, three banks were put in the rehabilitation status: Nova Ljubljanska Banka (NLB) since January 1993, Nova Kreditna Banka Maribor (NKBM) since April 1993, and Komercialna Banka Nova Gorica (KBNG) since January 1994. KBNG subsequently merged with NKBM in 1995.

Bad debts (DEM, 1,482 million) and potential obligations (DEM 392 million) were transferred to the BRA in 1993 in replacement for BRA's DEM nominated 8 percent bearing thirty-year maturity bonds. With this only about 85 percent of the 2.2 billion DEM package of bonds approved by the parliament was used. In 1995, to solve balance sheet valutary, maturity, and interest mismatch, these bonds were replaced with government bonds, marketable, denominated in SIT, with shorter and variable maturity but with lower interest rates.

Improvement of quality of assets can be illustrated (Table 9.8) also with the improvement in the classification of bank credits (on and off balance sheet, later meaning direct credit substitutes).

Major events in 1995 include:

substitution of rehabilitation bonds issued by BRA with rehabilitation bonds issued by the government of different quality,
annexation of Komercialna Banka Nova Gorica d.d. to Nova Kreditna Banka Maribor d.d.,
solution to the problems of foreign debts,
solution to loans given by NLB to a nuclear plant,
acquisition of E Banka by NLB,
preparation of acquisition of Posavska Banka Krško by NLB and acquisition in April 1996.

The results of internal measures by both banks under rehabilitation at the end of 1995 were:

a share in banking total assets of 40 percent,
a profit at NLB of 4.1 and at NKBM of 1.8 billion SIT,
a positive cash flow,
a capital adequacy ratio at NLB of 12 percent, at NKBM of 16 percent,
a valutary match between assets and liabilities at the level of 1 percent at NLB and 3 percent at NKBM,
a conservative provisioning policy,
decreased real interest rates from 12.5–13 percent (end of 1993) to 10.5 percent (end of 1995),
a reorganization of both banks, and
decreasing labor costs and number of employed.

Weaker points remain:

relatively expansive credit policy,
mismatch in terms of structure of interest rates and valutary mismatch, and
liquidity problems.

Quantification of Public Debt Caused by Bank Rehabilitation
Bad debt for government bond swaps were made in three banks under rehabilitation in the following amounts: 1.482,500 mio DEM for issued bonds for balance claims, 391,837 mio DEM for bonds reserved for out of balance potential liabilities, for a total of 1.874,337 mio DEM.

Total bonds outstanding in balances of banks in rehabilitation on 31 December 1995 were 155,562 million SIT = 1,767,750 DEM (at central bank exchange rate). It means that the amount of bonds repurchased is 107 million DEM.

Review of the Key State Rehabilitation Transactions

The bank rehabilitation process included four key state rehabilitation transactions.

1. A swap of bad assets for rehabilitation bonds, January 1993. The amount of financial resources earmarked for the rehabilitation of banks in the form of rehabilitation bonds (both the BRA bonds for bad assets and contingent liabilities as well as the Republic of Slovenia bonds for frozen foreign currency deposits) fell considerably short of the estimated amounts that would represent a full rehabilitation of the banks' balance sheets over a short period of time. Instead, the authorities set an absolute ceiling in the bond allocation for nonperforming assets and contingent liabilities. Consequently, even after the official initiation of the rehabilitation program, banks still retained nonperforming assets on and off the balance sheet. They were equivalent to more than 15 percent of the banks' total assets at the beginning of 1993. Thus, fast rehabilitation was impossible.

The restructuring program was agreed upon with the World Bank in mid-1993. It was clear that the program did not provide a sustainable solution to banks and that therefore the rehabilitation program as such could not be successfully concluded without further support from the state. It was envisaged that the additional actions would be taken by various agencies taking part in the rehabilitation process, as well as additional efforts by the banks and their management to rectify the situation in due course. The major shortfall of the restructuring program was the less than adequate treatment of the liquidity situation of the banks (partly stemming from the fact that bonds and not cash were used for carving out bad debts).

2. Formation of NLB and NKBM, July 1994. It was enacted with the enactment of Constitutional Law in July 1994. Its main objective was to remove certain assets and contingent liabilities the banks had in relation to the former Yugoslavia. NLB and NKBM were established with the Constitutional Law, which left them with around 10 percent smaller balance sheets, but with an increased capital. The main purpose of the transaction was to divide the balance sheets between old and new banks. Old banks

were left with all claims and liabilities to the former Yugoslavia and the solidarity clause liability. At the same time the new banks NLB and NKBM were given an additional rehabilitation assistance by the state in the amount of around 5 percent of the balance sum.

3. Exchange of rehabilitation bonds, October 1995 (valid on 1 January 1995). The rehabilitation bonds, given the way they were defined, caused serious mismatches in NLB's and NKBM's balance sheets with effects on their income statements and cash flow positions. In November 1995 old bonds were replaced with new ones, which decreased profits but eliminated serious currency, maturity, and interest mismatches. Instead of former BRA bonds, which were denominated in DEM with a thirty-year maturity, and an 8 percent interest rate, both banks obtained new government bonds denominated in tolars, with shorter and variable maturity, lower interest rates, but marketable immediately.

4. Resolving the issue of unconfirmed debt swaps under the "New Financial Agreement 1988," February 1996. A special separate agreement of Slovenia with foreign private creditors on repayment of debt of the former Yugoslavia, reached in spring 1996, helped to release Slovene banks in rehabilitation from the "joint and several liability clause" based on 1998 New Financial Agreement (NFA) between the former Yugoslavia and foreign private creditors. This helped Slovenia in improving its international financial position (low As in credit risk ratings of Slovenia by three major international grading agencies), but has a negative impact on banks in rehabilitation, which participated in debt swaps.

Because debt conversions, made under NFA by Slovene banks in the period immediately after proclamation of independence to minimize public debt, were not confirmed (by the NBY), banks in rehabilitation have to put on-balance-sheet deals under NFA, which were previously extinguished on the transaction day. Regarding deals made on customer accounts, banks will put NFA claims against clients or their banks on balance sheet. This will have (at least transitory, before claims against Slovene clients are cashed in) negative impact on the banks' balance sheets, but in an amount considerably smaller than 1 percent of their present balance sheet.

Banks had previously formed sufficient provisions for that

purpose. The stated negative impact on the banks' capital is more than offset by the amount of reduced Slovenia's public debt through this transaction and by the improved credit rating of Slovenia.

Management of Remaining Bad Debts by Banks in Rehabilitation

Around one-third of bad debts remained at the time in the balances of these banks. Through their intensive-care units, banks in rehabilitation are forced to participate directly in the process of enterprise restructuring (Štiblar 1995). In 1996, the share of nonperforming loans in these banks is far below 10 percent, an important indication that they are rehabilitated.

The collaboration of banks in rehabilitation in enterprise restructuring included the following acts (Deželak 1995, 121):

rescheduling old enterprises' obligations to banks, with longer maturity, moratoria on principle, and more favorable interest rates;
enabling enterprises to settle their obligations to banks by discount;
discharging some enterprises with legally determined write-offs; and
swapping bad loans for stakes in enterprise equity.

All this was done in the framework of formal procedure for each bad debtor in the intensive-care unit of the bank (with cooperation in plans and restructuring measures), using exact and stringent criteria for dealing with bad debtors (Štiblar 1995, 129).

The BRA's Management of Transferred Bad Loans

The BRA's major task is managing transferred bad loans to reduce public debt (or to use receipts for some other public goals – for instance, to finance the reform of the pension system). For around 110 enterprises, obligations were transferred to the BRA in the amount over 1 billion DEM. Over 40 of these enterprises were under restructuring and owned by the Development Fund.

Working with these enterprises the BRA succeeded in extracting around 100 million DEM from the sale of claims, collections, repayments of obligations, and repayments in liquidation and bankruptcy proceedings. Some of this comes from self-paying enterprises.

Involvement of the BRA in managing debtor enterprises includes agreements to reschedule their debts or conversion of claims into capital shares. Logical sequence of measures and instruments applied by the BRA in managing bad assets includes rescheduling enterprise's obligation (with better terms), transformation of claims into capital shares in the enterprise, and debt write-off.

The contradictory interests could appear in this process of the state as the owner and the lender to these enterprises. The BRA is not equipped well enough with human resources (quantity and quality) to be able to manage debtor enterprises adequately and to decide always correctly whether to extract debt or to relieve the debtor enterprise to be able to repay later, when (and if) it would be rehabilitated.

Concluding Comments

The Slovene approach seems to be appropriate, but its implementation was not always the best.

The Role of Bank Rehabilitation Agency (BRA)

The BRA did not play always and fully the role for which it was established. Among three major tasks the BRA was not able to fulfill the first: to produce ideas, laws, and institutional solutions for the process of bank rehabilitation. Strategic documents and their schemes of implementation are emerging outside the BRA.

Second, BRA is not sufficiently successful in management of bad assets obtained in return for government issued bonds. BRA was able to extract only a small portion of less than 10 percent of bad debts in its balances, while the usual world standards are 20–30 percent. Its role in managing companies-debtors is inadequate, which is indicated by the fact that the largest problematic enterprises are in its portfolio for years (as TAM, Adria Airways, Emona, Videm, Metalna, etc.), and there is conflict of interest present in managing BRA and presiding over supervisory boards of indebted enterprises at the same time.

In its third task, supervision of banks in rehabilitation, the BRA was and is overengaged in micromanaging these banks. While in the first contraction phase of the banks' divestment (1993–94) there could be some understanding for that, in the second phase (from 1995 on, when new strategies are needed to turn from the past to the future of banks) the BRA could not follow and became an important obstacle in the concluding phase of bank restructuring.

Evaluation of the Slovenian Rehabilitation of the Banking System

This evaluation leads to the following conclusions (Voljč 1995, 114):

While slow in getting started the program seems to be reasonably well thought out and pragmatic with learning-by-doing one of the important principles.

Only partial carving out of bad debts has had more positive effects (smaller public debt, which was retained in planned limits; stronger effort of banks) than negative effects (leaving banks with larger portions of substandard assets).

After initial uncertainty a rather cooperative approach was adopted among key actors (Ministry of Finance, the BOS, the BRA, bank's top management), while cooperation with institutions responsible for enterprise restructuring and privatization (Ministry of Economy, Privatization Agency, Development Fund) has been less fruitful.

The program imposed tight controls on banks and their management, leading to considerable improvement in corporate governance, organization, lending procedures, loan monitoring, and recovery.

Given a significant share of the banking sector in Slovenia put under rehabilitation (over 50 percent) and the rather restrictive (and successful) monetary policy, the BOS liquidity support to the program was reasonable, although not totally adequate, leading to adverse effects on interest rates.

The program has significantly benefited from external advice and technical assistance, provided by bilateral and multilateral sources, although this advice has been used selectively, taking into account local conditions and constraints dictated by political realities and bearing in mind that the bank rehabilitation in Slovenia was a "home-grown" program.

Completion of Bank Restructuring

After three years, conditions to terminate rehabilitation of banks, prescribed by the BOS in a special decree in June 1995, have been fulfilled and both banks already put forward their final reports on rehabilitation. This is one of the rare cases of a gradual bank restructuring that has been successful. The bad loans have not fallen dramatically as a share of the total loan portfolio; but this is because in Slovenia loans are indexed (indexation implies that bad loans will not be eroded by inflation, as they were, for example, in Poland) and the total (corporate) loan portfolio has not expanded much, and not because there are new loans going bad.

A very conservative provisioning policy has now shielded the banks' capital base almost completely from any downside risk in this respect – the bad loans are almost 100 percent provisioned against. Moreover, the restructuring of the recapitalization instruments has resulted in major improvements in terms of foreign-currency exposure. Banks are close to zero net foreign-exchange exposure, maturity mismatches have been much reduced, and the recapitalization bonds are now tradable. The banks have turned profitable in spite of continuing conservative provisioning practices. The outlook for strong profit growth in the future is very good, given the relatively low share of profits stemming from the foreign-exchange part of the balance sheet against banks' obvious potential in that area, and given the likely reduction in provisioning charges.

Accounting standards and information systems have clearly improved a great deal, while a strict loan classification system, in line with Western practice, leads to confidence in the assessed capital value for purposes of calculation of capital adequacy ratios. This ratio now exceeds 12 percent following Basel convention, clearly a dramatic improvement over the past. ROE and ROA coefficients attained in 1995 are for both banks in rehabilitation above the average in the Slovenian banking sector and above world standards. Liquidity is much improved, operational costs are under control, and provisioning is, in relation to conservative risk assessment, above standard.

The corporate governance has been improved a great deal and modern organizational structure put in place. Banks are introducing the newest and most sophisticated financial products and services, and their information technology (IT) is on an internationally comparable level.

In 1996 only factors related to events outside the banking sector prevented the final step in rehabilitation.

ACHIEVEMENTS IN REHABILITATION OF NOVA LJUBLJANSKA BANKA

The rehabilitation of Nova Ljubljanska Banka d.d. (NLB), which commenced formally in January 1993 when the present management team assumed responsibility, has come to a successful conclusion. Most of the problems that emanated from the transformation to a market economy and the emergence of Slovene independence have by and large been overcome. The bank is now in a sound financial condition with the prospect of substantial profit flows from several sources, making it potentially one of the most promising banks in Central Europe. NLB has succeeded in achieving an adequate capital base, introduced sufficient provisioning, developed sound financial and lending policies and procedures, and developed a well-qualified and motivated management team. (Internal sources of data are used in presenting the situation and developments in NLB.)

Summary of NLB's Achievements during Rehabilitation, 1993–96

NLB has made major strides during the three-year rehabilitation program in its financial performance, institutional strengthening, strategic planning, and human resource development. The bank's balance sheet in tolar (SIT) terms has almost doubled since 1992, but more importantly the quality of assets has dramatically improved (Tables 9.9 and 9.10). All nonearning and doubtful risk assets are graded, and provision levels comfortably exceed prudent requirements. In DEM equivalent the balance sheet has grown from DEM 3.7 billion in 1992 to DEM 5.3 billion by the end of 1995.

Throughout this period significant development has been made in creating a larger and more stable deposit base in addition to increasing the liquidity of assets. Since the beginning of the rehabilitation process, three new specialized subsidiaries have been

Table 9.9. *Consolidated balance sheet and net profit, unaudited (in billions SIT)*

		Balance sheet		Net profit	
Company	Incorporated	1992	1995	1992	1995
NLB d.d.	1994	214.4	423.5	−67.50	3.80
LB HIPO	1992	4.9	4.8	—	−0.20
PROTEUS Zurich	1989	4.6	15.5	0.02	0.08
LBS N.Y.	1986	18.2	29.2	0.06	0.16
LB Leasing	1990	0.9	3.9	0.26	0.21
LB Maksima	1994	—	1.1	—	0.86
LB Consulting	1995	—	—	—	—
LB Trading	1994	—	0.1	—	−0.05
Consolidation adjustments[a]		−17.3	−18.5	−8.00	−0.12
Total		225.6	459.6	−67.50	4.74

Notes: This table does not include LHB Frankfurt (46% ownership share of NLB) and Milano Branch (100% of NLB) due to problems with consolidation as well as NLB Svetovanje due to its establishment late in 1995.
[a] Intercompany adjustments, including associated companies.

established, complementing core business activities, with a view toward expanding the range of financial products and services on offer to the bank's clients. The bank group now consists of NLB d.d. (the bank) and seven subsidiaries, as well as a number of associated companies.

Financial Results

NLB had after-tax profit (using International Accounting Standards) of SIT 3.8 billion for the bank, and SIT 4.7 billion for the group in 1995 (Table 9.11). NLB has shown a constant increase in financial performance each year since rehabilitation began. Net income before provisions has improved but in 1993 and 1994, prior to the creation of NLB, as the bank created large provisions against potential losses, there were net losses after provisions. These provisions were related to the outstanding "bad" assets and contingent liabilities not provided for in the January 1993 rehabilitation transaction.

Throughout the rehabilitation period, the bank's management has been rigorous in terms of defining its business, streamlining its

Table 9.10. *Nova Ljubljanska Banka balance sheet, 1992–95, unconsolidated (in billions SIT)*

	1992	1993	1994	1995
Assets	277.7	365.8	371.7	431.0
Bonds	1.9	108.5	115.7	126.5
Loans to customers	118.0	102.8	107.7	154.1
Loans to banks	31.0	31.2	29.0	16.5
Deposits with banks	11.9	38.5	40.4	40.9
BOS	4.4	12.3	25.5	48.5
Fixed assets	11.7	12.7	14.5	14.6
Other assets	98.7	59.8	39.0	24.0
Liabilities	277.7	365.8	371.7	431.0
"Stable deposits"	42.8	62.7	92.2	114.0
"Unstable deposits"	34.5	57.4	71.3	85.0
Bank deposits	29.5	40.1	25.4	27.3
NLB securities				14.7
Liquidity borrowing	20.6	13.1	16.9	20.8
BOS	14.6	7.4	9.9	15.6
Interbank market	6.0	5.7	7.0	5.2
Other liabilities	193.6	185.8	146.7	143.1
Equity	−43.4	6.8	19.1	26.1
SIT/DEM	61.2	76.4	81.6	87.9

operations, and securing substantial reductions in operating expenses. Specific strategies include a successful redundancy program with a 27 percent decline in employee numbers and a reduction in the number of foreign representative offices from twenty-two to eight, resulting in excess of a 50 percent reduction in associated operating costs (Table 9.12). Also in this period special emphasis has been placed on cost control through a very effective budgetary control system in place right across the bank (Table 9.13).

One of the biggest issues the bank had to deal with at the beginning of rehabilitation was the management of cash flow. During the period the bank has continued to make significant progress in this area mainly through management's focus on generating liquidity by building up a stable deposit base (Table 9.14). It must be noted that significant support was provided to NLB by the central bank in overcoming a difficult beginning in 1993 and throughout the period. By 1995 the bank was generating positive cash flow from its operating activities; however, in the beginning

Table 9.11. *NLB accounting profit statement, 1992–95 (in billions SIT)*

	1992	1993	1994	1995
Net interest income	1.6	10.8	7.5	11.4
Other income	4.1	7.7	8.8	9.4
Total income	5.7	18.5	16.3	20.8
Staff costs	4.4	5.0	5.6	6.5
Other costs	3.2	4.0	6.7	7.1
Total costs	7.6	9.0	12.3	13.6
Operating surplus	−1.9	9.5	4.0	7.2
Provisions	−80.9	−23.7	−19.6	−2.8
Net profit/(loss) before taxation	−82.8	−14.2	−15.6	4.4
Taxation				0.3
profit after taxation	−82.8	−14.2	−15.6	4.1

Table 9.12. *Redundancy costs (in millions SIT)*

	Redundancy payments		Purchase of the insurance period		Total	
	Employee numbers	Amount	Employee numbers	Amount	Employee numbers	Amount
1992	153	147.8	92	150.0	245	297.8
1993	255	198.1	10	28.2	265	226.3
1994	91	73.0	2	6.2	93	79.2
1995	7	6.5	—	—	7	6.5
Total	506	425.4	104	184.4	610	609.8

of 1996 NLB still depends on the Bank of Slovenia (BOS) for special liquidity credits. A program is in place to eliminate these special liquidity credits in 1996 through additional efforts to increase liabilities and restrain the lending activities.

NLB began the rehabilitation program with negative capital in excess of SIT 43 billion. In the three-year period to the end of 1995, qualifying capital balances have increased to a positive level of more than SIT 19 billion (for the bank only; consolidated Group Capital Tier 1 and Tier 2 are in excess of SIT 28 billion). The bank's (unconsolidated) capital adequacy ratio at year end

Table 9.13. *NLB operating costs, 1992–95 (in billions SIT)*

	1991 (3,405)[a]	1992 (3,061)	1993 (2,601)	1994 (2,365)	1995 (2,473)
Staff costs	—	4.4	5.0	5.6	6.5
Special provision on unpaid salaries					0.6
Other operating costs	—	1.6	1.8	2.2	2.6
Fixed assets costs	—	1.6	2.3	3.2	3.9
Exceptional restructuring costs	—	—	—	1.3	—
Total costs	—	7.6	9.1	12.3	13.6
Increases in underlying employee costs					
Nominal	—	—	15%	12%	16%
Real	—	—	−8%	−6%	7.5%
Increases in underlying other operating costs					
Nominal	—	—	13%	22%	18%
Real	—	—	−10%	3%	9%
Increases in fixed assets expenses					
Nominal	—	—	12.5%	38.9%	0%
Real	—		−9.5%	19.9%	−8.0%

[a] Number of employees (at the year end).

Table 9.14. *NLB's liquidity statement, 1993–95 (in billions SIT)*

	1993	1994	1995
Net operating cash flow	−5.48	−1.25	+2.34
Rehabilitation transactions	−16.11	−5.04	−10.88
Other developments	+2.39	−22.78	−11.76
Core business developments	+30.70	+27.78	+27.60
Net liquidity position	+11.50	−1.29	+7.31
Funded by +/ appropriated to −			
Interbank market	−0.58	+1.29	−1.81
BOS liquidity loans	−10.92	0.00	+2.30
Short-term bank deposits		−7.81	
Total funding/appropriation	−11.50	+1.29	−7.31

Table 9.15. *Capital and capital adequacy ratio in the 1993–95 period (in billions SIT)*

	1993	1994	1995
Capital (including revaluation of capital)	12.8	12.8	15.5
Revenue reserves	0.5	2.8	
General provisions	1.9	1.8	2.0
Revaluation reserve (50%)	3.1	1.7	2.6
Fixed assets/investments in connected companies	−8.6	−3.3	−3.5
Total guarantee capital	9.2	13.5	19.4
Risk weighted assets	165.0	143.4	161.0
Capital adequacy ratio (%)	5.6	9.4	12.0

Table 9.16. *Summary of NLB's asset portfolio and provisions, 1992–95*

	1992	1993[a]	1993	1994	1995
Loan category (in billions SIT)					
A & B (on-off balance)	276.1	316.4	414.2	465.2	516.6
C, D, & E	84.2	44.0	59.8	48.9	37.0
Total	360.3	360.4	474.0	514.1	553.6
Provisions	68.6	21.3	45.4	47.4	35.2
Ratios (in %)					
Provisions as a % of C, D, & E assets		48.5	75.9	96.9	95.1
Loan portfolio structure (on and off balance sheet)					
A & B	76.6	87.8	87.4	90.5	93.3
C	4.1	4.1	5.4	1.4	1.7
D & E	19.3	8.1	7.2	8.1	5.0
Total	100.0	100.0	100.0	100.0	100.0

1995 stood at a comfortable 12.0 percent well in excess of the standard 8 percent requirement, while the consolidated ratio is 13.5 percent. (See Table 9.15.)

The quality of bank's asset portfolio has continuously improved during the rehabilitation period with doubtful and nonearning assets reduced from 23 percent of total assets in 1992 to 7 percent by 1995 year end (Table 9.16). This has been achieved through a program of conservative provisioning, even during a period of little growth in risk assets. Additionally, total provisions cover of doubtful and nonearning assets has increased from 48 percent at

Table 9.17. *NLB's deposit, loan flows, 1993–95 (in billions SIT)*

	1993	1994	1995	1993–95
Key deposits flows	+43.5	+25.8	+35.4	+104.7
Frozen	−16.4	−2.8	−0.4	−19.6
Retail	38.3	14.9	22.2	75.4
Corporate	11.2	16.9	16.7	44.8
Ministry of Finance	0.5	1.5	0.6	2.6
ZPIZ (Social Security Fund)	9.9	−4.7	−3.7	1.5
Flows of loans to Nonbank customers	−5.5	−1.0	41.7	35.2

Table 9.18. *NLB's divestment transactions, 1993–95 (in millions SIT)*

	1993	1994	1995	1993–95
Total fixed assets divestments	196.1	75.2	148.4	419.7
Real estate	178.8	67.2	127.4	373.4
Other fixed assets	17.3	5.3	21.0	43.6
Total capital divestments	58.9	5,905	201.8	6,165.9
In companies	0.8	841	201.8	1,043.9
In banks	58.1	5,064	—	5,122.0
Total divestments	255.0	5,977	350.2	6,582.9

the beginning of 1993 to 95 percent by year end 1995. (See also Table 9.17.)

NLB made divestments of SIT 255 billion (DEM 3.7 billion) in 1993, SIT 5,977 billion (DEM 75.3 billion) in 1994, and SIT 350 billion (DEM 4.2 billion) in 1995. In the 1993–95 period a total of DEM 83.2 billion divestments was made, of which 90 percent were divestments in banks (Table 9.18).

Institutional Strengthening

Since the commencement of rehabilitation in 1993, the bank has been the beneficiary of significant technical assistance provided by multilateral and developed-country aid agencies with headquarters within Europe and the United States. The bank has established internationally accepted operating policies and procedures for treasury, credit and risk management, financial accounting, and internal audit. A new and enhanced profit center approach to business and financial planning has been implemented with good results. Special emphasis has been placed on the development of human resources. Strategic planning has been established and a medium-term plan developed. Information technology (IT) has also been receiving special attention and a five-year IT strategic plan has been finalized. Additionally NLB has been the first Central Eastern European bank to complete a securitization deal successfully.

A well-qualified and highly motivated management team is now in place. A new organizational structure introduced in late 1994 has served to improve the efficiency and control of the bank's activities while simultaneously more clearly delineating responsibilities and encouraging interdepartmental communications.

The bank's domestic network has expanded in the period through acquisitions and the opening of new offices. The strategic goal is to have a branch network covering all the major towns and regions across Slovenia. Regarding NLB's international network, management has reduced the number of representative offices from twenty-two to eight, with the objective of retaining a presence in areas where Slovenia has significant intercountry trade relations. The main areas covered by NLB's subsidiaries, representative offices, and affiliated companies include the United States, Germany, Austria, Britain, Russia, and the Czech Republic, which give the bank a valuable competitive edge in comparison to its peer groups in the region.

Management of human resources has been an important factor in the rehabilitation process. In the first phase a successful redundancy program was implemented, resulting in a reduction in employee numbers from a high of 3,405 in 1991 to 2,365 by year end 1994. In 1995 numbers increased by 108 reflecting the bank's expansion in the domestic network, coupled with the selective recruitment of a number of staff (mainly university graduates) for employment within key sectors of the bank.

Fulfillment of Conditions to Conclude Rehabilitation Formally

In 1993 the BOS listed criteria on fulfillment, which will evaluate the success of appointed managers in rehabilitation procedure. In

July 1995 the BOS issued a formal list of seven conditions that banks need to fulfill for the formal termination of their rehabilitation status.

At the beginning of 1996, NLB has met the vast majority of the prudential banking requirements that were set out by the central bank, in order to exit from rehabilitation. Minimum capital and capital adequacy levels are satisfactory, monetary policy requirements have been met, and provisioning levels are more than comfortable. The outstanding issues are more of a technical than a business relevance.

With the special liquidity program, the bank will this year eliminate the need for special liquidity credits from the central bank. Regarding large credit exposures, the bank now has just one client exceeding central bank limits when exposures to banks are excluded. NLB has not yet met the legal requirement regarding nonbanking assets as a percentage of capital. However, significant progress has been made to date and a clear program to comply with requirements will be implemented fully by year end 1996.

Developments at the Beginning of 1996

In the first half of 1996 NLB added additional positive elements to the completion of rehabilitation. In the first four months of 1996 NLB's financial results are highly favorable: net interest income was 6.9 billion SIT; net noninterest income, 3.2 billion SIT; operating costs, 4.6 billion SIT; and increases in reservations, 2.0 billion SIT. Profit before taxes grossed to 3.5 billion SIT (around 40 million DEM).

Other major positive business developments in NLB at the beginning of 1996 include:

- obtaining a syndicated foreign loan to repay some liquidity credits of BOS,
- acquisition of Bank Krško,
- writing of a complete strategy for international banking of NLB, and
- measures to fulfill asset limitations (large loan exposure, maximum share of nonbanking assets).

NLB has prepared and presented to monetary authorities a plan to resolve the remaining open issues before the termination of rehabilitation. The bank is also intensively engaged in preparatory steps for privatization after that.

REFERENCES

Bole, V. 1995. "Sterilization in Slovene Monetary Sector." EIPF Working Paper, Ekonomski Institut Pravne Fakultete, Ljubljana.

Bollenbacher, G. M. 1992. *Bank Strategies for the 90s*. Dublin: Bankers.

Borak, N. (ed.). 1995. *Banke na razpotju*. Portoro: ZdruženJe Ekonomistov Slovenne.

Bremec, N. 1996. Konkurenca v slovenskem bančnem sistemu, Združenje bank Slovenije, Ljubljana, junij, 1–19.

Deželak, J. 1995. "Effectiveness of the Slovenian Banking System Rehabilitation Program Realized up to 1995." In Simoneti and Kavelec 1995.

EU Questionnaire. 1996. Reply by Government of Republic of Slovenia, Ljubljana, July.

"The Final Report on Rehabilitation of Nova Ljubljanska Banka, NLB." 1996. Internal material, Ljubljana, March.

Kraft, E. 1995. "Crisis, Rehabilitation and Restructuring: Banking in the Transition in Slovenia and Croatia." Mimeographed, Ekonomski institut Zagreb, Zagreb, May.

Mishkin, F. S. 1996. "Understanding Financial Crises: A Developing Country Perspective, Annual Conference on Development Economics." World Bank, Washington D.C., April, 1–71.

Repanšek, B. 1994. Regionalna analiza poslovanja bank v Republiki Sloveniji, Prikazi in analize, II/4, Banka Slovenije, Ljubljana.

Ribnikar, I. 1993. "Rehabilitation of Banks in Slovenia." *East-Ovest* 5 (1993): Studii e ricerche, Trieste.

Shleifer, Andre. 1995. "Corporate Governance: A Survey." Harvard University Working Paper. Cambridge, Mass.

Simoneti, M., and S. Kavalec (eds.). 1995. *Bank Rehabilitation and Enterprise Restructuring*, Conference proceedings, Budapest 1994. Ljubljana: CEEPN.

Štiblar, F. 1994. "Banking in Slovenia." *Vienna Institute Monthly Report*, Vienna Institute for Comparative Studies, 1: 32–39.

Štiblar, F. 1994. Tuje neposredne naložbe v slovenski bančni sektor, GG, EIPF, 6: Ljubljana, 24–40.

Štiblar, F. 1995. "Nova Ljubljanska banka d.d. – A Case Study." In Simoneti and Kavalec 1995, 125–35.

Štiblar, F. 1996. "Financial Restructuring Goes Forward: The Slovenian Case." Woodrow Wilson Center – East European Studies, Washington D.C., May.

Voljč, M. 1995. "Bank Rehabilitation and Private Sector Development." In Simoneti and Kavalec 1995.

CHAPTER 10

Liberalization and Financial Reforms: Lessons from the Israeli Experience

Jacob A. Frenkel

In this chapter, I discuss the experience of Israel regarding some of the issues covered in this volume, particularly with respect to the recent financial sector reforms and capital market liberalization. Although Israel does not, of course, belong to the group of countries covered here, its experience seems highly relevant for many economies in transition.

Modern Israeli economic history begins in 1985. Before that year, the country was experiencing an inflation rate of 450 percent that was reduced, within a year, to 18 percent. This relative stabilization was achieved by a deep budget cut by which the budget shifted from a deficit of about 15 percent GDR to a small surplus in a period of less than two years. This happened without any reduction in growth. While these and many other developments that accompanied the stabilization program are quite well documented, much less is known regarding the process of financial liberalization and deregulation that took place in the Israeli economy since that period. In my view, that process was no less important in securing the sustainability of the achievements of the stabilization program.

By the time of the beginning of the stabilization effort, and up to about 1987–88, the government was practically the sole player in the financial sector. The government determined the terms of borrowing, the financial spreads, and, as a matter of fact, the entire balance sheet of the banking sector. The balance sheet was practically fully determined by government decisions controlled through myriad central bank regulations: all the loans were directed and their terms and conditions were all set in advance. In

The author wishes to express his gratitude to Mario I. Blejer for his very helpful comments and assistance.

addition, there were widespread foreign-exchange controls and the government took it upon itself to determine who can buy, and who cannot buy foreign exchange and on what terms. And, following a number of financial crises at the time, the government also found itself, unexpectedly and unintendedly, the owner of all the banks in Israel. In this situation, a bold decision was taken: namely, to deregulate the financial sector.

REFORMING THE FINANCIAL SECTOR

The essence of the decision taken had a number of components. First, all the "special" financial programs were eliminated, and therefore, basically, all the sectors that had been shielded financially from the discipline of the markets became unshielded. As a result, the share of nondirected credit in total credit increased from 45 percent in 1987 to 95 percent in 1995. In other words, almost all credits became nondirected. Second, practically all nonprudential regulations that imposed various types of constraint on transactions were eliminated. Third, reserve requirements were reduced in a very fundamental manner. In 1987, the average reserve requirement was 63 percent. In 1995, the average reserve requirement was less than 10 percent and the marginal reserve requirement today is between 0 and 6 percent. These are magnitudes that would probably be appropriate in the normal course of business of a bank making the usual considerations. As far as foreign-exchange controls are concerned, they were gradually relaxed and, today, the corporate sector faces no restriction whatsoever in its foreign-exchange activities, while the rest of the economy is also free to a large extent, although there are still some foreign-exchange controls, particularly on institutional investors and on some household operations.

What were the results of these changes? Overall, it is possible to say that the various segments of the Israeli economy became much more integrated. Different types of saving instruments and loan operations became unified, financial business through banks and through securities markets became integrated, and almost no differences remain between the capacity of businesses to borrow domestically or internationally. As a result, financial spreads were very substantially narrowed, both regarding the spread between debitory and creditory rates, as well as between domestic and foreign rates. The decline in spread was remarkable. For example, spreads between borrowing and lending rates on domestic currency were about 34 percent in 1987, while today they are less than 8 percent. These spreads are, however, still high, but the trend has been clear, and it was determined by the structural changes mentioned earlier, particularly the decline in the reserve requirement ratio. At the Bank of Israel, today, reserve requirements are not viewed as a policy but rather as a distortion that has to be reduced. And, therefore, this requires the development of other policy instruments appropriately.

The policy instrument that emerged as crucial, following the reforms, was the interest rate. For a long time, during the old days, when the Bank of Israel changed its interest rates, its was practically unnoticed because that financial policy instrument was completely irrelevant, given that actions and financial decisions took place elsewhere and were determined elsewhere. But with the removal of most major distortions, suddenly the Bank of Israel rate, which is akin to a repo rate, became a very important element in the making of economic policy. It became very transparent, very explicit, and subject to public debate.

The reforms were therefore very successful. But if I had to ask myself, with the benefit of hindsight, what could have been done differently, I would point to one major issue: it would have been desired to move earlier and to move faster. We are all aware of the question of why policies that are widely recognized as useful and positive are, somehow, not being adopted. Of course, the issue is one of interest groups, rent seeking, and all the rest. This is true in many areas of public policy, it is true in trade liberalization, and it is true in any other area of reform. The fact of the matter is that there is no constituency for structural reforms, but since policy makers know that reforms should be carried out, they might as well do them fast, quickly, and early.

We can also now, with the benefits of time, talk about the benefits. The benefits of reform are not just to conform with the right norms. In countries that have been noncompetitive for a long time, either for political or for economic reasons, it is very difficult to introduce competition by itself. It is now becoming evident that the best way to introduce competition is to open up the economy to foreign competition. I see, therefore, the gains in competition, and therefore in efficiency, as a major benefit of the reform process. We have, however, still some way to go. In Israel much of the banking activity continues to be concentrated in three major groups of banks, and of course that is a highly concentrated structure that could explain the persistence of relatively high financial spreads.

EXCHANGE RATE POLICIES AND FINANCIAL REFORM

It could be said that in the not very distant past, it was the balance of trade that largely determined the exchange rate. The perspective about exchange rates in our days is that it is the capital account that really determines the external position. This, of course, changes the theory about exchange rates and, consequently, changes also the policy prescriptions. In this context, we can say that Israel went through the entire spectrum of exchange rate policies and approaches. During the stabilization program the currency was pegged to the U.S. dollar. But given the large bilateral exchange rate changes between the dollar and the deutsche mark, it was decided to peg the sheqel's exchange rate to a basket of currencies, representing Israel's trading patterns. Then, as it was perceived that the rate cannot really be maintained, it was decided to introduce a band. And as the band was perceived to be too narrow, it was decided to have a wider band. But within the band, as long as the inflation rate was higher than the one in the world, some adjustments had to be made periodically. And therefore, although formally Israel had a band, in practice the exchange rate behaved as an adjustable peg. And, then, Israel moved to what is now called the crawling band, where the slope of the band reflects the differential between the Israel inflation target and inflation abroad.

How does the band-cum-inflation-target work? At the beginning of each year, as part of the debate on the budget, an inflation target for the coming year is set. The difference between this target and the expected rate of inflation abroad determines the slope of the band. Of course the actual exchange rate may change freely within the band. Israel had a band of 14 percent, and within that band market forces played a significant role. With the passage of time, as Israel liberalized its capital markets and removed foreign-exchange controls, the band was widened to 30 percent.

Suppose your present inflation significantly exceeds your target. Obviously, you must tighten monetary policy by raising interest rates. However, this generates an incentive for capital inflow. These flows put pressure on the exchange rate generating currency appreciation. If your currency appreciates, the policy gets into a dilemma. The dilemma is between the erosion of export competitiveness and the violation of the inflation target. At the end of the day you have to make an assessment. The more the currency appreciates, the more successful your policy will be on the inflation front. But the more difficult it is as far as competitiveness is concerned, and maybe, therefore, the larger your trade balance deterioration. At some stage you may decide to intervene and slow down the appreciation. And when you intervene, you accumulate foreign-exchange reserves, at which point you obviously lose monetary control, unless you have the instruments to sterilize. To sterilize one needs to have both the instruments for the sterilization operation and the awareness that such sterilization carries some (quasi) budgetary cost. And if you sterilize, you must remember that sterilization policies are not viable in the long run. One always hopes, of course, that it will work in the short run. What is the necessary length of the short run? I believe that one needs to have the breathing space for the length of the period that is required for policies to bring back inflation to the target level. And, if inflation is higher than the target level, interest rates must be higher than the one prevailing in the next equilibrium. And that is exactly what has been done in Israel: some appreciation was allowed and then intervention took place. But, as a consequence of the intervention, foreign-exchange reserves were accumulated and then the Bank of Israel had to sterilize. And then people came and said: you accumulated so much reserves! Don't you worry that it will turn around at once and all your achievements will be gone? Your situation is very vulnerable.

I must confess that my answer to this complaint is the same answer that I got from the manager of the cloak room in the opera. I remember I went to the cloak room, and then I saw in the intermission that there were so many coats there. I asked the manager: "Tell me, don't you worry that at the end of the concert everyone will pick up a coat? That there will be a run on the coats?" He said: "No, why should I worry! Here they are. All the coats are here. When the owners come, they will get them." So, as long as you accumulate reserves and they are there, this should not be a major concern. As a matter of fact, in contrast with the situation for the owner of the cloak room, the central bank has one more degree of freedom. When they all come at the end of the concert, the manager cannot raise the price of the coats. The central bank, in contrast, need not supply the foreign exchange at the fixed price, and those who run on the bank will face currency depreciation. So, it is in this regard that the inflation target regime coupled with the exchange rate policy is making sense, provided that, as you try to sterilize and absorb liquidity, the budget policy does not create new liquidity. And indeed, I would not start the policy of raising interest rates, attracting capital, stopping appreciation, and sterilizing it unless I knew that this is a self-limiting process, namely that as far as the budget is concerned, there is no new injection of liquidity all the time.

In summary, if you have an inflation target, make sure that you have the instruments to attain it, because there is nothing worse than announcing a target and missing it more than once. If you miss it once, it is not a disaster because you can use the opportunity to build credibility because then you show the public that when you miss it, you use the instruments to correct the deviation. So, you raise interest rates, which in turn attracts capital. That means that you need to have the instruments to sterilize the excess supply of money; you need a government that runs a responsible budget policy that supports the process.

Disinflation policy is a long journey that requires maintaining relatively high rates of interest for a prolonged period. The market knew that the exchange rate is pegged through intervention and that risks were in a one-way direction. Capital flows came in, the exchange rate was maintained, and the foreign-exchange market was short because it is a market that is supposed to appraise risk and to have risk premia. Intervention policy interferes with the pricing mechanism as the currency market becomes a riskless market. But it is an illusion to believe that, by intervening, you reduce the risk in the system. In fact, you just transfer it elsewhere within the economy, maybe to a place where you do not see it. It is very likely that this has a negative consequence because you may have transferred the risk to a part of the system, which is less suitable for reflecting the risk – such as the labor market or some other market. Intervention policies do not reduce risk; they simply redirect the risk. The question from the economic perspective, therefore is: where do you want the risk to reveal itself? My presumption is that the foreign-exchange market is more suitable than other markets for it, because that market is capable of handling it through appropriate financial instruments. But this is, indeed, a debatable issue.

An additional issue in this context is the usefulness of imposing some type of limitation to capital flows. When capital flows in, there is the temptation to put some sand in the wheels: a tax on capital movements. My opinion and my lesson – because we have confronted it in Israel – is that this is a bad policy. Of course, I have been wondering why some policy makers in other places think that it may not be a bad policy. The only way I can reconcile this is to think of an asymmetric prescription. Namely, those countries that have already opened up their capital account will make a serious mistake by imposing capital taxes, because it signals that policy is going in the wrong direction as far as the strategy of reform is concerned: it is discrediting their opening-up strategy, and, furthermore, a system that has gotten used to working with an open capital account cannot be stopped doing so by the imposition of taxes. It will generate tax evasion and promote unrecorded capital flows through overinvoicing, underinvoicing, and all the things that we are familiar with. On the other hand, there is some discontinuity. Countries that have not yet opened up their capital account should consider the pace of opening up in a very prudent way. But what is prudence when it comes to economic policy? Does it mean hesitancy? No, there is one simple operational definition of prudence when it comes to economic policy. Consider all good news as being temporary, and all bad news as being permanent. If you implement your economic policy based on this presumption, then you will err in the right direction. And it is an important matter because I have seen more than once governments declaring victory at the first sign of light and recognizing danger only after the war was over.

To conclude these considerations, I would like to make one general statement about exchange rate systems: an exchange rate system can protect a country from bad policies. The opposite, however, may not be right. One may be tempted to say that, if you have the right policies, then it does not matter which exchange rate system you have. But I think that the right way to think about it is to ask what exchange rate system is most conducive to ensure the conduct of good policies and which exchange system is offering so many temptations to policy makers that they may end up implementing the wrong policies. The only way to assess this question is by observing a simple rule: one should not determine whether a system is good or bad according to its functioning in normal days, but rather according to its functioning in stormy days. Economic policy is very easy during normal days; under such circumstances it does not matter if the exchange rate is fixed or flexible – that is not the test. The test of a system is when you have a crisis. In a stormy day you should ask which system would withstand the storm more successfully. And the answer to this question requires much more information than a simple generalization could provide.

SOME IMPLICATIONS FOR TRANSITION ECONOMIES

It has been long recognized that underdeveloped capital markets inhibit the effectiveness of monetary and credit policies and hinder the stabilization process. From the Israeli experience we learn, indeed, that improving the functioning of capital markets enhances significantly the ability to conduct monetary policies, particularly during a period of significant structural reforms.

As I have discussed in joint work with Guillermo Calvo,[1] the main channel through which an early development of domestic capital markets enhances the effectiveness of monetary policy is through a reduction of its distortionary effects. By its nature, monetary policy is inherently unrefined: it affects healthy and unhealthy firms alike. Well-functioning credit markets, however, facilitate a separation between profitable and unprofitable firms. While strong firms can mitigate the contractionary effects of monetary policy by relying on other sources of finance, weaker firms cannot, because they do not have access to capital markets. Accordingly, the capacity of monetary policy to yield socially desirable outcomes is enhanced if it operates in an environment of well-functioning capital markets. In addition, the restructuring of capital markets should enhance the incentive effects of monetary

[1] The following discussion draws on the analysis in Calvo and Frenkel 1991.

and credit policies. Once enterprises are aware that access to credit markets is limited to economically viable firms, they are likely to respond more promptly and effectively to signals conveyed by monetary and credit policies.[2]

The quality and the openness of credit and capital markets also influence the benefits from trade liberalization. Trade liberalization provides the economy with useful price signals. Exposure to world prices helps to demonopolize the economy, enhance competition, and improve the allocation of resources. However, in adjusting to the removal of protection, even economically, viable firms may require credit. The adoption of hard budget constraints eliminates the automatic financing of enterprise deficits by the government. Without sufficient access to capital markets, even viable firms may be forced out of business, thereby reducing the benefits from trade liberalization. Moreover, in attempting to protect themselves, the viable but endangered enterprises may be tempted to join economically nonviable enterprises in lobbying against trade liberalization, thereby reducing the likelihood that liberalization will be adopted.

Furthermore, for trade liberalization to succeed in providing the discipline of world prices, unconstrained imports and exports should be permitted. Accordingly, a significant degree of current-account convertibility should be adopted. To enable the introduction of such convertibility, the financial system needs to be functional. These considerations imply that the benefits from, and support for, trade liberalization and currency convertibility can be enhanced by well-functioning domestic capital markets.

Another important implication from the Israeli experience is the crucial role played by a reforming government in enhancing its credibility and in creating a stable environment within which capital markets can function. Two elements of crediblility are needed. First, the economic program must be feasible, stand the test of professional scrutinity, and reflect the experience of and

[2] One of the salient features of transition economies in their early stages of transformation was the presence of a "monetary overhang." Such overhang could be reduced by three mechanisms: raising the demand for money, lowering the real supply through a rise in the price level, and reducing the nominal money stock (through monetary reform or open-market sales of state-owned assets). It is now clear that the effectiveness of these mechanisms (all of which amount to a tax of one form or another, underscoring the need for a well-developed tax system) was determined by the degree of development of credit and capital markets.

lessons from other episodes. Second, policy commitments must not be susceptible to the "time inconsistency" problem, providing incentives to change policy direction in midcourse. To acquire credibility, policy makers must demonstrate that they are willing to introduce a fundamental change in the manner by which policy is conducted. The adoption of a rule-based policy framework might reduce discretion and the perception of arbitrariness and, thereby, strengthen confidence in the policy-making process.

The advantages of rules (especially those that are simple and not excessively state-contingent) over discretion are particularly pronounced in transition economies, in which policy makers start giving a greater role to market signals. In this environment, discretionary actions may be counterproductive, since the structure of prices and other market signals reflect the prevailing distortions. Therefore, there is a danger that the discretionary actions are guided by the wrong signals. Simple policy rules are especially desirable where policy makers are untested. Furthermore, since discretion was the rule in these countries in the past, a clear statement favoring rules over discretion could help to signal a basic change in the regime. The key challenge, however, is how to make such a statement credible.

Note that the two elements of credibility – of the economic program and of the policy commitments – are interdependent. For example, a credible transformation program is likely to result in short-term hardships. It is liable, therefore, to generate political pressures and interest groups lobbying for midcourse changes, which may give rise to pressures to reverse course. This possibility, in turn, may be anticipated by the private sector already in the earlier stages of the economic transformation process, and incorporated into its behavior. If this problem of time inconsistency occurs, then market participants may end up giving excessive attention to the near term while discounting longer-term prospects heavily – thus generating a less-than-optimal equilibrium. To avoid such difficulties and enhance the likelihood that a better equilibrium ensues, policy makers may find it useful to tie their own hands and send a strong signal that the advantages of being the dominant player will not be used.

It is useful to classify the methods by which the authorities can tie their own hands into three categories. First, the early steps of the new policy regime must entail actions that are sufficiently significant to provide a clear signal that change in regime has occurred. The higher the political costs of policy reversals, the higher the credibility of policy pronouncements. This reflects the fact that in a democratic regime, politicians are aware that they might be held accountable for their policy statements. Once a credible signal is provided, it will influence the expectations of the private sector about the future course of the new policy regime and, in forming such expectations, the private sector is likely to lower the weight given to past policy failures. Thus, pressure to build a track record imposes internal political constraints on the ability of the government to reverse course.

Second, the various branches of the policy-making apparatus can be designed so as to provide effective checks and balances protecting from time inconsistency problems. Examples are the establishment of a legally independent central bank or, as implemented in Israel, a legal prohibition on central bank financing of government budget deficits, or a constitutional amendment legislating balanced budgets. Such mechanisms contribute to the credibility of policy commitments by imposing internal legal constraints on the ability of governments to abuse their role as dominant player.

Third, the government can tie its hands by entering into international agreements of various sorts. Examples are exchange rate commitments, like those undertaken by countries joining the Exchange Rate Mechanism (ERM) of the European Monetary System, or like those undertaken by countries joining the World Trade Organization (WTO). These commitments impose external legal constraints on the use of specific policy instruments: the exchange rate in the case of the ERM, and tariffs or quotas in the case of the WTO.

CREDIT MARKETS AND ECONOMIC TRANSFORMATION

This section outlines some general considerations regarding the relation between financial markets and the process of economic transition toward a well-functioning market economy. Imperfections in credit and financial markets can give rise to an equilibrium in which growth is low and the incentives to undertake efficient investments are stifled. In the previously centrally planned transition economies, credit and financial markets lack depth and breadth. The complex system of information necessary to assess risk and creditworthiness is underdeveloped, for there were no incentives to accumulate such information. In fact, in that system the concept of "creditworthiness" was less meaningful, since losses of enterprises were automatically financed.

In many cases, this implicit government insurance against losses also encouraged more extensive interenterprise credit. The interdependence among the balance sheets of enterprises is one of the key obstacles impeding the operation of the market system. In the Polish economy, the volume of interfirm credit in early 1990, was more than double the volume of bank credit for working capital. Such interfirm debts and assets create difficulties in distinguishing between enterprises that are efficient and viable and those that are neither, thereby adding to the complexity of assessing creditworthiness of individual firms. While a network of interenterprise credit is also prevalent in market economies, the informational difficulties associated with such a network are especially pronounced in the previously centrally planned economies, since the dramatic structural changes associated with the transformation process in these economies render the limited available information largely obsolete.

Furthermore, policy makers in these countries are typically untested, the structure of property rights is not fully defined, and the private sector is unaccustomed to "market rules." These factors are likely to reduce the expected profitability of enterprises and reduce the market value of installed capital. The greater uncertainty raises the uncertainty of the value of capital and, hence, makes borrowing, even against capital collateral, more difficult. These factors foreshadow the need for commitment.

The difficulties in assessing creditworthiness of individual enterprises can result in equilibrium in which socially profitable long-term investments are postponed, while less profitable short-term investments are undertaken. Such an equilibrium could arise if potential lenders lack the confidence that other lenders will stand ready to extend credit to cover the liquidity needs of enterprises. This lack of confidence may be especially likely in previously centrally planned economies, since there the information concerning the risk characteristics of specific enterprises is missing or not widely available to potential lenders.

In addition to the lack of information about specific firms, the previously centrally planned economies exhibit a relatively high degree of economy-wide systemic risk due to the large structural changes and the limited track record of the policy makers. The likelihood of systemic risk is enhanced in these countries since their capital markets are underdeveloped: risk that could be diversified in fully developed capital markets may remain undiversified. Furthermore, the network of interfirm credit increases the risk that firm-specific shocks are spread across enterprises and, thereby, are transformed into economy-wide shocks. All of these factors taken together contribute to shortening the planning horizon on lenders and borrowers, and account for the tendency to undertake short-term rather than long-term investment projects (like infrastructure investment) – even though the latter might be more desirable from the social point of view.

REFERENCE

Calvo, Guillermo, and Jacob A. Frenkel. 1991. "Credit Markets, Credibility, and Economic Transformation." *Journal of Economic Perspectives*, 5, no. 4 (1991): 139–48.

PART III
Afterword

CHAPTER 11

The Financial Sector in Transition

Mario Blejer

As the chapters in this volume have clearly revealed, the process of financial reform and capital market development is one of the most intricate aspects of the postsocialist transition and one that is probably among the most controversial and least understood. This is so not just because it encompasses the expansion of a set of economic activities that were totally neglected and therefore completely underdeveloped under the central planning regime, but also because it involves the promotion of institutional arrangements and the implementation of technical procedures for which there is no full consensus even in advanced market economies.

The studies collected here provide a thorough examination of the problems and the experiences related to the emerging financial sectors in transition economies. While an attempt to generalize and summarize conclusions cannot be all-encompassing, it could be useful to derive some inferences that seem to have general validity. Without seeking to be comprehensive, it is possible to organize the major questions dealt with in this volume around seven major issues, most of which raise new questions and should elicit further research and inquiry.

MONETARY POLICY: A SHIFT TOWARD INDIRECT INSTRUMENTS

The major modifications in the functioning of financial markets and financial institutions brought about by the post-Communist transition gave rise to drastic changes in the role and in the instrumentation of monetary policies. Monetary policy became an active policy tool, and there has been a marked shift throughout the region toward the introduction of more market-oriented monetary instruments. While the introduction of indirect instruments of monetary control, replacing direct intervention mechanisms, has also been taking place in advanced market economies, the transformation has been much faster and more systematic in transition economies, and currently the majority of these economies are, at least formally, relying heavily on market-oriented monetary instruments.

In this context, two questions arise: is this shift as striking as it appears and, if so, is the pace of transformation adequate and desirable? On the first question, the answer appears to be clear: the move toward indirect monetary instruments has not been fully accompanied by a commensurate reduction in the degree of intrusiveness of monetary management. Although it should be recognized that the ability of the monetary authority to abuse its discretionary powers has been significantly curtailed, the reliance on direct means of control, masked as market friendly instruments, has not been completely eliminated. For example, high dependence on reserve requirements, frequently not remunerated, persists throughout the region. Reserve requirements could only be seen as market-oriented instruments to the extent that they are low, uniform, stable, and remunerated, a description that would not characterize the current situation.

With respect to the desirability of the accelerated pace of introduction of indirect monetary instruments in the context of transition economies, the experience indicates that the adoption of these instruments has not enhanced significantly the efficiency of monetary policy and, to some extent, has resulted in a certain loss of monetary control. While this can be explained by the significant time lags in the operation of monetary policies that arise from the low development of credit markets in these economies, the appropriateness of adopting indirect instruments at a rapid pace could be questioned, particularly in the midst of the implementation of stabilization programs. However, there is a strong argument in favor of a fast shift toward indirect instruments based on structural considerations related to the development of financial markets. It could be reasonably claimed that emphasizing indirect monetary controls helps the process of financial reform and of institutional building in the financial sector, particularly by depoliticizing the process of credit allocation, and by enhancing the independence of the central bank (since the channels through which government interference could be effected become more restricted). Moreover, to the extent that financial reforms include a radical opening up of financial markets to foreign competition, the efficiency of direct monetary controls is largely eroded and the introduction of indirect controls becomes more imperative.

THE INGREDIENTS OF FINANCIAL REFORM

While the passage from a command to a market economy has resulted in a large number of systemic changes, practically in no other economic area has the transition implied a larger transformation than in the financial sector. This is so because the absence of a financial sector was a distinctive characteristic of a planned economy. Such a system had, indeed, little need for much of the functions performed by competitive financial intermediaries in a market economy, since those were, at least in theory, carried out by the central planner. Therefore, a priority for a successful transition is the creation, the development, the deepening, and the strengthening of financial markets and financial institutions.

From the postsocialist experience of the various transitional economies, it has become evident that the creation and growth of healthy financial sectors rest largely on three ingredients: the reform of the banking sector, the restructuring of the enterprise sector, and the attainment and preservation of macroeconomic stability. Banking sector reform, in turn, involves the selective implementation of four distinctive procedures: privatization, recapitalization, restructuring, and liquidation. These procedures could be in some cases alternatives to each other, and in others complementary, depending on the distinctive conditions of each institution.

A relevant question arising in this context is one of sequencing. Is it possible to attain macroeconomic stabilization without a sound banking system? Or, on the contrary, how feasible is it to reform the banking system under severe inflationary conditions or in the presence of pervasive soft budget constraints at the enterprise level? Moreover, how realistic is it to expect that enterprises would retool and restructure effectively in the absence of efficient financial intermediaries?

Clearly, the message emanating from the analytical and the

applied inquiry presented here is that this is not a question of optimal sequencing but rather an issue of practical feasibility: all three ingredients are essential and highly complementary. They should, therefore, be implemented, as much as possible, together. While it may not be reasonable to expect full simultaneity, it is evident that the development of the financial system in transition economies is more successful and progresses faster the more advanced the countries are in sustaining macroeconomic stability and in implementing critical enterprise reforms.

FINANCIAL DEEPENING

It is an accepted tenet, when analyzing economies in transition, that reaching a critical level of financial deepening is, for these countries, almost a precondition for redressing their many inherited distortions in resource allocation and for attaining sustained rates of economic growth. Most of the available evidence to date, however, seems to point out that, if gauged by standard – McKinnon/Shaw – types of measures (such as money/GDP ratios), financial deepening has, in fact, decreased over the past few years in many of the economies in transition.

While the elimination of existing monetary overhangs could explain part of this development, the apparent demonetization of some of these economies could still be seen as a puzzling result or, even worse, as a negative occurrence in the road toward a market economy. However, it is possible to contend that traditional quantitative measures of financial deepening are not all that meaningful anymore, and certainly are not particularly informative in transition economies. The financial developments of the past decade, encompassing the extensive opening of financial markets, deregulation, rapid increases in the cross-country flow of capital, and widespread currency substitution have made the conventional indicators of financial deepening either inaccurate or plainly obsolete. Moreover, it is becoming increasingly apparent that transition economies are able to "leapfrog," or jump ahead, into the advanced financial engineering of market economies and are quickly absorbing new payment technologies. The ample use of electronic transfers, the sweeping acceptance of credit cards and travelers checks, and the rapid incorporation of modern bank-clearing technologies are just examples of this catching-up process.

In the foregoing circumstance, the meaning and the measurement of financial deepening take a different dimension. The strength of the emerging financial markets in transition economies should be appraised and evaluated, first, by the spread and speed of absorption of new technologies and, second, by the degree of success achieved in the process of institutional building in the financial sector. Thus, the adoption of stable and transparent financial rules, the enactment and enforcement of an appropriate legal framework that ensures the property rights of financial agents, and the strengthening of monetary institutions – particularly the central bank – are much more relevant indicators of financial deepening than the conventional quantitative marks. Measured by such structural and institutional yardsticks, most transition economies have, indeed, experienced substantial progress in achieving financial maturity, although the cross-country dispersion in this area remains considerable.

BANKING CRISES

The experience to date seems to indicate that the occurrence of the banking crises during the process of transition is an almost unavoidable feature. A long list of reasons for such pessimistic determination has been compiled. Among these, special emphasis has been placed on the twin weight of the Communist inheritance: bad debt and bad habits, much of both resulting from the incestuous relation between bank owners, managers, and clients. But the close observation of country experiences seems to indicate that these inherited problems were largely compounded during the transition itself by the overextension of credit and by the general overexpansion of banking activities in an environment of weak supervision and inappropriate regulations.

Given the high degree of vulnerability of the banking sector in transition economies, a vital question is how to react to the threat, or to the actual emergence, of banking crises. While some observers have expressed the view that, given the lack of genuine constituencies for banking reforms, crises play, in fact, a positive role by forcing on the system the needed transformations, the high real costs of financial crises, both in economic and social terms, could derail the transition process. Bank runs and financial panics not only result in serious harm in terms of output losses but, probably more important, they cause deep reputation and credibility damage. The response to these crises should be, therefore, quick, decisive, and harsh. They should lead to fundamental reforms, including the liquidation and restructuring of inappropriate institutions and to the adoption and implementation of strict and nonarbitrary rules of the game.

At the same time, it is crucial to stress that banking crises should not induce a relaxation of monetary and macroeconomic conditions. The experience of market economies shows (as most recently demonstrated by the case of Venezuela) that financial problems are, in fact, compounded, when banking crises draw inadequate policy responses, particularly in the form of further softening of budget constraints and the unwarranted provision of liquidity. Although banking crises could, indeed, seriously hurt the attempts to achieve sustained economic recovery, they should not compromise the efforts to consolidate macroeconomic stabilization.

COMPETITION

Socialist economies were characterized by a high level of centralization of decision making and of concentration of economic institutions. It was therefore presumed from the beginning that encouraging decentralization and promoting competitive practices were part and parcel of the reform process. However, when observing developments in the financial sector, a paradox seems to emerge: the proliferation of banking institutions and the rapid growth of their activities, apparently stimulated by extended competition, resulted in an overexpansion that not only did not foster efficiency, but was clearly counterproductive, increasing the fragility of the system and raising the risks of financial crises.

This, of course, has been the result of the unchecked growth in the number of financial intermediaries operating within a tenuous environment, where professional capabilities were untested and the experience of economic agents was scanty. In these circumstances, the opportunities for dishonest, or at least irresponsible, behavior were open, leading to the mushrooming of substandard financial entities. Financial competition and free entry, by yielding too much of a faulty product, did not advance efficiency, nor were they conducive to a better allocation of resources.

Given these conditions and the consequent need for qualitative rather than quantitative expansion, what seems to be required is the promotion of contestability – that is, the threat of entry and the fear of competition. In this context, the question regarding the role of foreign banks arises. While it is clear that free foreign entry would greatly enhance market contestability, it could be also argued that the treatment of foreign banks should not be as liberal as the treatment of other foreign investments. This is so because the presence of externalities (reputation) and of economies of scale in the acquisition of informational technologies could result in the total displacement of domestic institutions. While restricting foreign entry in the financial sector in the context of economic liberalization is not a logical option, the special conditions of transition economies may call for some appropriate mechanisms that would encourage domestic participation in the financial sector.

Related to the issue of competition is the persistence of substantial bank spreads between lending and deposit rates. While high spreads indicate, in general, lack of enough competition, it seems that, in transition economies, high spreads reflect also high operational costs and the needed increase in profitability in a sector that was long neglected. In addition, it stands to reason that the level of risk prevailing in the credit markets of transition economies is higher than in Western industrial countries and, therefore, fast convergence of measured spreads cannot be expected quickly. Therefore, it would not be correct to infer that the current level of bank spreads in transition countries necessarily reflects lack of enough competition.

CAPITAL INFLOWS

Most of the transition economies, particularly those more advanced in their reform process, have experienced substantial inflows of foreign capital. Do these inflows exert a positive or a negative influence on the development of domestic financial markets? No clear-cut answer has emerged to this question, because the sources of capital inflows are very different and their effects vary accordingly. While short-term speculative capital movements (responding, e.g., to stabilization-induced high interests rates) could generate substantial financial business and stimulate the development of financial intermediaries, they could also turn out to be highly destabilizing and, eventually, harm the overall credibility of the banking system. Foreign direct investment, on the other hand, could be highly productive and stabilizing for the economy as a whole, but could dampen the development of domestic institutions if foreign investors rely solely on external intermediaries. Moreover, it could discourage the intermediation of domestic financial savings if local firms can safely rely on foreign financing (through equity and/or debt issues) for their investment needs.

THE ROLE OF THE GOVERNMENT

While a key word regarding the role of the government in the process of reforming postsocialist countries is disengagement, it is clear that, in fostering the development of the financial sector the government has an active part to play. Two elements of this role could be mentioned.

1. The government should withdraw from direct credit activities, from bank ownership and from bank management and it should strengthen its role in the regulatory and prudential areas. This is standard thinking. What should be, however, specially emphasized is that the concept of "withdrawal" encompasses more than the formal privatization of banking institutions and the official retreat from direct credit allocations. It involves the depolitization of banking activities and the decision to allow efficiency considerations to determine the allocation of financial resources. As a whole, it is crucial that the state stop abusing the banking sector through the imposition of requirements to conduct operations that are, in substance, purely fiscal.

2. Central banks should be strengthened and given independence. Central banks should, in turn, strengthen prudential practices and, more important, promote accounting and information standards that are conducive to improve transparency and accuracy. This is particularly important in transition economies because the lack of appropriate skills and experience makes it difficult to rely solely on market forces as the main source of financial disclosure.

Changing the role of the government lies, indeed, at the core of the transition. Its residual role in the financial market is, however, of crucial proportions, and striking the appropriate balance remains as one of the most imposing challenges.

Index

Page numbers printed in *italic* type refer to tables or figures

For EU product safety concerns, contact us at Calle de José Abascal, 56–1°, 28003 Madrid, Spain or eugpsr@cambridge.org.

www.ingramcontent.com/pod-product-compliance
Lightning Source LLC
LaVergne TN
LVHW052221200926
848481LV00001B/172

* 9 7 8 0 5 2 1 0 8 8 2 2 0 *